ALBERUNI'S INDIA

ALBERUNI'S INDIA

AN ACCOUNT OF THE RELIGION, PHILOSOPHY, LITERATURE, GEOGRAPHY, CHRONOLOGY, ASTRONOMY, CUSTOMS, LAWS AND ASTROLOGY OF INDIA ABOUT A.D. 1030

AN ENGLISH EDITION, WITH NOTES AND INDICES.

BY

DR. EDWARD C. SACHAU,

Professor in the Royal University of Berlin, and Principal of the Seminary for Oriental Languages; Member of the Royal Academy of Berlin, and Corresponding Member of the Imperial Academy of Vienna Honorary Member of the Asiatic Society of Great Britain and Ireland, London, and of the American Oriental Society, Cambridge, U.S.A.

In Two Volumes

Vol. I

GYAN

Published by

GYAN

Gyan Publishing House
5, Ansari Road
Daryaganj, New Delhi-110002
Phone: 011-47034999, 9811692060
E-mail: books@gyanbooks.com

Distribution Network
gyanbooks.com
India, USA, Canada, UK, Australia, France

ISBN : 978-81-212-3103-9 (Set)
ISBN : 978-81-212-4825-9 (PB)
First Published, 1910

2nd Impression 2020

Printed at: Gyan Press, Delhi.

Alberuni's India
Author: Dr. Edward C. Sachau

ALBERUNI'S INDIA.

AN ACCOUNT OF THE RELIGION, PHILOSOPHY, LITERATURE, GEOGRAPHY, CHRONOLOGY, ASTRONOMY, CUSTOMS, LAWS AND ASTROLOGY OF INDIA ABOUT A.D. 1030.

विष्णुः

An English Edition, with Notes and Indices.

BY

DR. EDWARD C. SACHAU,

Professor in the Royal University of Berlin, and Principal of the Seminary for Oriental Languages; Member of the Royal Academy of Berlin, and Corresponding Member of the Imperial Academy of Vienna Honorary Member of the Asiatic Society of Great Britain and Ireland, London, and of the American Oriental Society, Cambridge, U.S.A.

IN TWO VOLUMES.

VOL. I.

LONDON

KEGAN PAUL, TRENCH, TRÜBNER & CO. LTD

DRYDEN HOUSE, GERRARD STREET, W.

1910

Dedicated

TO

CHARLES SCHEFER,

MEMBRE DE L'INSTITUT, PARIS

AS

A HOMAGE BOTH TO

THE MAN AND THE SCHOLAR.

PREFACE.

I.

THE literary history of the East represents the court of King Maḥmûd at Ghazna, the leading monarch of Asiatic history between A.D. 997–1030, as having been a centre of literature, and of poetry in particular. There were four hundred poets chanting in his halls and gardens, at their head famous Unsurî, invested with the recently created dignity of a poet-laureate, who by his verdict opened the way to royal favour for rising talents; there was grand Firdausî, composing his heroic epos by the special orders of the king, with many more kindred spirits. Unfortunately history knows very little of all this, save the fact that Persian poets flocked together in Ghazna, trying their kasîdas on the king, his ministers and generals. History paints Maḥmûd as a successful warrior, but ignores him as a Mæcenas. With the sole exception of the lucubrations of bombastic Utbî, all contemporary records, the *Makâmât* of Abû-Naṣr Mishkânî, the *Ṭabakât* of his secretary Baihakî, the chronicles of Mullâ Muḥammad Ghaznavî, Maḥmûd Warrâk, and others, have perished, or not yet come to light, and the attempts at a literary history dating from a time 300–400 years later, the so-called *Tadhkiras*, weigh very light in the scale of matter-of-fact examination, failing almost invariably whenever they are applied to for information on some detail of ancient Persian literature. However this may be, Unsurî, the pane- Maḥmûd and Firdausî.

gyrist, does not seem to have missed the sun of royal favour, whilst Firdausî, immortal Firdausî, had to fly in disguise to evade the doom of being trampled to death by elephants. Attracted by the rising fortune of the young emperor, he seems to have repaired to his court only a year after his enthronisation, *i.e.* A.D. 998. But when he had finished his *Shâhnâma*, and found himself disappointed in his hopes for reward, he flung at him his famous satire, and fled into peaceless exile (A.D. 1010).[1] In the case of the king *versus* the poet the king has lost. As long as Firdausî retains the place of honour accorded to him in the history of the world's mental achievements, the stigma will cling to the name of Maḥmûd, that he who hoarded up perhaps more worldly treasures than were ever hoarded up, did not know how to honour a poet destined for immortality.

And how did the author of this work, as remarkable among the prose compositions of the East as the *Shâhnâma* in poetry, fare with the royal Mæcenas of Ghazna?

Mahmûd and Alberuni.

Alberuni, or, as his compatriots called him, Abû Raiḥân, was born A.D. 973, in the territory of modern Khiva, then called Khwârizm, or Chorasmia in antiquity.[2] Early distinguishing himself in science and literature, he played a political part as councillor of the ruling prince of his native country of the Ma'mûnî family. The counsels he gave do not seem always to have suited the plans of King Maḥmûd at Ghazna, who was looking out for a pretext for interfering in the affairs of independent Khiva, although its rulers were his own near relatives. This pretext was furnished by a military *émeute*.

[1] *Cf.* J. Mohl, *Le Livre des Rois*, traduit, &c. Publié par Mme. Mohl, 1876, préface, pp. xl. *seq.*

[2] There is a reminiscence of his native country, i. 166, where he speaks of a kind of measure used in Khwârizm.

Maḥmûd marched into the country, not without some fighting, established there one of his generals as provincial governor, and soon returned to Ghazna with much booty and a great part of the Khiva troops, together with the princes of the deposed family of Ma'mûn and the leading men of the country as prisoners of war or as hostages. Among the last was Abû-Raiḥân Muḥammad Ibn Aḥmad Alberuni.

This happened in the spring and summer of A.D. 1017. The Chorasmian princes were sent to distant fortresses as prisoners of state, the Chorasmian soldiers were incorporated in Maḥmûd's Indian army; and Alberuni—what treatment did *he* experience at Ghazna? From the very outset it is not likely that both the king and his chancellor, Aḥmad Ibn Hasan Maimandî, should have accorded special favours to a man whom they knew to have been their political antagonist for years. The latter, the same man who had been the cause of the tragic catastrophe in the life of Firdausî, was in office under Maḥmûd from A.D. 1007–1025, and a second time under his son and successor, Mas'ûd, from 1030–1033. There is nothing to tell us that Alberuni was ever in the service of the state or court in Ghazna. A friend of his and companion of his exile, the Christian philosopher and physician from Bagdad, Abulkhair Alkhammâr, seems to have practised in Ghazna his medical profession. Alberuni probably enjoyed the reputation of a great *munajjim*, *i.e.* astrologer-astronomer, and perhaps it was in this quality that he had relations to the court and its head, as Tycho de Brahe to the Emperor Rudolf. When writing the 'Ινδικά, thirteen years after his involuntary immigration to Afghanistan, he was a master of astrology, both according to the Greek and the Hindu system, and indeed Eastern writers of later centuries seem to consider him as having been the court astrologer of King Maḥmûd. In a book written five hundred years later (v. *Chresto-*

mathie Persane, &c., par Ch. Schefer, Paris, 1883, i. p. 107 of the Persian text), there is a story of a practical joke which Maḥmûd played on Alberuni as an astrologer. Whether this be historic truth or a late invention, anyhow the story does not throw much light on the author's situation in a period of his life which is the most interesting to us, that one, namely, when he commenced to study India, Sanskrit and Sanskrit literature.

Historic tradition failing us, we are reduced to a single source of information—the author's work—and must examine to what degree his personal relations are indicated by his own words. When he wrote, King Muḥmûd had been dead only a few weeks. *Le roi est mort*—but to whom was *Vive le roi* to be addressed?

Two heirs claimed the throne, Muḥammad and Mas'ûd, and were marching against each other to settle their claims by the sword. Under these circumstances it comes out as a characteristic fact that the book has no dedication whatever, either to the memory of Maḥmûd, or to one of the rival princes, or to any of the indifferent or non-political princes of the royal house. As a cautious politician, he awaited the issue of the contest; but when the dice had been thrown, and Mas'ûd was firmly established on the throne of his father, he at once hastened to dedicate to him the greatest work of his life, the *Canon Masudicus*. If he had been affected by any feeling of sincere gratitude, he might have erected in the Ἰνδικά a monument to the memory of the dead king, under whose rule he had made the necessary preparatory studies, and might have praised him as the great propagator of Islam, without probably incurring any risk. He has not done so, and the terms in which he speaks of Maḥmûd throughout his book are not such as a man would use when speaking of a deceased person who had been his benefactor.

He is called simply *The Amîr Maḥmûd*, ii. 13 (Arabic

text, p. 208, 9), *The Amîr Maḥmûd, may God's mercy be with him*, i. 116 (text, p. 56, 8), *The Amîr Maḥmûd, may the grace of God be with him*, ii. 103 (text, p. 252, 11). The title *Amîr* was nothing very complimentary. It had been borne by his ancestors when they were simply generals and provincial governors in the service of the Sâmânî king of Transoxiana and Khurasan. Speaking of Maḥmûd and his father Sabuktagîn, the author says, *Yamîn-aldaula Maḥmûd, may God's mercy be with them*, i. 22 (text, p. 11, 9). He had received the title *Yamîn-aldaula, i.e. The right hand of the dynasty* (of the Khalif), from the Khalif, as a recognition of the legitimacy of his rule, resembling the investiture of the German Emperor by the Pope in the Middle Ages. Lastly, we find at ii. 2 (text, p. 203, 20) the following terms: "*The strongest of the pillars* (of Islam), *the pattern of a Sultan, Maḥmûd, the lion of the world and the rarity of the age, may God's mercy be with him.*"

Whoever knows the style of Oriental authors when speaking of crowned heads, the style of their prefaces, which attains the height of absurdity at the court of the Moghul emperors at Delhi, will agree with me that the manner in which the author mentions the dead king is cold, cold in the extreme; that the words of praise bestowed upon him are meagre and stiff, a poor sort of praise for a man who had been the first man in Islam, and the founder of Islam in India; lastly, that the phrases of benediction which are appended to his name, according to a general custom of Islam, are the same as the author would have employed when speaking of any acquaintance of his in common life who had died. He says of Maḥmûd (i. 22): "He utterly ruined the prosperity of the country (of India), and performed those wonderful exploits by which the Hindus became like atoms of dust scattered in all directions, and like a tale of old in the mouth of the people." To criticise these words from a Muslim point of view, the passage of the ruining of the prosperity of the country was perfectly out of place in the glorification of a Ghâzî like Maḥmûd.

That it was not at all against the moral principles of Alberuni to write such dedications to princes is shown by two other publications of his, with dedications which exhibit the customary Byzantinism of the time. In the preface of the "Chronology of Ancient Nations" (translated, &c., by Edward Sachau, London, 1879), he extols with abundant praise the prince of Hyrcania or Jurjân, Shams-alma'âlî, who was a dwarf by the side of giant Maḥmûd. The studied character of the neglect of Maḥmûd in the Ἰνδικά comes out more strongly if we compare the unmerited praise which Alberuni lavishes upon his son and successor. The preface of his *Canon Masudicus* is a farrago of high-sounding words in honour of King Mas'ûd, who was a drunkard, and lost in less than a decennium most of what his father's sword and policy had gained in thirty-three years. The tenor of this preface, taken from the manuscript of the Royal Library in Berlin, is as follows:—

To those who lead the community of the believers in the place of the Prophet and by the help of the Word of God belongs "the king, the lord majestic and venerated, the helper of the representative of God, the furtherer of the law of God, the protector of the slaves of God, who punishes the enemies of God, Abû-Sa'îd Mas'ûd Ibn Yamîn-aldaula and 'Amîn-almilla Maḥmûd—may God give him a long life, and let him perpetually rise to glorious and memorable deeds. For a confirmation of what we here say of him lies in the fact that God, on considering the matter, restored the right (*i.e.* the right of being ruled by Mas'ûd) to his people, after it had been concealed. God brought it to light. After he had been in distress, God helped him. After he had been rejected, God raised him, and brought him the empire and the rule, after people from all sides had tried to get possession of it, speaking: 'How should he come to rule over us, as we have a better right to the rule than he?' But then they received (from God) an answer in the event (lit. sign) which followed. God carried out His promise relating to him (Mas'ûd), giving him the inheritance without his asking for it, as He gave the inheritance of David to Solomon without reserve. (That is, the dead King Maḥmûd had proclaimed as his successor his son Muḥammad, not Mas'ûd, but the latter contested the will of his father, and in the following contest with his brother he was the winner.) If God had not chosen him, the hearts of men would not have been gained (?) for him, and the intrigues of his enemies would not have missed their aim. In short, the souls of men hastened to meet him in order to live under his shadow. The order of God was an act of predestination, and his becoming king was written in the Book of Books in heaven (from all eternity).

"He—may God make his rule everlasting!—has conferred upon me a favour which was a high distinction to me, and has placed me under the obligation of everlasting gratitude. For although a benefactor may dispense with the thank-offerings for his deeds, &c., a sound heart inspires those who receive them with the fear that they might be lost (to general notice), and lays upon them the obligation of spreading them and making them known in the world. But already, before I received this favour, I shared with the inhabitants of all his countries the blessings of his rule, of peace and justice. However, then the *special service* (towards his Majesty) became incumbent upon me, after (until that time) obeying in general (his Majesty) had been incumbent on me. (This means, probably, that Mas'ûd conferred a special benefit (a pension?) on the author, not immediately after he had come to the throne, but some time later.) Is it not he who has enabled me for the rest of my life (Alberuni was then sixty-one years old) to devote myself entirely to the service of science, as he let me dwell under the shadow of his power and let the cloud of his favour rain on me, always personally distinguishing and befriending me, &c.? And with regard to this (the favour conferred upon me), he has deigned to send his orders to the treasury and the ministry, which certainly is the utmost that kings can do for their subjects. May God Almighty reward him both in this and in yonder world," &c.

Thereupon, finding that his Majesty did not require his actual service, and besides, finding that science stood in the highest favour with him, he composes a book on astronomy, to which he had been addicted all his life, and adorns it with the name of his Majesty, calling it *Canon Masudicus* (*Alḳânûn Almas'ûdî*), &c.

To put the phrases of this preface into plain language, the author was in favour with King Mas'ûd; he had access to the court—living, probably, near it—and received an income which enabled him to devote himself entirely to his scientific work. Besides, all this appears as a new state of things, the reverse of which had been the case under the king's predecessor, his father, Maḥmûd. We do not know the year in which this change in the life of Alberuni was brought about. Perhaps it was in some way connected with the fact that the chancellor, Maimandî, died A.D. 1033, and that after him one Abû-Naṣr Aḥmad Ibn Muḥammad Ibn 'Abdusṣamad became chancellor, who before, *i.e.* from 1017 to 1033, had administered Khwarizm, the native country of Alberuni. He and Maimandî had been political antagonists—not so he and 'Abdusṣamad.

The difference of the author's condition, as it appears to have been under Mas'ûd, from what it was under Maḥmûd when he prepared the Ἰνδικά, is further illustrated by certain passages in the book itself. When speaking of the difficulties with which he had to grapple in his efforts to learn everything about India, he continues: "What scholar, however, has the same favourable opportunities of studying this subject as I have? That would be only the case with one to whom the grace of God accords, what it did not accord to me, a perfectly free disposal of his own doings and goings; for it has never fallen to my lot in my own doings and goings to be perfectly independent, nor to be invested with sufficient power to dispose and to order as I thought best. However, I thank God for that which He has bestowed upon me, and which must be considered as sufficient for the purpose" (i. 24). These lines seem to say that the author, both at Ghazna and in India, at Multân, Peshâvar, &c., had the opportunity of conversing with pandits, of procuring their help, and of buying books; that, however, in other directions he was not his own master, but had to obey a higher will; and lastly, that he was not a man in authority.

In another place (i. 152) he explains that art and science require the protection of kings. "For they alone could free the minds of scholars from the daily anxieties for the necessities of life, and stimulate their energies to earn more fame and favour, the yearning for which is the pith and marrow of human nature. The present times, however, are not of this kind. They are the very opposite, and therefore it is quite impossible that a new science or any new kind of research should arise in our days. What we have of sciences is nothing but the scanty remains of bygone better times." Compare with this a dictum quoted (i. 188): "The scholars are well aware of the use of money, but the rich are ignorant of the nobility of science."

These are not the words of an author who basks in the sunshine of royal protection. The time he speaks of is the time of Maḥmûd, and it is Maḥmûd whom he accuses of having failed in the duties of a protector of art and science imposed upon him by his royal office. Firdausî, in his satire (Mohl, i. préf. p. xlv.), calls him "*un roi qui n'a ni foi ni loi ni manières*" (*royales*); and he says: "*Si le roi avait été un homme digne de renom, il aurait honoré le savoir,*" &c. It is most remarkable to what degree Firdausî and Alberuni agree in their judgment of the king. To neither of them had he been a Mæcenas.

In the absence of positive information, we have tried to form a chain of combinations from which we may infer, with a tolerable degree of certainty, that our author, during the thirteen years of his life from 1017 to 1030, after he had been carried from his native country to the centre of Maḥmûd's realm, did not enjoy the favours of the king and his leading men; that he stayed in different parts of India (as a companion of the princes of his native country?), probably in the character of a hostage or political prisoner kept on honourable terms; that he spent his leisure in the study of India; and that he had no official inducement or encouragement for this study, nor any hope of royal reward.

A radical change in all this takes place with the accession of Mas'ûd. There is no more complaint of the time and its ruler. Alberuni is all glee and exultation about the royal favours and support accorded to him and to his studies. He now wrote the greatest work of his life,[1] and with a swelling heart and overflowing words he proclaims in the preface the praise of his benefactor. Living in Ghazna, he seems to have forgotten India to a great extent. For in the *Canon Masudicus* he rarely refers to India; its chapter on Hindu eras does not prove any progress of his studies beyond that which he exhibits in the Ἰνδικά, and at the end of it he is even capable of confounding the era

[1] The *Canon Masudicus*, extant in four good copies in European libraries, waits for the patronage of some Academy of Sciences or some Government, and for the combination of two scholars, an astronomer and an Arabic philologist, for the purpose of an edition and translation.

of the astronomers, as used in the *Khaṇḍakhâdyaka* of Brahmagupta, with the Guptakâla.

The author's interest in India.

If the author and his countrymen had suffered and were still suffering from the oppression of King Mahmûd, the Hindus were in the same position, and perhaps it was this community of mishap which inspired him with sympathy for them. And certainly the Hindus and their world of thought have a paramount, fascinating interest for him, and he inquires with the greatest predilection into every Indian subject, howsoever heathenish it may be, as though he were treating of the most important questions for the souls of Muhammadans,—of free-will and predestination, of future reward and punishment, of the creation or eternity of the Word of God, &c. To Mahmûd the Hindus were infidels, to be dispatched to hell as soon as they refused to be plundered. To go on expeditions and to fill the treasury with gold, not to make lasting conquests of territories, was the real object of his famous expeditions; and it was with this view that he cut his way through enormous distances to the richest temples of India at Tanêshar, Mathurâ, Kanoj, and Somanâth.

To Alberuni the Hindus were excellent philosophers, good mathematicians and astronomers, though he naïvely believes himself to be superior to them, and disdains to be put on a level with them (i. 23).[1] He does not conceal whatever he considers wrong and unpractical with them, but he duly appreciates their mental achievements, takes the greatest pains to appropriate them to himself, even such as could not be of any use to him or to his readers, *e.g.* Sanskrit metrics; and whenever he hits upon something that is noble and grand both in science and in practical life, he never fails to lay it before his readers with warm-hearted words of approbation. Speaking of the construction of the ponds at holy bathing-places, he says: "In this

[1] For a similar trait of self-confidence *cf.* i. 277, last lines.

they have attained a very high degree of art, so that our people (the Muslims), when they see them, wonder at them, and are unable to describe them, much less to construct anything like them" (ii. 144).

Apparently Alberuni felt a strong inclination towards Indian philosophy. He seems to have thought that the philosophers both in ancient Greece and India, whom he most carefully and repeatedly distinguishes from the ignorant, image-loving crowd, held in reality the very same ideas, the same as seem to have been his own, *i.e.* those of a pure monotheism; that, in fact, originally all men were alike pure and virtuous, worshipping one sole Almighty God, but that the dark passions of the crowd in the course of time had given rise to the difference of religion, of philosophical and political persuasions, and of idolatry. "The first cause of idolatry was the desire of commemorating the dead and of consoling the living; but on this basis it has developed, and has finally become a foul and pernicious abuse" (i. 124).

He seems to have revelled in the pure theories of the *Bhagavadgîtâ*, and it deserves to be noticed that he twice mentions the saying of Vyâsa, "Learn twenty-five (*i.e.*, the elements of existence) by distinctions, &c. Afterwards adhere to whatever religion you like; your end will be salvation" (i. 44, and also i. 104). In one case he even goes so far as to speak of Hindu scholars as "*enjoying the help of God*," which to a Muslim means as much as *inspired by God, guided by divine inspiration* (ii. 108). These words are an addition of the author's in his paraphrase of the *Brihatsaṁhitâ* of Varâhamihira, v. 8. There can be scarcely any doubt that Muslims of later times would have found fault with him for going to such length in his interest for those heathenish doctrines, and it is a singular fact that Alberuni wrote under a prince who burned and impaled the Karmatians (*cf.* note to i. 31).

Still he was a Muslim; whether Sunnî or Shî'a

cannot be gathered from the 'Ινδικά. He sometimes takes an occasion for pointing out to the reader the superiority of Islam over Brahmanic India. He contrasts the democratic equality of men with the castes of India, the matrimonial law of Islam with degraded forms of it in India, the cleanliness and decency of Muslims with filthy customs of the Hindus. With all this, his recognition of Islam is not without a tacit reserve. He dares not attack Islam, but he attacks the Arabs. In his work on chronology he reproaches the ancient Muslims with having destroyed the civilisation of Eran, and gives us to understand that the ancient Arabs were certainly nothing better than the Zoroastrian Eranians. So too in the 'Ινδικά, whenever he speaks of a dark side in Hindu life, he at once turns round sharply to compare the manners of the ancient Arabs, and to declare that they were quite as bad, if not worse. This could only be meant as a hint to the Muslim reader not to be too haughty towards the poor bewildered Hindu, trodden down by the savage hordes of King Mahmûd, and not to forget that the founders of Islam, too, were certainly no angels.

The author's character.

Independent in his thoughts about religion and philosophy, he is a friend of clear, determined, and manly words. He abhors half-truths, veiled words, and wavering action. Everywhere he comes forward as a champion of his conviction with the courage of a man. As in religion and philosophy, so too in politics. There are some remarkable sentences of political philosophy in the introductions to chapters ix. and lxxi. As a politician of a highly conservative stamp, he stands up for throne and altar, and declares that "their union represents the highest development of human society, all that men can possibly desire" (i. 99). He is capable of admiring the mildness of the law of the Gospel: "To offer to him who has beaten your cheek the other cheek also, to bless your enemy and to pray for him. Upon my life, this is a noble philosophy; but the people of this world are not all philosophers. Most of them are ignorant and erring, who cannot be kept on the straight road save by the sword and the whip. And, indeed, ever since Constantine the Victorious became a Christian, both sword and whip have ever been employed, for without them it would be impossible to rule" (ii. 161). Although a scholar by profession, he is capable of taking the practical side of a case, and he applauds the Khalif Mu'âviya for having sold the golden gods of Sicily to the princes of Sindh for money's worth, instead of destroying them as heathen abominations, as bigoted Muslims would probably have liked him to do. His preaching the union of throne and altar does not prevent him from speaking with undisguised contempt of the "preconcerted tricks of the priests" having the purpose of enthralling the ignorant crowd (i. 123).

He is a stern judge both of himself and of others. Himself perfectly sincere, it is sincerity which he demands from others. Whenever he does not fully understand a subject, or only knows part of it, he will at once tell the reader so, either asking the reader's pardon for his ignorance, or promising, though a man of fifty-eight years, to continue his labours and to publish their results in time, as though he were acting under a moral responsibility to the public. He always sharply draws the limits of his knowledge; and although he has only a smattering of the metrical system of the Hindus, he communicates whatever little he knows, guided by the principle that the best must not be the enemy of the better (i. 200, 6–9), as though he were afraid that he should not live long enough to finish the study in question. He is not a friend of those who hate to avow their ignorance by a frank *I do not know*" (i. 177), and he is roused to strong indignation whenever he meets with want of sincerity. If Brahmagupta teaches two theories of the eclipses, the popular one of the dragon Râhu's devouring the luminous body, and the scientific one, he certainly committed the sin against conscience from undue concessions to the priests of the nation, and from fear of a fate like that which befell Socrates when he came into collision with the persuasions of the majority of his countrymen. *Cf.* chapter lix. In another place he accuses Brahmagupta of injustice and rudeness to his predecessor, Âryabhaṭa (i. 376). He finds in the works of Varâhamihira by the side of honest scientific work sentences which sound to him "*like the ravings of a madman*" (ii. 117), but he is kind enough to suggest that behind those passages there is perhaps an esoteric meaning, unknown to him, but more to the credit of the author. When, however, Varâhamihira seems to exceed all limits of common sense, Alberuni thinks that "*to such things silence is the only proper answer*" (ii. 114).

His professional zeal, and the principle that *learning is the fruit of repetition* (ii. 198), sometimes induce him to indulge in repetitions, and his thorough honesty sometimes misleads him to use harsh and even rude words. He cordially hates the verbosity of Indian authors or versifiers,[1] who use lots of words where a single one would be sufficient. He calls it "mere nonsense—a means of keeping people in the dark and throwing an air of mystery about the subject. And in any case this copiousness (of words denoting the same thing) offers painful difficulties to those who want to learn the whole language, and only results in a sheer waste of time" (i. 229, 299, 19). He twice explains the origin of the Dîbajat, *i.e.* Maledives and Laccadives (i. 233; ii. 106), twice the configuration of the borders of the Indian Ocean (i. 197, 270).

Whenever he suspects humbug, he is not backward in calling it by the right name. Thinking of the horrid practices of Rasâyana, *i.e.* the art of making gold, of

[1] *Cf.* his sarcasms on the versifying bias of Hindu authors, i. 137.

making old people young, &c., he bursts out into sarcastic words which are more coarse in the original than in my translation (i. 189). In eloquent words he utters his indignation on the same subject (i. 193): "The greediness of the ignorant Hindu princes for gold-making does not know any limit," &c. There is a spark of grim humour in his words on i. 237, where he criticises the cosmographic ravings of a Hindu author: "We, on our part, found it already troublesome enough to enumerate all the seven seas, together with the seven earths, and now this author thinks he can make the subject more easy and pleasant to us by inventing some more earths below those already enumerated by ourselves!" And when jugglers from Kanoj lectured to him on chronology, the stern scholar seems to have been moved to something like a grin. "I used great care in examining every single one of them, in repeating the same questions at different times in a different order and context. But lo! what different answers did I get! God is all-wise" (ii. 129).

The tendency of his work.

In the opening of his book Alberuni gives an account of the circumstances which suggested to him the idea of writing the Ἰνδικά. Once the conversation with a friend of his, else unknown, ran on the then existing literature on the history of religion and philosophy, its merits and demerits. When, in particular, the literature on the belief of the Hindus came to be criticised, Alberuni maintained that all of it was second-hand and thoroughly uncritical. To verify the matter, his friend once more examines the books in question, which results in his agreeing with our author, and his asking him to fill up this gap in the Arabic literature of the time. The book he has produced is not a polemical one. He will not convert the Hindus, nor lend a direct help to missionary zealots. He will simply describe Hinduism, without identifying himself with it. He takes care to inform the reader that *he* is not responsible for whatsoever repugnant detail he has to relate, but the Hindus themselves. He gives a repertory of information on Indian subjects, destined for the use of those who lived in peaceable intercourse with them, and wished to have an insight into their mode and world of thought (i. 7; ii. 246).

The author has nothing in common with the Muhammadan Ghâzî who wanted to convert the Hindus or to kill them, and his book scarcely reminds the reader of the incessant war between Islam and India, during which it had been prepared, and by which the possibility of writing such a book had first been given. It is like a magic island of quiet, impartial research in the midst of a world of clashing swords, burning towns, and plundered temples. The object which the author had in view, and never for a moment lost sight of, was to afford the necessary information and training to "*any one* (in Islam) *who wants to converse with the Hindus, and to discuss with them questions of religion, science, or literature, on the very basis of their own civilisation*" (ii. 246).

The author and his readers.

It is difficult to say what kind of readers Alberuni had, or expected to have, not only for the 'Ινδικά, but for all his other publications on Indian subjects. Probably educated, and not bigoted or fanatical Muslims in Sindh, in parts of the Panjab, where they were living by the side of Hindus and in daily intercourse with them; perhaps, also, for such in Kabul, the suburb of which had still a Hindu population in the second half of the tenth century, Ghazna, and other parts of Afghanistan. When speaking of the *Pulisasiddhânta*, a standard work on astronomy, he says: "A translation of his (Pulisa's) whole work into Arabic has not hitherto yet been undertaken, because in his mathematical problems there is an evident religious and theological tendency"[1] (i. 375). He

[1] Alberuni does not seem to have shared these scruples, for he translated it into Arabic (*cf.* i. 154).

does not tell us what this particular tendency was to which the readers objected, but we learn so much from this note that in his time, and probably also in his neighbourhood, there were circles of educated men who had an interest in getting the scientific works of India translated into Arabic, who at the same time were sufficiently familiar with the subject-matter to criticise the various representations of the same subject, and to give the preference to one, to the exclusion of another. That our author had a certain public among Hindus seems to be indicated by the fact that he composed some publications for people in Kashmîr; *cf.* preface to the edition of the text, p. xx. These relations to Kashmîr are very difficult to understand, as Muslims had not yet conquered the country, nor entered it to any extent, and as the author himself (i. 206) relates that it was closed to intercourse with all strangers save a few Jews. Whatever the interest of Muslims for the literature of and on India may have been, we are under the impression that this kind of literature has never taken deep root; for after Alberuni's death, in A.D. 1048, there is no more original work in this field; and even Alberuni, when he wrote, was quite alone in the field. Enumerating the difficulties which beset his study of India, he says: "I found it very hard to work into the subject, although I have a great liking for it, *in which respect I stand quite alone in my time*," &c. (i. 24). And certainly we do not know of any Indianist like him, before his time or after.

The author's method.

In general it is the method of our author not to speak himself, but to let the Hindus speak, giving extensive quotations from their classical authors. He presents a picture of Indian civilisation as painted by the Hindus themselves. Many chapters, not all, open with a short characteristic introduction of a general nature. The body of most chapters consists of three parts. The first is a *précis* of the question, as the author understands it.

The second part brings forward the doctrines of the Hindus, quotations from Sanskrit books in the chapters on religion, philosophy, astronomy, and astrology, and other kinds of information which had been communicated to him by word of mouth, or things which he had himself observed in the chapters on literature, historic chronology, geography, law, manners, and customs. In the third part he does the same as Megasthenes had already done; he tries to bring the sometimes very exotic subject nearer to the understanding of his readers by comparing it with the theories of ancient Greece, and by other comparisons. As an example of this kind of arrangement, *cf.* Chapter v. In the disposition of every single chapter, as well as in the sequence of the chapters, a perspicuous, well-considered plan is apparent. There is no patchwork nor anything superfluous, and the words fit to the subject as close as possible. We seem to recognise the professional mathematician in the perspicuity and classical order throughout the whole composition, and there was scarcely an occasion for him to excuse himself, as he does at the end of Chapter i. (i. 26), for not being able everywhere strictly to adhere to the geometrical method, as he was sometimes compelled to introduce an unknown factor, because the explanation could only be given in a later part of the book.

The author's critical mind.

He does not blindly accept the traditions of former ages; he wants to understand and to criticise them. He wants to sift the wheat from the chaff, and he will discard everything that militates against the laws of nature and of reason. The reader will remember that Alberuni was also a physical scholar, and had published works on most departments of natural science, optics, mechanics, mineralogy, and chemistry; *cf.* his geological speculation on the indications of India once having been a sea (i. 198), and a characteristic specimen of his natural philosophy (i. 400). That he believed in the action of the planets on the sublunary world I take for certain, though he nowhere says so. It would hardly be intelligible why he should have spent so much time and labour on the study of Greek and Indian astrology if he had not believed in the truth of the thing. He gives a sketch of Indian astrology in Chapter lxxx., because Muslim readers "are not acquainted with the Hindu methods of astrology, and have never had an opportunity of studying an Indian book" (ii. 211). Bardesanes, a Syrian philosopher and poet in the second half of the second Christian century, condemned astrology in plain and weighty words. Alberuni did not rise to this height, remaining entangled in the notions of Greek astrology.

He did not believe in alchemy, for he distinguishes between such of its practices as are of a chemical or mineralogical character, and such as are intentional deceit, which he condemns in the strongest possible terms (i. 187).

He criticises manuscript tradition like a modern philologist. He sometimes supposes the text to be corrupt, and inquires into the cause of the corruption; he discusses various readings, and proposes emendations. He guesses at *lacunæ*, criticises different translations, and complains of the carelessness and ignorance of the copyists (ii. 76; i. 162–163). He is aware that Indian works, badly translated and carelessly copied by the successive copyists, very soon degenerate to such a degree that an Indian author would hardly recognise his own work, if it were presented to him in such a garb. All these complaints are perfectly true, particularly as regards the proper names. That in his essays at emendation he sometimes went astray, that, *e.g.* he was not prepared fully to do justice to Brahmagupta, will readily be excused by the fact that at his time it was next to impossible to learn Sanskrit with a sufficient degree of accuracy and completeness.

When I drew the first sketch of the life of Alberuni ten years ago, I cherished the hope that more materials for his biography would come to light in the libraries of both the East and West. This has not been the case, so far as I am aware. To gain an estimate of his character we must try to read between the lines of his books, and to glean whatever minute indications may there be found. A picture of his character cannot therefore at the present be anything but very imperfect, and a detailed appreciation of his services in the advancement of science cannot be undertaken until all the numerous works of his pen have been studied and rendered accessible to the learned world. The principal domain of his work included astronomy, mathematics, chronology, mathematical geography, physics, chemistry, and mineralogy. By the side of this professional work he composed about twenty books on India, both translations and original compositions, and a number of tales and legends, mostly derived from the ancient lore of Eran and India. As probably most valuable contributions to the historic literature of the time, we must mention his history of his native country Khwârizm, and the history of the famous sect of the Karmatians, the loss of both of which is much to be deplored.

II.

On the origines of Arabic literature.

The court of the Khalifs of the house of Omayya at Damascus does not seem to have been a home for literature. Except for the practical necessities of administration, they had no desire for the civilisation of Greece, Egypt, or Persia, their thoughts being engrossed by war and politics and the amassing of wealth. Probably they had a certain predilection for poetry common to all Arabs, but they did not think of encouraging historiography, much to their own disadvantage. In many ways these Arab princes, only recently emerged from the rocky wilderness of the Hijâz, and suddenly raised to imperial power, retained much of the great Bedouin Shaikh of the desert. Several of them, shunning Damascus, preferred to stay in the desert or on its border, and we may surmise that in their households at Rusâfa and Khunâsara there was scarcely more thought of literature than at present in the halls of Ibn Arrashîd, the wily head of the Shammar at Hâil. The cradle of Arabic literature is not Damascus, but Bagdad, and the protection necessary for its rise and growth was afforded by the Khalifs of the house of Abbâs, whose Arab nature has been modified by the influence of Eranian civilisation during a long stay in Khurâsân.

The foundation of Arabic literature was laid between A.D. 750 and 850. It is only the tradition relating to their religion and prophet and poetry that is peculiar to the Arabs; everything else is of foreign descent. The development of a large literature, with numerous ramifications, is chiefly the work of foreigners, carried out with foreign materials, as in Rome the *origines* of the national literature mostly point to Greek sources. Greece, Persia, and India were taxed to help the sterility of the Arab mind.

What Greece has contributed by lending its Aristotle, Ptolemy, and Harpocrates is known in general. A detailed description of the influx and spread of Greek literature would mark a memorable progress in Oriental philology. Such a work may be undertaken with some chance of success by one who is familiar with the state of Greek literature at the centres of learning during the last centuries of Greek heathendom, although he would have to struggle against the lamentable fact that most Arabic books of this most ancient period are lost, and probably lost for ever.

Persian element in Arabic literature.

What did Persia, or rather the Sasanian empire, overrun by the Arab hordes, offer to its victors in literature?

It left to the east of the Khalifate the language of administration, the use of which during the following centuries, till recent times, was probably never much discontinued. It was this Perso-Sasanian language of administration which passed into the use of the smaller Eastern dynasties, reared under the Abbaside Khalifs, and became the language of literature at the court of one of those dynasties, that of the Sâmânî kings of Transoxiana and Khurâsân. Thus it has come to pass that the dialect of one of the most western parts of Eran first emerged as the language of literature in its farthest east. In a similar way modern German is an offspring of the language used in the chanceries of the Luxembourg emperors of Germany.

The bulk of the narrative literature, tales, legends, novels, came to the Arabs in translations from the Persian, *e.g.* the "Thousand and One Nights," the stories told by the mouth of animals, like *Kalîla and Dimna*, probably all of Buddhistic origin, portions of the national lore of Eran, taken from the *Khudâinâma*, or Lord's Book, and afterwards immortalised by Firdausî; but more than anything else love-stories. All this was the fashion under the Abbaside Khalifs, and is said to have attained the height of popularity during the rule of Almuḳtadir, A.D. 908–932. Besides, much favour was apparently bestowed upon didactic, parænetic compositions, mostly clothed in the garb of a testament of this or that Sasanian king or sage, *e.g.* Anushirvân and his minister Buzurjumihr, likewise upon collections of moralistic apothegms. All this was translated from Persian, or pretended to be so. Books on the science of war, the knowledge of weapons, the veterinary art, falconry, and the various methods of divination, and some books on medicine and *de rebus venereis*, were likewise borrowed from the Persians. It is noteworthy that, on the other hand, there are very few traces of the exact sciences, such as mathematics and astronomy, among the Sasanian Persians. Either they had only little of this kind, or the Arabs did not choose to get it translated.

An author by the name of 'Alî Ibn Ziyâd Altamîmî is said to have translated from Persian a book, *Zîj-alshahriyâr*, which, to judge by the title, must have been a system of astronomy. It seems to have been extant when Alberuni wrote his work on chronology; *vide* "Chronology of Ancient Nations," translated, &c., by Edward Sachau, London, 1876, p. 6, and note p. 368. Perhaps it was from this source that the famous Alkhwârizmî drew his knowledge of Persian astronomy, which he is said to have exhibited in his extract from the *Brahmasiddhânta*, composed by order of the Khalif Ma'mûn. For we are expressly told (*vide* Gildemeister, *Scriptorum Arabum de rebus Indicis loci*, &c., p. 101) that he used the *media*, *i.e.* the mean places of the planets as fixed by Brahmagupta, whilst in other things he deviated from him, giving the equations of the planetary revolutions according to the theory of the *Persians*, and the declination of the sun according to Ptolemy. Of what kind this Persian astronomy was we do not know, but we must assume that it was of a scientific character, based on observation and computation, else Alkhwârizmî would not have introduced its results into his own work. Of the terminology of Arabian astronomy, the word *jauzahar* = Caput draconis, is probably of Sasanian origin (*gaocithra*), as well as the word *zîj* (= canon), *i.e.* a collection of astronomical tables with the necessary explanations, perhaps also *kardaj, kardaja*, a measure in geometry equal to $\frac{1}{96}$ of the circumference of a circle, if it be identical with the Persian *karda*, *i.e. cut.*

Indian elements in Arabic literature.

What India has contributed reached Bagdad by two different roads. Part has come directly in translations from the Sanskrit, part has travelled through Eran, having originally been translated from Sanskrit (Palî? Prâkṛit?) into Persian, and farther from Persian into

Arabic. In this way, *e.g.* the fables of *Kalîla and Dimna* have been communicated to the Arabs, and a book on medicine, probably the famous *Caraka*. *Cf.* Fihrist, p. 303.

In this communication between India and Bagdad we must not only distinguish between two different roads, but also between two different periods.

As Sindh was under the actual rule of the Khalif Mansûr (A.D 753–774), there came embassies from that part of India to Bagdad, and among them scholars, who brought along with them two books, the *Brahmasiddhânta* to Brahmagupta (Sindhind), and his *Khaṇḍakhâdyaka* (Arkand). With the help of these pandits, Alfazârî, perhaps also Yakûb Ibn Târik, translated them. Both works have been largely used, and have exercised a great influence. It was on this occasion that the Arabs first became acquainted with a scientific system of astronomy. They learned from Brahmagupta earlier than from Ptolemy.

Another influx of Hindu learning took place under Harun, A.D. 786–808. The ministerial family Barmak, then at the zenith of their power, had come with the ruling dynasty from Balkh, where an ancestor of theirs had been an official in the Buddhistic temple *Naubehâr*, i.e. *nava vihâra* = the new temple (or monastery). The name Barmak is said to be of Indian descent, meaning *paramaka*, *i.e.* the superior (abbot of the *vihâra* ?). *Cf.* Kern, *Geschichte des Buddhismus in Indien*, ii. 445, 543. Of course, the Barmak family had been converted, but their contemporaries never thought much of their profession of Islam, nor regarded it as genuine. Induced probably by family traditions, they sent scholars to India, there to study medicine and pharmacology. Besides, they engaged Hindu scholars to come to Bagdad, made them the chief physicians of their hospitals, and ordered them to translate from Sanskrit into Arabic books on medicine, pharmacology, toxicology, philosophy, astrology, and other subjects. Still in later centuries Muslim scholars sometimes travelled for the same purposes as the emissaries of the Barmak, *e.g.* Almuwaffak not long before Alberuni's time (*Codex Vindobonensis, sive medici Abu Mansur liber fundamentorum pharmacologiæ*, ed. Seligmann, Vienna, 1859, pp. 6, 10, and 15, 9).

Soon afterwards, when Sindh was no longer politically dependent upon Bagdad, all this intercourse ceased entirely. Arabic literature turned off into other channels. There is no more mention of the presence of Hindu scholars at Bagdad nor of translations of the Sanskrit. Greek learning had already won an omnipotent sway over the mind of the Arabs, being communicated to them by the labours of Nestorian physicians, the philosophers of Harrân, and Christian scholars in Syria and other parts of the Khalifate. Of the more ancient or Indo-Arabian stratum of scientific literature nothing has reached our time save a number of titles of books, many of them in such a corrupt form as to baffle all attempts at decipherment.

Among the Hindu physicians of this time one ابن دهن is mentioned, *i.e. the son of DHN*, director of the hospital of the Barmaks in Bagdad. This name may be *Dhanya* or *Dhanin*, chosen probably on account of its etymological relationship with the name *Dhanvantari*, the name of the mythical physician of the gods in Manu's law-book and the epos (*cf.* A. Weber, *Indische Litteraturgeschichte*, pp. 284, 287). A similar relation seems to exist between the names *Kaṅka*, that of a physician of the same period, and *Kâṅkâyana*, an authority in Indian medicine (*cf.* Weber, *l. c.*, pp. 287 note, and 284 note, 302).

The name اطر, that of an author of a book on drinkables, may be identical with *Atri*, mentioned as a medical author by Weber, *l. c.*, p. 288.

There was a book by one بيدبا (also written بيدباه) on

wisdom or philosophy (*cf.* Fihrist, p. 305). According to Middle-Indian phonetics this name is = *vedavyâsa.*[1] A man of this name, also called *Vyâsa* or *Bâdarâyaṇa*, is, according to the literary tradition of India, the originator of the Vedânta school of philosophy (*cf.* Colebroke, Essays, i. 352), and this will remind the reader that in the Arabian Sufism the Indian Vedânta philosophy reappears.

Further, an author ساديرم, *Sadbrm,*[2] is mentioned, unfortunately without an indication of the contents of his book. Alberuni (i. 157) mentions one *Satya* as the author of a *jâtaka* (*cf.* Weber, *l. c.*, p. 278), and this name is perhaps an abbreviation of that one here mentioned, *i.e.* *Satyavarman.*

A work on astrology is attributed to one صنجهل, *SNGHL* (*vide* Fihrist, p. 271), likewise enumerated by Alberuni in a list of names (i. 158). The Indian equivalent of this name is not certain (*cf.* note to i. 158).

There is also mentioned a book on the signs of swords by one باجهر, probably identical with *Vyâghra*, which occurs as a name of Indian authors (*cf.* i. Fihrist, p. 315).

The famous Buddha legend in Christian garb, most commonly called *Joasaph and Barlaam*, bears in Fihrist, p. 300, the title بوداسف و بلوهر. The former word is generally explained as *Bodhisattva*, although there is no law in Indian phonetics which admits the change of *sattva* to *saf.* The second name is that of Buddha's spiritual teacher and guide, in fact, his *purohita*, and with this word I am inclined to identify the signs in question, *i.e.* بلوهد.

What Ibn Wâḍiḥ in his chronicle (ed. by Houtsma) relates of India, on pp. 92–106, is not of much value. His words on p. 105, "the king كوش = *Ghosha*, who

[1] Benfey in *Kalilag und Damnag, Einleitung*, p. xliii. note 3. The word has received currency in the form *Bidpai*.

[2] *Cf.* Benfey, *l. c.*, *Einleitung*, p. xl.

lived in the time of Sindbâd the sage, and this *Ghosha* composed the book on the cunning of the women," are perhaps an indication of some fables of Buddhaghosha having been translated into Arabic.

Besides books on astronomy, mathematics (الحساب الهندى), astrology, chiefly *jâtakas*, on medicine and pharmacology, the Arabs translated Indian works on snakes (*sarpavidyâ*), on poison (*vishavidyâ*), on all kinds of auguring, on talismans, on the veterinary art, *de arte amandi*, numerous tales, a life of Buddha, books on logic and philosophy in general, on ethics, politics, and on the science of war. Many Arab authors took up the subjects communicated to them by the Hindus and worked them out in original compositions, commentaries, and extracts. A favourite subject of theirs was Indian mathematics, the knowledge of which became far spread by the publications of Alkindî and many others.

The smaller dynasties which in later times tore the sovereignty over certain eastern countries of the Khalifate out of the hands of the successors of Mansûr and Harun, did not continue their literary commerce with India. The Banû-Laith (A.D. 872–903), owning great part of Afghanistan together with Ghazna, were the neighbours of Hindus, but their name is in no way connected with the history of literature. For the Buyide princes who ruled over Western Persia and Babylonia between A.D. 932 and 1055, the fables of Kalila and Dimna were translated. Of all these princely houses, no doubt, the Samanides, who held almost the whole east of the Khalifate under their sway during 892–999, had most relations with the Hindus, those in Kabul, the Panjab, and Sindh; and their minister, Aljaihânî, probably had collected much information about India. Originally the slave of the Samanides, then their general and provincial governor, Alptagîn, made himself practically independent in Ghazna a few years before Alberuni was born, and his successor, Sabuktagîn, Mahmûd's father, paved the road for the war with India (i. 22), and for the lasting establishment of Islam in India.

The author's study of India before he wrote the present book.

Some of the books that had been translated under the first Abbaside Khalifs were extant in the library of Alberuni when he wrote the Ἰνδικά, the *Brahmasiddhânta* or *Sindhind*, and the *Khaṇḍakhâdyaka* or *Arkand* in the editions of Alfazârî and of Yakûb Ibn Târik, the *Caraka* in the edition of 'Alî Ibn Zain, and the *Pañcatantra* or *Kalîla and Dimna*. He also used an Arabic translation of the *Karaṇasâra* by Vitteśvara (ii. 55), but we do not learn from him whether this was an old translation or a modern one made in Alberuni's time. These books offered to Alberuni—he complains of it repeatedly—the same difficulties as to us, viz., besides the faults of the translators, a considerable corruption of the text by the negligence of the copyists, more particularly as regards the proper names.

When Alberuni entered India, he probably had a good general knowledge of Indian mathematics, astronomy, and chronology, acquired by the study of Brahmagupta and his Arabian editors. What Hindu author was his teacher and that of the Arabs in pure mathematics (الحساب الهندى) is not known. Besides Alfazârî and Yakûb Ibn Târik, he learned from Alkhwârizmî, something from Abulhasan of Ahwâz, things of little value from Alkindî and Abû-Ma'shar of Balkh, and single details from the famous book of Aljaihânî. Of other sources which he has used in the Ἰνδικά, he quotes: (1.) A Muhammadan canon called *Alharkan*, i.e. *ahargaṇa*. I cannot trace the history of the book, but suppose that it was a practical handbook of chronology for the purpose of converting Arabian and Persian dates into Indian ones and *vice versâ*, which had perhaps been necessitated by the wants of the administration under Sabuktagîn and Mahmûd. The name of the author is not mentioned. (2.) Abû Ahmad Ibn Catlaghtagîn, quoted i. 317 as having computed the latitudes of Karlî and Tâneshar.

Two other authorities on astronomical subjects are quoted, but not in relation to Indian astronomy, Muhammad Ibn Ishâk, from *Sarakhs*, ii. 15, and a book called *Ghurrat-alzîjât*, perhaps derived from an Indian source, as the name is identical with *Karaṇatilaka*. The author is perhaps Abû-Muhammad Alnâib from Âmul (*cf.* note to ii. 90).

In India Alberuni recommenced his study of Indian astronomy, this time not from translations, but from Sanskrit originals, and we here meet with the remarkable fact that the works which about A.D. 770 had been the standard in India still held the same high position A.D. 1020, viz., the works of Brahmagupta. Assisted by learned pandits, he tried to translate them, as also the *Pulisasiddhânta* (*vide* preface to the edition of the text, § 5), and when he composed the Ἰνδικά, he had already come forward with several books devoted to special points of Indian astronomy. As such he quotes :—

(1.) A treatise on the determination of the lunar stations or *nakshatras*, ii. 83.

(2.) The *Khayâl-alkusûfaini*, which contained, probably beside other things, a description of the *Yoga* theory, ii. 208.

(3.) A book called *The Arabic Khaṇḍakhâdyaka*, on the same subject as the preceding one, ii. 208.

(4.) A book containing a description of the *Karaṇas*, the title of which is not mentioned, ii. 194.

(5.) A treatise on the various systems of numeration, as used by different nations, i. 174, which probably described also the related Indian subjects.

(6.) A book called "Key of Astronomy," on the question whether the sun rotates round the earth or the earth round the sun, i. 277. We may suppose that in this book he had also made use of the notions of Indian astronomers.

(7.) Lastly, several publications on the different methods for the computation of geographical longitude, i. 315. He does not mention their titles, nor whether they had any relation to Hindu methods of calculation.

Perfectly at home in all departments of Indian astronomy and chronology, he began to write the Ἰνδικά. In the chapters on these subjects he continues a literary movement which at his time had already gone on for centuries; but he surpassed his predecessors by going back upon the original Sanskrit sources, trying to check his pandits by whatever Sanskrit he had contrived to learn, by making new and more accurate translations, and by his conscientious method of testing the data of the Indian astronomers by calculation. His work represents a scientific *renaissance* in comparison with the aspirations of the scholars working in Bagdad under the first Abbaside Khalifs.

Alberuni seems to think that Indian astrology had not been transferred into the more ancient Arabic literature, as we may conclude from his introduction to Chapter lxxx.: "Our fellow-believers in these (Muslim) countries are not acquainted with the Hindu methods of astrology, and have never had an opportunity of studying an Indian book on the subject," ii. 211. We cannot prove that the works of Varâhamihira, *e.g.* his *Bṛihatsaṁhitâ* and *Laghujâtakam*, which Alberuni was translating, had already been accessible to the Arabs at the time of Mansûr, but we are inclined to think that Alberuni's judgment on this head is too sweeping, for books on astrology, and particularly on *jâtaka*, had already been translated in the early days of the Abbaside rule. *Cf.* Fihrist, pp. 270, 271.

As regards Indian medicine, we can only say that Alberuni does not seem to have made a special study of it, for he simply uses the then current translation of

Caraka, although complaining of its incorrectness, i. 159, 162, 382. He has translated a Sanskrit treatise on loathsome diseases into Arabic (*cf.* preface to the edition of the original, p. xxi. No. 18), but we do not know whether before the 'Ινδικά or after it.

What first induced Alberuni to write the Ινδικά was not the wish to enlighten his countrymen on Indian astronomy in particular, but to present them with an impartial description of the Indian theological and philosophical doctrines on a broad basis, with every detail pertaining to them. So he himself says both at the beginning and end of the book. Perhaps on this subject he could give his readers more perfectly new information than on any other, for, according to his own statement, he had in this only one predecessor, Aleranshahrî. Not knowing him or that authority which *he* follows, *i.e.* Zurkân, we cannot form an estimate as to how far Alberuni's strictures on them (i. 7) are founded. Though there can hardly be any doubt that Indian philosophy in one or other of its principal forms had been communicated to the Arabs already in the first period, it seems to have been something entirely new when Alberuni produced before his compatriots or fellow-believers the *Sâṁkhya* by Kapila, and the *Book of Patañjali* in good Arabic translations. It was this particular work which admirably qualified him to write the corresponding chapters of the 'Ινδικά. The philosophy of India seems to have fascinated his mind, and the noble ideas of the *Bhagavadgîtâ* probably came near to the standard of his own persuasions. Perhaps it was he who first introduced this gem of Sanskrit literature into the world of Muslim readers.

As regards the Purâṇas, Alberuni was perhaps the first Muslim who took up the study of them. At all events, we cannot trace any acquaintance with them on the part of the Arabs before his time. Of the literature of fables, he knew the *Pañcatantra* in the Arabic edition of Ibn Almukaffa.

Judging Alberuni in relation to his predecessors, we come to the conclusion that his work formed a most marked progress. His description of Hindu philosophy was probably unparalleled. His system of chronology and astronomy was more complete and accurate than had ever before been given. His communications from the Purâṇas were probably entirely new to his readers, as also the important chapters on literature, manners, festivals, actual geography, and the much-quoted chapter on historic chronology. He once quotes Râzî, with whose works he was intimately acquainted, and some Sûfî philosophers, but from neither of them could he learn much about India.

In the following pages we give a list of the Sanskrit books quoted in the Ἰνδικά:— His Sanskrit sources.

Sources of the chapters on theology and philosophy: *Sâṁkhya*, by Kapila; *Book of Patañjali*; *Gîtâ*, *i.e.* some edition of the *Bhagavadgîtâ*.

He seems to have used more sources of a similar nature, but he does not quote from them.

Sources of a Paurânic kind: *Vishṇu-Dharma*, *Vishṇu-Purâṇa*, *Matsya-Purâṇa*, *Vâyu-Purâṇa*, *Âditya-Purâṇa*.

Sources of the chapters on astronomy, chronology, geography, and astrology: *Pulisasiddhânta*; *Brahmasiddhânta*, *Khaṇḍakhâdyaka*, *Uttarakhaṇḍakhâdyaka*, by Brahmagupta; Commentary of the *Khaṇḍakhâdyaka*, by Balabhadra, perhaps also some other work of his; *Bṛihatsaṁhitâ*, *Pañcasiddhântikâ*, *Bṛihat-jâtakam*, *Laghu-jâtakam*, by Varâhamihira; Commentary of the *Bṛihatsaṁhitâ*, a book called *Srûdhava* (perhaps *Sarvadhara*), by Utpala, from Kashmîr; a book by Âryabhaṭa, junior; *Karaṇasâra*, by Vitteśvara; *Karaṇatilaka*, by Vijayanandin; *Srîpâla*; *Book of the Rishi* (sic) *Bhuvanakośa*; *Book of the Brâhman Bhaṭṭila*; *Book of Durlabha*, from Multan; *Book of Jîvaśarman; Book of Samaya; Book of Auliatta* (?), the son of Sahâwî (?); *The Minor Mânasa*, by Puñcala; *Srûdhava* (*Sarvadhara?*), by Mahâdeva Candrabîja; Calendar from Kashmîr.

As regards some of these authors, Śrîpâla, Jîvaśarman, Samaya (?), and Auliatta (?), the nature of the quotations leaves it uncertain whether Alberuni quoted from books of theirs or from oral communications which he had received from them.

Source on medicine: *Caraka*, in the Arabic edition of ʿAlî Ibn Zain, from Tabaristan.

In the chapter on metrics, a lexicographic work by one Haribhaṭa (?), and regarding elephants a "Book on the Medicine of Elephants," are quoted.

His communications from the *Mahâbhârata* and *Râmâyaṇa*, and the way in which he speaks of them, do not give us the impression that he had these books before him. He had some information of Jaina origin, but does not mention his source (Âryabhaṭa, jun.?) Once he quotes Manu's *Dharmaśâstra*, but in a manner which makes me doubt whether he took the words directly from the book itself.[1]

The quotations which he has made from these sources are, some of them, very extensive, *e.g.* those from the *Bhagavadgîtâ*. In the chapter on literature he mentions many more books than those here enumerated, but does not tell us whether he made use of them for the *'Ινδικά*. Sometimes he mentions Hindu individuals as his informants, *e.g.* those from Somanâth, i. 161, 165, and from Kanoj, i. 165; ii. 129.

In Chapter i. the author speaks at large of the radical difference between Muslims and Hindus in everything, and tries to account for it both by the history of India and by the peculiarities of the national character of its inhabitants (i. 17 *seq.*). Everything in India is just

[1] The places where mention of these books occurs are given in Index I. *Cf.* also the annotations on single cases.

the reverse of what it is in Islam, "and if ever a custom of theirs resembles one of ours, it has certainly just the opposite meaning" (i. 179). Much more certainly than to Alberuni, India would seem a land of wonders and monstrosities to most of his readers. Therefore, in order to show that there were other nations who held and hold similar notions, he compares Greek philosophy, chiefly that of Plato, and tries to illustrate Hindu notions by those of the Greeks, and thereby to bring them nearer to the understanding of his readers.

Greek and other parallels.

The rôle which Greek literature plays in Alberuni's work in the distant country of the Paktyes and Gandhari is a singular fact in the history of civilisation. Plato before the doors of India, perhaps in India itself! A considerable portion of the then extant Greek literature had found its way into the library of Alberuni, who uses it in the most conscientious and appreciative way, and takes from it choice passages to confront Greek thought with Indian. And more than this: on the part of his readers he seems to presuppose not only that they were acquainted with them, but also gave them the credit of first-rate authorities. Not knowing Greek or Syriac, he read them in Arabic translations, some of which reflect much credit upon their authors. The books he quotes are these:—

Plato, *Phædo.*
Timæus, an edition with a commentary.
Leges. In the copy of it there was an appendix relating to the pedigree of Hippokrates.
Proclus, Commentary on *Timæus* (different from the extant one).
Aristotle, only short references to his *Physica* and *Metaphysica.*
Letter to Alexander.
Johannes Grammaticus, *Contra Proclum.*
Alexander of Aphrodisias, Commentary on Aristotle's φυσικὴ ἀκρόασις.
Apollonius of Tyana.
Porphyry, *Liber historiarum philosophorum* (?).
Ammonius.

Aratus, *Phænomena*, with a commentary.
Galenus, *Protrepticus*.
περὶ συνθέσεως φαρμάκων τῶν κατὰ τόπους.
περὶ συνθέσεως φαρμάκων κατὰ γένη.
Commentary on the Apophthegms of Hippokrates.
De indole animæ.
Book of the Proof.
Ptolemy, *Almagest*.
Geography.
Kitâb-almanshûrât.
Pseudo-Kallisthenes, Alexander romance.
Scholia to the *Ars grammatica* of Dionysius Thrax.
A synchronistic history, resembling in part that of Johannes Malalas, in part the *Chronicon* of Eusebius. *Cf.* notes to i. 112, 105.

The other analogies which he draws, not taken from Greek, but from Zoroastrian, Christian, Jewish, Manichæan, and Sûfî sources, are not very numerous. He refers only rarely to Eranian traditions ; *cf.* Index II. (Persian traditions and Zoroastrian). Most of the notes on Christian, Jewish, and Manichæan subjects may have been taken from the book of Erânshahrî (*cf.* his own words, i. 6, 7), although he knew Christianity from personal experience, and probably also from the communications of his learned friends Abulkhair Alkhammâr and Abû-Sahl Almasîḥî, both Christians from the farther west (*cf. Chronologie Orientalischer Völker, Einleitung*, p. xxxii.). The interest he has in Mânî's doctrines and books seems rather strange. We are not acquainted with the history of the remnants of Manichæism in those days and countries, but cannot help thinking that the quotations from Mânî's "Book of Mysteries" and *Thesaurus Vivificationis* do not justify Alberuni's judgment in this direction. He seems to have seen in them venerable documents of a high antiquity, instead of the syncretistic ravings of a would-be prophet.

That he was perfectly right in comparing the Sûfî philosophy—he derives the word from σοφία, i. 33—

with certain doctrines of the Hindus is apparent to any one who is aware of the essential identity of the systems of the Greek Neo-Pythagoreans, the Hindu Vedânta philosophers, and the Sûfîs of the Muslim world. The authors whom he quotes, Abû Yazîd Albistâmî and Abû Bakr Alshiblî, are well-known representatives of Sufism. *Cf.* note to i. 87, 88.

As far as the present state of research allows one to judge, the work of Alberuni has not been continued. In astronomy he seems by his *Canon Masudicus* to represent the height, and at the same time the end, of the independent development of this science among the Arabs. But numerous scholars toiled on in his wake, whilst in the study of India, and for the translation of the standard works of Sanskrit literature, he never had a successor before the days of the Emperor Akbar. There followed some authors who copied from his 'Ινδικά, but there was none who could carry on the work in *his* spirit and method after he had died, eighteen years after the composition of the 'Ινδικά. We must here mention two authors who lived not long after him, under the same dynasty, and probably in the same place, Ghazna, viz., Gardêzî (*cf.* note to ii. 6), who wrote between A.D. 1049 and 1052, and Muhammad Ibn 'Uḳail, who wrote between A.D. 1089 and 1099 (*cf.* note to i. 5). Of the later authors who studied Alberuni's 'Ινδικά and copied from it, the most notorious is Rashîd-aldîn, who transferred, *e.g.* the whole geographical Chapter xviii. into his huge chronicle.

India at the author's time.

When Alberuni entered India, times were not favourable for opening friendly relations with native scholars. India recoiled from the touch of the impure barbarians. The Pâla dynasty, once ruling over Kabulistan and the Panjab, had disappeared from the theatre of history, and their former dominions were in the firm grasp of King Mahmûd and under the administration of his slaves, of Turkish descent. The princes of North-Western

India had been too narrow-minded, too blind in their self-conceit, duly to appreciate the danger threatening from Ghazna, and too little politic in due time to unite for a common defence and repulse of the enemy. Single-handed Ânandapâla had had to fight it out, and had succumbed; but the others were to follow, each one in his turn. All those who would not bear the yoke of the *mlecchas* fled and took up their abode in the neighbouring Hindu empires.

Kashmir was still independent, and was hermetically sealed to all strangers (i. 206). Ânandapâla had fled there. Mahmûd had tried the conquest of the country, but failed. About the time when Alberuni wrote, the rule passed from the hands of Saṅgrâmadeva, A.D. 1007–1030, into those of Anantadeva, A.D. 1030–1082.

Central and Lower Sindh were rarely meddled with by Mahmûd. The country seems to have been split into minor principalities, ruled by petty Muslim dynasties, like the Karmatian dynasty of Multan, deposed by Mahmûd.

In the conditions of the Gurjara empire, the capital of which was Anhilvâra or Pattan, the famous expedition of Mahmûd to Somanâth, A.D. 1025, in some ways resembling that of Napoleon to Moscow, does not seem to have produced any lasting changes. The country was under the sway of the Solanki dynasty, who in A.D. 980 had taken the place of the Câlukyas. King Câmuṇḍa fled before Mahmûd, who raised another prince of the same house, Devaśarman, to the throne; but soon after we find a son of Câmuṇḍa, Durlabha, as king of Gurjara till A.D. 1037.

Mâlava was ruled by the Prâmâra dynasty, who, like the kings of Kashmir, had afforded a refuge to a fugitive prince of the Pâla dynasty of Kabulistan. Bhojadeva of Mâlava, ruling between A.D. 997 and 1053, is mentioned by Alberuni. His court at Dhâr, where he had gone from Ujjain, was a rendezvous of the scholars of the time.

Kanoj formed at that time part of the realm of the Pâla princes of Gauḍa or Bengal, who resided in Mongîr. During the reign of Râjyapâla, Kanoj had been plundered and destroyed by Mahmûd, A.D. 1017, in consequence of which a new city farther away from the *mlecchas*, Bârî, had been founded, but does not seem to have grown to any importance. Residing in this place, the King Mahîpâla tried about A.D. 1026 to consolidate and to extend his empire. Both these rulers are said to have been Buddhists. *Cf.* Kern, *Geschichte des Buddhismus in Indien*, ii. 544.

The centres of Indian learning were Benares and Kashmir, both inaccessible to a barbarian like Alberuni (i. 22), but in the parts of India under Muslim administration he seems to have found the pandits he wanted, perhaps also at Ghazna among the prisoners of war.

India, as far as known to Alberuni, was Brahmanic, not Buddhistic. In the first half of the eleventh century all traces of Buddhism in Central Asia, Khurâsân, Afghanistan, and North-Western India seem to have disappeared; and it is a remarkable fact that a man of the inquisitive mind of Alberuni knew scarcely anything at all about Buddhism, nor had any means for procuring information on the subject. His notes on Buddhism are very scanty, all derived from the book of Eranshahrî, who, in his turn, had copied the book of one Zurkân, and this book he seems to indicate to have been a bad one. *Cf.* i. 7, 249, 326.

The author and Buddhism.

Buddha is said to be the author of a book called *Cûḍâmani* (not *Gûḍhâmana*, as I have written, i. 158), *i.e.* Jewel, on the knowledge of the supranaturalistic world.

The Buddhists or Shamanians, *i.e. śramaṇa*, are called *Muḥammira*, which I translate the *red-robe wearers*, taking it for identical with *raktapaṭa*. *Cf.* note to i. 21.

Mentioning the trinity of the Buddhistic system, *buddha, dharma, saṅgha,* he calls Buddha *Buddhodana,* which is a mistake for something like *the son of Śuddhodana.* *Cf.* note to i. 40 and i. 380, which latter passage is probably derived from the *Vishṅu-Dharma* (on which *vide* note to i. 54).

Of Buddhistic authors there are mentioned Candra, the grammarian, i. 135 (*cf.* Kern, *Geschichte des Buddhismus in Indien,* ii. 520), Sugrîva, the author of an astronomical work, and a pupil of his, i. 156.

Of the manners and customs of the Buddhists, only their practice of disposing of their dead by throwing them into flowing water is mentioned, ii. 169.

Alberuni speaks (ii. 11) of a building erected by King Kanishka in Peshavar, and called *Kanishkacaitya,* as existing in his time, most likely identical with that *stûpa* which he is reported to have built in consequence of a prophecy of no less a person than Buddha himself. *Cf.* Kern, *l. c.,* ii. 187. The word *bihâr, i.e. vihâra,* which Alberuni sometimes uses in the meaning of temple and the like, is of Buddhistic origin. *Cf.* Kern, *l. c.,* ii. 57.

Among the various kinds of writing used in India, he enumerates as the last one the "*Bhaikshukî, used in Udunpûr in Pûrvadeśa. This last is the writing of Buddha,*" i. 173. Was this Udunpûr (we may also read *Udannapûr*) the Buddhistic monastery in Magadha, *Udaṇḍapurî,* that was destroyed by the Muslims, A.D. 1200? *Cf.* Kern, *l. c.,* ii. 545.

The kosmographic views of the Buddhists, as given by Alberuni, i. 249, 326, ought to be examined as to their origin. Perhaps it will be possible to point out the particular Buddhistic book whence they were taken.

He speaks twice of an antagonism between Buddha and Zoroaster.

If Alberuni had had the same opportunity for travelling in India as Hiouen-Tsang had, he would easily have collected plenty of information on Buddhism.

Considering the meagreness of his notes on this subject, we readily believe that he never found a Buddhistic book, and never knew a Buddhist "from whom I might have learned their theories," i. 249. His Brahman pandits probably knew enough of Buddhism, but did not choose to tell him.

Lastly, India, as known to Alberuni, was in matters of religion Vishnuitic (*vaishnava*), not Sivaitic (*śaiva*). Vishṇu, or Nârâyaṇa, is the first god in the pantheon of his Hindu informants and literary authorities, whilst Śiva is only incidentally mentioned, and that not always in a favourable manner. This indicates a remarkable change in the religious history of those countries. For the predecessors of Mahmûd in the rule over Kabulistan and the Panjâb, the Pâla dynasty, were worshippers of Śiva (*cf.* Lassen, *Indische Alterthumskunde,* 3, 895), as we may judge from their coins, adorned with the image of Nanda, the ox of Śiva, and from the etymology of their names. *Cf.* note to ii. 13, and Lassen, *l. c.*, 3, 915. The image of Nanda reappears a second time on the coins of the last of the descendants of King Mahmúd on the throne of Ghazna.

Conclusion.

It was in the summer of 1883 that I began to work at the edition and translation of the 'Ινδικά, after having fulfilled the literary duties resulting from my journey in Syria and Mesopotamia in 1879 and 1880. A copy of the Arabic manuscript had been prepared in 1872, and collated in Stambul in the hot summer months of 1873.

In order to test my comprehension of the book, I translated it into German from beginning to end between February 1883 and February 1884. In the summer of the latter year the last hand was laid to the constitution of the Arabic text as it was to be printed.

In 1885–86 the edition of the Arabic original was printed. At the same time I translated the whole book a second time, into English, finishing the translation of every single sheet as the original was carried through the press.

In 1887 and the first half of 1888 the English translation, with annotations and indices, was printed.

My work during all these years was not uninterrupted.

Translating an Arabic book, written in the style of Alberuni, into English, is, for a person to whom English is not his mother-tongue, an act of temerity, which, when I was called upon to commit it, gravely affected my conscience to such a degree that I began to falter, and seriously thought of giving up the whole thing altogether. But then there rose up before "my mind's eye" the venerable figure of old MacGuckin de Slane, and as he had been gathered to his fathers, I could not get back the word I had given him. *Cf.* preface to the edition of the Arabic text, p. viii. Assuredly, to do justice to the words of Alberuni would require a command over English like that of Sir Theodore Martin, the translator of "Faust," or Chenery, the translator of *Harîrî*.

As regards my own translation, I can only say I have tried to find common sense in the author's language, and to render it as clearly as I could. In this I was greatly assisted by my friend the Rev. Robert Gwynne, Vicar of St. Mary's, Soho, London, whose training in Eastern languages and literature qualified him to cooperate in revising the entire manuscript and correcting the proof sheets.

Perhaps it will not be superfluous to point out to the reader who does not know Arabic that this language sometimes exhibits sentences perfectly clear as to the meaning of every single word and the syntactic construction, and nevertheless admitting of entirely different interpretations. Besides, a first translator who steers out on such a sea, like him who first tries to explain a difficult, hardly legible inscription, exposes himself to many dangers which he would easily have avoided had kind fortune permitted him to follow in the wake of other explorers. Under these circumstances, I do not flatter myself that I have caught the sense of the author everywhere, and I warn the reader not to take a translation, in particular a first translation, from Arabic for more than it is. It is nothing absolute, but only relative in many respects ; and if an Indianist does not find good Indian thought in my translation, I would advise him to consult the next Arabic philologist he meets. If the two can obtain a better insight into the subject-matter, they are very likely to produce a better rendering of the words.

My annotations do not pretend to be a running commentary on the book, for that cannot be written except by a professed Indianist. They contain some information as to the sources used by Alberuni, and as to those materials which guided me in translating. On the phonetic peculiarities of the Indian words as transcribed by Alberuni, the reader may compare a treatise of mine called *Indo-Arabische Studien*, and presented to the Royal Academy of Berlin on 21st June of this year.

My friend Dr. Robert Schram, of the University of Vienna, has examined all the mathematical details of chronology and astronomy. The results of his studies are presented to the reader in the annotations signed with his name. All this is Dr. Schram's special domain, in which he has no equal. My thanks are due to him for lending me his help in parts of the work where my own attempts at verification, after prolonged exertions in the same direction, proved to be insufficient.

Of the two indices, the former contains all words of Indian origin occurring in the book, some pure Sanskrit, some vernacular, others in the form exhibited by the

Arabic manuscript, howsoever faulty it may be. The reader will perhaps here and there derive some advantage from comparing the index of the edition of the Arabic original. The second index contains names of persons and places, &c., mostly of non-Indian origin.

It was the Committee of the Oriental Translation Fund, consisting at the time of Osmond de Beauvoir Priaulx, Edward Thomas, James Fergusson, Reinhold Rost, and Theodore Goldstücker, who first proposed to me to translate the *'Ινδικά*. Thomas, Goldstücker, and Fergusson are beyond the reach of human words, but to O. de Beauvoir Priaulx, Esq., and to Dr. Rost, I desire to express my sincerest gratitude for the generous help and the untiring interest which they have always accorded to me, though so many years have rolled on since I first pledged to them my word. Lastly, Her Majesty's India Office has extended its patronage from the edition of the Arabic original also to this edition of the work in an English garb.

Of the works of my predecessors, the famous publication of Reinaud, the *Mémoire géographique, historique et scientifique sur l'Inde*, Paris, 1849, has been most useful to me. Cf. on this and the labours of my other predecessors § 2 of the preface to the edition of the Arabic original.

The Sanskrit alphabet has been transliterated in the following way :—*a, â, i, î, u, û—ṛi, ai, au—k, kh, g, gh, ṅ—c, ch, j, jh, ñ—ṭ, ṭh, ḍ, ḍh, ṇ—t, th, d, dh, n—p, ph, b, bh, m—y, r, l, v—ś, sh, s, h.*

EDWARD SACHAU.

BERLIN, *August* 4, 1888.

TABLE OF CONTENTS.

(*For Alberuni's Synopsis of the Single Chapters of the Book, vide* pp. 9–16.)

ALBÊRÛNÎ'S INDIA

AN

ACCURATE DESCRIPTION OF ALL CATEGORIES OF HINDU THOUGHT,

AS WELL THOSE WHICH ARE ADMISSIBLE AS THOSE WHICH MUST BE REJECTED.

COMPOSED BY

'ABÛ-ALRAIHÂN MUHAMMAD IBN 'AHMAD

ALBÊRÛNÎ.

PREFACE.

In the Name of God, the Compassionate, the Merciful. Page 2.

No one will deny that in questions of historic authenticity *hearsay* does not equal *eye-witness*; for in the latter the eye of the observer apprehends the substance of that which is observed, both in the time when and in the place where it exists, whilst hearsay has its peculiar drawbacks. But for these, it would even be preferable to eye-witness; for the object of eye-witness can only be *actual* momentary existence, whilst hearsay comprehends alike the present, the past, and the future, so as to apply in a certain sense both to that which *is* and to that which is *not* (*i.e.* which either has ceased to exist or has not yet come into existence). Written tradition is one of the species of hearsay—we might almost say, the most preferable. How could we know the history of nations but for the everlasting monuments of the pen?

1. On tradition, hearsay and eye-witness.
2. The different kinds of reporters.
3. Praise of truthfulness.

The tradition regarding an event which in itself does not contradict either logical or physical laws will invariably depend for its character as true or false upon the character of the reporters, who are influenced by the divergency of interests and all kinds of animosities and antipathies between the various nations. We must distinguish different classes of reporters.

One of them tells a lie, as intending to further an

interest of his own, either *by lauding* his family or nation, because he is one of them, or *by attacking* the family or nation on the opposite side, thinking that thereby he can gain his ends. In both cases he acts from motives of objectionable cupidity and animosity.

Another one tells a lie regarding a class of people whom he likes, as being under obligations to them, or whom he hates because something disagreeable has happened between them. Such a reporter is near akin to the first-mentioned one, as he too acts from motives of personal predilection and enmity.

Another tells a lie because he is of such a base nature as to aim thereby at some profit, or because he is such a coward as to be afraid of telling the truth.

Another tells a lie because it is his nature to lie, and he cannot do otherwise, which proceeds from the essential meanness of his character and the depravity of his innermost being.

Lastly, a man may tell a lie from ignorance, blindly following others who told him.

If, now, reporters of this kind become so numerous as to represent a certain body of tradition, or if in the course of time they even come to form a consecutive series of communities or nations, both the first reporter and his followers form the connecting links between the hearer and the inventor of the lie; and if the connecting links are eliminated, there remains the originator of the story, one of the various kinds of liars we have enumerated, as the only person with whom we have to deal.

That man only is praiseworthy who shrinks from a lie and always adheres to the truth, enjoying credit even among liars, not to mention others.

It has been said in the Koran, "*Speak the truth, even if it were against yourselves*" (Sûra, 4, 134); and the Messiah
Page 3. expresses himself in the Gospel to this effect: "*Do not mind the fury of kings in speaking the truth before them.*

They only possess your body, but they have no power over your soul" (*cf.* St. Matt. x. 18, 19, 28; St. Luke xii. 4). In these words the Messiah orders us to exercise *moral courage.* For what the crowd calls courage—bravely dashing into the fight or plunging into an abyss of destruction—is only a *species* of courage, whilst the *genus*, far above all *species*, is *to scorn death*, whether by word or deed.

Now as justice (*i.e.* being just) is a quality liked and coveted for its own self, for its intrinsic beauty, the same applies to *truthfulness*, except perhaps in the case of such people as never tasted how sweet it is, or know the truth, but deliberately shun it, like a notorious liar who once was asked if he had ever spoken the truth, and gave the answer, "If I were not afraid to speak the truth, I should say, no." A liar will avoid the path of justice; he will, as matter of preference, side with oppression and false witness, breach of confidence, fraudulent appropriation of the wealth of others, theft, and all the vices which serve to ruin the world and mankind.

I. On the defects of Muslim works on religious and philosophical doctrines. II. Exemplified with regard to the Hindus. Criticism of the book of Erânshahrî. III. Bêrûnî asked to write a book on the subject. IV. He states his method.

When I once called upon the master 'Abû-Sahl 'Abd-Almun'im Ibn 'Alî Ibn Nûḥ At-tiflîsî, may God strengthen him! I found that he blamed the tendency of the author of a book on the Mu'tazila sect to misrepresent their theory. For, according to them, God is omniscient of himself, and this dogma that author had expressed in such a way as to say that *God has no knowledge* (like the knowledge of man), thereby misleading uneducated people to imagine that, according to the Mu'tazilites, *God is ignorant.* Praise be to God, who is far above all such and similar unworthy descriptions! Thereupon I pointed out to the master that precisely the same method is much in fashion among those who undertake the task of giving an account of religious and philosophical systems from which they slightly differ or to which they are entirely opposed. Such misrepresentation is easily detected in a report about dogmas comprehended within the frame of one single religion, because they are closely related and blended with each other. On the other hand, you would have great difficulty in detecting it in a report about entirely foreign systems of thought totally differing both in principle and details, for such a research is rather an out-of-the-way one, and there are few means of arriving at a thorough comprehension of it. The same tendency prevails throughout our whole literature on philosophical and religious sects. If such an author is not alive to the requirements of a strictly scientific method, he will procure some superficial information which will satisfy neither the adherents of the doctrine in question nor those who really know it. In such a case, if he be an honest character, he will simply retract and feel ashamed; but if he be so base as not to give due honour to truth, he will persist in litigious wrangling for his own original standing-point. If, on the contrary, an author has the right method, he will do his utmost to deduce the tenets of a sect from their legendary lore, things which people tell him, pleasant enough to listen to, but which he would never dream of taking for true or believing.

In order to illustrate the point of our conversation,
Page 4. one of those present referred to the religions and doctrines of the Hindus by way of an example. Thereupon I drew their attention to the fact that everything which exists on this subject in our literature is second-hand information which one has copied from the other, a farrago of materials never sifted by the sieve of critical examination. Of all authors of this class, I know only one who had proposed to himself to give a simple and exact report of the subject *sine irâ ac studio*, viz. 'Abû-al'abbâs Alêrânshahrî. He himself did not believe in any of the then existing religions, but was the sole believer in a religion invented by himself, which he tried to propagate. He has given a very good account of the doctrines of the Jews and Christians as well as

of the contents of both the Thora and the Gospel. Besides, he furnishes us with a most excellent account of the Manichæans, and of obsolete religions of bygone times which are mentioned in their books. But when he came in his book to speak of the Hindus and the Buddhists, his arrow missed the mark, and in the latter part he went astray through hitting upon the book of *Zarḳân*, the contents of which he incorporated in his own work. That, however, which he has not taken from *Zarḳân*, he himself has heard from common people among Hindus and Buddhists.

At a subsequent period the master 'Abû-Sahl studied the books in question a second time, and when he found the matter exactly as I have here described it, he incited me to write down what I know about the Hindus as a help to those who want to discuss religious questions with them, and as a repertory of information to those who want to associate with them. In order to please him I have done so, and written this book on the doctrines of the Hindus, never making any unfounded imputations against those, our religious antagonists, and at the same time not considering it inconsistent with my duties as a Muslim to quote their own words at full length when I thought they would contribute to elucidate a subject. If the contents of these quotations happen to be utterly heathenish, and *the followers of the truth*, *i.e.* the Muslims, find them objectionable, we can only say that such is the belief of the Hindus, and that they themselves are best qualified to defend it.

This book is not a *polemical* one. I shall not produce the arguments of our antagonists in order to refute such of them as I believe to be in the wrong. My book is nothing but *a simple historic record of facts.* I shall place before the reader the theories of the Hindus exactly as they are, and I shall mention in connection with them similar theories of the Greeks in order to show the relationship existing between them. For the

Greek philosophers, although aiming at truth in the abstract, never in all questions of popular bearing rise much above the customary exoteric expressions and tenets both of their religion and law. Besides Greek ideas we shall only now and then mention those of the Sûfîs or of some one or other Christian sect, because in their notions regarding the transmigration of souls and the pantheistic doctrine of the unity of God with creation there is much in common between these systems.

I have already translated two books into Arabic, one about the *origines* and a description of all created beings, called *Sâṁkhya*, and another about the emancipation of the soul from the fetters of the body, called *Patañjali* (*Pâtañjala ?*). These two books contain most of the elements of the belief of the Hindus, but not all the single rules derived therefrom. I hope that the present book will enable the reader to dispense with these two earlier ones, and with other books of the same kind; that it will give a sufficient representation of the subject, and will enable him to make himself thoroughly acquainted with it—God willing!

TABLE OF CONTENTS.

CHAPTER VIII.

CHAPTER IX.

CHAPTER X.

CHAPTER XI.

CHAPTER XII.

CHAPTER XIII.

CHAPTER XIV.

CHAPTER XV.

CHAPTER XVI.

CHAPTER XVII.

CHAPTER XVIII.

CHAPTER XIX.

CHAPTER XX.

CHAPTER XXI.

CHAPTER XXII.

CHAPTER XXIII.

CHAPTER XXIV.

CHAPTER XXV.

CHAPTER XXVI.

CHAPTER XXVII.

CHAPTER L.

CHAPTER LI.

CHAPTER LII.

CHAPTER LIII.

CHAPTER LIV.

CHAPTER LV.

CHAPTER LVI.

CHAPTER LVII.

CHAPTER LVIII.

CHAPTER LIX.

CHAPTER I.

ON THE HINDUS IN GENERAL, AS AN INTRODUCTION TO OUR ACCOUNT OF THEM.

Page 9.

Description of the barriers which separate the Hindus from the Muslims and make it so particularly difficult for a Muslim to study any Indian subject.

BEFORE entering on our exposition, we must form an adequate idea of that which renders it so particularly difficult to penetrate to the essential nature of any Indian subject. The knowledge of these difficulties will either facilitate the progress of our work, or serve as an apology for any shortcomings of ours. For the reader must always bear in mind that the Hindus entirely differ from us in every respect, many a subject appearing intricate and obscure which would be perfectly clear if there were more connection between us. The barriers which separate Muslims and Hindus rest on different causes.

First reason: Difference of the language and its particular nature.

First, they differ from us in everything which other nations have in common. And here we first mention the language, although the difference of language also exists between other nations. If you want to conquer this difficulty (*i.e.* to learn Sanskrit), you will not find it easy, because the language is of an enormous range, both in words and inflections, something like the Arabic, calling one and the same thing by various names, both original and derived, and using one and the same word for a variety of subjects, which, in order to be properly understood, must be distinguished from each other by various qualifying epithets. For nobody could distinguish between the various meanings of a word unless he understands the context in which it occurs, and its relation both to the following and the preceding parts of the sentence. The Hindus, like other people, boast of this enormous range of their language, whilst in reality it is a defect.

Further, the language is divided into a neglected vernacular one, only in use among the common people, and a classical one, only in use among the upper and educated classes, which is much cultivated, and subject to the rules of grammatical inflection and etymology, and to all the nicoties of grammar and rhetoric.

Besides, some of the sounds (consonants) of which the language is composed are neither identical with the sounds of Arabic and Persian, nor resemble them in any way. Our tongue and uvula could scarcely manage to correctly pronounce them, nor our ears in hearing to distinguish them from similar sounds, nor could we transliterate them with our characters. It is very difficult, therefore, to express an Indian word in our writing, for in order to fix the pronunciation we must change our orthographical points and signs, and must pronounce the case-endings either according to the common Arabic rules or according to special rules adapted for the purpose.

Add to this that the Indian scribes are careless, and do not take pains to produce correct and well-collated copies. In consequence, the highest results of the author's mental development are lost by their negligence, and his book becomes already in the first or second copy so full of faults, that the text appears as something entirely new, which neither a scholar nor one familiar with the subject, whether Hindu or Muslim, could any longer understand. It will sufficiently illustrate the matter if we tell the reader that we have sometimes written down a word from the mouth of Hindus, taking the greatest pains to fix its pronunciation, and that afterwards when we repeated it to them, they had great difficulty in recognising it.

As in other foreign tongues, so also in Sanskrit, two or three consonants may follow each other without an intervening vowel—consonants which in our Persian grammatical system are considered as having a *hidden* vowel. Since most Sanskrit words and names begin with such consonants without vowels, we find it very difficult to pronounce them.

Besides, the scientific books of the Hindus are composed in various favourite metres, by which they intend, considering that the books soon become corrupted by additions and omissions, to preserve them exactly as they are, in order to facilitate their being learned by heart, because they consider as canonical only that which is known by heart, not that which exists in writing. Now it is well known that in all metrical compositions there is much misty and constrained phraseology merely intended to fill up the metre and serving as a kind of patchwork, and this necessitates a certain amount of verbosity. This is also one of the reasons why a word has sometimes one meaning and sometimes another. Page 10.

From all this it will appear that the metrical form of literary composition is one of the causes which make the study of Sanskrit literature so particularly difficult.

Second reason: Their religious prejudices.

Secondly, they totally differ from us in religion, as we believe in nothing in which they believe, and *vice versâ*. On the whole, there is very little disputing about theological topics among themselves; at the utmost, they fight with words, but they will never stake their soul or body or their property on religious controversy. On the contrary, all their fanaticism is directed against those who do not belong to them—against all foreigners. They call them *mleccha*, *i.e.* impure, and forbid having any connection with them, be it by intermarriage or any other kind of relationship, or by sitting, eating, and drinking with them, because thereby, they think, they would be polluted. They consider as impure anything which touches the fire and the water of a foreigner; and no household can exist without these two elements. Besides, they never desire that a thing which once has been polluted should be purified and thus recovered, as, under ordinary circumstances, if anybody or anything has become unclean, he or it would strive to regain the state of purity. They are not allowed to receive anybody who does not belong to them, even if he wished it, or was inclined to their religion. This, too, renders any connection with them quite impossible, and constitutes the widest gulf between us and them.

Third reason: The radical difference of their manners and customs.

In the third place, in all manners and usages they differ from us to such a degree as to frighten their children with us, with our dress, and our ways and customs, and as to declare us to be devil's breed, and our doings as the very opposite of all that is good and proper. By the by, we must confess, in order to be just, that a similar depreciation of foreigners not only prevails among us and the Hindus, but is common to all nations towards each other. I recollect a Hindu who wreaked his vengeance on us for the following reason:—

Some Hindu king had perished at the hand of an enemy of his who had marched against him from our country. After his death there was born a child to him, which succeeded him, by the name of Sagara. On coming of age, the young man asked his mother about his father, and then she told him what had happened. Now he was inflamed with hatred, marched out of his country into the country of the enemy, and plentifully satiated his thirst of vengeance upon them. After having become tired of slaughtering, he compelled the survivors to dress in our dress, which was meant as an ignominious punishment for them. When I heard of it, I felt thankful that he was gracious enough not to compel us to Indianise ourselves and to adopt Hindu dress and manners.

Another circumstance which increased the already existing antagonism between Hindus and foreigners is that the so-called Shamaniyya (Buddhists), though they cordially hate the Brahmans, still are nearer akin to them than to others. In former times, Khurâsân, Persis, 'Irâk, Mosul, the country up to the frontier of Syria, was Buddhistic, but then Zarathustra went forth from Âdharbaijân and preached Magism in Balkh (Baktra). His doctrine came into favour with King Gushtasp, and his son Isfendiyâd spread the new faith both in east and west, both by force and by treaties. He founded fire-temples through his whole empire, from the frontiers of China to those of the Greek empire. The succeeding kings made their religion (*i.e.* Zoroastrianism) the obligatory state-religion for Persis and 'Irâk. In consequence, the Buddhists were banished from those countries, and had to emigrate to the countries east of Balkh. There are some Magians up to the present time in India, where they are called *Maga*. From that time dates their aversion towards the countries of Khurâsân. But then came Islam; the Persian empire perished, and the repugnance of the Hindus against foreigners increased more and more when the Muslims began to make their inroads into their country; for Muḥammad Ibn Elkâsim Ibn Elmunabbih entered Sindh from the side of Sijistân (Sakastene) and conquered the cities of Bahmanwâ and Mûlasthâna, the former of which he called *Al-manṣûra*, the latter *Al-ma'mûra*. He entered India proper, and penetrated even as far as Kanauj, marched through the country of Gandhâra, and on his way back, through the confines of Kashmîr, sometimes fighting sword in hand, sometimes gaining his ends by treaties, leaving to the people their ancient belief, except in the case of those who wanted to become Muslims. All these events planted a deeply rooted hatred in their hearts.

Fourth reason: Aversion of the Buddhists towards the countries of the West, whence they had been expelled. First inroads of the Muslims into India.

Page 11.

Muhammadan conquest of the country by Maḥmûd.

Now in the following times no Muslim conqueror passed beyond the frontier of Kâbul and the river Sindh until the days of the Turks, when they seized the power in Ghazna under the Sâmânî dynasty, and the supreme power fell to the lot of Nâṣir-addaula Sabuktagîn. This prince chose the holy war as his calling, and therefore called himself *Al-ghâzî* (i.e. *warring on the road of Allah*). In the interest of his successors he constructed, in order to weaken the Indian frontier, those roads on which afterwards his son Yamîn-addaula Maḥmûd marched into India during a period of thirty years and more. God be merciful to both father and son! Maḥmûd utterly ruined the prosperity of the country, and performed there wonderful exploits, by which the Hindus became like atoms of dust scattered in all directions, and like a tale of old in the mouth of the people. Their scattered remains cherish, of course, the most inveterate aversion towards all Muslims. This is the reason, too, why Hindu sciences have retired far away from those parts of the country conquered by us, and have fled to places which our hand cannot yet reach, to Kashmîr, Benares, and other places. And there the antagonism between them and all foreigners receives more and more nourishment both from political and religious sources.

Fifth reason: The self-conceit of the Hindus, and their depreciation of anything foreign.

In the fifth place, there are other causes, the mentioning of which sounds like a satire—peculiarities of their national character, deeply rooted in them, but manifest to everybody. We can only say, folly is an illness for which there is no medicine, and the Hindus believe that there is no country but theirs, no nation like theirs, no kings like theirs, no religion like theirs, no science like theirs. They are haughty, foolishly vain, self-conceited, and stolid. They are by nature niggardly in communicating that which they know, and they take the greatest possible care to withhold it from men of another caste among their own people, still much more, of course,

from any foreigner. According to their belief, there is no other country on earth but theirs, no other race of man but theirs, and no created beings besides them have any knowledge or science whatsoever. Their haughtiness is such that, if you tell them of any science or scholar in Khurâsân and Persis, they will think you to be both an ignoramus and a liar. If they travelled and mixed with other nations, they would soon change their mind, for their ancestors were not as narrow-minded as the present generation is. One of their scholars, Varâhamihira, in a passage where he calls on the people to honour the Brahmans, says: "*The Greeks, though impure, must be honoured, since they were trained in sciences, and therein excelled others. What, then, are we to say of a Brahman, if he combines with his* Page 12.
purity the height of science?" In former times, the Hindus used to acknowledge that the progress of science due to the Greeks is much more important than that which is due to themselves. But from this passage of Varâhamihira alone you see what a self-lauding man he is, whilst he gives himself airs as doing justice to others. At first I stood to their astronomers in the relation of a pupil to his master, being a stranger among them and not acquainted with their peculiar national and traditional methods of science. On having made some progress, I began to show them the elements on which this science rests, to point out to them some rules of logical deduction and the scientific methods of all mathematics, and then they flocked together round me from all parts, wondering, and most eager to learn from me, asking me at the same time from what Hindu master I had learnt those things, whilst in reality I showed them what they were worth, and thought myself a great deal superior to them, disdaining to be put on a level with them. They almost thought me to be a sorcerer, and when speaking of me to their leading men in their native tongue, they spoke of me as *the sea* or as

the water which is so acid that vinegar in comparison is sweet.

Personal relations of the author.

Now such is the state of things in India. I have found it very hard to work my way into the subject, although I have a great liking for it, in which respect I stand quite alone in my time, and although I do not spare either trouble or money in collecting Sanskrit books from places where I supposed they were likely to be found, and in procuring for myself, even from very remote places, Hindu scholars who understand them and are able to teach me. What scholar, however, has the same favourable opportunities of studying this subject as I have? That would be only the case with one to whom the grace of God accords, what it did not accord to me, a perfectly free disposal of his own doings and goings; for it has never fallen to my lot in my own doings and goings to be perfectly independent, nor to be invested with sufficient power to dispose and to order as I thought best. However, I thank God for that which He has bestowed upon me, and which must be considered as sufficient for the purpose.

The author declares his intention of comparing Greek theories, because of their being near akin, and of their strictly scientific character as contrasted with those of the Hindus.

The heathen Greeks, before the rise of Christianity, held much the same opinions as the Hindus; their educated classes thought much the same as those of the Hindus; their common people held the same idolatrous views as those of the Hindus. Therefore I like to confront the theories of the one nation with those of the other simply on account of their close relationship, not in order to correct them. For that which is not *the truth* (*i.e.* the true belief or monotheism) does not admit of any correction, and all heathenism, whether Greek or Indian, is in its pith and marrow one and the same belief, because it is only a deviation *from the truth*. The Greeks, however, had philosophers who, living in their country, discovered and worked out for them the elements of science, not of popular superstition, for it is the object of the upper classes to be guided by the results of science, whilst the common crowd will always be inclined to plunge into wrong-headed wrangling, as long as they are not kept down by fear of punishment. Think of Socrates when he opposed the crowd of his nation as to their idolatry and did not want to call the stars gods! At once eleven of the twelve judges of the Athenians agreed on a sentence of death, and Socrates died faithful to the truth.

The Hindus had no men of this stamp both capable and willing to bring sciences to a classical perfection. Therefore you mostly find that even the so-called scientific theorems of the Hindus are in a state of utter confusion, devoid of any logical order, and in the last instance always mixed up with the silly notions of the crowd, *e.g.* immense numbers, enormous spaces of time, and all kinds of religious dogmas, which the vulgar belief does not admit of being called into question. Therefore it is a prevailing practice among the Hindus *jurare in verba magistri*; and I can only compare their mathematical and astronomical literature, as far as I know it, to a mixture of pearl shells and sour dates, or of pearls Page 13.
and dung, or of costly crystals and common pebbles. Both kinds of things are equal in their eyes, since they cannot raise themselves to the methods of a strictly scientific deduction.

The author's method.

In most parts of my work I simply relate without criticising, unless there be a special reason for doing so. I mention the necessary Sanskrit names and technical terms once where the context of our explanation demands it. If the word is an *original* one, the meaning of which can be rendered in Arabic, I only use the corresponding Arabic word; if, however, the Sanskrit word be more practical, we keep this, trying to transliterate it as accurately as possible. If the word is a secondary or *derived* one, but in general use, we also keep it, though there be a corresponding term in Arabic, but before using it we explain its signification. In this way we have tried to facilitate the understanding of the terminology.

Lastly, we observe that we cannot always in our discussions strictly adhere to the geometrical method, only referring to that which precedes and never to that which follows, as we must sometimes introduce in a chapter an unknown factor, the explanation of which can only be given in a later part of the book, God helping us!

CHAPTER II.

ON THE BELIEF OF THE HINDUS IN GOD.

The nature of God.

THE belief of educated and uneducated people differs in every nation; for the former strive to conceive abstract ideas and to define general principles, whilst the latter do not pass beyond the apprehension of the senses, and are content with derived rules, without caring for details, especially in questions of religion and law, regarding which opinions and interests are divided.

The Hindus believe with regard to God that he is one, eternal, without beginning and end, acting by free-will, almighty, all-wise, living, giving life, ruling, preserving; one who in his sovereignty is unique, beyond all likeness and unlikeness, and that he does not resemble anything nor does anything resemble him. In order to illustrate this we shall produce some extracts from their literature, lest the reader should think that our account is nothing but hearsay.

Quotation from Patañjali.

In the book of Patañjali the pupil asks:

"Who is the worshipped one, by the worship of whom blessing is obtained?"

The master says:

"It is he who, being eternal and unique, does not for his part stand in need of any human action for which he might give as a recompense either a blissful repose, which is hoped and longed for, or a troubled existence, which is feared and dreaded. He is unattainable to thought, being sublime beyond all unlikeness which is abhorrent and all likeness which is sympathetic. He by his essence knows from all eternity. *Knowledge*, in the human sense of the term, has as its object that which was *unknown* before, whilst *not knowing* does not at any time or in any condition apply to God."

Further the pupil speaks:

"Do you attribute to him other qualities besides those you have mentioned?"

The master says:

"He is height, absolute in the idea, not in *space*, for he is sublime beyond all existence *in any space*. He is the pure absolute good, longed for by every created being. He is the knowledge free from the defilement of forgetfulness and not-knowing."

The pupil speaks:

"Do you attribute to him speech or not?"

The master says:

"As he knows, he no doubt also speaks."

The pupil asks:

"If he *speaks* because he *knows*, what, then, is the difference between him and the *knowing* sages who have *spoken* of their *knowing?*"

The master says:

Page 14. "The difference between them is time, for they have learned in time and spoken in time, after having been not-knowing and not-speaking. By speech they have transferred their knowledge to others. Therefore their speaking and acquiring knowledge take place in time. And as divine matters have no connection with time, God is *knowing, speaking* from eternity. It was he who spoke to Brahman, and to others of the first beings in different ways. On the one he bestowed a book; for the other he opened a door, a means of communicating with him; a third one he inspired so that he obtained by cogitation what God bestowed upon him."

The pupil asks:

"Whence has he this knowing?"

The master answers:

"His knowing is the same from all eternity, for ever and ever. As he has never been not-knowing, he is *knowing* of himself, having never acquired any knowledge which he did not possess before. He speaks in the Veda which he sent down upon Brahman:

"'*Praise and celebrate him who has spoken the Veda, and was before the Veda.*'"

The pupil asks:

"How do you worship him to whom the perception of the senses cannot attain?"

The master says:

"His name proves his existence, for where there is a report there must be something to which it refers, and where there is a name there must be something which is named. He is hidden to the senses and unperceivable by them. However, the soul perceives him, and thought comprehends his qualities. This meditation is identical with worshipping him exclusively, and by practising it uninterruptedly beatitude is obtained."

In this way the Hindus express themselves in this very famous book.

The following passage is taken from the book *Gîtâ*, a part of the book *Bhârata*, from the conversation between Vâsudeva and Arjuna:— Quotation from the book *Gîtâ*.

"I am the universe, without a beginning by being born, or without an end by dying. I do not aim by whatever I do at any recompense. I do not specially belong to one class of beings to the exclusion of others, as if I were the friend of one and the enemy of others. I have given to each one in my creation what is sufficient for him in all his functions. Therefore whoever knows me in this capacity, and tries to become similar to me by keeping desire apart from his action, his fetters will be loosened, and he will easily be saved and freed."

This passage reminds one of the definition of philosophy as *the striving to become as much as possible similar to God.*

Further, Vâsudeva speaks in the same book :—

"It is desire which causes most men to take refuge with God for their wants. But if you examine their case closely, you will find that they are very far from having an accurate knowledge of him; for God is not apparent to every one, so that he might perceive him with his senses. Therefore they do not know him. Some of them do not pass beyond what their senses perceive; some pass beyond this, but stop at the knowledge of the *laws of nature*, without learning that above them there is one who did not give birth nor was born, the essence of whose being has not been comprehended by the knowledge of any one, while *his* knowledge comprehends everything."

On the notions of the action and the agent.

The Hindus differ among themselves as to the definition of what is *action*. Some who make God the source of action consider him as the universal cause; for as the existence of the *agents* derives from him, he is the cause of their action, and in consequence it is his own action coming into existence through their intermediation. Others do not derive action from God, but from other sources, considering them as the *particular causes* which in the last instance—according to external observation—produce the action in question.

Quotation from the book *Sâṁkhya.*

In the book *Sâṁkhya* the devotee speaks: "Has there been a difference of opinion about *action* and the *agent*, or not?"

The sage speaks: "Some people say that the soul is not alive and the matter not living; that God, who is self-sufficing, is he who unites them and separates them
Page 15. from each other; that therefore in reality he himself is the *agent*. *Action* proceeds from him in such a way that he causes both the soul and the matter to move, like as that which is living and powerful moves that which is dead and weak.

"Others say that the union of *action* and the *agent* is effected by nature, and that such is the usual process in everything that increases and decreases.

"Others say the agent is the soul, because in the Véda it is said, 'Every being comes from Purusha.' According to others, the agent is time, for the world is tied to time as a sheep is tied to a strong cord, so that its motion depends upon whether the cord is drawn tight or slackened. Still others say that action is nothing but a recompense for something which has been done before.

"All these opinions are wrong. The truth is, that action entirely belongs to matter, for matter binds the soul, causes it to wander about in different shapes, and then sets it free. Therefore matter is the agent, all that belongs to matter helps it to accomplish action. But the soul is not an agent, because it is devoid of the different faculties."

This is what educated people believe about God. They call him *íśvara*, *i.e.* self-sufficing, beneficent, who gives without receiving. They consider the unity of God as absolute, but that everything beside God which may appear as a unity is really a plurality of things. The existence of God they consider as a real existence, because everything that exists exists through him. It is not impossible to think that the existing beings are *not* and that he *is*, but it is impossible to think that he *is not* and that they *are*.

Philosophical and vulgar notions about the nature of God.

If we now pass from the ideas of the educated people among the Hindus to those of the common people, we must first state that they present a great variety. Some of them are simply abominable, but similar errors also occur in other religions. Nay, even in Islam we must decidedly disapprove, *e.g.* of the anthropomorphic doctrines, the teachings of the Jabriyya sect, the prohibition of the discussion of religious topics, and such like. Every religious sentence destined for the people at large must be carefully worded, as the following example shows. Some Hindu scholar calls God *a point*, meaning to say thereby that the qualities of bodies do not apply to him. Now some uneducated man reads this and imagines, God is as small as *a point*, and he does not find out what the word *point* in this sentence was really intended to express. He will not even stop with this offensive comparison, but will describe God as much larger, and will say, "He is twelve fingers long and ten fingers broad." Praise be to God, who is far above measure and number! Further, if an uneducated man hears what we have mentioned, that God comprehends the universe so that nothing is concealed from him, he will at once imagine that this comprehending is effected by means of eyesight; that eyesight is only possible by means of an eye, and that two eyes are better than only one; and in consequence he will describe God as having a thousand eyes, meaning to describe his omniscience.

Similar hideous fictions are sometimes met with among the Hindus, especially among those castes who are not allowed to occupy themselves with science, of whom we shall speak hereafter.

CHAPTER III.

ON THE HINDU BELIEF AS TO CREATED THINGS, BOTH "INTELLIGIBILIA" AND "SENSIBILIA."

ON this subject the ancient Greeks held nearly the same view as the Hindus, at all events in those times before philosophy rose high among them under the care of the seven so-called *pillars of wisdom*, viz. Solon of Athens, Bias of Priene, Periander of Corinth, Thales of Miletus, Chilon of Lacedæmon, Pittacus of Lesbos, and Cleobulus of Lindos, and their successors. Some of them thought that all things are *one*, and this *one* thing is according to some τὸ λανθάνειν, according to others ἡ δύναμις; that *e.g.* man has only this prerogative before a stone and the inanimate world, that he is by one degree nearer than they to the *First Cause*. But this he would not be anything better than they.

Notions of the Greeks and the Ṣûfî philosophers as to the *First Cause*.

Page 16.

Others think that only *the First Cause* has real existence, because it alone is self-sufficing, whilst everything else absolutely requires it; that a thing which for its existence stands in need of something else has only a dream-life, no real life, and that reality is only that *one* and *first* being (*the First Cause*).

This is also the theory of the *Ṣûfîs*, i.e. *the sages*, for *ṣûf* means in Greek *wisdom* (σοφία). Therefore a philosopher is called *pailâsôpâ* (φιλόσοφος), *i.e.* loving wisdom. When in Islam persons adopted something like the doctrines of these *philosophers*, they also adopted their name; but some people did not understand the meaning of the word, and erroneously combined it with

Origin of the word Ṣûfî.

the Arabic word *ṣuffa*, as if the *Ṣûfi* (= φιλόσοφοι) were identical with the so-called *'Ahl-aṣṣuffa* among the companions of Muḥammad. In later times the word was corrupted by misspelling, so that finally it was taken for a derivation from *ṣûf*, i.e. *the wool of goats.* Abû-alfatḥ Albustî made a laudable effort to avoid this mistake when he said, "From olden times people have differed as to the meaning of the word *ṣûfi*, and have thought it a derivative from *ṣûf*, *i.e.* wool. I, for my part, understand by the word a youth who is *ṣâfi*, *i.e.* pure. This *ṣâfi* has become *ṣûfi*, and in this form the name of a class of thinkers, the *Ṣûfi*."

Further, the same Greeks think that the existing world is only *one* thing; that the First Cause appears in it under various shapes; that the power of the First Cause is inherent in the parts of the world under different circumstances, which cause a certain difference of the things of the world notwithstanding their original unity.

Others thought that he who turns with his whole being towards the First Cause, striving to become as much as possible similar to *it*, will become united with *it* after having passed the intermediate stages, and stripped of all appendages and impediments. Similar views are also held by the *Ṣûfi*, because of the similarity of the dogma.

As to the souls and spirits, the Greeks think that they exist by themselves before they enter bodies; that they exist in certain numbers and groups, which stand in various relations to each other, knowing each other and not knowing; that they, whilst staying in bodies, earn by the actions of their free-will that lot which awaits them after their separation from the bodies, *i.e.* the faculty of ruling the world in various ways. Therefore they called them gods, built temples in their names and offered them sacrifices; as Galenus says in his book called προτρεπτικὸς εἰς τὰς τέχνας: "Excel-

Galenus.

lent men have obtained the honour of being reckoned among the deified beings only for the noble spirit in which they cultivated the arts, not for their prowess in wrestling and discus-throwing. *E.g.* Asclepius and Dionysos, whether they were originally human beings in bygone times and afterwards deified, or were divine beings from the very beginning, deserved in any case the greatest of honours, because the one taught mankind the science of medicine, the other the art of the cultivation of the vine." Page 17.

Galenus says in his commentary on the aphorisms of Hippocrates: "As regards the offerings to Asclepius, we have never heard that anybody offered him a goat, because the weaving of goat's-hair is not easy, and much goat's-meat produces epilepsy, since the humours of the goats are bad. People only offer him a cock, as also Hippocrates has done. For this divine man acquired for mankind the art of medicine, which is much superior to that which Dionysos and Demeter have invented, *i.e.* the wine and the cereals whence bread is prepared. Therefore cereals are called by the name of Demeter and the vine is called by the name of Dionysos."

Plato says in his *Timaeus*: "The θεοί whom the barbarians call *gods*, because of their not dying, are the δαίμονες, whilst they call *the* god *the first god*." Plato.

Further he says: "God spoke to the gods, 'You are not of yourselves exempt from destruction. Only you will not perish by death. You have obtained from my will at the time when I created you, the firmest covenant.'"

In another passage of the same book he says: "God is in the single number; there are no gods in the plural number."

These quotations prove that the Greeks call in general *god* everything that is glorious and noble, and the like usage exists among many nations. They go even so far as to call *gods* the mountains, the seas, &c. Secondly, they apply the term *god* in a special sense to the *First Cause*, to the angels, and to their souls. According to a third usage, Plato calls gods the *Sekînât* (= Μοῦσαι). But on this subject the terms of the interpreters are not perfectly clear; in consequence of which we only know the name, but not what it means. Johannes Grammaticus says in his refutation of Proclus: "The Greeks gave the name of gods to the visible bodies in heaven, as many barbarians do. Afterwards, when they came to philosophise on the abstract ideas of the world of thought, they called these by the name of gods."

Johannes Grammaticus.

Hence we must necessarily infer that being deified means something like the state of angels, according to our notions. This Galenus says in clear words in the same book: "If it is true that Asclepius was a man in bygone times, and that then God deigned to make him one of the angels, everything else is idle talk."

Galenus.

In another passage of the same book he says: "God spoke to Lycurgus, 'I am in doubt concerning you, whether to call you a man or an angel, but I incline to the latter.'"

Difference of denominating God in Arabic, Hebrew, and Syriac.

There are, however, certain expressions which are offensive according to the notions of one religion, whilst they are admissible according to those of another, which may pass in one language, whilst they are rejected by another. To this class belongs the word *apotheosis*, which has a bad sound in the ears of Muslims. If we consider the use of the word *god* in the Arabic language, we find that all the names by which the *pure truth*, *i.e.* Allâh, has been named, may somehow or other be applied to other beings besides him, except the word *Allâh*, which only applies to *God*, and which has been called his *greatest name*.

Page 18.

If we consider the use of the word in Hebrew and

Syriac, in which two languages the sacred books before the Koran were revealed, we find that in the Thora and the following books of prophets which are reckoned with the Thora as one whole, that word *Rabb* corresponds to the word *Allâh* in Arabic, in so far as it cannot in a genitive construction be applied to anybody besides God, and you cannot say the *rabb* of the house, the *rabb* of the property (which in Arabic is allowed). And, secondly, we find that the word *'Eloah* in Hebrew corresponds in its usage there to the word *Rabb* in Arabic (*i.e.* that in Hebrew the word אֱלֹהַ may apply to other beings but *God*, like the word رَبّ in Arabic). The following passages occur in those books:—

"The sons of *Elohim* came in unto the daughters of men" (Gen. vi. 4), before the deluge, and cohabited with them.

"Satan entered together with the sons of *Elohim* into their meeting" (Job i. 6).

In the Thora of Moses God speaks to him: "I have made thee a *god* to Pharaoh" (Exod. vii. 1).

In the 82d Psalm of the Psalter of David the following occurs: "God standeth in the congregation of the *gods*" (Ps. lxxxii. 1), *i.e.* of the angels.

In the Thora the idols are called *foreign gods.* If the Thora had not forbidden to worship any other being but God, if it had not forbidden people to prostrate themselves before the idols, nay, even to mention them and to think of them, one might infer from this expression (*foreign gods*) that the order of the Bible refers only to the abolition of *foreign gods,* which would mean *gods that are not Hebrew ones* (as if the Hebrews had adored *national gods,* in opposition to the *gods* of their neighbours). The nations round Palestine were idol worshippers like the heathen Greeks, and the Israelites always rebelled against God by worshipping the idol of Baal (lit. *Ba'lâ*) and the idol of Ashtârôth, *i.e.* Venus.

From all this it is evident that the Hebrews used to

apply the term *being god*, grammatically a term like *being king*, to the angels, to the souls invested with divine power (v. p. 34); by way of comparison, also, to the images which were made to represent the bodies of those beings; lastly, metaphorically, to kings and to other great men.

Passing from the word *God* to those of *father* and *son*, we must state that Islam is not liberal in the use of them; for in Arabic the word *son* means nearly always as much as a *child* in the natural order of things, and from the ideas involved in parentage and birth can never be derived any expression meaning the Eternal Lord of creation. Other languages, however, take much more liberty in this respect; so that if people address a man by *father*, it is nearly the same as if they addressed him by *sir*. As is well known, phrases of this kind have become so prevalent among the Christians, that anybody who does not always use the words *father* and *son* in addressing people would scarcely be considered as one of them. By *the son* they understand most especially Jesus, but apply it also to others besides him. It is Jesus who orders his disciples to say in prayer, "O our *father* which art in heaven" (St. Matt. vi. 9); and informing them of his approaching death, he says that he is going to his *father* and to their *father* (St. John xx. 17). In most of his speeches he explains the word *the son* as meaning himself, that he is *the son of man*.

Besides the Christians, the Jews too use similar ex-
Page 19. pressions; for the 2d Book of Kings relates that God consoled David for the loss of his son, who had been borne to him by the wife of Uriah, and promised him another son from her, whom he would *adopt as his own son* (1 Chron. xxii. 9, 10). If the use of the Hebrew language admits that Salomo is by adoption a *son* of God, it is admissible that he who adopted was a *father*, viz. God.

The Manichæans stand in a near relationship to the Christians. Mânî expresses himself in a similar way in the book called *Kanz-al'iḥyâ* (*Thesaurus Vivificationis*): "The resplendent hosts will be called young women and virgins, fathers and mothers, sons, brothers, and sisters, because such is the custom in the books of the prophets. In the country of joy there is neither male nor female, nor are there organs of generation. All are invested with living bodies. Since they have divine bodies, they do not differ from each other in weakness and force, in length and shortness, in figure and looks; they are like similar lamps, which are lighted by the same lamp, and which are nourished by the same material. The cause of this kind of name-giving arises, in the last instance, from the rivalry of the two realms in mixing up with each other. When the low dark realm rose from the abyss of chaos, and was seen by the high resplendent realm as consisting of pairs of male and female beings, the latter gave similar outward forms to its own children, who started to fight that other world, so that it placed in the fight one kind of beings opposite the same kind of the other world." Note on the Manichæans.

The educated among the Hindus abhor anthropomorphisms of this kind, but the crowd and the members of the single sects use them most extensively. They go even beyond all we have hitherto mentioned, so as to speak of wife, son, daughter, of the rendering pregnant and other physical processes, all in connection with God. They are even so little pious, that, when speaking of these things, they do not even abstain from silly and unbecoming language. However, nobody minds these classes and their theories, though they be numerous. The main and most essential point of the Hindu world of thought is that which the Brahmans think and believe, for they are specially trained for preserving and maintaining their religion. And this it is which we shall explain, viz. the belief of the Brahmans. Notions of the educated Hindus. All created beings are a unity.

Regarding the whole creation (τὸ ὄν), they think that it is a unity, as has already been declared, because Vâsudeva speaks in the book called *Gîtâ*: "To speak accurately, we must say that all things are divine; for Vishṇu made himself the earth that the living beings should rest thereupon; he made himself water to nourish them thereby; he made himself fire and wind in order to make them grow; and he made himself the heart of every single being. He presented them with recollection and knowledge and the two opposite qualities, as is mentioned in the Veda."

How much does this resemble the expression of the author of the book of Apollonius, *De Causis Rerum*, as if the one had been taken from the other! He says: "There is in all men a divine power, by which all things, both material and immaterial, are apprehended." Thus in Persian the immaterial Lord is called *Khudhâ*, and in a derivative sense the word is also used to mean a man, *i.e.* a human lord.

Purusha.

I. Those Hindus who prefer clear and accurate definitions to vague allusions call the soul *purusha*, which means *man*, because it is the living element in the existing world. Life is the only attribute which they give to it. They describe it as alternately knowing and not knowing, as not knowing ἐν πράξει (actually), and as knowing ἐν δυνάμει (potentially), gaining knowledge by acquisition. The not-knowing of *purusha* is the cause why action comes into existence, and its knowing is the cause why action ceases.

Page 20.

Avyakta.

II. Next follows the general matter, *i.e.* the abstract ὕλη, which they call *avyakta*, *i.e.* a shapeless thing. It is dead, but has three powers potentially, not actually, which are called *sattva*, *rajas*, and *tamas*. I have heard that Buddhodana (*sic*), in speaking to his adherents the Shamanians, calls them *buddha*, *dharma*, *saṅgha*, as it were *intelligence*, *religion*, and *ignorance* (*sic*). The first power is rest and goodness, and hence come existing and growing. The second is exertion and fatigue, and hence come firmness and duration. The third is languor and irresolution, and hence come ruin and perishing. Therefore the first power is attributed to the angels, the second to men, the third to the animals. The ideas *before*, *afterwards*, and *thereupon* may be predicated of all these things only in the sense of a certain sequence and on account of the inadequacy of language, but not so as to indicate any ordinary notions of time.

III. Matter proceeding from δύναμις into πρᾶξις under the various shapes and with the *three primary forces* is called *vyakta*, i.e. *having shape*, whilst the union of the *abstract* ὕλη and of the *shaped matter* is called *prakṛiti*. This term, however, is of no use to us; we do not want to speak of an *abstract* matter, the term *matter* alone being sufficient for us, since the one does not exist without the other. Vyakta and prakṛiti.

IV. Next comes *nature*, which they call *ahaṅkâra*. The word is derived from the ideas of *overpowering*, *developing*, and *self-assertion*, because matter when assuming shape causes things to develop into new forms, and this growing consists in the changing of a foreign element and assimilating it to the growing one. Hence it is as if *Nature* were trying to overpower those *other* or foreign elements in this process of changing them, and were subduing that which is changed. Ahaṅkâra.

V.–IX. As a matter of course, each compound presupposes simple elements from which it is compounded and into which it is resolved again. The universal existences in the world are the five elements, *i.e.* according to the Hindus: heaven, wind, fire, water, and earth. They are called *mahâbhûta*, i.e. *having great natures*. They do not think, as other people do, that the fire is a hot dry body near the bottom of the ether. They understand by fire the common fire on earth which comes from an inflammation of smoke. The *Vâyu Purâṇa* says: "In the beginning were earth, water, wind, Mahâbhûta Annotation from *Vâyu Purâṇa*.

and heaven. Brahman, on seeing sparks under the earth, brought them forward and divided them into three parts: the first, *pârthiva*, is the common fire, which requires wood and is extinguished by water; the second is *divya*, *i.e.* the sun; the third, *vidyut*, *i.e.* the lightning. The sun attracts the water; the lightning shines through the water. In the animals, also, there is fire in the midst of moist substances, which serve to nourish the fire and do not extinguish it."

Pañca mátáras. **Page 21.**

X.–XIV. As these elements are compound, they presuppose simple ones which are called *pañca mátáras*, *i.e.* five mothers. They describe them as the functions of the senses. The simple element of heaven is *śabda*, *i.e.* that which is heard; that of the wind is *sparśa*, *i.e.* that which is touched; that of the fire is *rûpa*, *i.e.* that which is seen; that of the water is *rasa*, *i.e.* that which is tasted; and that of the earth is *gandha*, *i.e.* that which is smelled. With each of these *mahâbhúta* elements (earth, water, &c.) they connect, firstly, *one* of the *pañca-mátáras* elements, as we have here shown; and, secondly, all those which have been attributed to the *mahâbhúta* elements previously mentioned. So the earth has all five qualities; the water has them *minus* the smelling (= four qualities); the fire has them *minus* the smelling and tasting (*i.e.* three qualities); the wind has them *minus* smelling, tasting, and seeing (*i.e.* two qualities); heaven has them *minus* smelling, tasting, seeing, and touching (*i.e.* one quality).

I do not know what the Hindus mean by bringing *sound* into relation with heaven. Perhaps they mean something similar to what Homer, the poet of the ancient Greeks, said, "*Those invested with the seven melodies speak and give answer to each other in a pleasant tone.*" Thereby he meant the seven planets; as another poet says, "*The spheres endowed with different melodies are seven, moving eternally, praising the Creator, for it is he who holds them and embraces them unto the farthest end of the starless sphere.*"

Porphyry says in his book on the opinions of the most prominent philosophers about the nature of the sphere: "The heavenly bodies moving about in forms and shapes and with wonderful melodies, which are fixed for ever, as Pythagoras and Diogenes have explained, point to their Creator, who is without equal and without shape. People say that Diogenes had such subtle senses that he, and *he* alone, could hear the sound of the motion of the sphere."

All these expressions are rather hints than clear speech, but admitting of a correct interpretation on a scientific basis. Some successor of those philosophers, one of those who did not grasp the full truth, says: "Sight is watery, hearing airy, smelling fiery, tasting earthy, and touching is what the soul bestows upon everybody by uniting itself with it." I suppose this philosopher connects the sight with the water because he had heard of the moist substances of the eye and of their different classes (*lacuna*); he refers the smelling to the fire on account of frankincense and smoke; the tasting to the earth because of his nourishment which the earth yields him. As, then, the four elements are finished, he is compelled for the fifth sense, the touching, to have recourse to the soul.

The result of all these elements which we have enumerated, *i.e.* a compound of all of them, is the animal. The Hindus consider the plants as a species of animal as Plato also thinks that the plants have a sense, because they have the faculty of distinguishing between that which suits them and that which is detrimental to them. The animal is an animal as distinguished from a stone by virtue of its possession of the senses.

XV.–XIX. The senses are five, called *indriyáṇi*, the hearing by the ear, the seeing by the eye, the smelling by the nose, the tasting by the tongue, and the touching by the skin. Indriyáṇi.

XX. Next follows the will, which directs the senses Mansa.

in the exercise of their various functions, and which dwells in the heart. Therefore they call it *manas*.

Karmendriyâṇi.

XXI.–XXV. The animal nature is rendered perfect by five *necessary functions*, which they call *karmendriyâṇi, i.e.* the senses of action. The former senses bring about learning and knowledge, the latter action and work. We shall call them the *necessaria*. They are: 1. To produce a sound for any of the different wants and wishes a man may have; 2. To throw the hands with force, in order to draw towards or to put away; 3. To walk with the feet, in order to seek something or to fly from it; 4, 5. The ejection of the superfluous elements of nourishment by means of the two openings created for the purpose.

Page 22.

Recapitulation of the twenty-five elements.

The whole of these elements are twenty-five, viz.:—

1. The general soul.
2. The abstract ὕλη.
3. The shaped matter.
4. The overpowering nature.

5–9. The simple mothers.

10–14. The primary elements.

15–19. The senses of apperception.

20. The directing will.

21–25. The instrumental *necessaria*.

The totality of these elements is called *tattva*, and all knowledge is restricted to them. Therefore Vyâsa the son of Parâśara speaks: "Learn twenty-five by distinctions, definitions, and divisions, as you learn a logical syllogism, and something which is a certainty, not merely studying with the tongue. Afterwards adhere to whatever religion you like; your end will be salvation."

CHAPTER IV.

FROM WHAT CAUSE ACTION ORIGINATES, AND HOW THE SOUL IS CONNECTED WITH MATTER.

The soul longing to be united with the body, is so united by intermediary spirits.

VOLUNTARY actions cannot originate in the body of any animal, unless the body be living and exist in close contact with that which is living of itself, *i.e.* the soul. The Hindus maintain that the soul is ἐν πράξει, not ἐν δυνάμει, ignorant of its own essential nature and of its material substratum, longing to apprehend what it does not know, and believing that it cannot exist unless by matter. As, therefore, it longs for the good which is duration, and wishes to learn that which is hidden from it, it starts off in order to be united with matter. However, substances which are dense and such as are *tenuous*, if they have these qualities in the very highest degree, can mix together only by means of intermediary elements which stand in a certain relation to each of the two. Thus the air is the medium between fire and water, which are opposed to each other by these two qualities, for the air is related to the fire in tenuity and to the water in density, and by either of these qualities it renders the one capable of mixing with the other. Now, there is no greater antithesis than that between *body* and *not-body*. Therefore the soul, being what it is, cannot obtain the fulfilment of its wish but by similar media, spirits which derive their existence from the *matres simplices* in the worlds called *Bhûrloka*, *Bhuvarloka*, and *Svarloka*. The Hindus call them *tenuous bodies* over which the soul rises like the sun over the earth, in order to distinguish them from the *dense bodies* which derive their existence from the common five elements. The soul, in consequence of this union with the media, uses them as its vehicles. Thus the image of the sun, though he is only *one*, is represented in many mirrors which are placed opposite to him, as also in the water of vessels placed opposite. The sun is seen alike in each mirror and each vessel, and in each of them his warming and light-giving effect is perceived.

When, now, the various bodies, being from their nature compounds of different things, come into existence, being composed of *male* elements, viz. bones, veins, and sperma, and of *female* elements, viz. flesh, blood, and hair, and being thus fully prepared to receive life, then those spirits unite themselves with them, and the bodies are to the spirits what castles or fortresses are to the various affairs of princes. In a farther stage of development five winds enter the bodies. By the first and second of them the inhaling and exhaling are effected, by the third the mixture of the victuals in the stomach, by the fourth the locomotion of the body from one place to the other, by the fifth the transferring of the apperception of the senses from one side of the body to the other.

Page 23.

Five winds regulating the functions of the body.

The difference of the souls depending upon the difference of the bodies and their interaction.

The spirits here mentioned do not, according to the notions of the Hindus, differ from each other in substance, but have a precisely identical nature. However, their individual characters and manners differ in the same measure as the bodies with which they are united differ, on account of the three forces which are in them striving with each other for supremacy, and on account of their harmony being disturbed by the passions of envy and wrath.

Such, then, is the supreme highest cause of the soul's starting off into action.

On the other hand, the *lowest* cause, as proceeding

from matter, is this: that matter for its part seeks for perfection, and always prefers that which is better to that which is less good, viz. proceeding from δύναμις into πρᾶξις. In consequence of the vainglory and ambition which are its pith and marrow, matter produces and shows all kinds of possibilities which it contains to its pupil, the soul, and carries it round through all classes of vegetable and animal beings. Hindus compare the soul to a dancing-girl who is clever in her art and knows well what effect each motion and pose of hers has. She is in the presence of a sybarite most eager of enjoying what she has learned. Now she begins to produce the various kinds of her art one after the other under the admiring gaze of the host, until her programme is finished and the eagerness of the spectator has been satisfied. Then she stops suddenly, since she could not produce anything but a repetition; and as a repetition is not wished for, he dismisses her, and action ceases. The close of this kind of relation is illustrated by the following simile: A caravan has been attacked in the desert by robbers, and the members of it have fled in all directions except a blind man and a lame man, who remain on the spot in helplessness, despairing of their escape. After they meet and recognise each other, the lame speaks to the blind: "I cannot move, but I can lead the way, whilst the opposite is the case with you. Therefore put me on your shoulder and carry me, that I may show you the way and that we may escape together from this calamity." This the blind man did. They obtained their purpose by helping each other, and they left each other on coming out of the desert.

On matter seeking the union with the soul.

Illustrations of this particular kind of union.

Further, the Hindus speak in different ways of the *agent*, as we have already mentioned. So the *Vishṇu Purâṇa* says: "Matter is the origin of the world. Its action in the world rises from an innate disposition, as a tree sows its own seed by an innate disposition, not

Action of matter rising from an innate disposition.

intentionally, and the wind cools the water though it only intends blowing. *Voluntary* action is only due to Vishṇu." By the latter expression the author means the living being who is above matter (God). Through him matter becomes an *agent* toiling for him as a friend toils for a friend without wanting anything for himself.

On this theory Mâni has built the following sentence: "The Apostles asked Jesus about the life of inanimate nature, whereupon he said, 'If that which is inanimate is separated from the living element which is commingled with it, and appears alone by itself, it is again

Page 24.

inanimate and is not capable of living, whilst the living element which has left it, retaining its vital energy unimpaired, never dies.'"

On matter as the cause of action according to the Sâṁkhya school of philosophers.

The book of Sâṁkhya derives action from matter, for the difference of forms under which matter appears depends upon the *three primary forces*, and upon whether one or two of them gain the supremacy over the remainder. Those forces are the *angelic*, the *human*, and the *animal*. The three forces belong only to matter, not to the soul. The task of the soul is to learn the actions of matter like a spectator, resembling a traveller who sits down in a village to repose. Each villager is busy with his own particular work, but he looks at them and considers their doings, disliking some, liking others, and taking an example from them. In this way he is busy without having himself any share in the business going on, and without being the cause which has brought it about.

The book of Sâṁkhya brings action into relation with the soul, though the soul has nothing to do with action, only in so far as it resembles a man who happens to get into the company of people whom he does not know. They are robbers returning from a village which they have sacked and destroyed, and he has scarcely marched with them a short distance, when they are overtaken by the avengers. The whole party are taken prisoners, and together with them the innocent man is dragged off; and being treated precisely as they are, he receives the same punishment, without having taken part in their action.

People say the soul resembles the rain-water which comes down from heaven, always the same and of the same nature. However, if it is gathered in vessels placed for the purpose, vessels of different materials, of gold, silver, glass, earthenware, clay, or bitter-salt earth, it begins to differ in appearance, taste, and smell. Thus the soul does not influence matter in any way, except in this, that it gives matter life by being in close contact with it. When, then, matter begins to act, the result is different, in conformity with the one of the *three primary forces* which happens to preponderate, and conformably to the mutual assistance which the other two latent forces afford to the former. This assistance may be given in various ways, as the fresh oil, the dry wick, and the smoking fire help each other to produce light. The soul is in matter like the rider on a carriage, being attended by the senses, who drive the carriage according to the rider's intentions. But the soul for its part is guided by the intelligence with which it is inspired by God. This *intelligence* they describe as that by which the reality of things is apprehended, which shows the way to the knowledge of God, and to such actions as are liked and praised by everybody.

CHAPTER V.

ON THE STATE OF THE SOULS, AND THEIR MIGRATIONS THROUGH THE WORLD IN THE METEMPSYCHOSIS.

As *the word of confession*, "There is no god but God, Muḥammad is his prophet," is the shibboleth of Islam, the Trinity that of Christianity, and the institute of the Sabbath that of Judaism, so metempsychosis is the shibboleth of the Hindu religion. Therefore he who does not believe in it does not belong to them, and is not reckoned as one of them. For they hold the following belief:—

Beginning, development, and ultimate result of metempsychosis. Page 25.

The soul, as long as it has not risen to the highest absolute intelligence, does not comprehend the totality of objects at once, or, as it were, in no time. Therefore it must explore all particular beings and examine all the possibilities of existence; and as their number is, though not unlimited, still an enormous one, the soul wants an enormous space of time in order to finish the contemplation of such a multiplicity of objects. The soul acquires knowledge only by the contemplation of the individuals and the species, and of their peculiar actions and conditions. It gains experience from each object, and gathers thereby new knowledge.

However, these actions differ in the same measure as the three primary forces differ. Besides, the world is not left without some direction, being led, as it were, by a bridle and directed towards a definite scope. Therefore the imperishable souls wander about in perishable bodies conformably to the difference of their actions, as they prove to be good or bad. The object of the migration through the world of *reward* (*i.e.* heaven) is to direct the attention of the soul to the good, that it should become desirous of acquiring as much of it as possible. The object of its migration through the world of *punishment* (*i.e.* hell) is to direct its attention to the bad and abominable, that it should strive to keep as far as possible aloof from it.

The migration begins from low stages, and rises to higher and better ones, not the contrary, as we state on purpose, since the one is *a priori* as possible as the other. The difference of these lower and higher stages depends upon the difference of the actions, and this again results from the quantitative and qualitative diversity of the temperaments and the various degrees of combinations in which they appear.

This migration lasts until the object aimed at has been completely attained both for the soul and matter; the *lower* aim being the disappearance of the shape of matter, except any such new formation as may appear desirable; the *higher* aim being the ceasing of the desire of the soul to learn what it did not know before, the insight of the soul into the nobility of its own being and its independent existence, its knowing that it can dispense with matter after it has become acquainted with the mean nature of matter and the instability of its shapes, with all that which matter offers to the senses, and with the truth of the tales about its delights. Then the soul turns away from matter; the connecting links are broken, the union is dissolved. Separation and dissolution take place, and the soul returns to its home, carrying with itself as much of the bliss of knowledge as sesame develops grains and blossoms, afterwards never separating from its oil. The intelligent being, intelligence and its object, are united and become one.

It is now our duty to produce from their literature

Quotations from the book *Gîtâ*.

some clear testimonies as to this subject and cognate theories of other nations.

Vâsudeva speaks to Arjuna instigating him to the battle, whilst they stand between the two lines: "If you believe in predestination, you must know that neither they nor we are mortal, and do not go away without a return, for the souls are immortal and unchangeable. They migrate through the bodies, while man changes from childhood into youth, into manhood and infirm age, the end of which is the death of the body. Thereafter the soul proceeds on its return."

Further he says: "How can a man think of death and being killed who knows that the soul is eternal, not having been born and not perishing; that the soul is something stable and constant; that no sword can cut it, no fire burn it, no water extinguish it, and no wind wither it? The soul migrates from its body, after it has become old, into another, a different one, as the body, when its dress has become old, is clad in another. What then is your sorrow about a soul which does not perish? If it were perishable, it would be more becoming that you should not sorrow about a thing which may be dispensed with, which does not exist, and does not return into existence. But if you look more to your body than to your soul, and are in anxiety about its perishing, you must know that all that which is born dies, and that all that which dies returns into another existence. However, both life and death are not your concern. They are in the hands of God, from whom all things come and to whom they return."

Page 26.

In the further course of conversation Arjuna speaks to Vâsudeva: "How did you dare thus to fight Brahman, Brahman who was before the world was and before man was, whilst you are living among us as a being, whose birth and age are known?"

Thereupon Vâsudeva answered: "Eternity (pre-existence) is common to both of us and to him. How often have we lived together, when I knew the times of our life and death, whilst they were concealed from you! When I desire to appear in order to do some good, I array myself in a body, since one cannot be with man except in a human shape."

People tell a tale of a king, whose name I have forgotten, who ordered his people after his death to bury his body on a spot where never before had a dead person been buried. Now they sought for such a spot, but could not find it; finally, on finding a rock projecting out of the ocean, they thought they had found what they wanted. But then Vâsudeva spoke unto them, "This king has been burned on this identical rock already many times. But now do as you like; for the king only wanted to give you a lesson, and this aim of his has now been attained."

Vâsudeva says: "He who hopes for salvation and strives to free himself from the world, but whose heart is not obedient to his wish, will be rewarded for his action in the worlds of those who receive a good reward; but he does not attain his last object on account of his deficiency, therefore he will return to this world, and will be found worthy of entering a new shape of a kind of beings whose special occupation is devotion. Divine inspiration helps him to raise himself in this new shape by degrees to that which he already wished for in the first shape. His heart begins to comply with his wish; he is more and more purified in the different shapes, until he at last obtains salvation in an uninterrupted series of new births."

Further, Vâsudeva says: "If the soul is free from matter, it is knowing; but as long as it is clad in matter, the soul is not-knowing, on account of the turbid nature of matter. It thinks that it is an agent, and that the actions of the world are prepared for its sake. Therefore it clings to them, and it is stamped with the impressions of the senses. When, then, the soul leaves the body, the traces of the impressions of the senses remain in it, and are not completely eradicated, as it longs for the world of sense and returns towards it. And since it in these stages undergoes changes entirely opposed to each other, it is thereby subject to the influences of the *three primary forces*. What, therefore, can the soul do, its wing being cut, if it is not sufficiently trained and prepared?"

Vâsudeva says: "The best of men is the perfectly
Page 27. wise one, for he loves God and God loves him. How many times has he died and been born again! During his whole life he perseveringly seeks for perfection till he obtains it."

Vishṇu-Dharma. In the *Vishṇu-Dharma*, Mârkaṇḍeya, speaking of the spiritual beings, says: "Brahman, Kârttikeya, son of Mahâdeva, Lakshmî, who produced the Amṛita, Daksha, who was beaten by Mahâdeva, Umâdevî, the wife of Mahâdeva, each of them has been in the middle of this *kalpa*, and they have been the same already many times."

Varâhamihira speaks of the influences of the comets, and of the calamities which befall men when they appear. These calamities compel them to emigrate from their homes, lean from exhaustion, moaning over their mishap, leading their children by the hand along the road, and speaking to each other in low tones, "We are punished for the sins of our kings;" whereupon others answer, "Not so. This is the retribution for what we have done in the former life, before we entered these bodies."

Mânî. When Mânî was banished from Êrânshahr, he went to India, learned metempsychosis from the Hindus, and transferred it into his own system. He says in the *Book of Mysteries*: "Since the Apostles knew that the souls are immortal, and that in their migrations they array themselves in every form, that they are shaped in every animal, and are cast in the mould of every figure, they asked Messiah what would be the end of those souls which did not receive the truth nor learn the origin of their existence. Whereupon he said, 'Any weak soul which has not received all that belongs to her of truth perishes without any rest or bliss.'" By *perishing* Mânî means her being punished, not her total disappearance. For in another place he says: "The partisans of Bardesanes think that the living soul rises and is purified in the carcase, not knowing that the latter is the enemy of the soul, that the carcase prevents the soul from rising, that it is a prison, and a painful punishment to the soul. If this human figure were a real existence, its creator would not let it wear out and suffer injury, and would not have compelled it to reproduce itself by the sperma in the uterus."

The following passage is taken from the book of Patañjali:—"The soul, being on all sides tied to ignorance, which is the cause of its being fettered, is like rice in its cover. As long as it is there, it is capable of growing and ripening in the transition stages between being born and giving birth itself. But if the cover is taken off the rice, it ceases to develop in this way, and becomes stationary. The retribution of the soul depends on the various kinds of creatures through which it wanders, upon the extent of life, whether it be long or short, and upon the particular kind of its happiness, be it scanty or ample." Patañjali.

The pupil asks: "What is the condition of the spirit when it has a claim to a recompense or has committed a crime, and is then entangled in a kind of new birth either in order to receive bliss or to be punished?"

The master says: "It migrates according to what it has previously done, fluctuating between happiness and misfortune, and alternately experiencing pain or pleasure." Page 28.

The pupil asks: "If a man commits something which

necessitates a retribution for him in a different shape from that in which he has committed the thing, and if between both stages there is a great interval of time and the matter is forgotten, what then?"

The master answers: "It is the nature of action to adhere to the spirit, for action is its product, whilst the body is only an instrument for it. Forgetting does not apply to spiritual matters, for they lie outside of time, with the nature of which the notions of long and short duration are necessarily connected. Action, by adhering to the spirit, frames its nature and character into a condition similar to that one into which the soul will enter on its next migration. The soul in its purity knows this, thinks of it, and does not forget it; but the light of the soul is covered by the turbid nature of the body as long as it is connected with the body. Then the soul is like a man who remembers a thing which he once knew, but then forgot in consequence of insanity or an illness or some intoxication which overpowered his mind. Do you not observe that little children are in high spirits when people wish them a long life, and are sorry when people imprecate upon them a speedy death? And what would the one thing or the other signify to them, if they had not tasted the sweetness of life and experienced the bitterness of death in former generations through which they had been migrating to undergo the due course of retribution?"

Quotations from Plato and Proclus.

The ancient Greeks agreed with the Hindus in this belief. Socrates says in the book *Phaedo:* "We are reminded in the tales of the ancients that the souls go from here to Hades, and then come from Hades to here; that the living originates from the dead, and that altogether things originate from their contraries. Therefore those who have died are among the living. Our souls lead an existence of their own in Hades. The soul of each man is glad or sorry at something, and contemplates this thing. This impressionable nature ties the soul to the body, nails it down in the body, and gives it, as it were, a bodily figure. The soul which is not pure cannot go to Hades. It quits the body still filled with its nature, and then migrates hastily into another body, in which it is, as it were, deposited and made fast. Therefore, it has no share in the living of the company of the unique, pure, divine essence."

Further he says: "If the soul is an independent being, our learning is nothing but remembering that which we had learned previously, because our souls were in some place before they appeared in this human figure. When people see a thing to the use of which they were accustomed in childhood, they are under the influence of this impressionability, and a cymbal, for instance, reminds them of the boy who used to beat it, whom they, however, had forgotten. Forgetting is the vanishing of knowledge, and knowing is the soul's remembrance of that which it had learned before it entered the body."

Proclus says: "Remembering and forgetting are peculiar to the soul endowed with reason. It is evident that the soul has always existed. Hence it follows that it has always been both knowing and for- Page 29.
getting, knowing when it is separated from the body, forgetting when it is in connection with the body. For, being separated from the body, it belongs to the realm of the spirit, and therefore it is knowing; but being connected with the body, it descends from the realm of the spirit, and is exposed to forgetting because of some forcible influence prevailing over it."

The same doctrine is professed by those Ṣûfî who *Ṣûfî doctrine.* teach that this world is a sleeping soul and yonder world a soul awake, and who at the same time admit that God is immanent in certain places—*e.g.* in heaven —in the *seat* and the *throne* of God (mentioned in the Koran). But then there are others who admit that

God is inmanent in the whole world, in animals, trees, and the inanimate world, which they call his *universal appearance.* To those who hold this view, the entering of the souls into various beings in the course of metempsychosis is of no consequence.

CHAPTER VI.

ON THE DIFFERENT WORLDS, AND ON THE PLACES OF RETRIBUTION IN PARADISE AND HELL.

The three *lokas.*

THE Hindus call the world *loka.* Its primary division consists of the upper, the low, and the middle. The upper one is called *svarloka, i.e.* paradise; the low. *nâgaloka, i.e.* the world of the serpents, which is hell; besides they call it *naraloka,* and sometimes also *pâtâla, i.e.* the lowest world. The middle world, that one in which we live, is called *madhyaloka* and *manushyaloka, i.e.* the world of men. In the latter, man has to earn, in the upper to receive his reward; in the low, to receive punishment. A man who deserves to come to *svarloka* or *nâgaloka* receives there the full recompense of his deeds during a certain length of time corresponding to the duration of his deeds, but in either of them there is only the soul, the soul free from the body.

For those who do not deserve to rise to heaven and to sink as low as hell there is another world called *tiryagloka,* the irrational world of plants and animals, through the individuals of which the soul has to wander in the metempsychosis until it reaches the human being, rising by degrees from the lowest kinds of the vegetable world to the highest classes of the sensitive world. The stay of the soul in this world has one of the following causes: either the award which is due to the soul is not sufficient to raise it into heaven or to sink it into hell, or the soul is in its wanderings on the way back from hell; for they believe that a soul returning to the human world from heaven at once adopts a human body, whilst that one which returns there from hell has first to wander about in plants and animals before it reaches the degree of living in a human body.

Quotation from the *Vishṇu-Purâṇa.*

The Hindus speak in their traditions of a large number of hells, of their qualities and their names, and for each kind of sin they have a special hell. The number of hells is 88,000 according to the *Vishṇu-Purâṇa.* We shall quote what this book says on the subject:—

"The man who makes a false claim and who bears false witness, he who helps these two and he who ridicules people, come into the *Raurava* hell.

"He who sheds innocent blood, who robs others of their rights and plunders them, and who kills cows, comes into *Rodha.* Those also who strangle people come here.

"Whoso kills a Brahman, and he who steals gold,
Page 30. and their companions, the princes who do not look after their subjects, he who commits adultery with the family of his teacher, or who lies down with his mother-in-law, come into *Taptakumbha.*

"Whoso connives at the shame of his wife for greediness, commits adultery with his sister or the wife of his son, sells his child, is stingy towards himself with his property in order to save it, comes into *Mahâjwâla.*

"Whoso is disrespectful to his teacher and is not pleased with him, despises men, commits incest with animals, contemns the Veda and Purâṇas, or tries to make a gain by means of them in the markets, comes into *Śavala.*

"A man who steals and commits tricks, who opposes the straight line of conduct of men, who hates his father, who does not like God and men, who does not honour the gems which God has made glorious, and who considers them to be like other stones, comes into *Kṛimîśa.*

"Whoso does not honour the rights of parents and

grandparents, whoso does not do his duty towards the angels, the maker of arrows and spear-points, come to *Lâlâbhaksha*.

"The maker of swords and knives comes to *Viśasana*.

"He who conceals his property, being greedy for the presents of the rulers, and the Brahman who sells meat or oil or butter or sauce or wine, come to *Adhomukha*.

"He who rears cocks and cats, small cattle, pigs, and birds, comes to *Rudhirândha*.

"Public performers and singers in the markets, those who dig wells for drawing water, a man who cohabits with his wife on holy days, who throws fire into the houses of men, who betrays his companion and then receives him, being greedy for his property, come to *Rudhira*.

"He who takes the honey out of the beehive comes to *Vaitaraṇî*.

"Whoso takes away by force the property and women of others in the intoxication of youth comes to *Kṛishṇa*.

"Whoso cuts down the trees comes to *Asipatravana*.

"The hunter, and the maker of snares and traps, come to *Vahnijwâla*.

"He who neglects the customs and rules, and he who violates the laws—and he is the worst of all—come to *Sandaṁśaka*."

We have given this enumeration only in order to show what kinds of deeds the Hindus abhor as sins.

Some Hindus believe that the middle world, that one for earning, is the human world, and that a man wanders about in it, because he has received a reward which does not lead him into heaven, but at the same time saves him from hell. They consider heaven as a higher stage, where a man lives in a state of bliss which must be of a certain duration on account of the good deeds he has done. On the contrary, they consider the wandering about in plants and animals as a lower stage,

According to some Hindus, the migration through plants and animals takes the place of hell.

where a man dwells for punishment for a certain length of time, which is thought to correspond to the wretched deeds he has done. People who hold this view do not know of another hell, but this kind of degradation below the degree of living as a human being.

Page 31.

Moral principles of metempsychosis.

All these degrees of retribution are necessary for this reason, that the seeking for salvation from the fetters of matter frequently does not proceed on the straight line which leads to absolute knowledge, but on lines chosen by guessing or chosen because others had chosen them. Not one action of man shall be lost, not even the last of all; it shall be brought to his account after his good and bad actions have been balanced against each other. The retribution, however, is not according to the deed, but according to the intention which a man had in doing it; and a man will receive his reward either in the form in which he lives on earth, or in that form into which his soul will migrate, or in a kind of intermediary state after he has left his shape and has not yet entered a new one.

Here now the Hindus quit the path of philosophical speculation and turn aside to traditional fables as regards the two places where reward or punishment is given, *e.g.* that man exists there as an incorporeal being, and that after having received the reward of his actions he again returns to a bodily appearance and human shape, in order to be prepared for his further destiny.

The *Sâṁkhya* criticises metempsychosis.

Therefore the author of the book *Sâṁkhya* does not consider the reward of paradise a special gain, because it has an end and is not eternal, and because this kind of life resembles the life of this our world; for it is not free from ambition and envy, having in itself various degrees and classes of existence, whilst cupidity and desire do not cease save where there is perfect equality.

Ṣûfî parallel.

The Ṣûfî, too, do not consider the stay in paradise a special gain for another reason, because there the soul delights in other things but the Truth, *i.e.* God, and its thoughts are diverted from the Absolute Good by things which are not the Absolute Good.

On the soul leaving the body, according to popular views.

We have already said that, according to the belief of the Hindus, the soul exists in these two places without a body. But this is only the view of the educated among them, who understand by the soul an independent being. However, the lower classes, and those who cannot imagine the existence of the soul without a body, hold about this subject very different views. One is this, that the cause of the agony of death is the soul's waiting for a shape which is to be prepared. It does not quit the body before there has originated a cognate being of similar functions, one of those which nature prepares either as an embryo in a mother's womb or as a seed in the bosom of the earth. Then the soul quits the body in which it has been staying.

Others hold the more traditional view that the soul does not wait for such a thing, that it quits its shape on account of its weakness whilst another body has been prepared for it out of the elements. This body is called *ativâhika*, i.e. *that which grows in haste*, because it does not come into existence by being born. The soul stays in this body a complete year in the greatest agony, no matter whether it has deserved to be rewarded or to be punished. This is like the Barzakh of the Persians, an intermediary stage between the periods of acting and earning and that of receiving award. For this reason the heir of the deceased must, according to Hindu use, fulfil the rites of the year for the deceased, duties which end with the end of the year, for then the soul goes to that place which is prepared for it.

Quotations from *Vishṇu Purâṇa* and the Sâṁkhya school.

We shall now give some extracts from their literature to illustrate these ideas. First from the *Vishṇu Purâṇa*.

"Maitreya asked Parâśara about the purpose of hell and the punishment in it, whereupon he answered: 'It is for distinguishing the good from the bad, knowledge

Page 32. from ignorance, and for the manifestation of justice. But not every sinner enters hell. Some of them escape hell by previously doing works of repentance and expiation. The greatest expiation is uninterruptedly thinking of Vishṇu in every action. Others wander about in plants, filthy insects and birds, and abominable dirty creeping things like lice and worms, for such a length of time as they desire it.' "

In the book *Sâṁkhya* we read: "He who deserves exaltation and reward will become like one of the angels, mixing with the hosts of spiritual beings, not being prevented from moving freely in the heavens and from living in the company of their inhabitants, or like one of the eight classes of spiritual beings. But he who deserves humiliation as recompense for sins and crimes will become an animal or a plant, and will wander about until he deserves a reward so as to be saved from punishment, or until he offers himself as expiation, flinging away the vehicle of the body, and thereby attaining salvation."

Muslim authors on metempsychosis.

A theosoph who inclines towards metempsychosis says: "The metempsychosis has four degrees:

"1. The *transferring*, *i.e.* the procreation as limited to the human species, because it *transfers* existence from one individual to another; the opposite of this is—

"2. The *transforming*, which concerns men in particular, since they are *transformed* into monkeys, pigs, and elephants.

"3. A stable condition of existence, like the condition of the plants. This is worse than *transferring*, because it is a stable condition of life, remains as it is through all time, and lasts as long as the mountains.

"4. The *dispersing*, the opposite of number 3, which applies to the plants that are plucked, and to animals immolated as sacrifice, because they vanish without leaving posterity."

Abû-Ya'ḳûb of Sijistân maintains in his book, called "*The disclosing of that which is veiled*," that the species are preserved; that metempsychosis always proceeds in one and the same species, never crossing its limits and passing into another species.

This was also the opinion of the ancient Greeks; for Johannes Grammaticus relates as the view of Plato that the rational souls will be clad in the bodies of animals, and that in this regard he followed the fables of Pythagoras.

Quotations from Johannes Grammaticus and Plato.

Socrates says in the book *Phædo:* "The body is earthy, ponderous, heavy, and the soul, which loves it, wanders about and is attracted towards the place, to which it looks from fear of the shapeless and of Hades, the gathering-place of the souls. They are soiled, and circle round the graves and cemeteries, where souls have been seen appearing in shadowy forms. This phantasmagoria only occurs to such souls as have not been entirely separated, in which there is still a part of that towards which the look is directed."

Further he says: "It appears that these are not the souls of the good, but the souls of the wicked, which wander about in these things to make an expiation for the badness of their former kind of rearing. Thus they remain until they are again bound in a body on account of the desire for the bodily shape which has followed them. They will dwell in bodies the character of which is like the character which they had in the world. Whoso, *e.g.* only cares for eating and drinking will enter the various kinds of asses and wild animals; and he who preferred wrong and oppression will enter the various kinds of wolves, and falcons, and hawks."

Further he says about the gathering-places of the souls after death: "If I did not think that I am going first to gods who are wise, ruling, and good, then afterwards to men, deceased ones, better than those here, I should be wrong not to be in sorrow about death."

Page 33.

Further, Plato says about the two places of reward and

of punishment: "When a man dies, a *daimon, i.e.* one of the guardians of hell, leads him to the tribunal of judgment, and a guide whose special office it is brings him, together with those assembled there, to Hades, and there he remains the necessary number of many and long cycles of time. Telephos says, 'The road of Hades is an even one.' I, however, say, 'If the road were even or only a single one, a guide could be dispensed with.' Now that soul which longs for the body, or whose deeds were evil and not just, which resembles souls that have committed murder, flies from there and encloses itself in every species of being until certain times pass by. Thereupon it is brought by necessity to that place which is suitable to it. But the pure soul finds companions and guides, gods, and dwells in the places which are suitable to it."

Further he says: "Those of the dead who led a middle sort of life travel on a vessel prepared for them over Acheron. After they have received punishment and have been purified from crime, they wash and receive honour for the good deeds which they did according to merit. Those, however, who had committed great sins, *e.g.* the stealing from the sacrifices of the gods, robberies on a great scale, unjust killing, repeatedly and consciously violating the laws, are thrown into Tartarus, whence they will never be able to escape."

Further: "Those who repented of their sins already during their lifetime, and whose crimes were of a somewhat lower degree, who, *e.g.* committed some act of violence against their parents, or committed a murder by mistake, are thrown into Tartarus, being punished there for a whole year; but then the wave throws them out to a place whence they cry to their antagonists, asking them to abstain from further retaliation, that they may be saved from the horrors of punishment. If those now agree, they *are* saved; if not, they are sent back into

Tartarus. And this, their punishment, goes on until their antagonists agree to their demands for being relieved. Those whose mode of life was virtuous are liberated from *these* places on *this* earth. They feel as though released from prison, and they will inhabit the pure earth."

Tartarus is a huge deep ravine or gap into which the rivers flow. All people understand by the punishment of hell the most dreadful things which are known to them, and the Western countries, like Greece, have sometimes to suffer deluges and floods. But the description of Plato indicates a place where there are glaring flames, and it seems that he means the sea or some part of the ocean, in which there is a whirlpool (*durdûr*, a pun upon *Tartarus*). No doubt these descriptions represent the belief of the men of those ages.

CHAPTER VII.

ON THE NATURE OF LIBERATION FROM THE WORLD, AND ON THE PATH LEADING THERETO.

First part: Moksha in general.

If the soul is bound up with the world, and its being bound up has a certain cause, it cannot be liberated from this bond save by the opposite of this identical cause. Now according to the Hindus, as we have already explained (p. 55), the reason of the bond is *ignorance*, and therefore it can only be liberated by *knowledge*, by comprehending all things in such a way as to define them both in general and in particular, rendering superfluous any kind of deduction and removing all doubts. For the soul distinguishing between things (τὰ ὄντα) by means of definitions, recognises its own self, and recognises at the same time that it is its noble lot to last for ever, and that it is the vulgar lot of matter to change and to perish in all kinds of shapes. Then it dispenses with matter, and perceives that that which it held to be good and delightful is in reality bad and painful. In this manner it attains real knowledge and turns away from being arrayed in matter. Thereby action ceases, and both matter and soul become free by separating from each other.

Page 34.

Moksha according to *Patañjali*.

The author of the book of *Patañjali* says: "The concentration of thought on the unity of God induces man to notice something besides that with which he is occupied. He who wants God, wants the good for the whole creation without a single exception for any reason whatever; but he who occupies himself exclusively with his own self, will for its benefit neither inhale, breathe, nor exhale it (*śvâsa* and *praśvâsa*). When a man attains to this degree, his spiritual power prevails over his bodily power, and then he is gifted with the faculty of doing eight different things by which detachment is realised; for a man can only dispense with that which he is able to do, not with that which is outside his grasp. These eight things are:—

"1. The faculty in man of making his body so thin that it becomes invisible to the eyes.

"2. The faculty of making the body so light that it is indifferent to him whether he treads on thorns or mud or sand.

"3. The faculty of making his body so big that it appears in a terrifying miraculous shape.

"4. The faculty of realising every wish.

"5. The faculty of knowing whatever he wishes.

"6. The faculty of becoming the ruler of whatever religious community he desires.

"7. That those over whom he rules are humble and obedient to him.

"8. That all distances between a man and any far-away place vanish."

Ṣûfî parallel.

The terms of the Ṣûfî as to the *knowing* being and his attaining the *stage of knowledge* come to the same effect, for they maintain that he has two souls—an eternal one, not exposed to change and alteration, by which he knows that which is hidden, the transcendental world, and performs wonders; and another, a human soul, which is liable to being changed and being born. From these and similar views the doctrines of the Christians do not much differ.

The different degrees of knowledge according to *Patañjali*.

The Hindus say: "If a man has the faculty to perform these things, he can dispense with them, and will reach the goal by degrees, passing through several stages:—

"1. The knowledge of things as to their names and

qualities and distinctions, which, however, does not yet afford the knowledge of definitions.

"2. Such a knowledge of things as proceeds as far as the definitions by which particulars are classed under the category of universals, but regarding which a man must still practise distinction.

"3. This distinction (*viveka*) disappears, and man comprehends things at once as a whole, but within *time*.

"4. This kind of knowledge is raised above *time*, and he who has it can dispense with names and epithets, which are only instruments of human imperfection. In this stage the *intellectus* and the *intelligens* unite with the *intellectum*, so as to be one and the same thing."

This is what *Patañjali* says about the knowledge which liberates the soul. In Sanskrit they call its liberation *Moksha*—i.e. *the end*. By the same term they call the last contact of the eclipsed and eclipsing bodies, or their separation in both lunar and solar eclipses, because it is *the end* of the eclipse, the moment when the two luminaries which were in contact with
Page 35. each other separate.

According to the Hindus, the organs of the senses have been made for acquiring knowledge, and the pleasure which they afford has been created to stimulate people to research and investigation, as the pleasure which eating and drinking afford to the taste has been created to preserve the individual by means of nourishment. So the pleasure of *coitus* serves to preserve the species by giving birth to new individuals. If there were not special pleasure in these two functions, man and animals would not practise them for these purposes.

On knowledge according to the book *Gîtâ*.

In the book *Gîtâ* we read: "Man is created for the purpose of *knowing*; and because *knowing* is always the same, man has been gifted with the same organs.

If man were created for the purpose of *acting*, his organs would be *different*, as actions are *different* in consequence of the difference of the *three primary forces*. However, bodily nature is bent upon *acting* on account of its essential opposition to *knowing*. Besides, it wishes to invest action with *pleasures* which in reality are *pains*. But knowledge is such as to leave this nature behind itself prostrated on the earth like an opponent, and removes all darkness from the soul as an eclipse or clouds are removed from the sun."

Quotation from Plato's *Phædo*.

This resembles the opinion of Socrates, who thinks that the soul "being with the body, and wishing to inquire into something, then is deceived by the body. But by cogitations something of its desires becomes clear to it. Therefore, its cogitation takes place in that time when it is not disturbed by anything like hearing, seeing, or by any pain or pleasure, when it is quite by itself, and has as much as possible quitted the body and its companionship. In particular, the soul of the philosopher scorns the body, and wishes to be separate from it."

"If we in this our life did not make use of the body, nor had anything in common with it except in cases of necessity, if we were not inoculated with its nature, but were perfectly free from it, we should come near *knowledge* by getting rest from the ignorance of the body, and we should become pure by knowing ourselves as far as God would permit us. And it is only right to acknowledge that this is the truth."

The process of knowledge according to *Gîtâ* and another source.

Now we return and continue our quotation from the book *Gîtâ*.

"Likewise the other organs of the senses serve for acquiring knowledge. The *knowing person* rejoices in turning them to and fro on the field of knowledge, so that they are his spies. The apprehension of the senses is different according to time. The *senses* which serve the heart perceive only that which is present. The heart reflects over that which is present and remembers also the past. The *nature* takes hold of the present, claims it for itself in the past, and prepares to wrestle with it in future. The *reason* understands the nature of a thing, no regard being had of time or date, since past and future are the same for it. Its nearest helpers are *reflection* and *nature*; the most distant are the five senses. When the *senses* bring before reflection some particular object of knowledge, *reflection* cleans it from the errors of the functions of the senses, and hands it over to reason. Thereupon reason makes universal what was before particular, and communicates it to the *soul*. Thus the soul comes to know it."

Further, the Hindus think that a man becomes *knowing* in one of three ways:—

1. By being inspired, not in a certain course of time, but at once, at birth, and in the cradle, as, *e.g.* the sage Kapila, for he was born knowing and wise.

2. By being inspired after a certain time, like the children of Brahman, for they were inspired when they came of age.

3. By learning, and after a certain course of time, like all men who learn when their mind ripens.

Page 36

Cupidity, wrath, and ignorance are the chief obstacles to Moksha.

Liberation through knowledge can only be obtained by abstaining from *evil*. The branches of evil are many, but we may classify them as *cupidity*, *wrath*, and *ignorance*. If the roots are cut the branches will wither. And here we have first to consider the rule of the two forces of *cupidity* and *wrath*, which are the greatest and most pernicious enemies of man, deluding him by the pleasure of eating and the delight of revenge, whilst in reality they are much more likely to lead him into pains and crimes. They make a man similar to the wild beasts and the cattle, nay, even to the demons and devils.

Next we have to consider that man must prefer the reasoning force of mind, by which he becomes similar to the highest angels, to the forces of cupidity and wrath; and, lastly, that he must turn away from the actions of the world. He cannot, however, *give up* these actions unless he does away with their causes, which are his lust and ambition. Thereby the second of the *three primary forces* is cut away. However, the abstaining *from action* takes place in two different ways:—

1. By laziness, procrastination, and ignorance according to the *third force.* This mode is not desirable, for it will lead to a blamable end.

2. By judicious selection and by preferring that which is better to that which is good, which way leads to a laudable end.

The abstaining from actions is rendered perfect in this way, that a man quits anything that might occupy him and shuts himself up against it. Thereby he will be enabled to restrain his senses from extraneous objects to such a degree that he does not any more know that there exists anything besides himself, and be enabled to stop all motions, and even the breathing. It is evident that a greedy man strains to effect his object, the man who strains becomes tired, and the tired man pants; so the panting is the result of greediness. If this greediness is removed, the breathing becomes like the breathing of a being living at the bottom of the sea, that does not want breath; and then the heart quietly rests on one thing, viz. the search for liberation and for arriving at the absolute unity.

Further quotations from *Gîtâ.*

In the book *Gîtâ* we read: "How is a man to obtain liberation who disperses his heart and does not concentrate it alone upon God, who does not exclusively direct his action towards him? But if a man turns away his cogitation from all other things and concentrates it upon the One, the light of his heart will be steady like the light of a lamp filled with clean oil, standing in a corner where no wind makes it flicker, and he will be occupied in such a degree as not to perceive anything that gives pain, like heat or cold, knowing that everything besides the One, *the Truth*, is a vain phantom."

In the same book we read: "Pain and pleasure have no effect on the real world, just as the continuous flow of the streams to the ocean does not affect its water. How could anybody ascend this mountain pass save him who has conquered *cupidity* and *wrath* and rendered them inert?"

On account of what we have explained it is necessary that cogitation should be continuous, not in any way to be defined by number; for a number always denotes *repeated times*, and repeated times presuppose a break in the cogitation occurring between two consecutive times. This would interrupt the continuity, and would prevent cogitation becoming united with the object of cogitation. And this is not the object kept in view, which is, on the contrary, *the continuity of cogitation*.

This goal is attained either in a *single shape*, *i.e.* a single stage of metempsychosis, or *in several shapes*, in this way, that a man perpetually practises virtuous behaviour and accustoms the soul thereto, so that this virtuous behaviour becomes to it a nature and an essential quality.

The nine commandments of the Hindu religion.

Virtuous behaviour is that which is described by the religious law. Its principal laws, from which they derive many secondary ones, may be summed up in the following nine rules:—

1. A man shall not kill.
2. Nor lie.
3. Nor steal.
4. Nor whore.
5. Nor hoard up treasures.
6. He is perpetually to practise holiness and purity.
7. He is to perform the prescribed fasting without an interruption and to dress poorly.

Page 37.

8. He is to hold fast to the adoration of God with praise and thanks.

9. He is always to have in mind the word *ôm*, the word of creation, without pronouncing it.

The injunction to abstain from killing as regards animals (No. 1) is only a special part of the general order to *abstain from doing anything hurtful.* Under this head falls also the robbing of another man's goods (No. 3), and the telling lies (No. 2), not to mention the foulness and baseness of so doing.

The abstaining from hoarding up (No. 5) means that a man is to give up toil and fatigue; that he who seeks the bounty of God feels sure that he is provided for; and that, starting from the base slavery of material life, we may, by the noble liberty of cogitation, attain eternal bliss.

Practising purity (No. 6) implies that a man knows the filth of the body, and that he feels called upon to hate it, and to love cleanness of soul. Tormenting oneself by poor dress (No. 7) means that a man should reduce the body, allay its feverish desires, and sharpen its senses. Pythagoras once said to a man who took great care to keep his body in a flourishing condition and to allow it everything it desired, "Thou art not lazy in building thy prison and making thy fetter as strong as possible."

The holding fast to meditation on God and the angels means a kind of familiar intercourse with them. The book *Sâṁkhya* says: "Man cannot go beyond anything in the wake of which he marches, it being a scope to him (*i.e.* thus engrossing his thoughts and detaining him from meditation on God)." The book *Gîtâ* says: "All that which is the object of a man's continuous meditating and bearing in mind is stamped upon him, so that he even unconsciously is guided by it. Since, now, the time of heath is the time of remembering what we love, the soul on leaving the body is united with that object which we love, and is changed into it."

However, the reader must not believe that it is only the union of the soul with any forms of life that perish and return into existence that is perfect *liberation*, for the same book, *Gîtâ*, says: "He who knows when dying that God is everything, and that from him everything proceeds, *is liberated*, though his degree be lower than that of the saints."

Quotations from *Gîtâ*.

The same book says: "Seek deliverance from this world by abstaining from any connection with its follies, by having sincere intentions in all actions and when making offerings by fire to God, without any desire for reward and recompense; further, by keeping aloof from mankind." The real meaning of all this is that you should not prefer one because he is your friend to another because he is your enemy, and that you should beware of negligence in sleeping when others are awake, and in waking when others are asleep; for this, too, is a kind of being *absent* from them, though outwardly you are *present* with them. Further: Seek deliverance by guarding soul from soul, for the soul is an enemy if it be addicted to lusts; but what an excellent friend it is when it is *chaste!*"

Greek and Ṣûfî parallels.

Socrates, caring little for his impending death and being glad at the prospect of coming to his Lord, said: "My degree must not be considered by any one of you lower than that of the swan," of which people say that it is the bird of Apollo, the sun, and that it therefore knows what is hidden; that is, when feeling that it will soon die, sings more and more melodies from joy at the prospect of coming to its Lord. "At least my joy at my prospect of coming to the object of my adoration must not be less than the joy of this bird."

For similar reasons the Ṣûfî define *love* as being engrossed by the creature to the exclusion of God.

Second part: The *practical* path leading to Moksha

In the book of *Patañjali* we read: "We divide the path of liberation into three parts:—

"I. *The practical one* (*kriyâ-yoga*), a process of habituating the senses in a gentle way to detach themselves from the external world, and to concentrate themselves upon the internal one, so that they exclusively occupy themselves with God. This is in general the path of him who does not desire anything save what is sufficient to sustain life."

according to *Patañjali*, *Vishṇu-Dharma*, and *Gîtâ*.

Page 38.

In the book *Vishṇu-Dharma* we read: "The king Parîksha, of the family of Bhṛigu, asked Śatânîka, the head of an assembly of sages, who stayed with him, for the explanation of some notion regarding the deity, and by way of answer the sage communicated what *he* had heard from Śaunaka, Śaunaka from Uśanas, and Uśanas from Brahman, as follows: 'God is without first and without last; he has not been born from anything, and he has not borne anything save that of which it is impossible to say that it is *He*, and just as impossible to say that it is *Not-he*. How should I be able to ponder on the absolute good which is an outflow of his benevolence, and of the absolute bad which is a product of his wrath; and how could I know him so as to worship him as is his due, save by turning away from the world in general and by occupying myself exclusively with him, by perpetually cogitating on him?'

"It was objected to him: 'Man is weak and his life is a trifling matter. He can hardly bring himself to abstain from the necessities of life, and this prevents him from walking on the path of liberation. If we were living in the *first* age of mankind, when life extended to thousands of years, and when the world was good because of the non-existence of evil, we might hope that that which is necessary on this path should be done. But since we live in the *last* age, what, according to your opinion, is there in this revolving world that might protect him against the floods of the ocean and save him from drowning?'

"Thereupon Brahman spoke: 'Man wants nourishment, shelter, and clothing. Therefore in *them* there is no harm to him. But happiness is only to be found in abstaining from things besides them, from superfluous and fatiguing actions. Worship God, him alone, and venerate him; approach him in the place of worship with presents like perfumes and flowers; praise him and attach your heart to him so that it never leaves him. Give alms to the Brahmans and to others, and vow to God vows—special ones, like the abstaining from meat; general ones, like fasting. Vow to him animals which you must not hold to be something different from yourselves, so as to feel entitled to kill them. Know that he is everything. Therefore, whatever you do, let it be for his sake; and if you enjoy anything of the vanities of the world, do not forget him in your intentions. If you aim at the fear of God and the faculty of worshipping him, thereby you will obtain liberation, not by anything else.'"

The book *Gîtâ* says: "He who mortifies his lust does not go beyond the necessary wants; and he who is content with that which is sufficient for the sustaining of life will not be ashamed nor be despised."

The same book says: "If man is not without wants as regards the demands of human nature, if he wants nourishment to appease thereby the heat of hunger and exhaustion, sleep in order to meet the injurious influences of fatiguing motions and a couch to rest upon, let the latter be clean and smooth, everywhere equally high above the ground and sufficiently large that he may stretch out his body upon it. Let him have a place of temperate climate, not hurtful by cold nor by heat, and where he is safe against the approach of reptiles. All this helps him to sharpen the functions of his heart, that he may without any interruption concentrate his cogitation on the unity. For all things besides the necessities of life in the way of eating and clothing are pleasures of a kind which, in reality, are disguised pains. To acquiesce in them is impossible, and would end in the gravest inconvenience. There is pleasure only to him who kills the two intolerable enemies, *lust* and *wrath*, already during his life and not when he dies, who derives his rest and bliss from within, not from without; and who, in the final result, is able altogether to dispense with his senses." Page 39.

Vâsudeva spoke to Arjuna: "If you want the absolute good, take care of the nine doors of thy body, and know what is going in and out through them. Constrain thy heart from dispersing its thoughts, and quiet thy soul by thinking of the upper membrane of the child's brain, which is first soft, and then is closed and becomes strong, so that it would seem that there were no more need of it. Do not take perception of the senses for anything but the nature immanent in their organs, and therefore beware of following it."

The path of renunciation as the second part of the path of liberation according to *Gîtâ*.

II. The second part of the path of liberation is renunciation (the *via omissionis*), based on the knowledge of the evil which exists in the changing things of creation and their vanishing shapes. In consequence the heart shuns them, the longing for them ceases, and a man is raised above the *three primary forces* which are the cause of actions and of their diversity. For he who accurately understands the affairs of the world knows that the good ones among them are evil in reality, and that the bliss which they afford changes in the course of recompense into pains. Therefore he avoids everything which might aggravate his condition of being entangled in the world, and which might result in making him stay in the world for a still longer period.

The book *Gîtâ* says: "Men err in what is ordered and what is forbidden. They do not know how to distinguish between good and evil in actions. Therefore, giving up acting altogether and keeping aloof from it, this is *the* action."

The same book says: "The purity of knowledge is high above the purity of all other things, for by knowledge ignorance is rooted out and certainty is gained in exchange for doubt, which is a means of torture, for there is no rest for him who doubts."

It is evident from this that the first part of the path of liberation is instrumental to the second one.

Worship as the third part of the path of liberation according to *Gîtâ*.

III. The third part of the path of liberation which is to be considered as instrumental to the preceding two is *worship*, for this purpose, that God should help a man to obtain liberation, and deign to consider him worthy of such a shape of existence in the metempsychosis in which he may effect his progress towards beatitude.

The author of the book *Gîtâ* distributes the duties of worship among the *body*, the *voice*, and the *heart*.

What the *body* has to do is fasting, prayer, the fulfilment of the law, the service towards the angels and the sages among the Brahmans, keeping clean the body, keeping aloof from killing under all circumstances, and never looking at another man's wife and other property.

What the *voice* has to do is the reciting of the holy texts, praising God, always to speak the truth, to address people mildly, to guide them, and to order them to do good.

What the *heart* has to do is to have straight, honest intentions, to avoid haughtiness, always to be patient, to keep your senses under control, and to have a cheerful mind.

On Rasâyana as a path leading to Moksha.

The author (Patañjali) adds to the three parts of the path of liberation a fourth one of an illusory nature, called *Rasâyana*, consisting of alchemistic tricks with various drugs, intended to realise things which by nature are impossible. We shall speak of these things afterwards (*vide* chap. xvii.). They have no other relation to the theory of *Moksha* but this, that also in the tricks of Rasâyana everything depends upon the intention, the well-understood determination to carry them out, this determination resting on the firm belief in them, and resulting in the endeavour to realise them.

According to the Hindus, liberation is union with God; for they describe God as a being who can dispense with hoping for a recompense or with fearing opposition, unattainable to thought, because he is sublime beyond all unlikeness which is abhorrent and all likeness which is sympathetic, knowing himself not by a knowledge which comes to him like an accident, regarding something which had not in every phase before been known to him. And this same description the Hindus apply to *the liberated one*, for he is equal to God in all these things except in the matter of beginning, since he has not existed from all eternity, and except this, that before liberation he existed in *the world of entanglement*, knowing the objects of knowledge only by a phantasmagoric kind of knowing which he had acquired by absolute exertion, whilst the object of his knowing is still covered, as it were, by a veil. On the contrary, in the world of liberation all veils are lifted, all covers taken off, and obstacles removed. There the being is absolutely knowing, not desirous of learning anything unknown, separated from the soiled perceptions of the senses, united with the everlasting ideas. Therefore in the end of the book of *Patañjali*, after the pupil has asked about the nature of liberation, the master says: "If you wish, say, Liberation is the cessation of the functions of *the three forces*, and their returning to that home whence they had come. Or if you wish, say, It is the return of the soul as a *knowing* being into its own nature."

On the nature of Moksha itself.

Page 40.

Quotations from *Patañjali*.

The two men, pupil and master, disagree regarding him who has arrived at the stage of liberation. The anchorite asks in the book of Sâṁkhya, "Why does not *death* take place when *action* ceases?" The sage replies, "Because the cause of the separation is a certain condition of the soul whilst the spirit is still in the body. Soul and body are separated by a natural condition which severs their union. Frequently when

From *Sâṁkhya*.

the cause of an effect has already ceased or disappeared, the effect itself still goes on for a certain time, slackening, and by and by decreasing, till in the end it ceases totally; *e.g.* the silk-weaver drives round his wheel with his mallet until it whirls round rapidly, then he leaves it; however, it does not stand still, though the mallet that drove it round has been removed; the motion of the wheel decreases by little and little, and finally it ceases. It is the same case with the body. After the action of the body has ceased, its effect is still lasting until it arrives, through the various stages of motion and of rest, at the cessation of physical force and of the effect which had originated from preceding causes. Thus liberation is finished when the body has been completely prostrated."

From *Patañjali.*

In the book of Patañjali there is a passage which expresses similar ideas. Speaking of a man who restrains his senses and organs of perception, as the turtle draws in its limbs when it is afraid, he says that "he is not fettered, because the fetter has been loosened, and he is not liberated, because his body is still with him."

There is, however, another passage in the same book which does not agree with the theory of liberation as expounded above. He says: "The bodies are the snares of the souls for the purpose of acquiring recompense. He who arrives at the stage of liberation has acquired, in his actual form of existence, the recompense for all the doings of the past. Then he ceases to labour to acquire a title to a recompense in the future. He frees himself from the snare; he can dispense with the particular form of his existence, and moves in it quite freely without being ensnared by it. He has even the faculty of moving wherever he likes, and if he like, he might rise above the face of death. For the thick, cohesive bodies cannot oppose an obstacle to his *form* of existence (as, *e.g.* a mountain could not prevent him from passing through). How, then, could his body oppose an obstacle to his soul?"

Similar views are also met with among the Ṣûfî. Some Ṣûfî author relates the following story: "A company of Ṣûfî came down unto us, and sat down at some distance from us. Then one of them rose, prayed, and on having finished his prayer, turned towards me and spoke: 'O master, do you know here a place fit for us *to die* on?' Now I thought he meant *sleeping*, and so I pointed out to him a place. The man went there, threw himself on the back of his head, and remained motionless. Now I rose, went to him and shook him, but lo! he was already cold." Ṣûfî parallels.

The Ṣûfî explains the Koranic verse, "We have made room for him on earth" (Sûra 18, 83), in this way: "If he wishes, the earth rolls itself up for him; if he wishes, he can walk on the water and in the air, which offer him sufficient resistance so as to enable him to walk, whilst the mountains do not offer him any resistance when he wants to pass through them." Page 41.

We next speak of those who, notwithstanding their greatest exertions, do not reach the stage of liberation. There are several classes of them. The book *Sâṁkhya* says: "He who enters upon the world with a virtuous character, who is liberal with what he possesses of the goods of the world, is recompensed in it in this way, that he obtains the fulfilment of his wishes and desires, that he moves about in the world in happiness, happy in body and soul and in all other conditions of life. For in reality good fortune is a recompense for former deeds, done either in the same shape or in some preceding shape. Whoso lives in this world piously but without knowledge will be raised and be rewarded, but not be liberated, because the means of attaining it are wanting in his case. Whoso is content and acquiesces in possessing the faculty of practising the above-men- On those who do not reach Moksha according to *Sâṁkhya*.

tioned eight commandments (*sic*, *vide* p. 74), whoso glories in them, is successful by means of them, and believes that *they* are liberation, will remain in the same stage."

A parable showing people in the various degrees of knowledge.

The following is a parable characterising those who vie with each other in the progress through the various stages of knowledge:—A man is travelling together with his pupils for some business or other towards the end of the night. Then there appears something standing erect before them on the road, the nature of which it is impossible to recognise on account of the darkness of night. The man turns towards his pupils, and asks them, one after the other, what it is? The first says: "I do not know what it is." The second says: "I do not know, and I have no means of learning what it is." The third says: "It is useless to examine what it is, for the rising of the day will reveal it. If it is something terrible, it will disappear at daybreak; if it is something else, the nature of the thing will anyhow be clear to us." Now, none of them had attained to knowledge, the first, because he was ignorant; the second, because he was incapable, and had no means of knowing; the third, because he was indolent and acquiesced in his ignorance.

The fourth pupil, however, did not give an answer. He stood still, and then he went on in the direction of the object. On coming near, he found that it was pumpkins on which there lay a tangled mass of something. Now he knew that a living man, endowed with free will, does not stand still in his place until such a tangled mass is formed on his head, and he recognised at once that it was a lifeless object standing erect. Further, he could not be sure if it was not a hidden place for some dunghill. So he went quite close to it, struck against it with his foot till it fell to the ground. Thus all doubt having been removed, he returned to his master and gave him the exact account. In such a way the master obtained the knowledge through the intermediation of his pupils.

Parallels from Greek authors, Ammonius, Plato, and Proclus.

With regard to similar views of the ancient Greeks we can quote Ammonius, who relates the following as a sentence of Pythagoras: "Let your desire and exertion in this world be directed towards the union with *the First Cause*, which is the cause of the cause of your existence, that you may endure for ever. You will be saved from destruction and from being wiped out; you will go to the world of the true sense, of the true joy, of the true glory, in everlasting joy and pleasures."

Further, Pythagoras says: "How can you hope for the state of detachment as long as you are clad in bodies? And how will you obtain liberation as long as you are incarcerated in them?"

Ammonius relates: "Empedocles and his successors as far as Heracles (*sic*) think that the soiled souls always remain commingled with the world until they ask the universal soul for help. The universal soul intercedes Page 42. for it with the *Intelligence*, the latter with the Creator. The Creator affords something of his light to Intelligence; Intelligence affords something of it to the universal soul, which is immanent in this world. Now the soul wishes to be enlightened by Intelligence, until at last the individual soul recognises the universal soul, unites with it, and is attached to its world. But this is a process over which many ages must pass. Then the soul comes to a region where there is neither place nor time, nor anything of that which is in the world, like transient fatigue or joy."

Socrates says: "The soul on leaving space wanders to the holiness (τὸ καθαρόν) which lives for ever and exists eternally, being related to it. It becomes like holiness in duration. because it is by means of something like contact able to receive impressions from holiness. This, its susceptibility to impressions, is called *Intelligence*."

Further, Socrates says: "The soul is very similar to the divine substance which does not die nor dissolve, and is the only *intelligibile* which lasts for ever; the body is the contrary of it. When soul and body unite, nature orders body to serve, the soul to rule; but when they separate, the soul goes to another place than that to which the body goes. There it is happy with things that are suitable to it; it reposes from being circumscribed in space, rests from folly, impatience, love, fear, and other human evils, on this condition, that it had always been pure and hated the body. If, however, it has sullied itself by connivance with the body, by serving and loving it so that the body was subservient to its lusts and desires, in this case it does not experience anything more real than the species of bodily things (τὸ σωματοειδές) and the contact with them."

Proclus says: "The body in which the rational soul dwells has received the figure of a globe, like the ether and its individual beings. The body in which both the rational and the irrational souls dwell has received an erect figure like man. The body in which only the irrational soul dwells has received a figure erect and curved at the same time, like that of the irrational animals. The body in which there is neither the one nor the other, in which there is nothing but the nourishing power, has received an erect figure, but it is at the same time curved and turned upside down, so that the head is planted in the earth, as is the case with the plants. The latter direction being the contrary to that of man, man is a heavenly tree, the root of which is directed towards its home, *i.e.* heaven, whilst the root of vegetables is directed towards *their* home, *i.e.* the earth."

Brahman compared to an Aśvattha tree according to *Patañjali.*

The Hindus hold similar views about nature. Arjuna asks, "What is Brahman like in the world?" Whereupon Vâsudeva answers, "Imagine him like an *Aśvattha* tree." This is a huge precious tree, well known among them, standing upside down, the roots being above, the branches below. If it has ample nourishment, it becomes quite enormous; the branches spread far, cling to the soil, and creep into it. Roots and branches above and below resemble each other to such a degree that it is difficult to say which is which.

"Brahman is the upper roots of this tree, its trunk is the Veda, its branches are the different doctrines and schools, its leaves are the different modes of interpretation; its nourishment comes from *the three forces;* the tree becomes strong and compact through the senses. The intelligent being has no other keen desire but that of felling this tree, *i.e.* abstaining from the world and its vanities. When he has succeeded in felling it, he wishes to settle in the place where it has grown, a place in which there is no returning in a further stage of metempsychosis. When he obtains this, he leaves behind himself all the pains of heat and cold, and coming from the light of sun and moon and common fires, he attains to the divine lights." Page 43.

The doctrine of *Patañjali* is akin to that of the Ṣûfî regarding being occupied in meditation on *the Truth* (*i.e.* God), for they say, "As long as you point to something, you are not a *monist;* but when *the Truth* seizes upon the object of your pointing and annihilates it, then there is no longer an indicating person nor an object indicated." Ṣûfî parallels.

There are some passages in their system which show that they believe in the pantheistic union; *e.g.* one of them, being asked what is *the Truth* (God), gave the following answer: "How should I not know the being which is *I* in essence and *Not-I* in space? If I return once more into existence, thereby I am separated from him; and if I am neglected (*i.e.* not born anew and sent into the world), thereby I become light and become accustomed to the *union*" (*sic*).

Abû-Bekr Ash-shiblî says: "Cast off all, and you

will attain to us completely. Then you will exist; but you will not report about us to others as long as your doing is like ours."

Abû-Yazîd Albistâmî once being asked how he had attained *his* stage in Ṣufism, answered: "I cast off my own self as a serpent casts off its skin. Then I considered my own self, and found that *I* was *He*," *i.e.* God.

The Ṣûfî explain the Koranic passage (Sûra 2, 68), "*Then we spoke: Beat him with a part of her*," in the following manner: "The order to kill that which is dead in order to give life to it indicates that the heart does not become alive by the lights of knowledge unless the body be killed by ascetic practice to such a degree that it does not any more exist as a reality, but only in a formal way, whilst your heart is a reality on which no object of the formal world has any influence."

Further they say: "Between man and God there are a thousand stages of light and darkness. Men exert themselves to pass through darkness to light, and when they have attained to the stations of light, there is no return for them."

CHAPTER VIII.

ON THE DIFFERENT CLASSES OF CREATED BEINGS, AND ON THEIR NAMES.

The various classes of creatures according to *Sâṁkhya.*

THE subject of this chapter is very difficult to study and understand accurately, since we Muslims look at it from without, and the Hindus themselves do not work it out to scientific perfection. As we, however, want it for the further progress of this treatise, we shall communicate all we have heard of it until the date of the present book. And first we give an extract from the book *Sâṁkhya.*

"The anchorite spoke: 'How many classes and species are there of living bodies?'

"The sage replied: 'There are three classes of them—the spiritual ones in the height, men in the middle, and animals in the depth. Their species are fourteen in number, eight of which belong to the spiritual beings: Brahman, Indra, Prajâpati, Saumya, Gandharva, Yaksha, Râkshasa, and Piśâca. Five species are those of the animals—cattle, wild beasts, birds, creeping things, and *growing things, i.e.* the trees. And, lastly, *one* species is represented by man.'"

The author of the same book has in another part of it given the following enumeration with different names: "Brahman, Indra, Prajâpati, Gandharva, Yaksha, Râkshasa, Pitaras, Piśâca."

The Hindus are people who rarely preserve one and the same order of things, and in their enumeration of things there is much that is arbitrary. They use or invent numbers of names, and who is to hinder or to control them?

In the book *Gîtâ*, Vâsudeva says: "When the *first* of
Page 44. the *three primary forces* prevails, it particularly applies itself to developing the intellect, purifying the senses, and producing *action* for the angels. Blissful rest is one of the consequences of this force, and liberation one of its results.

"When the *second* force prevails, it particularly applies itself to developing cupidity. It will lead to fatigue, and induce to actions for the Yaksha and Râkshasa. In this case the recompense will be according to the action.

"If the *third* force prevails, it particularly applies itself to developing ignorance, and making people easily beguiled by their own wishes. Finally, it produces wakefulness, carelessness, laziness, procrastination in fulfilling duties, and sleeping too long. If man acts, he acts for the classes of the Bhûta and Piśâca, the devils, for the Preta who carry the spirits in the air, not in paradise and not in hell. Lastly, this force will lead to punishment; man will be lowered from the stage of humanity, and will be changed into animals and plants."

In another place the same author says: "Belief and virtue are in the Deva among the spiritual beings. Therefore that man who resembles them believes in God, clings to him, and longs for him. Unbelief and vice are in the demons called Asura and Râkshasa. That man who resembles them does not believe in God nor attend to his commandments. He tries to make the world godless, and is occupied with things which are harmful in this world and in the world beyond, and are of no use."

The author enumerates eight classes of spiritual beings.

If we now combine these statements with each other, it will be evident that there is some confusion both in the names and in their order. According to the most popular view of the majority of the Hindus, there are the following eight classes of *spiritual* beings :—

1. The *Deva*, or angels, to whom the north belongs. They specially belong to the Hindus. People say that Zoroaster made enemies of the Shamaniyya or Buddhists by calling the devils by the name of the class of angels which *they* consider the highest, *i.e. Deva*. And this usage has been transmitted from Magian times down to the Persian language of our days.

2. *Daitya 'dânava*, the demons who live in the south. To them everybody belongs who opposes the religion of the Hindus and persecutes the cows. Notwithstanding the near relationship which exists between them and the Deva, there is, as Hindus maintain, no end of quarrelling and fighting among them.

3. *Gandharva*, the musicians and singers who make music before the Deva. Their harlots are called Apsaras.

4. *Yaksha*, the treasurers or guardians of the Deva.

5. *Râkshasa*, demons of ugly and deformed shapes.

6. *Kinnara*, having human shapes but horses' heads, being the contrary of the centaurs of the Greek, of whom the lower half has the shape of a horse, the upper half that of a man. The latter figure is that of the Zodiacal sign of *Arcitenens*.

7. *Nâga*, beings in the shape of serpents.

8. *Vidyâdhara*, demon-sorcerers, who exercise a certain witchcraft, but not such a one as to produce permanent results.

Criticisms on this list.

If we consider this series of beings, we find the angelic power at the upper end and the demoniac at the lower, and between them there is much interblending. The qualities of these beings are different, inasmuch as they have attained this stage of life in the course of metempsychosis by *action*, and actions are different on account of the *three primary forces*. They live very long, since they have entirely stripped off the bodies,

since they are free from all exertion, and are able to do things which are impossible to man. They serve man
Page 45. in whatever he desires, and are near him in cases of need.

However, we can learn from the extract from *Sâṁkhya* that this view is not correct. For Brahman, Indra, and Prajâpati are not names of species, but of individuals. Brahman and Prajâpati very nearly mean the same, but they bear different names on account of some quality or other. Indra is the ruler of the worlds. Besides, Vâsudeva enumerates the Yaksha and Râkshasa together in one and the same class of demons, whilst the Purâṇas represent the Yaksha as guardian-angels and the servants of guardian-angels.

On the Devas.

After all this, we declare that the spiritual beings which we have mentioned are one category, who have attained their present stage of existence by action during the time when they were human beings. They have left their bodies behind them, for bodies are weights which impair the power and shorten the duration of life. Their qualities and conditions are different, in the same measure as one or other of the *three primary forces* prevails over them. The first force is peculiar to the Deva, or angels who live in quietness and bliss. The predominant faculty of their mind is the comprehending of an idea *without matter*, as it is the predominant faculty of the mind of man to comprehend the idea *in matter*.

The *third force* is peculiar to the Piśâca and Bhûta, whilst the second is peculiar to the classes between them.

The Hindus say that the number of Deva is thirty-three *koṭi* or *crore*, of which eleven belong to Mahâdeva. Therefore this number is one of his surnames, and his name itself (Mahâdeva) points in this direction. The sum of the number of angels just mentioned would be 330,000,000.

Further, they represent the Deva as eating and drinking, cohabiting, living and dying, since they exist within matter, though in the most subtle and most simple kind of it, and since they have attained this by action, not by knowledge. The book *Patañjali* relates that Nandikeśvara offered many sacrifices to Mahâdeva, and was in consequence transferred into paradise in his human shape; that Indra, the ruler, had intercourse with the wife of Nahusha the Brahmin, and therefore was changed into a serpent by way of punishment.

On the Pitaras and Ṛishis.

After the Deva comes the class of the *Pitaras*, the deceased ancestors, and after them the *Bhûta*, human beings who have attached themselves to the *spiritual beings* (Deva), and stand in the middle between them and mankind. He who holds this degree, but without being free from the body, is called either *Ṛishi* or *Siddha* or *Muni*, and these differ among themselves according to their qualities. *Siddha* is he who has attained by his action the faculty to do in the world whatever he likes, but who does not aspire further, and does not exert himself on the path leading to liberation. He may ascend to the degree of a Ṛishi. If a Brahmin attains this degree, he is called *Brahmarshi*; if the Kshatriya attains it, he is called *Râjarshi*. It is not possible for the lower classes to attain this degree. Ṛishis are the sages who, though they are only human beings, excel the angels on account of their knowledge. Therefore the angels learn from them, and above them there is none but Brahman.

After the Brahmarshi and Râjarshi come those classes of the populace which exist also among us, the castes, to whom we shall devote a separate chapter.

Vishṇu the unity of Brahman, Nârâyaṇa, and Rudra.

All these latter beings are ranged under matter. Now, as regards the notion of that which is above matter, we say that the ὕλη is the middle between matter and the spiritual divine ideas that are above matter, and that the *three primary forces* exist in the ὕλη dynamically (ἐν δυνάμει). So the ὕλη, with all that is comprehended in it, is a bridge from above to below.

Any life which circulates in the ὕλη under the exclusive influence of the *First Cause* is called *Brahman*, Page 46. *Prajâpati*, and by many other names which occur in their religious law and tradition. It is identical with nature in so far as it is active, for all bringing into existence, the creation of the world also, is attributed by them to Brahman.

Any life which circulates in the ὕλη under the influence of the *second force* is called *Nârâyaṇa* in the tradition of the Hindus, which means nature in so far as it has reached the end of its action, and is now striving to preserve that which has been produced. Thus Nârâyaṇa strives so to arrange the world that it should endure.

Any life which circulates in the ὕλη under the influence of the *third force* is called *Mahâdeva* and *Śaṁkara*, but his best-known name is *Rudra*. His work is destruction and annihilation, like nature in the last stages of activity, when its power slackens.

These three beings bear different names, as they circulate through the various degrees to above and below, and accordingly their actions are different.

But prior to all these beings there is one source whence everything is derived, and in this unity they comprehend all three things, no more separating one from the other. This unity they call *Vishṇu*, a name which more properly designates the *middle force*; but sometimes they do not even make a distinction between this *middle force* and *the first cause* (*i.e.* they make Nârâyaṇa the *causa causarum*).

Here there is an analogy between Hindus and Christians, as the latter distinguish between the Three *Persons* and give them separate names, Father, Son, and Holy Ghost, but unite them into one substance.

This is what clearly results from a careful examination of the Hindu doctrines. Of their traditional accounts, which are full of silly notions, we shall speak hereafter in the course of our explanation. You must not wonder if the Hindus, in their stories about the class of the Deva, whom we have explained as *angels*, allow them all sorts of things, unreasonable in themselves, some perhaps not objectionable, others decidedly objectionable, both of which the theologians of Islam would declare to be incompatible with the dignity and nature of angels.

If you compare these traditions with those of the Greeks regarding their own religion, you will cease to find the Hindu system strange. We have already mentioned that they called the angels gods (p. 36). Now consider their stories about Zeus, and you will understand the truth of our remark. As for anthropomorphisms and traits of animal life which they attribute to him, we give the following tradition: "When he was born, his father wanted to devour him; but his mother took a stone, wrapped rags round it, and gave him the stone to swallow, whereupon he went away." This is also mentioned by Galenus in his *Book of Speeches*, where he relates that Philo had in an enigmatical way described the preparation of the φιλώνειον φάρμακον in a poem of his by the following words:— Greek parallels. Stories about Zeus.

> "*Take red hair, diffusing sweet odour, the offering to the gods,*
> *And of man's blood weigh weights of the number of the mental faculties.*"

The poet means *five* pounds of saffron, because the senses are *five*. The weights of the other ingredients of the mixture he describes in similar enigmatic terms, of which Galenus gives a commentary. In the same poem occurs the following verse:—

> "*And of the pseudonymous root which has grown in the district in which Zeus was born.*"

To which Galenus adds: "This is *Andropogon Nardus*, which *bears a false name*, because it is called *an ear* of corn, although it is not an ear, but a root. The poet

prescribes that it should be Cretan, because the mythologists relate that Zeus was born on the mountain
Page 47. Δικταῖον in Creta, where his mother concealed him from his father Kronos, that he should not devour him as he had devoured others."

Besides, well-known story-books tell that he married certain women one after the other, cohabited with others, doing violence to them and not marrying them; among them Europa, the daughter of Phœnix, who was taken from him by Asterios, king of Crete. Afterwards she gave birth to two children from him, Minos and Rhadamanthus. This happened long before the Israelites left the desert and entered Palestine.

Another tradition is that he died in Crete, and was buried there at the time of Samson the Israelite, being 780 years of age; that he was called *Zeus* when he had become old, after he had formerly been called *Dios;* and that the first who gave him this name was Cecrops, the first king of Athens. It was common to all of them to indulge in their lusts without any restraint, and to favour the business of the pander; and so far they were not unlike Zoroaster and King Gushtâsp when they desired to consolidate the realm and the rule (*sic*).

Chroniclers maintain that Cecrops and his successors are the source of all the vices among the Athenians, meaning thereby such things as occur in the story of Alexander, viz. that Nectanebus, king of Egypt, after having fled before Artaxerxes the Black and hiding in the capital of Macedonia, occupied himself with astrology and soothsaying; that he beguiled Olympias, the wife of King Philip, who was absent. He cunningly contrived to cohabit with her, showing himself to her in the figure of the god Ammon, as a serpent with two heads like rams' heads. So she became pregnant with Alexander. Philip, on returning, was about to disclaim the paternity, but then he dreamt that it was the child of the god Ammon. Thereupon he recognised the child as his, and spoke, "Man cannot oppose the gods." The combination of the stars had shown to Nectanebus that he would die at the hands of his *son*. When then he died at the hands of Alexander from a wound in the neck, he recognised that he was his (Alexander's) father.

The tradition of the Greeks is full of similar things. We shall relate similar subjects when speaking of the marriages of the Hindus.

Now we return to our subject. Regarding that part of the nature of Zeus which has no connection with humanity, the Greeks say that he is Jupiter, the son of Saturn; for Saturn alone is eternal, not having been born, according to the philosophers of the Academy, as Galenus says in the *Book of Deduction*. This is sufficiently proved by the book of Aratos on the *Φαινόμενα*, for he begins with the praise of Zeus: Quotations from Aratos.

"We, mankind, do not leave him, nor can we do without him;
Of him the roads are full,
And the meeting-places of men.
He is mild towards them;
He produces for them what they wish, and incites them to work.
Reminding them of the necessities of life,
He indicates to them the times favourable
For digging and ploughing for a good growth,
Who has raised the signs and stars in heaven.
Therefore we humiliate ourselves before him first and last."

And then he praises the spiritual beings (the Muses). If you compare Greek theology with that of the Hindus, you will find that Brahman is described in the same way as Zeus by Aratos.

The author of the commentary on the *Φαινόμενα* of Aratos maintains that he deviated from the custom of the poets of his time in beginning with the gods; that it was his intention to speak of the celestial sphere. Further, he makes reflections on the origin of Asclepius, Page 48.
like Galenus, and says: "We should like to know

which Zeus Aratos meant, the mystical or the physical one. For the poet Krates called the celestial sphere *Zeus*, and likewise Homer says:

'As pieces of snow are cut off from *Zeus*.'"

Aratos calls the ether and the air *Zeus* in the passage: "The roads and the meeting-places are full of him, and we all must inhale him."

Therefore the philosophers of the Stoa maintain that Zeus is the spirit which is dispersed in the ὕλη, and similar to our souls, *i.e.* the nature which rules every natural body. The author supposes that he is mild, since he is the cause of the good; therefore he is right in maintaining that he has not only created men, but also the gods.

CHAPTER IX.

ON THE CASTES, CALLED "COLOURS" (VARṆA), AND ON THE CLASSES BELOW THEM.

Throne and altar.

If a new order of things in political or social life is created by a man naturally ambitious of ruling, who by his character and capacity really deserves to be a ruler, a man of firm convictions and unshaken determination, who even in times of reverses is supported by good luck, in so far as people then side with him in recognition of former merits of his, such an order is likely to become consolidated among those for whom it was created, and to continue as firm as the deeply rooted mountains. It will remain among them as a generally recognised rule in all generations through the course of time and the flight of ages. If, then, this new form of state or society rests in some degree on religion, these twins, state and religion, are in perfect harmony, and their union represents the highest development of human society, all that men can possibly desire.

The kings of antiquity, who were industriously devoted to the duties of their office, spent most of their care on the division of their subjects into different classes and orders, which they tried to preserve from intermixture and disorder. Therefore they forbade people of different classes to have intercourse with each other, and laid upon each class a particular kind of work or art and handicraft. They did not allow anybody to transgress the limits of his class, and even punished those who would not be content with their class.

Castes of the ancient Persians.

All this is well illustrated by the history of the ancient Chosroes (Khusrau), for they had created great institutions of this kind, which could not be broken through by the special merits of any individual nor by bribery. When Ardashîr ben Bâbak restored the Persian empire, he also restored the classes or castes of the population in the following way:—

The first class were the knights and princes.

The second class the monks, the fire-priests, and the lawyers.

The third class the physicians, astronomers, and other men of science.

The fourth class the husbandmen and artisans.

And within these classes there were subdivisions, distinct from each other, like the species within a genus. All institutions of this kind are like a pedigree, as long as their origin is remembered; but when once their origin has been forgotten, they become, as it were, the stable property of the whole nation, nobody any more questioning its origin. And forgetting is the necessary result of any long period of time, of a long succession of centuries and generations.

Among the Hindus institutions of this kind abound. We Muslims, of course, stand entirely on the other side of the question, considering all men as equal, except in piety; and this is the greatest obstacle which prevents any approach or understanding between Hindus and Muslims.

The four castes.

The Hindus call their castes *varṇa*, i.e. *colours*, and from a genealogical point of view they call them *jâtaka*, i.e. *births*. These castes are from the very beginning only four.

Page 49.

I. The highest caste are the Brâhmaṇa, of whom the books of the Hindus tell that they were created from the head of Brahman. And as Brahman is only another name for the force called *nature*, and the head is the highest part of the animal body, the Brâhmaṇa are the choice part of the whole genus. Therefore the Hindus consider them as the very best of mankind.

II. The next caste are the Kshatriya, who were created, as they say, from the shoulders and hands of Brahman. Their degree is not much below that of the Brâhmaṇa.

III. After them follow the Vaiśya, who were created from the thigh of Brahman.

IV. The Śûdra, who were created from his feet.

Between the latter two classes there is no very great distance. Much, however, as these classes differ from each other, they live together in the same towns and villages, mixed together in the same houses and lodgings.

After the Śûdra follow the people called *Antyaja*, who render various kinds of services, who are not reckoned amongst any caste, but only as members of a certain craft or profession. There are eight classes of them, who freely intermarry with each other, except the fuller, shoemaker, and weaver, for no others would condescend to have anything to do with them. These eight guilds are the fuller, shoemaker, juggler, the basket and shield maker, the sailor, fisherman, the hunter of wild animals and of birds, and the weaver. The four castes do not live together with them in one and the same place. These guilds live near the villages and towns of the four castes, but outside them. Low-caste people.

The people called Hâḍî, Ḍoma (Ḍomba), Caṇḍâla, and Badhatau (*sic*) are not reckoned amongst any caste or guild. They are occupied with dirty work, like the cleansing of the villages and other services. They are considered as one sole class, and distinguished only by their occupations. In fact, they are considered like illegitimate children; for according to general opinion they descend from a Śûdra father and a Brâhmaṇî mother as the children of fornication; therefore they are degraded outcasts.

Different occupations of the castes and guilds.

The Hindus give to every single man of the four castes characteristic names, according to their occupations and modes of life. *E.g.* the Brâhmaṇa is in general called by this name as long as he does his work staying at home. When he is busy with the service of one fire, he is called *ishṭin;* if he serves three fires, he is called *agnihôtrin;* if he besides offers an offering to the fire, he is called *dîkshita.* And as it is with the Brâhmaṇa, so is it also with the other castes. Of the classes *beneath* the castes, the Hâḍî are the best spoken of, because they keep themselves free from everything unclean. Next follow the Ḍôma, who play on the lute and sing. The still lower classes practise as a trade killing and the inflicting of judicial punishments. The worst of all are the Badhatau, who not only devour the flesh of dead animals, but even of dogs and other beasts.

Customs of the Brahmins.

Each of the four castes, when eating together, must form a group for themselves, one group not being allowed to comprise two men of different castes. If, further, in the group of the Brâhmaṇa there are two men who live at enmity with each other, and the seat of the one is by the side of the other, they make a barrier between the two seats by placing a board between them, or by spreading a piece of dress, or in some other way; and if there is only a line drawn between them, they are considered as separated. Since it is forbidden to eat the remains of a meal, every single man must have his own food for himself; for if any one of the party who are eating should take of the food from one and the same plate, that which remains in the plate becomes, after the first eater has taken part, to him who wants to take as the second, *the remains of the meal,* and such is forbidden.

Page 50.

Such is the condition of the four castes. Arjuna

asked about the nature of the four castes and what must be their moral qualities, whereupon Vâsudeva answered:

"The Brâhmaṇa must have an ample intellect, a quiet heart, truthful speech, much patience; he must be master of his senses, a lover of justice, of evident purity, always directed upon worship, entirely bent upon religion.

"The Kshatriya must fill the hearts with terror, must be brave and high-minded, must have ready speech and a liberal hand, not minding dangers, only intent upon carrying the great tasks of his calling to a happy end.

"The Vaiśya is to occupy himself with agriculture, with the acquisition of cattle, and with trade.

"The Śûdra is to endeavour to render services and attention to each of the preceding classes, in order to make himself liked by them.

"If each member of these castes adheres to his customs and usages, he will obtain the happiness he wishes for, supposing that he is not negligent in the worship of God, not forgetting to remember him in his most important avocations. But if anybody wants to quit the works and duties of his caste and adopt those of another caste, even if it would bring a certain honour to the latter, it is a sin, because it is a transgression of the rule."

Further, Vâsudeva speaks, inspiring him with courage to fight the enemy: "Dost thou not know, O man with the long arm, that thou art a Kshatriya; that thy race has been created brave, to rush boldly to the charge, to care little for the vicissitudes of time, never to give way whenever their soul has a foreboding of coming misfortune? for only thereby is the reward to be obtained. If he conquers, he obtains power and good fortune. If he perishes, he obtains paradise and bliss. Besides, thou showest weakness in the presence of the enemy, and seemest melancholy at the prospect of killing this host; but it will be infinitely worse if thy name will spread as that of a timid, cowardly man, that thy reputation among the heroes and the experienced warriors will be gone, that thou wilt be out of their sight, and thy name no longer be remembered among them. I do not know a worse punishment than such a state. Death is better than to expose thyself to the consequences of ignominy. If, therefore, God has ordered thee to fight, if he has deigned to confer upon thy caste the task of fighting and has created thee for it, carry out his order and perform his will with a determination which is free from any desire, so that thy action be exclusively devoted to him."

Moksha and the various castes.

Hindus differ among themselves as to which of these castes is capable of attaining to liberation; for, according to some, only the Brâhmaṇa and Kshatriya are capable of it, since the others cannot learn the Veda, whilst according to the Hindu philosophers, liberation is common to all castes and to the whole human race, if their intention of obtaining it is perfect. This view is based on the saying of Vyâsa: "Learn to know the twenty-five things thoroughly. Then you may follow whatever religion you like; you will no doubt be liberated." This view is also based on the fact that Vâsudeva was a descendant of a Śûdra family, and also on the following saying of his, which he addressed to Arjuna: "God distributes recompense without injustice and without partiality. He reckons the good as bad if people in doing good forget him; he reckons the bad as good if people in doing bad remember him and do not forget him, whether those people be Vaiśya or Śûdra or women. How much more will this be the case when they are Brâhmaṇa or Kshatriya."

Page 51.

CHAPTER X.

ON THE SOURCE OF THEIR RELIGIOUS AND CIVIL LAW, ON PROPHETS, AND ON THE QUESTION WHETHER SINGLE LAWS CAN BE ABROGATED OR NOT.

Law and religion among the Greeks founded by their sages.

THE ancient Greeks received their religious and civil laws from sages among them who were called to the work, and of whom their countrymen believed that they received divine help, like Solon, Draco, Pythagoras, Minos, and others. Also their kings did the same; for Mianos (*sic*), when ruling over the islands of the sea and over the Cretans about two hundred years after Moses, gave them laws, pretending to have received them from Zeus. About the same time also Minos (*sic*) gave his laws.

At the time of Darius I., the successor of Cyrus, the Romans sent messengers to the Athenians, and received from them the laws in twelve books, under which they lived till the rule of Pompilius (Numa). This king gave them new laws; he assigned to the year twelve months, whilst up to that time it had only had ten months. It appears that he introduced his innovations against the will of the Romans, for he ordered them to use as instruments of barter in commerce pieces of pottery and hides instead of silver, which seems on his part to betray a certain anger against rebellious subjects.

Quotation from Plato's *Laws*.

In the first chapter of the *Book of Laws* of Plato, the Athenian stranger says: "Who do you think was the first who gave laws to you? Was he an angel or a man?" The man of Cnossus said: "He was an angel. In truth, with us it was Zeus, but with the Lacedæmonians, as they maintain, the legislator was Apollo."

Further, he says in the same chapter: "It is the duty of the legislator, if he comes from God, to make the acquisition of the greatest virtues and of the highest justice the object of his legislation."

He describes the laws of the Cretans as rendering perfect the happiness of those who make the proper use of them, because by them they acquire all the human good which is dependent upon the divine good.

The Athenian says in the second chapter of the same book: "The gods, pitying mankind as born for trouble, instituted for them feasts to the gods, the Muses, Apollo the ruler of the Muses, and to Dionysos, who gave men wine as a remedy against the bitterness of old age, that old men should again be young by forgetting sadness, and by bringing back the character of the soul from the state of affliction to the state of soundness."

Further he says: "They have given to men by inspiration the arrangements for dancing, and the equally weighed rhythm as a reward for fatigues, and that they may become accustomed to live together with them in feasts and joy. Therefore they call one kind of their music *praises*, with an implied allusion to the prayers to the gods."

The Rishis, the authors of Hindu law. Page 52.

Such was the case with the Greeks, and it is precisely the same with the Hindus. For they believe that their religious law and its single precepts derive their origin from Ṛishis, their sages, the pillars of their religion, and not from the prophet, *i.e.* Nârâyaṇa, who, when coming into this world, appears in some human figure. But he only comes in order to cut away some evil matter which threatens the world, or to set the world right again when anything has gone wrong. Further, no law can be exchanged or replaced by another, for they use the laws simply as they find them. Therefore they can dispense with prophets, as far as law and worship are concerned, though in other affairs of the creation they sometimes want them.

Whether laws may be abrogated or not.

As for the question of the abrogation of laws, it seems that this is not impossible with the Hindus, for they say that many things which are now forbidden were allowed before the coming of Vâsudeva, *e.g.* the flesh of cows. Such changes are necessitated by the change of the nature of man, and by their being too feeble to bear the whole burden of their duties. To these changes also belong the changes of the *matrimonial system* and of *the theory of descent*. For in former times there were three modes of determining descent or relationship:

Different matrimonial systems.

1. The child born to a man by his legitimate wife is the child of the father, as is the custom with us and with the Hindus.

2. If a man marries a woman and has a child by her; if, further, the marriage-contract stipulates that the children of the woman will belong to *her* father, the child is considered as the child of its grandfather who made that stipulation, and not as the child of its father who engendered it.

3. If a stranger has a child by a married woman, the child belongs to her husband, since the wife being, as it were, the soil in which the child has grown, is the property of the husband, always presupposing that the sowing, *i.e.* the cohabitation, takes place with his consent.

The story of Pâṇḍu and Vyâsa.

According to this principle, Pâṇḍu was considered as the son of Śântanu; for this king had been cursed by an anchorite, and in consequence was unable to cohabit with his wives, which was the more provoking to him as he had not yet any children. Now he asked Vyâsa, the son of Parâśara, to procreate for him children from his wives in his place. Pâṇḍu sent him one, but she was afraid of him when he cohabited with her, and trembled, in consequence of which she conceived a sickly child of yellow hue. Then the king sent him a second woman; she, too, felt much reverence for him, and wrapped herself up in her veil, and in consequence she gave birth to Dhṛitarâshṭra, who was blind and unhealthy. Lastly, he sent him a third woman, whom he enjoined to put aside all fear and reverence with regard to the saint. Laughing and in high spirits, she went in to him, and conceived from him a child of moon-like beauty, who excelled all men in boldness and cunning.

Birth of Vyâsa.

The four sons of Pâṇḍu had one wife in common, who stayed one month with each of them alternately. In the books of the Hindus it is told that Parâśara, the hermit, one day travelled in a boat in which there was also a daughter of the boatman. He fell in love with her, tried to seduce her, and finally she yielded; but there was nothing on the bank of the river to hide them from the looks of the people. However, instantaneously there grew a tamarisk-tree to facilitate their purpose. Now he cohabited with her behind the tamarisk, and made her conceive, whereupon she became pregnant with this his excellent son Vyâsa.

All these customs have now been abolished and abrogated, and therefore we may infer from their tradition that in principle *the abrogation of a law is allowable.*

Various kinds of marriage with Tibetans and Arabs.

As regards unnatural kinds of marriage, we must state that such exist still in our time, as they also existed in the times of Arab heathendom; for the people inhabiting the mountains stretching from the region of Panchîr into the neighbourhood of Kashmîr live under the rule that several brothers have one wife in common. Among the heathen Arabs, too, marriage was of different kinds:—

Page 53.

1. An Arab ordered his wife to be sent to a certain

man to demand sexual intercourse with him; then he abstained from her during the whole time of her pregnancy, since he wished to have from her a generous offspring. This is identical with the third kind of marriage among the Hindus.

2. A second kind was this, that the one Arab said to the other, "Cede me your wife, and I will cede you mine," and thus they exchanged their wives.

3. A third kind is this, that several men cohabited with one wife. When, then, she gave birth to a child, she declared who was the father; and if she did not know it, the fortune-tellers had to know it.

4. The *Nikâḥ-elmakt* (= *matrimonium exosum*), *i.e.* when a man married the widow of his father or of his son, the child of such a marriage was called *ḍaizan*. This is nearly the same as a certain Jewish marriage, for the Jews have the law that a man must marry the widow of his brother, if the latter has not left children, and create a line of descent for his deceased brother; and the offspring is considered as that of the deceased man, not as that of the real father. Thereby they want to prevent his memory dying out in the world. In Hebrew they call a man who is married in this way *Yâbhâm*.

Marriage among the ancient Iranians.

There was a similar institution among the Magians. In the book of Tausar, the great *herbadh*, addressed to Padashvâr-girshâh, as an answer to his attacks on Ardashîr the son of Bâbak, we find a description of the institution of a man's being married as the substitute for another man, which existed among the Persians. If a man dies without leaving male offspring, people are to examine the case. If he leaves a wife, they marry her to his nearest relative. If he does not leave a wife, they marry his daughter or the nearest related woman to the nearest related male of the family. If there is no woman of his family left, they woo by means of the money of the deceased a woman for his family, and marry her to some male relative. The child of such a marriage is considered as the offspring of the deceased.

Whoever neglects this duty and does not fulfil it, kills innumerable souls, since he cuts off the progeny and the name of the deceased to all eternity.

We have here given an account of these things in order that the reader may learn by the comparative treatment of the subject how much superior the institutions of Islam are, and how much more plainly this contrast brings out all customs and usages, differing from those of Islam, in their essential foulness.

CHAPTER XI.

ABOUT THE BEGINNING OF IDOL-WORSHIP, AND A DESCRIPTION OF THE INDIVIDUAL IDOLS.

It is well known that the popular mind leans towards the sensible world, and has an aversion to the world of abstract thought which is only understood by highly educated people, of whom in every time and every place there are only few. And as common people will only acquiesce in pictorial representations, many of the leaders of religious communities have so far deviated from the right path as to give such imagery in their books and houses of worship, like the Jews and Christians, and, more than all, the Manichæans. These words of mine would at once receive a sufficient illustration if, for example, a picture of the Prophet were made, or of Mekka and the Ka'ba, and were shown to an uneducated man or woman. Their joy in looking at the thing would bring them to kiss the picture, to rub their cheeks against it, and to roll themselves in the dust before it, as if they were seeing not the picture, but the original, and were in this way, as if they were present in the holy places, performing the rites of pilgrimage, the great and the small ones.

Origin of idol-worship in the nature of man.

This is the cause which leads to the manufacture of idols, monuments in honour of certain much venerated persons, prophets, sages, angels, destined to keep alive their memory when they are absent or dead, to create for them a lasting place of grateful veneration in the hearts of men when they die. But when much time passes by after the setting up of the monument, generations and centuries, its origin is forgotten, it becomes a matter of custom, and its veneration a rule for general practice. This being deeply rooted in the nature of man, the legislators of antiquity tried to influence them from this weak point of theirs. Therefore they made the veneration of pictures and similar monuments obligatory on them, as is recounted in historic records, both for the times before and after the Deluge. Some people even pretend to know that all mankind, before God sent them his prophets, were one large idolatrous body.

Page 54.

Story of Romulus and Remus.

The followers of the Thora fix the beginning of idolatry in the days of Serûgh, the great-grandfather of Abraham. The Romans have, regarding this question, the following tradition:—Romulus and Romanus (!), the two brothers from the country of the Franks, on having ascended the throne, built the city of Rome. Then Romulus killed his brother, and the consequence was a long succession of intestine troubles and wars. Finally, Romulus humiliated himself, and then he dreamt that there would only be peace on condition that he placed his brother on the throne. Now he got a golden image made of him, placed it at his side, and henceforward he used to say, "*We* (not *I*) have ordered thus and thus," which since has become the general use of kings. Thereupon the troubles subsided. He founded a feast and a play to amuse and to gain over those who bore him ill-will on account of the murder of his brother. Besides, he erected a monument to the sun, consisting of four images on four horses, the green one for the earth, the blue for the water, the red for the fire, and the white for the air. This monument is still in Rome in our days.

Idol-worship as restricted to the low classes of people.

Since, however, here we have to explain the system and the theories of the Hindus on the subject, we shall now mention their ludicrous views; but we declare at once that they are held only by the common uneducated people. For those who march on the path to liberation, or those who study philosophy and theology, and who desire abstract truth which they call *sâra*, are entirely free from worshipping anything but God alone, and would never dream of worshipping an image manufactured to represent him. A tradition illustrative of this is that which Śaunaka told the king Parîksha in these words:—

Story of King Ambarîsha and Indra.

There was once a king called Ambarîsha, who had obtained an empire as large as he had wished for. But afterwards he came to like it no longer; he retired from the world, and exclusively occupied himself with worshipping and praising God for a long time. Finally, God appeared to him in the shape of Indra, the prince of the angels, riding on an elephant. He spoke to the king: "Demand whatever you like, and I will give it you."

The king answered: "I rejoice in seeing thee, and I am thankful for the good fortune and help thou hast given; but I do not demand anything from thee, but only from him who created thee."

Indra said: "The object of worship is to receive a noble reward. Realise, therefore, your object, and accept the reward from him from whom hitherto you have obtained your wishes, and do not pick and choose, saying, 'Not from thee, but from another.'"

The king answered: "The earth has fallen to my lot, but I do not care for all that is in it. The object of my worship is to see the Lord, and that thou canst not give me. Why, therefore, should I demand the fulfilment of my desire from thee?"

Indra said: "The whole world and whoever is upon it are obedient to me. Who are you that you dare to oppose me?"

The king answered: "I, too, hear and obey, but I worship *him* from whom thou hast received this power, who is the lord of the universe, who has protected thee against the attacks of the two kings, Bali and Hiraṇyâksha. Therefore let me do as *I* like, and turn away from me with my farewell greeting."

Indra said: "If you will absolutely oppose me, I will kill you and annihilate you."

The king answered: "People say that happiness is envied, but not so misfortune. He who retires from the world is envied by the angels, and therefore they will try to lead him astray. I am one of those who have retired from the world and entirely devoted themselves to worship, and I shall not give it up as long as
Page 55. I live. I do not know myself to be guilty of a crime for which I should deserve to be killed by thee. If thou killest me without any offence on my part, it is thy concern. What dost thou want from me? If my thoughts are entirely devoted to God, and nothing else is blended with them, thou art not able to do me any harm. Sufficient for me is the worship with which I am occupied, and now I return to it."

As the king now went on worshipping, the Lord appeared to him in the shape of a man of the grey lotus colour, riding on a bird called Garuḍa, holding in one of the four hands the *śaṅkha*, a sea-shell which people blow when riding on elephants; in the second hand the *cakra*, a round, cutting, orbicular weapon, which cuts everything it hits right through; in the third an amulet, and in the fourth *padma*, *i.e.* the red lotus. When the king saw him, he shuddered from reverence, prostrated himself and uttered many praises. The Lord quieted his terrified mind and promised him that he should obtain everything he wished for. The king spoke: "I had obtained an empire which nobody disputed with me; I was in conditions of life not troubled by sorrow or sickness. It was as if the whole world belonged to me. But then I turned away from it, after I had understood that the good of the world is really bad in the end. I do not wish for anything except what I now have. The only thing I now wish for is to be liberated from this fetter."

The Lord spoke: "That you will obtain by keeping aloof from the world, by being alone, by uninterrupted meditation, and by restraining your senses to yourself."

The king spoke: "Supposing that I am able to do so through that sanctity which the Lord has deigned to bestow upon me, how should any other man be able to do so? for man wants eating and clothing, which connects him with the world. How is he to think of anything else?"

The Lord spoke: "Occupy yourself with your empire in as straightforward and prudent a way as possible: turn your thoughts upon me when you are engaged in civilising the world and protecting its inhabitants, in giving alms, and in everything you do. And if you are overpowered by human forgetfulness, make to yourself an image like that in which you see me; offer to it perfumes and flowers, and make it a memorial of me, so that you may not forget me. If you are in sorrow, think of me; if you speak, speak in my name; if you act, act for me."

The king spoke: "Now I know what I have to do in general, but honour me further by instructing me in the details."

The Lord spoke: "That I have done already. I have inspired your judge Vasishṭha with all that is required. Therefore rely upon him in all questions."

Then the figure disappeared from his sight. The king returned into his residence and did as he had been ordered.

From that time, the Hindus say, people make idols, some with four hands like the appearance we have described, others with two hands, as the story and description require, and conformably to the being which is to be represented.

Nârada and the voice from the fire.

Another story of theirs is the following:—Brahman had a son called Nârada, who had no other desire but that of seeing the Lord. It was his custom, when he walked about, to hold a stick. If he threw it down, it became a serpent, and he was able to do miracles with it. He never went without it. One day being engrossed in meditation on the object of his hopes, he saw a fire from afar. He went towards it, and then a voice spoke to him out of the fire: "What you demand and wish is impossible. You cannot see me save thus." When he looked in that direction, he saw a fiery appearance in something like human shape. Henceforward it has been the custom to erect idols of certain shapes.

Page 56.

The idol of Multân called Âditya.

A famous idol of theirs was that of Multân, dedicated to the sun, and therefore called *Âditya*. It was of wood and covered with red Cordovan leather; in its two eyes were two red rubies. It is said to have been made in the last Kṛitayuga. Suppose that it was made in the very end of Kṛitayuga, the time which has since elapsed amounts to 216,432 years. When Muhammad Ibn Alḳâsim Ibn Almunabbih conquered Multân, he inquired how the town had become so very flourishing and so many treasures had there been accumulated, and then he found out that this idol was the cause, for there came pilgrims from all sides to visit it. Therefore he thought it best to have the idol where it was, but he hung a piece of cow's-flesh on its neck by way of mockery. On the same place a mosque was built. When then the Ḳarmatians occupied Multân, Jalam Ibn Shaibân, the usurper, broke the idol into pieces and killed its priests. He made his mansion, which was a castle built of brick on an elevated place, the mosque instead of the old mosque, which he ordered to be shut from hatred against anything that had been done under the dynasty of the Caliphs of the house of 'Umayya. When afterwards the blessed Prince Maḥmûd swept away their rule from those countries, he made again the old mosque the place of the Friday-worship, and the second one was left to decay. At present it is only a barn-floor, where bunches of Ḥinnâ (*Lawsonia inermis*) are bound together.

If we now subtract from the above-mentioned number of years the hundreds, tens, and units, *i.e.* the 432 years, as a kind of arbitrary equivalent for the sum of about 100 years, by which the rise of the Karmatians preceded our time, we get as the remainder 216,000 years for the time of the end of the Kṛitayuga, and about the epoch of the era of the Hijra. How, then, could wood have lasted such a length of time, and particularly in a place where the air and the soil are rather wet? God knows best!

The idol of Tâneshar called Cakrasvâmin.

The city of Tâneshar is highly venerated by the Hindus. The idol of that place is called *Cakrasvâmin*, *i.e.* the owner of the *cakra*, a weapon which we have already described (page 114). It is of bronze, and is nearly the size of a man. It is now lying in the hippodrome in Ghazna, together with the *Lord of Somanâth*, which is a representation of the *penis* of Mahâdeva, called *Linga*. Of Somanâth we shall hereafter speak in the proper place. This Cakrasvâmin is said to have been made in the time of Bhârata as a memorial of wars connected with this name.

The idol Śârada in Kashmîr.

In Inner Kashmîr, about two or three days' journey from the capital in the direction towards the mountains of Bolor, there is a wooden idol called *Śârada*, which is much venerated and frequented by pilgrims.

Quotation from the Saṁhitâ of Varâhamihira.

We shall now communicate a whole chapter from the book *Saṁhitâ* relating to the construction of idols, which will help the student thoroughly to comprehend the present subject.

Varâhamihira says: "If the figure is made to represent Râma the son of Daśaratha, or Bali the son of Virocana, give it the height of 120 digits," *i.e.* of *idol digits*, which must be reduced by one-tenth to become *common digits*, in this case 108.

"To the idol of Vishṇu give eight hands, or four, or two, and on the left side under the breast give him the figure of the woman Śrî. If you give him eight hands, place in the right hands a sword, a club of gold or iron, an arrow, and make the fourth hand as if it were drawing water; in the left hands give him a shield, a bow, a *cakra*, and a conch.

Page 57.

"If you give him four hands, omit the bow and the arrow, the sword and shield.

"If you give him two hands, let the right hand be drawing water, the left holding a conch.

"If the figure is to represent Baladeva, the brother of Nârâyaṇa, put earrings into his ears, and give him eyes of a drunken man.

"If you make both figures, Nârâyaṇa and Baladeva, join with them their sister *Bhagavatî* (Durgâ = Ekânanśâ), her left hand resting on her hip a little away from the side, and her right hand holding a lotus.

"If you make her four-handed, place in the right hands a rosary and a hand drawing water; in the left hands, a book and a lotus.

"If you make her eight-handed, place in the left hands the *kamaṇḍalu, i.e.* a pot, a lotus, bow and book; in the right hands, a rosary, a mirror, an arrow, and a water-drawing hand.

"If the figure is to represent Sâmba, the son of Vishṇu, put only a club in his right hand. If it is to represent Pradyumna, the son of Vishṇu, place in his right hand an arrow, in his left hand a bow. And if you make their two wives, place in their right hand a sword, in the left a buckler.

"The idol of Brahman has four faces towards the four sides, and is seated on a lotus.

"The idol of Skanda, the son of Mahâdeva, is a boy riding on a peacock, his hand holding a *śakti*, a weapon like a double-edged sword, which has in the middle a pestle like that of a mortar.

"The idol Indra holds in its hand a weapon called *vajra* of diamond. It has a similar handle to the *śakti*, but on each side it has two swords which join at the handle. On his front place a third eye, and make him ride on a white elephant with four tusks.

"Likewise make on the front of the idol of Mahâdeva a third eye right above, on his head a crescent, in his hand a weapon called *śûla*, similar to the club but with three branches, and a sword; and let his left hand hold his wife Gaurî, the daughter of Himavant, whom he presses to his bosom from the side.

"To the idol Jina, *i.e.* Buddha, give a face and limbs as beautiful as possible, make the lines in the palms of his hands and feet like a lotus, and represent him seated on a lotus; give him grey hair, and represent him with a placid expression, as if he were the father of creation.

"If you make Arhant, the figure of another body of Buddha, represent him as a naked youth with a fine face, beautiful, whose hands reach down to the knees, with the figure of Śrî, his wife, under the left breast.

"The idol of Revanta, the son of the sun, rides on a horse like a huntsman.

"The idol of Yima, the angel of death, rides on a buffalo, and holds a club in his hand.

"The idol of Kubera, the treasurer, wears a crown, has a big stomach and wide hips, and is riding on a man.

"The idol of the sun has a red face like the pith of the red lotus, beams like a diamond, has protruding limbs, rings in the ears, the neck adorned with pearls which hang down over the breast, wears a crown of several compartments, holds in his hands two lotuses, and is clad in the dress of the Northerners which reaches down to the ankle.

"If you represent the Seven Mothers, represent several of them together in one figure, Brahmâṇî with four faces Page 58.

towards the four directions, Kaumârî with six faces, Vaishṇavî with four hands, Vârâhi with a hog's head on a human body, Indrâṇî with many eyes and a club in her hand, Bhagavatî (Durgâ) sitting as people generally sit, Câmuṇḍâ ugly, with protruding teeth and a slim waist. Further join with them the sons of Mahâdeva, Kshetrapâla with bristling hair, a sour face, and an ugly figure, but Vinâyaka with an elephant's head on a human body, with four hands, as we have heretofore described."

The worshippers of these idols kill sheep and buffaloes with axes (*kuṭâra*), that they may nourish themselves with their blood. All idols are constructed according to certain measures determined by *idol-fingers* for every single limb, but sometimes they differ regarding the measure of a limb. If the artist keeps the right measure and does not make anything too large nor too small, he is free from sin, and is sure that the being which he represented will not visit him with any mishap. "If he makes the idol one cubit high and together with the throne two cubits, he will obtain health and wealth. If he makes it higher still, he will be praised.

"But he must know that making the idol too large, especially that of the Sun, will hurt the ruler, and making it too small will hurt the artist. If he gives it a thin belly, this helps and furthers the famine in the country; if he gives it a lean belly, this ruins property.

"If the hand of the artist slips so as to produce something like a wound, he will have a wound in his own body which will kill him.

"If it is not completely even on both sides, so that the one shoulder is higher than the other, his wife will perish.

"If he turns the eye upward, he will be blind for lifetime; if he turns it downward, he will have many troubles and sorrows."

If the statue is made of some precious stone, it is better than if it were made of wood, and wood is better than clay. "The benefits of a statue of precious stone will be common to all the men and women of the empire. A golden statue will bring power to him who erected it, a statue of silver will bring him renown, one of bronze will bring him an increase of his rule, one of stone the acquisition of landed property."

The Hindus honour their idols on account of those who erected them, not on account of the material of which they are made. We have already mentioned that the idol of Multân was of wood. *E.g.* the *linga* which Râma erected when he had finished the war with the demons was of sand, which he had heaped up with his own hand. But then it became petrified all at once, since the astrologically correct moment for the erecting of the monument fell before the moment when the workmen had finished the cutting of the stone monument which Râma originally had ordered. Regarding the building of the temple and its peristyle, the cutting of the trees of four different kinds, the astrological determination of the favourable moment for the erection, the celebration of the rites due on such an occasion, regarding all this Râma gave very long and tedious instructions. Further, he ordered that servants and priests to minister to the idols should be nominated from different classes of the people. "To the idol of Vishnu are devoted the class called Bhâgavata; to the idol of the Sun, the Maga, *i.e.* the Magians; to the idol of Mahâdeva, a class of saints, anchorites with long hair, who cover their skin with ashes, hang on their persons the bones of dead people, and swim in the pools. The Brâhmaṇa are devoted to the Eight Page 59.
Mothers, the Shamanians to Buddha, to Arhant the class called *Nagna*. On the whole, to each idol certain people are devoted who constructed it, for those know best how to serve it."

Quotations from *Gîtâ* showing that God is not to be confounded with the idols.

Our object in mentioning all this mad raving was to teach the reader the accurate description of an idol, if he happens to see one, and to illustrate what we have said before, that such idols are erected only for uneducated low-class people of little understanding; that the Hindus never made an idol of any supernatural being, much less of God; and, lastly, to show how the crowd is kept in thraldom by all kinds of priestly tricks and deceits. Therefore the book *Gîtâ* says: "Many people try to approach me in their aspirations through something which is different from me; they try to insinuate themselves into my favour by giving alms, praise, and prayer to something besides me. I, however, confirm and help them in all these doings of theirs, and make them attain the object of their wishes, because I am able to dispense with them."

In the same book Vâsudeva speaks to Arjuna: "Do you not see that most of those who wish for something address themselves in offering and worshipping to the several classes of *spiritual beings*, and to the sun, moon, and other celestial bodies? If now God does not disappoint their hopes, though he in no way stands in need of their worship, if he even gives them more than they asked for, and if he gives them their wishes in such a way as though they were receiving them from that to which they had addressed their prayers—viz. the idol—they will proceed to worship those whom they address, because they have not learned to know him, whilst *he*, by admitting this kind of intermediation, carries their affairs to the desired end. But that which is obtained by desires and intermediation is not lasting, since it is only as much as is deserved for any particular merit. Only that is lasting which is obtained from God alone, when people are disgusted with old age, death, and birth (and desire to be delivered therefrom by *Mokska*)."

This is what Vâsudeva says. When the ignorant crowd

get a piece of good luck by accident or something at which they had aimed, and when with this some of the preconcerted tricks of the priests are brought into connection, the darkness in which they live increases vastly, not their intelligence. They will rush to those *figures* of idols, maltreating their own figures before them by shedding their own blood and mutilating their own bodies.

The ancient Greeks, also, considered the idols as mediators between themselves and the *First Cause*, and worshipped them under the names of the stars and the highest substances. For they described the First Cause, not with positive, but only with negative predicates, since they considered it too high to be described by human qualities, and since they wanted to describe it as free from any imperfection. Therefore they could not address it in worship.

When the heathen Arabs had imported into their country idols from Syria, they also worshipped them, hoping that they would intercede for them with God.

Plato says in the fourth chapter of the *Book of Laws*: "It is necessary to any one who gives perfect honours (to the gods) that he should take trouble with the *mystery* of the gods and Sakînât, and that he should not make special idols masters over the ancestral gods. Further, it is the greatest duty to give honours as much as possible to the parents while they live."

By *mystery* Plato means a special kind of *devotion*. The word is much used among the Ṣâbians of Ḥarrân, the dualistic Manichæans, and the theologians of the Hindus.

Galenus says in the book *De Indole Animæ*: "At the time of the Emperor Commodus, between 500–510 years after Alexander, two men went to an idol-merchant and bargained with him for an idol of Hermes. The one wanted to erect it in a temple as a memorial of Hermes, the other wanted to erect it on a tomb as a Page 60.

memorial of the deceased. However, they could not settle the business with the merchant, and so they postponed it until the following day. The idol-merchant dreamt the following night that the idol addressed him and spoke to him: 'O excellent man! I am thy work. I have received through the work of thy hands a figure which is thought to be the figure of a star. Now I am no longer a stone, as people called me heretofore; I am now known as Mercury. At present it stands in thy hands to make me either a memorial of something imperishable or of something that has perished already.'"

There is a treatise of Aristotle in which he answers certain questions of the Brahmins which Alexander had sent him. There he says: "If you maintain that some Greeks have fabled that the idols speak, that the people offer to them and think them to be spiritual beings, of all this we have no knowledge, and we cannot give a sentence on a subject we do not know." In these words he rises high above the class of fools and uneducated people, and he indicates by them that he does not occupy himself with such things. It is evident that the first cause of idolatry was the desire of commemorating the dead and of consoling the living; but on this basis it has developed, and has finally become a foul and pernicious abuse.

The former view, that idols are only memorials, was also held by the Caliph Mu'âwiya regarding the idols of Sicily. When, in the summer of A.H. 53, Sicily was conquered, and the conquerors sent him golden idols adorned with crowns and diamonds which had been captured there, he ordered them to be sent to Sind, that they should be sold there to the princes of the country; for he thought it best to sell them as objects costing sums of so-and-so many denars, not having the slightest scruple on account of their being objects of abominable idolatry, but simply considering the matter from a political, not from a religious point of view.

CHAPTER XII.

ON THE VEDA, THE PURÂṆAS, AND OTHER KINDS OF THEIR NATIONAL LITERATURE.

VEDA means knowledge of that which was before unknown. It is a religious system which, according to the Hindus, comes from God, and was promulgated by the mouth of Brahman. The Brahmins recite the Veda without understanding its meaning, and in the same way they learn it by heart, the one receiving it from the other. Only few of them learn its explanation, and still less is the number of those who master the contents of the Veda and their interpretation to such a degree as to be able to hold a theological disputation. Sundry notes relating to the Veda.

The Brahmins teach the Veda to the Kshatriyas. The latter learn it, but are not allowed to teach it, not even to a Brahmin. The Vaiśya and Śûdra are not allowed to hear it, much less to pronounce and recite it. If such a thing can be proved against one of them, the Brahmins drag him before the magistrate, and he is punished by having his tongue cut off.

The Veda contains commandments and prohibitions, detailed statements about reward and punishment intended to encourage and to deter; but most of it contains hymns of praise, and treats of the various kinds of sacrifices to the fire, which are so numerous and difficult that you could hardly count them.

They do not allow the Veda to be committed to writing, because it is recited according to certain modu- The Veda transmitted by memory.

lations, and they therefore avoid the use of the pen, since it is liable to cause some error, and may occasion an addition or a defect in the written text. In consequence it has happened that they have several times forgotten the Veda and lost it. For they maintain that the following passage occurs in the conversations between God and Brahman relating to the beginning of all things, according to the report of Śaunaka who had received it from the planet Venus: "You will forget the Veda at the time when the earth will be submerged; it will then go down to the depths of the earth, and none but the fish will be able to bring it out again. Therefore I shall send the fish, and it will deliver the Veda into your hands. And I shall send the boar to raise the earth with its tusks and to bring it out of the water."

Page 61.

Further, the Hindus maintain that the Veda, together with all the rites of their religion and country, had been obliterated in the last Dvâpara-yuga, a period of time of which we shall speak in the proper place, until it was renewed by Vyâsa, the son of Parâśara.

The *Vishṇu Purâṇa* says: "At the beginning of each Manvantara period there will be created anew a lord of a period whose children will rule over the whole earth, and a prince who will be the head of the world, and angels to whom men will bring fire-offerings, and the *Great Bear*, who will renew the Veda which is lost at the end of each period."

Vasukra commits the Veda to writing.

This is the reason why, not long before our time, Vasukra, a native of Kashmîr, a famous Brahmin, has of his own account undertaken the task of explaining the Veda and committing it to writing. He has taken on himself a task from which everybody else would have recoiled, but he carried it out because he was afraid that the Veda might be forgotten and entirely vanish out of the memories of men, since he observed that the characters of men grew worse and worse, and that they did not care much for virtue, nor even for duty.

There are certain passages in the Veda which, as they maintain, must not be recited within dwellings, since they fear that they would cause an abortion both to women and the cattle. Therefore they step out into the open field to recite them there. There is hardly a single verse free from such and similar minatory injunctions.

As we have already mentioned, the books of the Hindus are metrical compositions like the Rajaz poems of the Arabs. Most of them are composed in a metre called *śloka*. The reason of this has already been explained. Galenus also prefers metrical composition, and says in his book Κατὰ γένη: "The single signs which denote the weights of medicines become corrupt by being copied; they are also corrupted by the wanton mischief of some envious person. Therefore it is quite right that the books of Damocrates on medicines should be preferred to others, and that they should gain fame and praise, since they are written in a Greek metre. If all books were written in this way it would be the best;" the fact being that a prose text is much more exposed to corruption than a metrical one.

The Veda, however, is not composed in this common metre, śloka, but in another. Some Hindus say that no one could compose anything in the same metre. However, their scholars maintain that this is possible indeed, but that they refrain from trying it merely from veneration for the Veda.

The four pupils of Vyâsa and the four Vedas.

According to their tradition, Vyâsa divided it into four parts: *Ṛigveda*, *Yajurveda*, *Sâmaveda*, and *Atharvaṇaveda*.

Vyâsa had four *śishya*, *i.e.* pupils. He taught a separate Veda to each of them, and made him carry it in his memory. They are enumerated in the same order as the four parts of the Veda: *Paila*, *Vaiśampâyana*, *Jaimini*, *Sumantu*.

On the Ṛigveda. Each of the four parts has a peculiar kind of recitation. The first is Ṛigveda, consisting of metrical compositions called *ṛic*, which are of different lengths. It is called Ṛigveda as being the totality of the *ṛic*. Page 62. It treats of the sacrifices to the fire, and is recited in three different ways. First, in a uniform manner of reading, just as every other book is read. Secondly, in such a way that a pause is made after every single word. Thirdly, in a method which is the most meritorious, and for which plenty of reward in heaven is promised. First you read a short passage, each word of which is distinctly pronounced; then you repeat it together with a part of that which has not yet been recited. Next you recite the added portion alone, and then you repeat it together with the next part of that which has not yet been recited, &c., &c. Continuing to do so till the end, you will have read the whole text twice.

On the Yajurveda. The Yajurveda is composed of *kâṇḍin*. The word is a derivative noun, and means *the totality of the kâṇḍin*. The difference between this and the Ṛigveda is that it may be read as a text connected by the rules of Saṁdhi, which is not allowed in the case of Ṛigveda. The one as well as the other treats of works connected with the fire and the sacrifices.

I have heard the following story about the reason why the Ṛigveda cannot be recited as a text connected by the rules of Saṁdhi:—

The story of Yâjnavalkya. Yâjnavalkya stayed with his master, and his master had a Brahmin friend who wanted to make a journey. Therefore he asked the master to send somebody to his house to perform there during his absence the rites to *Homa*, *i.e.* to his fire, and to prevent it from being extinguished. Now the master sent his pupils to the house of his friend one after the other. So it came to be the turn of Yâjnavalkya, who was beautiful to look at and handsomely dressed. When he began the work which he was sent for, in a place where the wife of the absent man was present, she conceived an aversion to his fine attire, and Yâjnavalkya became aware of it, though she concealed it. On having finished, he took the water to sprinkle it over the head of the woman, for this holds with them the place of the blowing after an incantation, since blowing is disliked by them and considered as something impure. Then the woman said, "Sprinkle it over this column." So he did, and at once the column became green. Now the woman repented having missed the blessing of his pious action; therefore on the following day she went to the master, asking him to send her the same pupil whom he had sent the day before. Yâjnavalkya, however, declined to go except in his turn. No urging had any effect upon him; he did not mind the wrath of his master, but simply said, "Take away from me all that you have taught me." And scarcely had he spoken the word, when on a sudden he had forgotten all he knew before. Now he turned to the Sun and asked him to teach him the Veda. The Sun said, "How is that possible, as I must perpetually wander, and you are incapable of doing the same?" But then Yâjnavalkya clung to the chariot of the Sun and began to learn the Veda from him; but he was compelled to interrupt the recitation here and there on account of the irregularity of the motion of the chariot.

Sâmaveda and Âtharvaṇaveda.

The Sâmaveda treats of the sacrifices, commandments, and prohibitions. It is recited in a tone like a chant, and hence its name is derived, because *sâman* means *the sweetness of recitation.* The cause of this kind of recital is, that Nârâyaṇa, when he appeared on earth in the shape of Vâmana, and came to the king Bali, changed himself into a Brahman and began to recite the Sâmaveda with a touching melody, by which he exhilarated the king, in consequence of which there happened to him the well-known story.

The Âtharvaṇaveda is as a text connected by the

rules of Saṁdhi. It does not consist of the same compositions as the Ṛig and Yajur Vedas, but of a third kind called *bhara*. It is recited according to a melody with a nasal tone. This Veda is less in favour with the Hindus than the others. It likewise treats of the sacrifices to the fire, and contains injunctions regarding the dead and what is to be done with them.

List of the Purâṇas.

As to the Purâṇas, we first mention that the word means *first, eternal*. There are eighteen Purâṇas, most of them called by the names of animals, human or

Page 63.

angelic beings, because they contain stories about them, or because the contents of the book refer in some way to them, or because the book consists of answers which the creature whose name forms the title of the book has given to certain questions.

The Purâṇas are of human origin, composed by the so-called Ṛishis. In the following I give a list of their names, as I have heard them, and committed them to writing from dictation :—

1. *Âdi-purâṇa*, *i.e.* the first.
2. *Matsya-purâṇa*, *i.e.* the fish.
3. *Kûrma-purâṇa*, *i.e.* the tortoise.
4. *Varâha-purâṇa*, *i.e.* the boar.
5. *Narasiṁha-purâṇa*, *i.e.* a human being with a lion's head.
6. *Vâmana-purâṇa*, *i.e.* the dwarf.
7. *Vâyu-purâṇa*, *i.e.* the wind.
8. *Nanda-purâṇa*, *i.e.* a servant of Mahâdeva.
9. *Skanda-purâṇa*, *i.e.* a son of Mahâdeva.
10. *Âditya-purâṇa*, *i.e.* the sun.
11. *Soma-purâṇa*, *i.e.* the moon.
12. *Sâmba-purâṇa*, *i.e.* the son of Vishṇu.
13. *Brahmâṇḍa-purâṇa*, *i.e.* heaven.
14. *Mârkandeya-purâṇa*, *i.e.* a great Rishi.
15. *Târkshya-purâṇa*, *i.e.* the bird Garuḍa.
16. *Vishṇu-purâṇa*, *i.e.* Nârâyaṇa.
17. *Brahma-purâṇa*, *i.e.* the nature charged with the preservation of the world.
18. *Bhavishya-purâṇa*, *i.e.* future things.

Of all this literature I have only seen portions of the Matsya, Âditya, and Vâyu Purâṇas.

Another somewhat different list of the Purâṇas has been read to me from the *Vishṇu-Purâṇa*. I give it here *in extenso*, as in all questions resting on tradition it is the duty of an author to give those traditions as completely as possible :—

1. *Brahma*.
2. *Padma*, *i.e.* the red lotus.
3. *Vishṇu*.
4. *S'iva*, *i.e.* Mahâdeva.
5. *Bhâgavata*, *i.e.* Vâsudeva.
6. *Nârada*, *i.e.* the son of Brahma.
7. *Mârkaṇḍeya*.
8. *Agni*, *i.e.* the fire.
9. *Bhavishya*, *i.e.* the future.
10. *Brahmavaivarta*, *i.e.* the wind.
11. *Liṅga*, *i.e.* an image of the *αἰδοῖα* of Mahâdeva.
12. *Varâha*.
13. *Skanda*.
14. *Vâmana*.
15. *Kûrma*.
16. *Matsya*, *i.e.* the fish.
17. *Garuḍa*, *i.e.* the bird on which Vishṇu rides.
18. *Brahmâṇḍa*.

These are the names of the Purâṇas according to the *Vishṇu-Purâṇa*.

The book *Smṛiti* is derived from the Veda. It contains commandments and prohibitions, and is composed by the following twenty sons of Brahman :— A list *Smṛiti* books.

1. Âpastamba.
2. Parâśara.
3. Śâtâtapa.
4. Saṁvarta.
5. Daksha.
6. Vasishṭha.
7. Aṅgiras.
8. Yama.
9. Vishṇu.
10. Manu.
11. Yâjnavalkya.
12. Atri.
13. Hârita.
14. Likhita.
15. Śaṅkha.
16. Gautama.
17. Vṛihaspati.
18. Kâtyâyana.
19. Vyâsa.
20. Uśanas.

Besides, the Hindus have books about the jurisprudence of their religion, on theosophy, on ascetics, on the process of becoming god and seeking liberation from the world, as, *e.g.* the book composed by Gauḍa the anchorite, which goes by his name; the book *Sáṁkhya*, composed by Kapila, on divine subjects; the book of *Patañjali*, on the search for liberation and for the union of the soul with the object of its meditation; the book *Nyâyabhâshâ*, composed by Kapila, on the Veda and its interpretation, also showing that it has been created, and distinguishing within the Veda between such injunctions as are obligatory only in certain cases, and those which are obligatory in general; further, the book *Mîmâṁsâ*, composed by Jaimini, on the same subject; the book *Laukâyata*, composed by Bṛihaspati, treating of the subject that in all investigations we must exclusively rely upon the apperception of

Page 64. the senses; the book *Agastyamata*, composed by Agastya, treating of the subject that in all investigations we must use the apperception of the senses as well as tradition; and the book *Vishṇu-dharma*. The word *dharma* means *reward*, but in general it is used for *religion*; so that this title means *The religion of God*, who in this case is understood to be Nârâyaṇa. Further, there are the books of the six pupils of Vyâsa, viz. *Devala*, *Śukra*, *Bhârgava*, *Vṛihaspati*, *Yâjnavalkya*, and *Manu*. The Hindus have numerous books about all the branches of science. How could anybody know the titles of all of them, more especially if he is not a Hindu, but a foreigner?

Mahâbhârata.

Besides, they have a book which they hold in such veneration that they firmly assert that everything which occurs in other books is found also in this book, but not all which occurs in this book is found in other books. It is called *Bhârata*, and composed by Vyâsa the son of Parâśara at the time of the great war between the children of Pâṇḍu and those of Kuru. The title itself gives an indication of those times. The book has 100,000 Ślokas in eighteen parts, each of which is called *Parvan*. Here we give the list of them:—

1. *Sabhâ-parva*, *i.e.* the king's dwelling.
2. *Aranya*, *i.e.* going out into the open field, meaning the exodus of the children of Pâṇḍu.
3. *Virâṭa*, *i.e.* the name of a king in whose realm they dwelt during the time of their concealment.
4. *Udyoga*, *i.e.* the preparing for battle.
5. *Bhîshma.*
6. *Droṇa* the Brahmin.
7. *Karṇa* the son of the Sun.
8. *S'alya* the brother of *Duryodhana*, some of the greatest heroes who did the fighting, one *always* coming forward after his predecessor had been killed.
9. *Gadâ*, *i.e.* the club.
10. *Sauptika*, *i.e.* the killing of the sleepers, when Aśvatthâman the son of Droṇa attacked the city of Pâñcâla during the night and killed the inhabitants.
11. *Jalapradânika*, *i.e.* the successive drawing of water for the dead, after people have washed off the impurity caused by the touching of the dead.
12. *Strî*, *i.e.* the lamentations of the women.
13. *S'ânti*, containing 24,000 Ślokas on eradicating hatred from the heart, in four parts:
    (1.) *Râjadharma*, on the reward of the kings.
    (2.) *Dânadharma*, on the reward for almsgiving.
    (3.) *Âpaddharma*, on the reward of those who are in need and trouble.
    (4.) *Mokshadharma*, on the reward of him who is liberated from the world.
14. *Aśvamedha*, *i.e.* the sacrifice of the horse which is sent out together with an army to wander through the world. Then they proclaim in public that it belongs to the king of the world, and that he who does not agree thereto is to come forward to fight. The Brahmans follow the horse, and celebrate sacrifices to the fire in those places where the horse drops its dung.
15. *Mausala*, *i.e.* the fighting of the Yâdavas, the tribe of Vâsudeva, among themselves.
16. *Âśramavâsa*, *i.e.* leaving one's own country.
17. *Prasthâna*, *i.e.* quitting the realm to seek liberation.
18. *Svargârohaṇa*, *i.e.* journeying towards Paradise.

These eighteen parts are followed by another one which is called *Harivaṁśa-Parvan*, which contains the traditions relating to Vâsudeva.

In this book there occur passages which, like riddles, admit of manifold interpretations. As to the reason of Page 65.

this the Hindus relate the following story:—Vyâsa asked Brahman to procure him somebody who might write for him the *Bhârata* from his dictation. Now he intrusted with this task his son Vinâyaka, who is represented as an idol with an elephant's head, and made it obligatory on him never to cease from writing. At the same time Vyâsa made it obligatory on him to write only that which he understood. Therefore Vyâsa, in the course of his dictation, dictated such sentences as compelled the writer to ponder over them, and thereby Vyâsa gained time for resting awhile.

CHAPTER XIII.

THEIR GRAMMATICAL AND METRICAL LITERATURE.

THE two sciences of grammar and metrics are auxiliary to the other sciences. Of the two, the former, grammar, holds the first place in their estimate, called *vyâkaraṇa*, *i.e.* the law of the correctness of their speech and etymological rules, by means of which they acquire an eloquent and classical style both in writing and reading. We Muslims cannot learn anything of it, since it is a branch coming from a root which is not within our grasp—I mean the language itself. That which I have been told as to titles of books on this science is the following:— List of books on grammar.

1. *Aindra*, attributed to Indra, the head of the angels.
2. *Cândra*, composed by Candra, one of the red-robe-wearing sect, the followers of Buddha.
3. *S'âkaṭa*, so called by the name of its author. His tribe, too, is called by a name derived from the same word, viz. *S'âkaṭâyana*.
4. *Pâṇini*, so called from its author.
5. *Kâtantra*, composed by Śarvavarman.
6. *S'aśidevavṛitti*, composed by Śaśideva.
7. *Durgavivṛitti*.
8. *S'ishyahitâvṛitti*, composed by Ugrabhûti.

I have been told that the last-mentioned author was the teacher and instructor of Shâh Ânandapâla, the son of Jayapâla, who ruled in our time. After having composed the book he sent it to Kashmîr, but the people there did not adopt it, being in such things haughtily conservative. Now he complained of this to the Shâh, and Shâh Ânandapâla and his master Ugrabhûti.

the Shâh, in accordance with the duty of a pupil towards his master, promised him to make him attain his wish. So he gave orders to send 200,000 *dirham* and presents of a similar value to Kashmîr, to be distributed among those who studied the book of his master. The consequence was that they all rushed upon the book, and would not copy any other grammar but this one, showing themselves in the baseness of their avarice. The book became the fashion and highly prized.

Tale relating to the origin of grammar.

Of the origin of grammar they give the following account:—One of their kings, called Samalvâhana, *i.e.* in the classical language, Sâtavâhana, was one day in a pond playing with his wives, when he said to one of them "*Mâudakaṁ dehi*," i.e. *do not sprinkle the water on me*. The woman, however, understood it as if he had said *modakaṁ dehi*, i.e. *bring sweetmeats*. So she went away and brought him sweetmeats. And when the king disapproved of her doing so, she gave him an angry reply, and used coarse language towards him. Now he was deeply offended, and, in consequence, as is their custom, he abstained from all food, and concealed himself in some corner until he was called upon by a sage, who consoled him, promising him that he would teach people grammar and the inflexions of the language. Thereupon the sage went off to Mahâdeva, praying, praising, and fasting devoutly. Mahâdeva appeared to him, and communicated to him some few rules, the like of which Abul'aswad Addu'alî has given for the Arabic language. The god also promised to assist him in the further development of this science. Then the sage returned to the king and taught it to him. This was the beginning of the science of grammar.

The predilection of the Hindus for metrical compositions.

Grammar is followed by another science, called *chandas*, *i.e.* the metrical form of poetry, corresponding to our metrics—a science indispensable to them, since all their books are in verse. By composing their books in metres they intend to facilitate their being learned

Page 66.

by heart, and to prevent people in all questions of science ever recurring to a *written* text, save in a case of bare necessity. For they think that the mind of man sympathises with everything in which there is symmetry and order, and has an aversion to everything in which there is no order. Therefore most Hindus are passionately fond of their verses, and always desirous of reciting them, even if they do not understand the meaning of the words, and the audience will snap their fingers in token of joy and applause. They do not want prose compositions, although it is much easier to understand them.

Most of their books are composed in *Śloka*, in which I am now exercising myself, being occupied in composing for the Hindus a translation of the books of Euclid and of the Almagest, and dictating to them a treatise on the construction of the astrolabe, being simply guided herein by the desire of spreading science. If the Hindus happen to get some book which does not yet exist among them, they set at work to change it into *Ślokas*, which are rather unintelligible, since the metrical form entails a constrained, affected style, which will become apparent when we shall speak of their method of expressing numbers. And if the verses are not sufficiently affected, their authors meet with frowning faces, as having committed something like mere prose, and then they will feel extremely unhappy. God will do me justice in what I say of them.

The first who invented this art were Piṅgala and چلت (*? C L T*). The books on the subject are numerous. The most famous of them is the book *Gaisita* (? G—AI—S—T), so called from its author, famous to such a degree that even the whole science of metrics has been called by this name. Other books are that of Mṛigalâñchana, that of Piṅgala, and that of اولياند (? Û (Au)—L—Y—Â—N—D). I, however, have not seen any of these books, nor do I know much of the chapter

Books on metrics.

of the *Brahma-siddhânta* which treats of metrical calculations, and therefore I have no claim to a thorough knowledge of the laws of their metrics. Nevertheless, I do not think it right to pass by a subject of which I have only a smattering, and I shall not postpone speaking of it until I shall have thoroughly mastered it.

On the meaning of the technical terms *laghu* and *guru*.

In counting the syllables (*gaṇachandas*) they use similar figures to those used by Alkhalîl Ibn Aḥmad and our metricians to denote the *consonant without vowel* and the *consonant with vowel*, viz. these two signs, | and >, the former of which is called *laghu*, *i.e.* light; the latter, *guru*, *i.e.* heavy. In measuring (*mâtrâchandas*), the *guru* is reckoned double of a *laghu*, and its place may be filled by two *laghu*.

Further, they have a syllable which they call long (*dîrgha*), the measure or prosody of which is equal to that of a *guru*. This, I think, is a syllable with a long vowel (like *kâ, kî, kû*). Here, however, I must confess that up to the present moment I have not been able to gain a clear idea of the nature of both *laghu* and *guru*, so as to be able to illustrate them by similar elements in Arabic. However, I am inclined to think that *laghu* does *not* mean a *consonant without vowel*, nor *guru* a *consonant with vowel*, but that, on the contrary, *laghu* means a consonant with a short vowel (e.g. *ka, ki, ku*), and *guru* means the same with a vowelless consonant (e.g. *kat, kit, kut*), like an element in Arabic metrics called *Sabab* (*i.e.* — or ⏑⏑, a long syllable the place of which may be taken by two short ones). That which makes me doubt as to the first-mentioned definition of *laghu* is this circumstance, that the Hindus use *many laghu* one after the other in an uninterrupted succession. The Arabs are not capable of pronouncing two vowelless consonants one after the other, but in other languages this is possible. The Persian metricians, for instance, call such a consonant *moved by a light vowel* (*i.e.* pronounced with a sound like the Hebrew Schwa). But, in any case, if such consonants are more than three in number, they are most difficult, nay, even impossible to pronounce; whilst, on the other hand, there is not the slightest difficulty in pronouncing an uninterrupted series of short syllables consisting of a consonant with a short vowel, as when you say in Arabic, "*Badanuka kamathali ṣifatika wafamuka bisa'ati shafatika*" (*i.e.* Thy body is like thy description, and thy mouth depends upon the width of thy lip). Further, although it is difficult to pronounce Page 67. a vowelless consonant at the beginning of a word, most nouns of the Hindus begin, if not exactly with vowelless consonants, still with such consonants as have only a Schwa-like vowel-sound to follow them. If such a consonant stands at the beginning of a verse, they drop it in counting, since the law of the *guru* demands that in it the vowelless consonant shall not *precede* but *follow* the vowel (*ka-t, ki-t, ku-t*).

Further, as our people have composed out of the *feet* (افاعيل) certain schemes or types, according to which verses are constructed, and have invented signs to denote the component parts of a foot, *i.e.* the consonant *with* and *without* a vowel, in like manner also the Hindus use certain names to denote the feet which are composed of *laghu* and *guru*, either the former preceding and the latter following or *vice versâ*, in such a way, however, that the *measure* must always be the same, whilst the *number* of syllables may vary. By these names they denote a certain conventional prosodic unity (*i.e.* certain *feet*). By *measure*, I mean that *laghu* is reckoned = one *mâtrâ*, *i.e.* measure, and *guru* = two *mâtrâ*. If they represent a foot in writing, they only express the *measure* of the syllables, not their number, as, *e.g.* (in Arabic) a double consonant (*kka*) is counted as a consonant *without* vowel *plus* a consonant *with* vowel, and a consonant followed by Tanwîn (*kun*) is counted as a consonant with a vowel *plus* a consonant

Definition of *mâtrâ*.

without vowel, whilst in writing both are represented as one and the same thing (*i.e.* by the sign of the consonant in question).

Names of laghu and guru.

Taken alone by themselves, *laghu* and *guru* are called by various names: the former, *la*, *kali*, *rûpa*, *câmara*, and *graha*; the latter, *ga*, *nîvra*, and a *half aṁśaka*. The latter name shows that a complete *aṁśaka* is equal to two *guru* or their equivalent. These names they have invented simply to facilitate the versification of their metrical books. For this purpose they have invented so many names, that one may fit into the metre if others will not.

The single feet.

The feet arising out of combinations of *laghu* and *guru* are the following:—

Twofold both in number and measure is the foot | |, *i.e.* two syllables and two *mâtrâ*.

Twofold in number, not in measure, are the feet, | < and < |; in measure they are = three *mâtrâ* | | | (but, in number, only two syllables).

The second foot < | (a trochee) is called *kṛittikâ*.

The quaternary feet are in each book called by different names:

< < *paksha*, *i.e.* the half month.
| | < *jvalana*, *i.e.* the fire.
| < | *madhya* (? *madhu*).
< | | *parvata*, *i.e.* the mountain, also called *hâra* and *rasa*.
| | | | *ghana*, *i.e.* the cube.

The feet consisting of five *mâtrâ* have manifold forms; those of them which have special names are the following:—

| < < *hastin*, *i.e.* the elephant.	< < | (? lacuna).
< | < *kâma*, *i.e.* the wish.	| | | < *kusuma*.

A foot consisting of six *mâtrâ* is < < <.

Some people call these feet by the names of the chess figures, viz.:

jvalana = the elephant.	*parvata* = the pawn.
madhya = the tower.	*ghana* = the horse.

In a lexicographical work to which the author هرود (? Haribhaṭṭa) has given his own name, the feet composed of three *laghu* or *guru* are called by single consonants, which in the following diagram are written on their left :— On the arrangement of the feet. Quotation from Haribhaṭṭa.

Diagram.

m	< < <	sixfold (*i.e.* containing six *mátrá*).
y	| < <	*hastin.*
r	< | <	*káma.*
t	< < |	(? lacuna).
s	| | <	*jvalana.*
j	| < |	*madhya.*
bh	< | |	*parvata.*
n	| | |	threefold (*i.e.* containing three *mátrá*).

By means of these signs the author teaches how to construct these eight feet by an inductive method (a kind of algebraic permutation), saying:

"Place one of the two kinds (*guru* and *laghu*) in the first line unmixed (that would be <<<, if we begin with a *guru*). Then mix it with the second kind, and place one of this at the beginning of the second line, whilst the two other elements are of the first kind (|<<). Then place this element of admixture in the middle of the third line (<|<), and lastly at the end of the fourth line (<<|). Then you have finished the first half. Page 68.

"Further, place the second kind in the lowest line, unmixed (| | |), and mix up with the line above it one of the first kind, placing it at the beginning of the line (< | |), then in the middle of the next following line (| < |), and lastly at the end of the next following line (| | <). Then the second half is finished, and all the possible combinations of three *mátra* have been exhausted."

1. < < <	First half.	5. | | <	Second half.
2. | < <		6. | < |	
3. < | <		7. < | |	
4. < < |		8. | | |	

This system of composition or permutation is correct,

but his calculation showing how to find that place which every single foot occupies in this series of permutations is not in accordance with it. For he says:

"Place the numeral 2 to denote each element of a foot (*i.e.* both *guru* and *laghu*), once for all, so that every foot is represented by 2, 2, 2. Multiply the left (number) by the middle, and the product by the right one. If this *multiplier* (*i.e.* this number of the right side) is a *laghu*, then leave the product as it is; but if it is a *guru*, subtract *one* from the product."

The author exemplifies this with the sixth foot, *i.e.* | < |. He multiplies 2 by 2, and from the product (4) he subtracts 1. The remaining 3 he multiplies by the third 2, and he gets the product of 6.

This, however, is not correct for most of the feet, and I am rather inclined to believe that the text of the manuscript is corrupt.

The proper order of the feet would accordingly be the following:

<table>
<tr><th></th><th>I.</th><th>II.</th><th>III.</th><th></th><th>I.</th><th>II.</th><th>III.</th></tr>
<tr><td>1.</td><td><</td><td><</td><td><</td><td>5.</td><td><</td><td><</td><td>|</td></tr>
<tr><td>2.</td><td>|</td><td><</td><td><</td><td>6.</td><td>|</td><td><</td><td>|</td></tr>
<tr><td>3.</td><td><</td><td>|</td><td><</td><td>7.</td><td><</td><td>|</td><td>|</td></tr>
<tr><td>4.</td><td>|</td><td>|</td><td><</td><td>8.</td><td>|</td><td>|</td><td>|</td></tr>
</table>

The *mixture* of the first line (No. I.) is such that one kind always follows the other. In the *second* line (No. II.) two of one kind are followed by two of the other; and in the third line (No. III.) four of one kind are followed by four of the other.

Then the author of the above-mentioned calculation goes on to say: "If the first element of the foot is a *guru*, subtract *one* before you multiply. If the multiplier is a *guru*, subtract one from the product. Thus you find the place which a foot occupies in this order."

On the *pádas.* As the Arabic verse is divided into two halves or hemistichs by the *ʿarûḍ*, *i.e.* the last foot of the first hemistich, and the *ḍarb*, *i.e.* the last foot of the second hemistich, in like manner the verses of the Hindus are divided into two halves, each of which is called *foot* (*pâda*). The Greeks, too, call them *feet* (*lacuna*),—those words which are composed of it, συλλάβη, and the consonants *with* or *without* vowels, with long, short, or doubtful vowels.

On the metre Aryâ.

The verse is divided into three, or more commonly into four *pâda*. Sometimes they add a fifth *pâda* in the middle of the verse. The *pâdas* have no rhyme, but there is a kind of metre, in which the 1 and 2 *pâdas* end with the same consonant or syllable as if rhyming on it, and also the *pâdas* 3 and 4 end with the same consonant or syllable. This kind is called *Âryâ*. At the end of the *pâda* a *laghu* may become a *guru*, though in general this metre ends with a *laghu*. Page 69.

The different poetical works of the Hindus contain a great number of metres. In the metre of 5 *pâda*, the fifth *pâda* is placed between *pâdas* 3 and 4. The names of the metres differ according to the number of syllables, and also according to the verses which follow. For they do not like all the verses of a long poem to belong to one and the same metre. They use many metres in the same poem, in order that it should appear like an embroidered piece of silk.

The construction of the four *pâdas* in the four-*pâda* metre is the following:—

PÂDA I.	< <	paksha = 1 aṁśaka.	< <	paksha.	PÂDA III.
	< | |	parvata.	< | |	parvata.	
	| | <	jvalana.	< <	paksha.	
PÂDA II.	< <	paksha.	< <	paksha.	PÂDA IV.
	| | <	jvalana.	| | <	jvalana.	
	| < |	madhya.	| < |	madhya.	
	< | |	parvata.	< | |	parvata.	
	< <	paksha.	| | <	jvalana.	

This is a representation of a species of their metres, called *Skandha*, containing four *pâda*. It consists of two halves; and each half has eight *aṁśaka*.

Of the single *aṁśaka*, the 1st, 3d, and 5th can never be a *madhya*, *i.e.* < |, and the 6th must always be either a *madhya* or a *ghana*. If this condition is adhered to, the other *aṁśakas* may be anything at all, just as accident or the fancy of the poet wills it. However, the metre must always be complete, neither more nor less. Therefore, observing the rules as to the formation of certain *aṁśakas* in the single *pâdas*, we may represent the four *pâdas* in the following manner:—

Pâda I. < <   < | | | | <.
Pâda II. < < | | < | < | < | | < <.
Pâda III. < <   < | < <.
Page 70. Pâda IV. < < | < < | < | < | | | | <.

According to this pattern the verse is composed.

Arab and Hindu notation of a metre.

If you represent an Arabic metre by these signs of the Hindus, you will find that they mean something entirely different from what the Arabic signs mean which denote a consonant *with* a short vowel and a consonant *without* a vowel. (The Arabic sign | means a consonant without a vowel; the Hindu sign | means a short syllable; the Arabic sign o means a consonant followed by a short vowel; the Hindu sign < means a long syllable.) As an example, we give a representation of the regular complete *Khafîf* metre, representing each foot by derivations of the root فعل.

Metrum Khafîf.

(1.) فَاعِلَاتُنْ   مُسْتَفْعِلُنْ   فَاعِلَاتُنْ,

represented by derivations of the root فعل.

(2.) |o|oo|o |oo|o|o |o|oo|o,

represented by Arabic signs.

(3.) < < | <   < | < <   < < | <,

represented by the signs of the Hindus.

We give the latter signs in an inverted order, since the Hindus read from the left to the right.

I have already once pleaded as my excuse, and do so here a second time, that my slender knowledge of this science does not enable me to give the reader a complete insight into the subject. Still I take the greatest pains with it, though I am well aware that it is only very little I can give.

On the metre *Vṛitta.*

The name *Vṛitta* applies to each four-*pâda* metre in which the signs of both the prosody and the number of the syllables are like each other, according to a certain correspondence of the *pâdas* among themselves, so that if you know one *pâda*, you know also the other ones, for they are like it. Further, there is a law that a *pâda* cannot have less than four syllables, since a *pâda* with less does not occur in the Veda. For the same reason the smallest number of the syllables of a *pâda* is four, the largest twenty-six. In consequence, there are twenty-three varieties of the *Vṛitta* metre, which we shall here enumerate:—

1. The *pâda* has four *heavy* syllables (*guru*), and here you *cannot* put two *laghu* in the place of one *guru*.
2. The nature of the second kind of the *pâda* is not clear to me, so I omit it.
3. This *pâda* is built of
   ghana + *paksha.*
   | | | | < <
4. = 2 *guru* + 2 *laghu* + 3 *guru.*
   < < | | < < <
   It would be better to describe this *pâda* as = *paksha* + *jvalana* + *paksha.*
5. = 2 *krittikâ* + *jvalana* + *paksha.*
   < | < | | | <   < <
6. = *ghana* + *madhya* + *paksha.* Page 71.
   | | | | | < | < <
7. = *ghana* + *parvata* + *jvalana.*
   | | | | < | | | | <

8. = *kâma*, *kusuma*, *jvalana*, *guru*.
<|< |||< ||< <

9. = *paksha*, *hastin*, *jvalana*, *madhya*, 2 *guru*.
<< |<< ||< |<| <<

10. = *paksha*, *parvata*, *jvalana*, *madhya*, *paksha*.
<< <|| ||< |<| <<

11. = *paksha*, *madhya*, 2 *jvalana*, *hastin*.
<< |<| ||< ||< |<<

12. = *ghana*, *jvalana*, *paksha*, 2 *hastin*.
|||| ||< << |<<|<<

13. = *parvata*, *kâma*, *kusuma*, *madhya*, *jvalana*.
<|| <|< |||< |<| ||<

14. = *hastin*, *paksha*, *parvata*, *kusuma*, *parvata*, *laghu*, *guru*.
|<< << <|| |||< <|| | <

15. = 2 *paksha*, *parvata*, *kusuma*, 2 *kâma*, *guru*.
<<<< <|| |||< <|< <|< <

16. = *paksha*, *parvata*, *kâma*, *kusuma*, *paksha*, *laghu*, *guru*.
<< <|| <|< |||< << | <

17. = 2 *paksha*, *parvata*, *ghana*, *jvalana*, *paksha*, *kusuma*.
<< << <|| |||| ||< << |||<

18. = 2 *paksha*, *parvata*, *ghana*, *jvalana*, 2 *kâma*, *guru*.
<< << <|| |||| ||< <|< <|< <

19. = *guru*, 2 *paksha*, *parvata*, *ghana*, *jvalana*, 2 *kâma*, *guru*.
< << << <|| |||| ||< <|< <|< <

20. = 4 *paksha*, *jvalana*, *madhya*, *paksha*, 2 *madhya*, *guru*.
<<<<<<<< ||< |<| << |<||<| <

21. = 4 *paksha*, 3 *jvalana*, 2 *madhya*, *guru*.
<<<<<<<< ||< ||V.||< |<||<| <

22. = 4 *paksha*, *kusuma*, *madhya*, *jvalana*, 2 *madhya*, *guru*.
<<<<<<<< |||< |<| ||< |<||<| <

23. = 8 *guru*, 10 *laghu*, *kâma*, *jvalana*, *laghu*, *guru*.
<<<<<<<< |||||||||| <|< ||< | <

We have given such a lengthy account, though it be only of scanty use, in order that the reader may see for himself the example of an accumulation of *laghus*, which shows that *laghu* means *a consonant followed by a short vowel*, not a consonant without a vowel. Further, he will thereby learn the way in which they represent a metre and the method of their scanning a verse. Lastly, he will learn that Alkhalîl Ibn Aḥmad exclusively drew from his own genius when he invented the Arabic metrics, though, possibly, he may have heard, as some people think, that the Hindus use certain metres in their poetry. If we here take so much trouble with Indian metrics, we do it for the purpose of fixing the laws of the Śloka, since most of their books are composed in it.

Theory of the Śloka.

The *Śloka* belongs to the four-*páda* metres. Each *páda* has eight syllables, which are different in all four *pádas*. The last syllable of each of the four *pádas* must be the same, viz. a *guru*. Further, the fifth syllable in each *páda* must always be *laghu*, the sixth syllable *guru*. The seventh syllable must be *laghu* in the second and fourth *páda*, *guru* in the first and third *pádas*. The other syllables are entirely dependent upon accident or the writer's fancy.

Quotation from Brahmagupta.

In order to show in what way the Hindus use arithmetic in their metrical system, we give in the following a quotation from Brahmagupta: "The first kind of poetry is *gáyatrî*, a metre consisting of two *pádas*. If we now suppose that the number of the syllables of this metre may be 24, and that the smallest number of the syllables of one *páda* is 4, we describe the two *pádas* by 4 + 4, representing their smallest possible number of syllables. As, however, their largest possible number is 24, we add the difference between these 4 + 4 and 24, *i.e.* 16, to the right-side number, and get 4 + 20. If the metre had three *pádas*, it would be represented by 4 + 4 + 16. The right-side *páda* is always distinguished from the others and called by a separate name; but the preceding *pádas* also are connected, so as to form one whole, and likewise called by a separate name. If the metre had four *pádas*, it would be represented by 4 + 4 + 4 + 12.

"If, however, the poet does not use the *pádas* of 4, *i.e.* the smallest possible number of syllables, and if we Page 72. want to know the number of combinations of the 24 syllables which may occur in a two-*páda* metre, we write 4 to the left and 20 to the right; we add 1 to 4, again 1 to the sum, &c.; we subtract 1 from 20, again 1 from the remainder, &c.; and this we continue until we get both the same numbers with which we commenced, the small number in the line which commenced with the greater number, and the greater number in the line which commenced with the small number. See the following scheme:—

4	20
5	19
6	18
7	17
8	16
9	15
10	14
11	13
12	12
13	11
14	10
15	9
16	8
17	7
18	6
19	5
20	4

The number of these combinations is 17, *i.e.* the difference between 4 and 20 *plus* 1.

"As regards the three-*páda* metre with the presupposed number of syllables, *i.e.* 24, its first species is that in which all three *pâdas* have the smallest possible number of syllables, *i.e.* 4 + 4 + 16.

"The right-side number and the middle number we write down as we have done with the *pâdas* of the two-*pâda* metre, and we make with them the same calculation as we have done above. Besides, we add the left-side number in a separate column, but do not make it undergo any changes. See the following scheme:—

4	4	16
4	5	15
4	6	14
4	7	13
4	8	12
4	9	11
4	10	10
4	11	9
4	12	8
4	13	7
4	14	6
4	15	5
4	16	4

"This gives the number of 13 permutations, but by changing the places of the numbers forwards and backwards in the following method, the number may be increased sixfold, *i.e.* to 78:—

"I. The right-side number keeps its place; the two other numbers exchange their places, so that the middle number stands at the left side; the left-side number occupies the middle:—

I.

4	4	16
5	4	15
6	4	14
7	4	13 &c.

"II.–III. The right-side number is placed in the middle between the other two numbers, which first keep their original places, and then exchange them with each other:—

II.

4	16	4
4	15	5
4	14	6
4	13	7 &c.

III.

4	16	4
5	15	4
6	14	4
7	13	4 &c.

"IV.–V. The right-side number is placed to the left, and the other two numbers first keep their original places, and then exchange them with each other:—

IV.

16	4	4
15	4	5
14	4	6
13	4	7 &c.

V.

16	4	4
15	5	4
14	6	4
13	7	4 &c.

"Because, further, the numbers of the syllables of a *pâda* rise like the square of 2, for after 4 follows 8, we may represent the syllables of the three *pâdas* in this way: 8+8+8 (=4+4+16). However, their arithmetical peculiarities follow another rule. The four-*pâda* metre follows the analogy of the three-*pâda* metre."

Of the above-mentioned treatise of Brahmagupta I have only seen a single leaf: it contains, no doubt, important elements of arithmetic. God affords help and sustains by his mercy, *i.e.* I hope one day to learn those things. As far as I can guess with regard to the literature of the Greeks, they used in their poetry similar *feet* to the Hindus; for Galenus says in his book *κατὰ γένη*: "The medicine prepared with saliva discovered by Menecrates has been described by Damocrates in a poem composed in a metre consisting of three parts." Page 73.

CHAPTER XIV.

HINDU LITERATURE IN THE OTHER SCIENCES, ASTRONOMY, ASTROLOGY, ETC.

Times unfavourable to the progress of science.

THE number of sciences is great, and it may be still greater if the public mind is directed towards them at such times as they are in the ascendancy and in general favour with all, when people not only honour science itself, but also its representatives. To do this is, in the first instance, the duty of those who rule over them, of kings and princes. For they alone could free the minds of scholars from the daily anxieties for the necessities of life, and stimulate their energies to earn more fame and favour, the yearning for which is the pith and marrow of human nature.

The present times, however, are not of this kind. They are the very opposite, and therefore it is quite impossible that a new science or any new kind of research should arise in our days. What we have of sciences is nothing but the scanty remains of bygone better times.

If a science or an idea has once conquered the whole earth, every nation appropriates part of it. So do also the Hindus. Their belief about the cyclical revolutions of times is nothing very special, but is simply in accordance with the results of scientific observation.

On the Siddhântas.

The science of astronomy is the most famous among them, since the affairs of their religion are in various ways connected with it. If a man wants to gain the title of an astronomer, he must not only know scientific or mathematical astronomy, but also astrology. The book known among Muslims as *Sindhind* is called by them *Siddhânta*, i.e. *straight*, not crooked nor changing. By this name they call every standard book on astronomy, even such books as, according to our opinion, do not come up to the mark of our so-called *Zîj*, *i.e.* handbooks of mathematical astronomy. They have five Siddhântas :—

I. *Sûrya-siddhânta*, *i.e.* the Siddhânta of the sun, composed by Lâṭa.

II. *Vasishṭha-siddhânta*, so called from one of the stars of the Great Bear, composed by Vishṇucandra.

III. *Pulisa-siddhânta*, so called from Paulisa, the Greek, from the city of Saintra, which I suppose to be Alexandria, composed by Pulisa.

IV. *Romaka-siddhânta*, so called from the Rûm, *i.e.* the subjects of the Roman Empire, composed by Śrîsheṇa.

V. *Brahma-siddhânta*, so called from Brahman, composed by Brahmagupta, the son of Jishṇu, from the town of Bhillamâla between Multân and Anhilwâra, 16 *yojana* from the latter place (?).

The authors of these books draw from one and the same source, the Book *Paithâmaha*, so called from *the first father*, *i.e.* Brahman.

Varâhamihira has composed an astronomical handbook of small compass called *Pañca-siddhântikâ*, which name ought to mean that it contains the pith and marrow of the preceding five Siddhântas. But this is not the case, nor is it so much better than they as to be called the most correct one of the five. So the name does not indicate anything but the fact that the number of Siddhântas is five.

Brahmagupta says: "Many of the Siddhântas are Sûrya, others Indu, Pulisa, Romaka, Vasishṭha, and Yavana, *i.e.* the Greeks; and though the Siddhântas are many, they differ only in words, not in the subject-matter. He who studies them properly will find that they agree with each other."

Up to the present time I have not been able to procure any of these books save those of Pulisa and of Brahmagupta. I have commenced translating them, but have not yet finished my work. Meanwhile I shall give here a table of contents of the *Brahma-siddhânta*, which in any case will be useful and instructive.

Page 74.

Contents of the *Brahma-siddhânta*.

Contents of the twenty-four chapters of the *Brahma-siddhânta*—

1. On the nature of the globe and the figure of heaven and earth.

2. On the revolutions of the planets; on the calculation of time, *i.e.* how to find the time for different longitudes and latitudes; how to find the mean places of the planets; how to find the sine of an arc.

3. On the correction of the places of the planets.

4. On three problems: how to find the shadow, the bygone portion of the day and the *ascendens,* and how to derive one from the other.

5. On the planets becoming visible when they leave the rays of the sun, and their becoming invisible when entering them.

6. On the first appearance of the moon, and about her two cusps.

7. On the lunar eclipse.

8. On the solar eclipse.

9. On the shadow of the moon.

10. On the meeting and conjunction of the planets.

11. On the latitudes of the planets.

12. A critical investigation for the purpose of distinguishing between correct and corrupt passages in the texts of astronomical treatises and handbooks.

13. On arithmetic; on plane measure and cognate subjects.

14. Scientific calculation of the mean places of the planets.

15. Scientific calculation of the correction of the places of the planets.

16. Scientific calculation of the three problems (v. chap. 4).

17. On the deflection of eclipses.

18. Scientific calculation of the appearance of the new moon and her two cusps.

19. On *Kuṭṭaka, i.e.* the pounding of a thing. The pounding of oil-producing substances is here compared with *the most minute and detailed research.* This chapter treats of algebra and related subjects, and besides it contains other valuable remarks of a more or less arithmetical nature.

20. On the shadow.

21. On the calculation of the measures of poetry and on metrics.

22. On cycles and instruments of observation.

23. On time and the four measures of time, the *solar*, the *civil*, the *lunar*, and the *sidereal.*

24. About numeral notation in the metrical books of this kind.

These, now, are twenty-four chapters, according to his own statement, but there is a twenty-fifth one, called *Dhyâna-graha-adhyâya,* in which he tries to solve the problems by speculation, not by mathematical calculation. I have not enumerated it in this list, because the pretensions which he brings forward in this chapter are repudiated by mathematics. I am rather inclined to think that that which he produces is meant to be the *ratio metaphysica* of all astronomical methods, otherwise how could any problem of this science be solved by anything save by mathematics?

Such books as do not reach the standard of a Siddhânta are mostly called *Tantra* or *Karaṇa.* The former means *ruling under a governor*, the latter means *following, i.e.* following behind the Siddhânta. Under *governors* they understand the *Âcâryas, i.e.* the sages, anchorites, the followers of Brahman. On the literature of Tantras and Karaṇas.

There are two famous *Tantras* by *Âryabhaṭa* and *Balabhadra*, besides the *Rasâyana-tantra* by *Bhânu-yaśas* (?). About what Rasâyana means we shall give a separate chapter (chap. xvii.).

As for *Karaṇas*, there is one (*lacuna*) called by his name, besides the *Karaṇa-khaṇḍa-khâdyaka* by Brahmagupta. The last word, *khaṇḍa*, means a kind of their sweetmeats. With regard to the reason why he gave his book this title, I have been told the following:—

Sugrîva, the Buddhist, had composed an astronomical handbook which he called *Dadhi-sâgara, i.e.* the sea of sour-milk; and a pupil of his composed a book of the same kind which he called *Kûra-babayâ* (?), *i.e.* a mountain of rice. Afterwards he composed another book which he called *Lavaṇa-mushṭi, i.e.* a handful of salt. Therefore Brahmagupta called his book the *Sweetmeat—khâdyaka*—in order that all kinds of victuals (sour-milk, rice, salt, &c.) should occur in the titles of the books on this science.

The contents of the book *Karaṇa-khaṇḍa-khâdyaka*
Page 75. represent the doctrine of Âryabhaṭa. Therefore Brahmagupta afterwards composed a second book, which he called *Uttara-khaṇḍa-khâdyaka, i.e.* the explanation of the *Khaṇḍa-khâdyaka.* And this book is again followed by another one called *Khaṇḍa-khâdyaka-tippâ* (*sic*), of which I do not know whether it is composed by Brahmagupta or somebody else. It explains the reasons and the nature of the calculations employed in the *Khaṇḍa-khâdyaka.* I suppose it is a work of Balabhadra's.

Further, there is an astronomical handbook composed by Vijayanandin, the commentator, in the city of Benares, entitled *Karaṇa-tilaka, i.e.* the blaze on the front of the Karaṇas; another one by Vitteśvara the son of Bhadatta (? Mihdatta), of the city of Nâgarapura, called *Karaṇa-sâra, i.e.* that which has been derived from the Karaṇa; another one, by Bhânuyaśas (?), is called *Karaṇa-para-tilaka*, which shows, as I am told, how the corrected places of the stars are derived from one another.

There is a book by Utpala the Kashmirian called *Râhunrâkaraṇa* (?), *i.e.* breaking the Karaṇas; and another called *Karaṇa-pâta*, *i.e.* killing the Karaṇas. Besides there is a book called *Karaṇa-cûḍâmaṇi* of which I do not know the author.

There are more books of the same kind with other titles, *e.g.* the great *Mânasa*, composed by Manu, and the commentary by Utpala; the small *Mânasa*, an epitome of the former by Puñcala (?), from the southern country; *Daśagîtikâ*, by Âryabhaṭa; *Âryâshṭaśata*, by the same; *Lokânanda*, so called from the name of the author; *Bhaṭṭilâ* (?), so called from its author, the Brahman Bhaṭṭila. The books of this kind are nearly innumerable.

As for astrological literature, each one of the following authors has composed a so-called *Saṃhitâ*, viz.:— On astrological literature, the so-called Saṁhitâs.

Mâṇḍavya.
Parâśara.
Garga.
Brahman.
Balabhadra.
Divyatattva.
Varâhamihira.

Saṃhitâ means *that which is collected*, books containing something of everything, *e.g.* forewarnings relating to a journey derived from meteorological occurrences; prophecies regarding the fate of dynasties; the knowledge of lucky and unlucky things; prophesying from the lines of the hand; interpretation of dreams, and taking auguries from the flight or cries of birds. For Hindu scholars believe in such things. It is the custom of their astronomers to propound in their Saṁhitâs also the whole science of meteorology and cosmology.

Each one of the following authors has composed a book, *Jâtaka*, *i.e.* book of nativities, viz.:— The Jâtakas, *i.e.* books on nativities

Parâśara.
Satya.
Maṇittha.
Jîvaśarman.
Mau, the Greek.

Varâhamihira has composed two Jâtakas, a small and a large one. The latter of these has been explained by Balabhadra, and the former I have translated into Arabic. Further, the Hindus have a large book on the science of the astrology of nativities called *Sârâvalî*, *i.e.* the chosen one, similar to the *Vazîdaj* (= Persian *guzîda* ?), composed by Kalyâṇa-Varman, who gained high credit for his scientific works. But there is another book still larger than this, which comprehends the whole of astrological sciences, called *Yavana*, *i.e.* belonging to the Greeks.

Of Varâhamihira there are several small books, *e.g.* *Shaṭ-pañcâśikâ*, fifty-six chapters on astrology; *Horâ-pañca-hotriya* (?), on the same subject.

Travelling is treated of in the book *Yogayâtrâ* and the book *Tikanî*(?)-*yâtrâ*, marriage and marrying in the book *Virâha-paṭala*, architecture in the book (*lacuna*).

The art of taking auguries from the flight or cries of birds, and of the foretelling by means of piercing a needle into a book, is propounded in the work called *Srudhava* (? śrotavya), which exists in three different copies. Mahâdeva is said to be the author of the first, Vimalabuddhi the author of the second, and Baṅgâla the author of the third. Similar subjects are treated in the book *Gûḍhâmana* (?), *i.e.* the knowledge of the unknown, composed by Buddha, the originator of the sect of the red robe-wearers, the Shamanians; and in the book *Praśna Gûḍhâmana* (?), *i.e.* questions of the science of the unknown, composed by Utpala.

Besides, there are Hindu scholars of whom we know
Page 76. the names, but not the title of any book of theirs, viz. :—

Pradyumna.	Sârasvata.
Saṅgahila (Śṛiṅkhala ?).	Pîruvâna (?).
Divâkara.	Devakîrtti.
Parêśvara.	Prithûdaka-svâmin.

Medical literature.

Medicine belongs to the same class of sciences as astronomy, but there is this difference, that the latter stands in close relation to the religion of the Hindus. They have a book called by the name of its author, *i.e. Caraka*, which they consider as the best of their whole literature on medicine. According to their belief, Caraka was a Ṛishi in the last Dvâpara-yuga, when his name was *Agniveśa*, but afterwards he was called *Caraka*, *i.e.* the intelligent one, after the first elements of medicine had been laid down by certain Ṛishis, the children of *Sûtra*. These latter had received them from Indra, Indra from Aśvin, one of the two physicians of the Devas, and Aśvin had received them from Prajâpati, *i.e.* Brahman, *the first father*. This book has been translated into Arabic for the princes of the house of the Barmecides.

On Pañcatantra.

The Hindus cultivate numerous other branches of science and literature, and have a nearly boundless literature. I, however, could not comprehend it with my knowledge. I wish I could translate the book *Pañcatantra*, known among us as the book of Kalila and Dimna. It is far spread in various languages, in Persian, Hindî, and Arabic—in translations of people who are not free from the suspicion of having altered the text. For instance, 'Abdallâh Ibn Almuḳaffa' has added in his Arabic version the chapter about Barzôya, with the intention of raising doubts in the minds of people of feeble religious belief, and to gain and prepare them for the propagation of the doctrines of the Manichæans. And if he is open to suspicion in so far as he has added something to the text which he had simply to translate, he is hardly free from suspicion in his capacity as translator.

CHAPTER XV.

NOTES ON HINDU METROLOGY, INTENDED TO FACILITATE THE UNDERSTANDING OF ALL KINDS OF MEASUREMENTS WHICH OCCUR IN THIS BOOK.

The Hindu system of weights.

COUNTING is innate to man. The measure of a thing becomes known by its being compared with another thing which belongs to the same species and is assumed as a unit by general consent. Thereby the difference between the object and this standard becomes known.

By weighing, people determine the amount of gravity of heavy bodies, when the tongue of the scales stands at right angles on the horizontal plane. Hindus want the scales very little, because their *dirhams* are determined by number, not by weight, and their fractions, too, are simply counted as so-and-so many *fulûs*. The coinage of both *dirhams* and *fulûs* is different according to towns and districts. They weigh gold with the scales only when it is in its natural state or such as has been worked, *e.g.* for ornaments, but not coined. They use as a weight of gold the *suvarṇa* = $1\frac{1}{3}$ *tola*. They use the *tola* as frequently as we use the *mithḳâl*. According to what I have been able to learn from them, it corresponds to three of our *dirhams*, of which 10 equal 7 *mithḳâl*.

Therefore 1 *tola* = $2\frac{1}{10}$ of our *mithḳâl*.

The greatest fraction of a *tola* is $\frac{1}{12}$, called *mâsha*. Therefore 16 *mâsha* = 1 *suvarṇa*.

Further,

> 1 *másha* = 4 *aṇḍî* (*eraṇḍa*), *i.e.* the seed of a tree called *Gaura*.
> 1 *aṇḍî* = 4 *yava*.
> 1 *yava* = 6 *kalâ*.
> 1 *kalâ* = 4 *pâda*.
> 1 *pâda* = 4 *mdrî* (?).

Arranged differently we have—

1 *suvarṇa* = 16 *mâsha* = 64 *aṇḍî* = 256 *yava* = 1600 *kalâ* = 6400 *pâda* = 25,600 *mdrî* (?).

Six *mâshas* are called 1 *draṅkshaṇa*. If you ask them about this weight, they will tell you that 2 *draṅkshaṇa* = 1 *mithḳâl*. But this is a mistake; for 1 *mithḳâl* = $5\frac{5}{7}$ *mâsha*. The relation between a *draṅkshaṇa* and a *mithḳâl* is as 20 to 21, and therefore 1 *draṅkshaṇa* = $1\frac{1}{20}$ *mithḳâl*. If, therefore, a man gives the answer which we have just mentioned, he seems to have in mind the notion of a *mithḳâl* as a weight which does not much differ from a *draṅkshaṇa*; but by doubling the amount, saying 2 *draṅkshaṇas* instead of 1, he entirely spoils the comparison.

Since the unit of measure is not a natural unit, but a conventional one assumed by general consent, it admits of both practical and imaginary division. Its subdivisions or fractions are different in different places at one and the same time, and at different periods in one and the same country. Their names, too, are different according to places and times; changes which are produced either by the organic development of languages or by accident. Page 77.

A man from the neighbourhood of Somanâth told me that their *mithḳâl* is equal to ours; that

> 1 *mithḳâl* = 8 *ruvu*.
> 1 *ruvu* = 2 *pâli*.
> 1 *pâli* = 16 *yava*, *i.e.* barley-corn.

Accordingly 1 *mithḳâl* = 8 *ruvu* = 16 *pâli* = 256 *yava*.

This comparison shows that the man was mistaken

in comparing the two *mithkâls;* that what he called *mithkâls* is in reality the *tola,* and that he calls the *mâsha* by a different name, viz. *ruvu.*

Varâhamihira on weights.

If the Hindus wish to be particularly painstaking in these things, they give the following scale, based on the measurements which Varâhamihira prescribes for the constructiou of idols:—

1 *reṇu* or particle of dust	=	1 *raja.*
8 *raja*	=	1 *bâlâgra, i.e.* the end of a hair.
8 *bâlâgra*	=	1 *likhyâ, i.e.* the egg of a louse.
8 *likhyâ*	=	1 *yûkâ, i.e.* a louse.
8 *yûkâ*	=	1 *yava, i.e.* a barley-corn.

Hence, Varâhamihira goes on to enumerate the measures for distances. His measures of weight are the same as those which we have already mentioned. He says:

4 *yava*	=	1 *anḍî.*
4 *anḍî*	=	1 *mâsha.*
16 *mâsha*	=	1 *suvarṇa, i.e.* gold.
4 *suvarṇa*	=	1 *pala.*

The measures of dry substances are the following:—

4 *pala*	=	1 *kuḍava.*
4 *kuḍava*	=	1 *prastha.*
4 *prastha*	=	1 *âḍhaka.*

The measures of liquid substances are the following:—

8 *pala*	=	1 *kuḍava.*
8 *kuḍava*	=	1 *prastha.*
4 *prastha*	=	1 *aḍhaka.*
4 *âḍhaka*	=	1 *droṇa.*

Weights according to the book *Caraka.*

The following weights occur in the book *Caraka.* I give them here according to the Arabic translation, as I have not received them from the Hindus *vivâ voce.* The Arabic copy seems to be corrupt, like all other books of this kind which I know. Such corruption must of necessity occur in our Arabic writing, more particularly at a period like ours, when people care

so little about the correctness of what they copy.
"Âtreya says:

6 particles of dust	=	1 *marîci.*
6 *marîci*	=	1 mustard-seed (*râjikâ*).
8 mustard-seeds	=	1 red rice-corn.
2 red rice-corns	=	1 pea.
2 peas	=	1 *aṇḍî.*

And 1 *aṇḍî* is equal to $\frac{1}{8}$ *dânak,* according to the scale by which 7 *dânak* are equal to one *dirham.* Further:

4 *aṇḍî*	=	1 *mâsha.*
8 *mâsha*	=	1 *caṇa* (?).
2 *caṇa*	=	1 *karsha* or *suvarṇa* of the weight of 2 *dirhams.*
4 *suvarṇa*	=	1 *pala.*
4 *pala*	=	1 *kuḍava.*
4 *kuḍava*	=	1 *prastha.*
4 *prastha*	=	1 *âḍhaka.*
4 *âḍhaka*	=	1 *droṇa.*
2 *droṇa*	=	1 *śûrpa.*
2 *śûrpa*	=	1 *janâ* (?)."

The weight *pala* is much used in all the business dealings of the Hindus, but it is different for different wares and in different provinces. According to some, 1 *pala* = $\frac{1}{15}$ *manâ;* according to others, 1 *pala* = 14 *mithḳâl;* but the *manâ* is not equal to 210 *mithḳâl.* According to others, 1 *pala* = 16 *mithḳâl,* but the *manâ* is not equal to 240 *mithḳâl.* According to others, 1 *pala* = 15 *dirham,* but the *manâ* is not equal to 225 *dirham.* In reality, however, the relation between the *pala* and the *manâ* is different.

Further, Âtreya says: "1 *âḍhaka* = 64 *pala* = 128 *dirham* = 1 *raṭl.* But if the *aṇḍî* is equal to $\frac{1}{8}$ *dânak,* one *suvarṇa* contains 64 *aṇḍî,* and then a *dirham* has 32 *aṇḍî,* which, as each *aṇḍî* is equal to $\frac{1}{8}$ *dânak,* are equal to 4 *dânak.* The double amount of it is $1\frac{1}{3}$ *dirham*" (*sic*). Page 78.

Such are the results when people, instead of translating, indulge in wild conjecture and mingle together different theories in an uncritical manner.

As regards the first theory, resting on the assumption of one *suvarṇa* being equal to three of our *dirhams*, people in general agree in this—that

1 *suvarṇa* = $\frac{1}{4}$ *pala*.
1 *pala* = 12 *dirham*.
1 *pala* = $\frac{1}{15}$ *manâ*.
1 *manâ* = 180 *dirham*.

This leads me to think that 1 *suvarṇa* is equal to 3 of our *mithḳâl*, not to 3 of our *dirham*.

Various authors on weights.

Varâhamihira says in another place of his Saṁhitâ: "Make a round vase of the diameter and height of one yard, and then expose it to the rain until it ceases. All the water that has been collected in it of the weight of 200 *dirham* is, if taken fourfold, equal to 1 *âḍhaka*."

This, however, is only an approximate statement, because, as we have above mentioned in his own words, 1 *âḍhaka* is equal to 768 either *dirham*, as *they* say, or *mithḳâl*, as *I* suppose.

Śrîpâla relates, on the authority of Varâhamihira, that 50 *pala* = 256 *dirham* = 1 *âḍhaka*. But he is mistaken, for here the number 256 does not mean *dirhams*, but the number of the *suvarṇa* contained in one *âḍhaka*. And the number of *pala* contained in 1 *âḍhaka* is 64, not 50.

As I have been told, Jîvaśarman gives the following detailed account of these weights:

4 *pala* = 1 *kuḍava*.
4 *kuḍava* = 1 *prastha*.
4 *prastha* = 1 *âḍhaka*.
4 *âḍhaka* = 1 *droṇa*.
20 *droṇa* = 1 *khârî*.

The reader must know that 16 *mâsha* are 1 *suvarṇa*, but in weighing wheat or barley they reckon 4 *suvarṇa* = 1 *pala*, and in weighing water and oil they reckon 8 *suvarṇa* = 1 *pala*.

The Hindu balance.

The balances with which the Hindus weigh things are χαριστίωνες, of which the weights are immovable, whilst the scales move on certain marks and lines.

Therefore the balance is called *tulâ*. The first lines mean the units of the weight from 1 to 5, and farther on to 10; the following lines mean the tenths, 10, 20, 30, &c. With regard to the cause of this arrangement they relate the following saying of Vâsudeva:—

"I will not kill Śiśupâla, the son of my aunt, if he has not committed a crime, but will pardon him *until ten*, and then I shall call him to account."

We shall relate this story on a later opportunity.

Alfazârî uses in his astronomical handbook the word *pala* for *day-minutes* (*i.e.* sixtieth parts of a day). I have not found this use anywhere in Hindu literature, but they use the word to denote *a correction* in a mathematical sense.

The Hindus have a weight called *bhâra*, which is mentioned in the books about the conquest of Sindh. It is equal to 2000 *pala*; for they explain it by 100 × 20 *pala*, and as nearly equal to the weight of an ox.

This is all I have lighted on as regards Hindu weights.

By measuring (with dry measures) people determine the body and the bulk of a thing, if it fills up a certain measure which has been gauged as containing a certain quantity of it, it being understood that the way in which the things are laid out in the measure, the way in which their surface is determined, and the way in which, on the whole, they are arranged within the measure, are in every case identical. If two objects which are to be weighed belong to the same species, they then prove to be equal, not only in bulk, but also in weight; but if they do not belong to the same species, their bodily extent is equal, but not their weight. Dry measures. Page 79.

They have a measure called *bîsî* (? *sibî*), which is mentioned by every man from Kanauj and Somanâth. According to the people of Kanauj—

4 *bîsî* = 1 *prastha*.
¼ *bîsî* = 1 *kuḍava*.

According to the people of Somanâth—

16 *bisi*	=	1 *punti*.
12 *punti*	=	1 *moru*.

According to another theory—

12 *bisi*	=	1 *kalaśi*.
¼ *bisi*	=	1 *mânu*.

From the same source I learnt that a *mâna* of wheat is nearly equal to 5 *manâ*. Therefore 1 *bisi* (?) is equal to 20 *manâ*. The *bisi* corresponds to the Khwârizmian measure *sukhkh*, according to old style, whilst the *kalaśi* corresponds to the Khwârizmian *ghûr*, for 1 *ghûr* = 12 *sukhkh*.

Measures of distances.

Mensuration is the determination of distances by lines and of superficies by planes. A plane ought to be measured by part of a plane, but the mensuration by means of lines effects the same purpose, as lines determine the limits of planes. When, in quoting Varâhamihira, we had come so far as to determine the weight of a barley-corn (p. 162), we made a digression into an exposition of weights, where we used his authority about gravity, and now we shall return to him and consult him about distances. He says—

8 barley-corns put together	=	1 *aṅgula*, *i.e.* finger.
4 fingers	=	1 *râma* (?), *i.e.* the fist.
24 fingers	=	1 *hattha*, *i.e.* yard, also called *dasta*.
4 yards	=	1 *dhanu*, *i.e.* arc = a fathom.
40 arcs	=	1 *nalva*.
25 *nalva*	=	1 *krośa*.

Hence it follows that 1 *kroh* = 4000 yards; and as our mile has just so many yards, 1 mile = 1 *kroh*. Pulisa the Greek also mentions in his Siddhânta that 1 *kroh* = 4000 yards.

The *yard* is equal to 2 *mikyâs* or 24 fingers; for the Hindus determine the *śaṅku*, *i.e.* *mikyâs*, by idol-fingers. They do not call the twelfth part of a *mikyâs* a *finger* in general, as *we* do, but their *mikyâs* is always a *span*. The span, *i.e.* the distance between the ends of the thumb and the small finger at their widest possible stretching, is called *vitasti* and also *kishku*.

The distance between the ends of the fourth or ring-finger and the thumb, both being stretched out, is called *gokarṇa*.

The distance between the ends of the index-finger and of the thumb is called *karabha*, and is reckoned as equal to two-thirds of a span.

The distance between the tops of the middle finger and of the thumb is called *tâla*. The Hindus maintain that the height of a man is eight times his *tâla*, whether he be tall or small; as people say with regard to the foot, that it is one-seventh of the height of a man.

Regarding the construction of idols, the book *Saṁhitâ* says:—

"The breadth of the palm has been determined as 6, the length as 7; the length of the middle finger as 5, that of the fourth finger as the same; that of the index-finger as the same *minus* $\frac{1}{6}$ (*i.e.* $4\frac{1}{6}$); that of the small finger as the same *minus* $\frac{1}{3}$ (*i.e.* $3\frac{1}{3}$); that of the thumb as equal to two-thirds of the length of the middle finger (*i.e.* $3\frac{1}{3}$), so that the two last fingers are of equal length."

By the measurements and numbers of this passage, the author means *idol-fingers*. Page 80.

The relation between *yojana*, mile, and *farsakh*.

After the measure of the *krośa* has been fixed and found to be equal to our *mile*, the reader must learn that they have a measure of distances, called *yojana*, which is equal to 8 miles or to 32,000 yards. Perhaps somebody might believe that 1 *kroh* is = $\frac{1}{4}$ *farsakh*, and maintain that the *farsakhs* of the Hindus are 16,000 yards long. But such is not the case. On the contrary, 1 *kroh* = $\frac{1}{8}$ *yojana*. In the terms of this measure, Alfazârî has determined the circumference of the earth in his astronomical handbook. He calls it *jûn*, in the plural *'ajwân*.

Relation between

The elements of the calculations of the Hindus on the circumference of the circle rest on the assumption circumference and diameter.

that it is *thrice its diameter*. So the *Matsya-Purâṇa* says, after it has mentioned the diameters of the sun and moon in *yojanas*: "The circumference is thrice the diameter."

The *Âditya-Purâṇa* says, after it has mentioned the breadth of the *Dvîpas*, *i.e.* the islands and of their surrounding seas: "The circumference is thrice the diameter."

The same occurs also in the *Vâyu-Purâṇa*. In later times, however, Hindus have become aware of the fraction following after the three wholes. According to Brahmagupta, the circumference is $3\frac{1}{7}$ times the diameter; but he finds this number by a method peculiar to himself. He says: "As the root of 10 is nearly $3\frac{1}{7}$, the relation between the diameter and its circumference is like the relation between 1 and the root of 10." Then he multiplies the diameter by itself, the product by 10, and of this product he takes the root. Then the circumference is *solid*, *i.e.* consists of integers, in the same way as the root of ten. This calculation, however, makes the fraction larger than it really is. Archimedes defined it to be something between $\frac{10}{70}$ and $\frac{11}{70}$. Brahmagupta relates with regard to Âryabhaṭa, criticising him, that he fixed the circumference as 3393; that he fixed the diameter in one place as 1080, in another place as 1050. According to the first statement, the relation between diameter and circumference would be like $1 : 3\frac{17}{120}$. This fraction ($\frac{17}{120}$) is by $\frac{1}{17}$ smaller than $\frac{1}{7}$. However, as regards the second statement, it contains no doubt a blunder in the text, not of the author; for according to the text, the relation would be like $1 : 3\frac{1}{4}$ and something over.

Pulisa employs this relation in his calculations in the proportion of $1 : 3\frac{177}{1250}$.

This fraction is here by so much smaller than one-seventh as it is according to Âryabhaṭa, *i.e.* by $\frac{1}{17}$.

The same relation is derived from the old theory, which Ya'kûb Ibn Ṭâriḳ mentions in his book, *Compositio Sphærarum*, on the authority of his Hindu informant, viz. that the circumference of the zodiac is 1,256,640,000 *yojana*, and that its diameter is 400,000,000 *yojana*.

These numbers presuppose the relation between circumference and diameter to be as 1 : 3 $\frac{56,640,000}{400,000,000}$. These two numbers may be reduced by the common divisor of 360,000. Thereby we get 177 as numerator and 1250 as denominator. And this is the fraction ($\frac{177}{1250}$) which Pulisa has adopted.

CHAPTER XVI.

NOTES ON THE WRITING OF THE HINDUS, ON THEIR ARITHMETIC AND RELATED SUBJECTS, AND ON CERTAIN STRANGE MANNERS AND CUSTOMS OF THEIRS.

Page 81.

On various kinds of writing material.

THE tongue communicates the thought of the speaker to the hearer. Its action has therefore, as it were, a momentary life only, and it would have been impossible to deliver by oral tradition the accounts of the events of the past to later generations, more particularly if they are separated from them by long periods of time. This has become possible only by a new discovery of the human mind, by the art of writing, which spreads news over space as the winds spread, and over time as the spirits of the deceased spread. Praise therefore be unto Him who has arranged creation and created everything for the best!

The Hindus are not in the habit of writing on hides, like the Greeks in ancient times. Socrates, on being asked why he did not compose books, gave this reply: "I do not transfer knowledge from the living hearts of men to the *dead* hides of sheep." Muslims, too, used in the early times of Islam to write on hides, *e.g.* the treaty between the Prophet and the Jews of Khaibar and his letter to Kisrâ. The copies of the Koran were written on the hides of gazelles, as are still nowadays the copies of the Thora. There occurs this passage in the Koran (Sûra vi. 91): "They make it *karâṭîs*," *i.e.* *τομάρια*. The *kirṭâs* (or *charta*) is made in Egypt, being cut out of the papyrus stalk. Written on this material, the orders of the Khalifs went out into all the world until shortly before our time. Papyrus has this advantage over vellum, that you can neither rub out nor change anything on it, because thereby it would be destroyed. It was in China that paper was first manufactured. Chinese prisoners introduced the fabrication of paper into Samarkand, and thereupon it was made in various places, so as to meet the existing want.

The Hindus have in the south of their country a slender tree like the date and cocoa-nut palms, bearing edible fruits and leaves of the length of one yard, and as broad as three fingers one put beside the other. They call these leaves *târî* (*tâla* or *tâṛ*=*Borassus flabelliformis*), and write on them. They bind a book of these leaves together by a cord on which they are arranged, the cord going through all the leaves by a hole in the middle of each.

In Central and Northern India people use the bark of the *tûz* tree, one kind of which is used as a cover for bows. It is called *bhûrja*. They take a piece one yard long and as broad as the outstretched fingers of the hand, or somewhat less, and prepare it in various ways. They oil and polish it so as to make it hard and smooth, and then they write on it. The proper order of the single leaves is marked by numbers. The whole book is wrapped up in a piece of cloth and fastened between two tablets of the same size. Such a book is called *pûthî* (cf. *pusta*, *pustaka*). Their letters, and whatever else they have to write, they write on the bark of the *tûz* tree.

On the Hindu alphabet.

As to the writing or alphabet of the Hindus, we have already mentioned that it once had been lost and forgotten; that nobody cared for it, and that in consequence people became illiterate, sunken into gross ignorance, and entirely estranged from science. But then Vyâsa, the son of Parâśara, rediscovered their alphabet of fifty letters by an inspiration of God. A letter is called *akshara*.

Some people say that originally the number of their letters was less, and that it increased only by degrees. This is possible, or I should even say necessary. As for the Greek alphabet, a certain *Asídhas* (*sic*) had formed sixteen characters to perpetuate science about the time when the Israelites ruled over Egypt. Thereupon *Kímush* (*sic*) and *Agenon* (*sic*) brought them to the Greeks. By adding four new signs they obtained an alphabet of twenty letters. Later on, about the time when Socrates was poisoned, Simonides added four
Page 82. other signs, and so the Athenians at last had a complete alphabet of twenty-four letters, which happened during the reign of Artaxerxes, the son of Darius, the son of Artaxerxes, the son of Cyrus, according to the chronographers of the West.

The great number of the letters of the Hindu alphabet is explained, firstly, by the fact that they express every letter by a separate sign if it is followed by a vowel or a diphthong or a *hamza* (*viśarga*), or a small extension of the sound beyond the measure of the vowel; and, secondly, by the fact that they have consonants which are not found together in any other language, though they may be found scattered through different languages—sounds of such a nature that *our* tongues, not being familiar with them, can scarcely pronounce them, and that *our* ears are frequently not able to distinguish between many a cognate pair of them.

The Hindus write from the left to the right like the Greeks. They do not write on the basis of a line, above which the heads of the letters rise whilst their tails go down below, as in Arabic writing. On the contrary, their ground-line is above, a straight line above every single character, and from this line the letter hangs down and is written under it. Any sign *above* the line is nothing but a grammatical mark to denote the pronunciation of the character above which it stands.

On the local alphabets of the Hindus.

The most generally known alphabet is called *Siddhamâtṛikâ*, which is by some considered as originating from Kashmîr, for the people of Kashmîr use it. But it is also used in Varânaṣî. This town and Kashmîr are the high schools of Hindu sciences. The same writing is used in Madhyadeśa, *i.e.* the middle country, the country all around Kanauj, which is also called Âryâvarta.

In Mâlava there is another alphabet called *Nâgara*, which differs from the former only in the shape of the characters.

Next comes an alphabet called *Ardhanâgarî*, *i.e. half-nâgara*, so called because it is compounded of the former two. It is used in Bhâtiya and some parts of Sindh.

Other alphabets are the *Malwârî*, used in Malwashau, in Southern Sind, towards the sea-coast; the *Saindhava*, used in Bahmanwâ or Almanṣûra; the *Karnâṭa*, used in Karnâṭadeśa, whence those troops come which in the armies are known as *Kannara;* the *Aṇdhrî*, used in Andhradeśa; the *Dirwarî* (*Drâviḍî*), used in Dirwaradeśa (Draviḍadeśa); the *Lârî*, used in Lâradeśa (Lâṭadeśa); the *Gaurî* (*Gauḍî*), used in Pûrvadeśa, *i.e.* the Eastern country; the *Bhaikshukî*, used in Uduṇpûr in Pûrvadeśa. This last is the writing of Buddha.

On the word Om.

The Hindus begin their books with *Om*, the word of creation, as we begin them with "In the name of God." The figure of the word *om* is  This figure does not consist of letters; it is simply an image invented to represent this word, which people use, believing that it will bring them a blessing, and meaning thereby a confession of the unity of God. Similar to this is the manner in which the Jews write the name of God, viz. by three Hebrew *yods*. In the Thora the word is written *YHVH* and pronounced

Adonai; sometimes they also say *Yah.* The word *Adonai,* which they pronounce, is not expressed in writing.

On their numeral signs.

The Hindus do not use the letters of their alphabet for numerical notation, as we use the Arabic letters in the order of the Hebrew alphabet. As in different parts of India the letters have different shapes, the numeral signs, too, which are called *aṅka,* differ. The numeral signs which *we* use are derived from the finest forms of the Hindu signs. Signs and figures are of no use if people do not know what they mean, but the people of Kashmîr mark the single leaves of their books with figures which look like drawings or like the Chinese characters, the meaning of which can only be learned by a very long practice. However, they do not use them when reckoning in the sand.

Page 83.

In arithmetic all nations agree that all the *orders* of numbers (*e.g.* one, ten, hundred, thousand) stand in a certain relation to the ten; that each order is the tenth part of the following and the tenfold of the preceding. I have studied the names of the *orders* of the numbers in various languages with all kinds of people with whom I have been in contact, and have found that no nation goes beyond the thousand. The Arabs, too, stop with the thousand, which is certainly the most correct and the most natural thing to do. I have written a separate treatise on this subject.

Those, however, who go beyond the thousand in their numeral system are the Hindus, at least in their arithmetical technical terms, which have been either freely invented or derived according to certain etymologies, whilst in others both methods are blended together. They extend the names of the *orders* of numbers until the 18th *order* for religious reasons, the mathematicians being assisted by the grammarians with all kinds of etymologies.

The 18th *order* is called *Parârdha, i.e.* the half of

heaven, or, more accurately, *the half of that which is above.* For if the Hindus construct periods of time out of Kalpas, the unit of this *order* is *a day of God* (*i.e.* a half *nychthemeron*). And as we do not know any body larger than heaven, half of it (*parârdha*), as *a half of the greatest body*, has been compared with *a half of the greatest day.* By doubling it, by uniting night to day, we get the *whole* of the greatest day. There can be no doubt that the name *Parârdha* is accounted for in this way, and that *parâr* means *the whole of heaven.*

The following are the names of the eighteen *orders* of numbers:— The eighteen orders of numeration.

1. *Ekam.*
2. *Daśam.*
3. *Śatam.*
4. *Sahasram.*
5. *Ayuta.*
6. *Laksha.*
7. *Prayuta.*
8. *Koṭi.*
9. *Nyarbuda.*
10. *Padma.*
11. *Kharva.*
12. *Nikharva.*
13. *Mahâpadma.*
14. *Śaṅku.*
15. *Samudra.*
16. *Madhya.*
17. *Antya.*
18. *Parârdha.*

I shall now mention some of their differences of opinion relating to this system.

Variations occurring in the eighteen orders.

Some Hindus maintain *that there is a 19th order beyond the Parârdha, called Bhûri, and that this is the limit of reckoning.* But in reality *reckoning* is unlimited; it has only a technical limit, which is conventionally adopted as the last of the *orders* of numbers. By the word *reckoning* in the sentence above they seem to mean *nomenclature*, as if they meant to say that the language has no *name* for any reckoning beyond the 19th *order.* It is known that the unit of this *order*, *i.e.* one *bhûri*, is equal to one-fifth of the *greatest day*, but on this subject they have no tradition. In their tradition there are only traces of combinations of the *greatest day*, as we shall hereafter explain. Therefore this 19th order is an addition of an artificial and hyper-accurate nature.

Page 84. According to others, the limit of reckoning is *koṭi*; and starting from *koṭi* the succession of the *orders* of numbers would be *koṭi*, thousands, hundreds, tenths; for the number of Devas is expressed in *kôṭis*. According to their belief there are thirty-three *kotis* of Devas; eleven of which belong to each of the three beings, Brahman, Narâyaṇa, and Mahâdeva.

The names of the *orders* beyond that of the 18th have been invented by the grammarians, as we have said already (p. 174).

Further, we observe that the popular name of the 5th *order* is *Daśa sahasra*, that of the 7th *order*, *Daśa laksha*; for the two names which we have mentioned in the list above (*Ayuta Prayuta*) are rarely used.

The book of Âryabhaṭa of Kusumapura gives the following names of the *orders* from the ten till 10 *koṭi*:—

Ayutaṁ.	*Koṭi padma.*
Niyutaṁ.	*Parapadma.*
Prayutaṁ.	

Further, it is noteworthy that some people establish a kind of etymological relationship between the different names; so they call the 6th *order Niyuta*, according to the analogy of the 5th, which is called *Ayuta*. Further, they call the 8th *order Arbuda*, according to the analogy of the 9th, which is called *Nyarbuda*.

There is a similar relation between *Nikharva* and *Kharva*, the names of the 12th and 11th *orders*, and between *Śaṅku* and *Mahâśaṅku*, the names of the 13th and 14th *orders*. According to this analogy *Mahâpadma* ought to follow immediately after *Padma*, but this latter is the name of the 10th, the former the name of the 13th *order*.

These are differences of theirs which can be traced back to certain reasons; but besides, there are many differences without any reason, which simply arise from people dictating these names without observing any fixed order, or from the fact that they hate to avow their ignorance by a frank *I do not know*,—a word which is difficult to them in any connection whatsoever.

The *Pulisa-siddhânta* gives the following list of the *orders* of the numbers:—

4. *Sahasram.*	8. *Koṭi.*
5. *Ayutam.*	9. *Arbudam.*
6. *Niyutam.*	10. *Kharva.*
7. *Prayutam.*	

The following *orders*, from the 11th till the 18th, are the same as those of the above-mentioned list.

The Hindus use the numeral signs in arithmetic in the same way as we do. I have composed a treatise showing how far, possibly, the Hindus are ahead of us in this subject. We have already explained that the Hindus compose their books in Ślokas. If, now, they wish, in their astronomical handbooks, to express some numbers of the various *orders*, they express them by words used to denote certain numbers either in one *order* alone or at the same time in two *orders* (*e.g.* a word meaning either 20 or both 20 and 200). For each number they have appropriated quite a great quantity of words. Hence, if one word does not suit the metre, you may easily exchange it for a synonym which suits. Brahmagupta says: "If you want to write *one*, express it by everything which is unique, as *the earth, the moon; two* by everything which is double, as, *e.g. black* and *white; three* by everything which is threefold; the *nought* by *heaven*, the *twelve* by the names of the sun." Numeral notation.

I have united in the following table all the expressions for the numbers which I used to hear from them; for the knowledge of these things is most essential for deciphering their astronomical handbooks.

Whenever I shall come to know all the meanings of these words, I will add them, if God permits! Page

0 = *śûnya* and *kha*, both meaning *point*.
gagana, *i.e.* heaven.
viyat, *i.e.* heaven.
âkâśa, *i.e.* heaven.
ambara, *i.e.* heaven.
abhra, *i.e.* heaven.

1 = *âdi*, *i.e.* the beginning.
śaśin.
indu.
śîtâ.
urvarâ, *dharaṇî*.
pitâmaha, *i.e.* the first father.
candra, *i.e.* the moon.
śîtâṁśu, *i.e.* the moon.
rûpa.
raśmi.

2 = *yama*.
aśvin.
ravicandra.
locana, *i.e.* the two eyes.
akshi.
dasra.
yamala.
paksha, *i.e.* the two halves of a month.
netra, *i.e.* the two eyes.

3 = *trikâla*, *i.e.* the three parts of time.
trijagat.
trayaṁ.
pâvaka, *vaiśvânara*, *dahana*, *tapana*, *hutâśana*, *jvalana*, *agni*, *i.e.* fire.
[*triguṇa*,] *i.e.* the three first forces.
loka, *i.e.* the worlds, earth, heaven and hell.
trikaṭu.

4 = *veda*, *i.e.* their sacred code, because it has four parts.
samudra, *sâgara*, *i.e.* the sea.
abdhi.
dadhi.
diś, *i.e.* the four cardinal points.
jalâśaya.
kṛita. Page 86.

5 = *śara*.
artha.
indriya, *i.e.* the five senses.
sâyaka.
إخون
vâṇa.
bhûta.
ishu.
Pâṇḍava, *i.e.* the five royal brothers.
pattrin, *mârgaṇa*.

6 = *rasa*.
aṅga.
shaṭ.
الدرم (?) *i.e.* the year.
ṛitu (?).
mâsârdhaṁ.

7 = *aga*.
mahîdhara.
parvata, *i.e.* the mountains.
saptan.
naga, *i.e.* the mountains.
adri.
muni.

8 = *vasu*, *ashṭa*.
dhî, *maṅgala*.
gaja, *nâga*.
dantin.

9 = *go*, *chidra*.
nanda, *pavana*.
randhra, *antara*.
navan = 9. Page 87.

10 = *diś, khendu.*
âśâ, Râvaṇa-śiras.

11 = *Rudra*, the destroyer of the world.
Mahâdeva, *i.e.* the prince of the angels.
īśvara.
akshauhiṇī, *i.e.* the army Kuru had.

12 = *sûrya*, because there are twelve suns.
âditya.
arka, *i.e.* the sun.
mâsa, bhânu.
sahasrâṁśu.

13 = *viśva.*

14 = *manu*, the lords of the fourteen *manvantaras.*

15 = *tithi*, *i.e.* the lunar days in each half month.

16 = *ashṭi, nṛipa, bhûpa.*

17 = *atyashṭi.*

18 = *dhṛiti.* Page 88.

19 = *atidhṛiti.*

20 = *nakha, kṛiti.*

21 = *utkṛiti.*

22 =

23 =

24 =

25 = *tattva*, *i.e.* the twenty-five things, through the knowledge of which liberation is obtained.

As far as I have seen and heard of the Hindus, they do not usually go beyond twenty-five with this kind of numerical notation.

Strange manners and customs of the Hindus. Page 89.

We shall now speak of certain strange manners and customs of the Hindus. The strangeness of a thing evidently rests on the fact that it occurs but rarely, and that we seldom have the opportunity of witnessing it. If such strangeness reaches a high degree, the thing becomes a curiosity, or even something like a miracle, which is no longer in accordance with the ordinary laws of nature, and which seems chimerical as long as it has not been witnessed. Many Hindu customs differ from those of our country and of our time to such a degree as to appear to us simply monstrous. One might almost think that they had intentionally changed them into the opposite, for *our* customs do not resemble theirs, but are the very reverse; and if ever a custom of *theirs* resembles one of *ours*, it has certainly just the opposite meaning.

They do not cut any of the hair of the body. Originally they went naked in consequence of the heat, and by not cutting the hair of the head they intended to prevent sunstroke.

They divide the moustache into single plaits in order to preserve it. As regards their not cutting the hair of the genitals, they try to make people believe that the cutting of it incites to lust and increases carnal desire. Therefore such of them as feel a strong desire for cohabitation never cut the hair of the genitals.

They let the nails grow long, glorying in their idleness, since they do not use them for any business or work, but only, while living a *dolce far niente* life, they scratch their heads with them and examine the hair for lice.

The Hindus eat singly, one by one, on a tablecloth of dung. They do not make use of the remainder of a meal, and the plates from which they have eaten are thrown away if they are earthen.

They have red teeth in consequence of chewing arecanuts with betel-leaves and chalk.

They drink wine before having eaten anything, then they take their meal. They sip the stall of cows, but they do not eat their meat.

They beat the cymbals with a stick.

They use turbans for trousers. Those who want little dress are content to dress in a rag of two fingers' breadth, which they bind over their loins with two cords; but those who like much dress, wear trousers lined with so much cotton as would suffice to make a number of counterpanes and saddle-rugs. These trousers have no (visible) openings, and they are so huge that the feet are not visible. The string by which the trousers are fastened is at the back.

Their *ṣidâr* (a piece of dress covering the head and the upper part of breast and neck) is similar to the trousers, being also fastened at the back by buttons.

The lappets of the *kurṭakas* (short shirts from the shoulders to the middle of the body with sleeves, a female dress) have slashes both on the right and left sides.

They keep the shoes tight till they begin to put them on. They are turned down from the calf before walking (?).

In washing they begin with the feet, and then wash the face. They wash themselves before cohabiting with their wives.

Cœunt stantes velut palus vitis, dum mulieres ab imo sursum moventur velut occupatæ in arando, maritus vero plane otiosus manet.

On festive days they besmear their bodies with dung instead of perfumes.

The men wear articles of female dress; they use cosmetics, wear earrings, arm-rings, golden seal-rings on the ring-finger as well as on the toes of the feet.

Miseret eos catamiti et viri qui rebus venereis frui non potest pushaṇḍila *dicti, qui penem bucca devorans semen elicit sorbendum.*

In cacando faciem vertunt versus murum retegentes pudenda ut videantur a prætereuntibus.

Sacra faciunt virilibus liṅga *dictis, quæ est imago veretri Mahadevæ.*

They ride without a saddle, but if they put on a saddle, they mount the horse from its right side. In travelling they like to have somebody riding behind them.

They fasten the *kuṭhâra, i.e.* the dagger, at the waist on the right side.

They wear a girdle called *yajnopavîta*, passing from the left shoulder to the right side of the waist.

In all consultations and emergencies they take the advice of the women. Page 90.

When a child is born people show particular attention to the man, not to the woman.

Of two children they give the preference to the younger, particularly in the eastern parts of the country;

for they maintain that the elder owes his birth to predominant lust, whilst the younger owes his origin to mature reflection and a calm proceeding.

In shaking hands they grasp the hand of a man from the convex side.

They do not ask permission to enter a house, but when they leave it they ask permission to do so.

In their meetings they sit cross-legged.

They spit out and blow their noses without any respect for the elder ones present, and they crack their lice before them. They consider the *crepitus ventris* as a good omen, sneezing as a bad omen.

They consider as unclean the weaver, but as clean the cupper and the flayer, who kills dying animals for money either by drowning or by burning.

They use black tablets for the children in the schools, and write upon them along the long side, not the broad side, writing with a white material from the left to the right. One would think that the author of the following verses had meant the Hindus:—

> "How many a writer uses paper as black as charcoal,
> Whilst his pen writes on it with white colour.
> By writing he places a bright day in a dark night,
> Weaving like a weaver, but without adding a woof."

They write the title of a book at the end of it, not at the beginning.

They magnify the nouns of their language by giving them the feminine gender, as the Arabs magnify them by the diminutive form.

If one of them hands over a thing to another, he expects that it should be thrown to him as we throw a thing to the dogs.

If two men play at *Nard* (backgammon), a third one throws the dice between them.

They like the juice which flows over the cheeks of

the rutting elephant, which in reality has the most horrid smell.

On the Indian chess.

In playing chess they move the elephant straight on, not to the other sides, one square at a time, like the pawn, and to the four corners also one square at a time, like the queen (*firzân*). They say that these five squares (*i.e.* the one straight forward and the others at the corners) are the places occupied by the trunk and the four feet of the elephant.

They play chess—four persons at a time—with a pair of dice. Their arrangement of the figures on the chess-board is the following:—

Tower (*rukh*).	Horse.	Elephant.	King.			Pawn.	Tower.
Pawn.	Pawn.	Pawn.	Pawn.			Pawn.	Horse.
						Pawn.	Elephant.
						Pawn.	King.
King.	Pawn.						
Elephant.	Pawn.						
Horse.	Pawn.			Pawn.	Pawn.	Pawn.	Pawn.
Tower.	Pawn.			King.	Elephant.	Horse.	Tower.

As this kind of chess is not known among us, I shall here explain what I know of it.

Page 91. The four persons playing together sit so as to form a square round a chess-board, and throw the two dice alternately. Of the numbers of the dice the five and six are blank (*i.e.* do not count as such). In that case, if the dice show five or six, the player takes one instead of the five, and four instead of the six, because the figures of these two numerals are drawn in the following manner:—

6   5
4   3   2   1

so as to exhibit a certain likeness of form to 4 and 1, viz. in the Indian signs.

The name *Shâh* or *king* applies here to the *queen* (*firzân*).

Each number of the dice causes a move of one of the figures.

The 1 moves either the pawn or the king. Their moves are the same as in the common chess. The king may be taken, but is not required to leave his place.

The 2 moves the tower (*rukh*). It moves to the third square in the direction of the diagonal, as the elephant moves in *our* chess.

The 3 moves the horse. Its move is the generally known one to the third square in oblique direction.

The 4 moves the elephant. It moves in a straight line, as the tower does in our chess, unless it be prevented from moving on. If this is the case, as sometimes happens, one of the dice removes the obstacle, and enables it to move on. Its smallest move is one square, the greatest fifteen squares, because the dice sometimes show two 4, or two 6, or a 4 and a 6. In consequence of one of these numbers, the elephant moves along the whole side of the margin on the chessboard; in consequence of the other number, it moves along the other side on the other margin of the board, in case there is no impediment in its way. In consequence of these two numbers, the elephant, in the course of his moves, occupies the two ends of the diagonal.

The pieces have certain values, according to which the player gets his share of the stake, for the pieces are taken and pass into the hands of the player. The value of the king is 5, that of the elephant 4, of the horse 3, of the tower 2, and of the pawn 1. He who takes a king gets 5. For two kings he gets 10, for three kings 15, if the winner is no longer in possession of his own king. But if he has still his own king, and takes all three kings, he gets 54, a number which represents a progression based on general consent, not on an algebraic principle.

If the Hindus claim to differ from us, and to be something better than we, as we on our side, of course, do *vice versâ*, we might settle the question by an experiment to be made with their boys. I never knew a Hindu boy who had only recently come into Muhammadan territory who was not thoroughly versed in the manners and customs of the people, but at the same time he would place the shoes before his master in a wrong order, the right one to the left foot, and *vice versâ*; he would, in folding, turn his master's garments inside out, and spread the carpets so that the under part is uppermost, and more of the kind. All of which is a consequence of the innate perversity of the Hindu nature.

The innate perversity of the Hindu character.

However, I must not reproach the Hindus only with their heathen practices, for the heathen Arabs too committed crimes and obscenities. They cohabited with menstruating and pregnant women; several men agreed to cohabit with the same woman in the same period of menstruation; they adopted the children of others, of their guests, of the lover of their daughter, not to men-

Customs of the heathen Arabs.

tion that in some kinds of their worship they whistled on their fingers and clapped with their hands, and that they ate unclean and dead animals. Islam has abolished all those things among the Arabs, as it has also abolished them in those parts of India the people of which have become Muḥammadans. Thanks be unto God!

CHAPTER XVII.

ON HINDU SCIENCES WHICH PREY ON THE IGNORANCE OF PEOPLE.

We understand by witchcraft, making by some kind of delusion a thing appear to the senses as something different from what it is in reality. Taken in this sense, it is far spread among people. Understood, however, as common people understand it, as the producing of something which is impossible, it is a thing which does not lie within the limits of reality. For as that which is impossible cannot be produced, the whole affair is nothing but a gross deception. Therefore witchcraft in this sense has nothing whatever to do with science.

On alchemy among the Hindus in general.

Page 92.

One of the species of witchcraft is alchemy, though it is generally not called by this name. But if a man takes a bit of cotton and makes it appear as a bit of gold, what would you call this but a piece of witchcraft? It is quite the same as if he were to take a bit of silver and make it appear as gold, only with this difference, that the latter is a generally-known process, *i.e.* the gilding of silver, the former is not.

The Hindus do not pay particular attention to alchemy, but no nation is entirely free from it, and one nation has more bias for it than another, which must not be construed as proving intelligence or ignorance; for we find that many intelligent people are entirely given to alchemy, whilst ignorant people ridicule the art and its adepts. Those intelligent people, though boisterously exulting over their make-believe science, are not to be blamed for occupying themselves with alchemy, for their motive is simply excessive eagerness for acquiring fortune and for avoiding misfortune. Once a sage was asked why scholars always flock to the doors of the rich, whilst the rich are not inclined to call at the doors of scholars. "The scholars," he answered, "are well aware of the use of money, but the rich are ignorant of the nobility of science." On the other hand, ignorant people are not to be praised, although they behave quite quietly, simply because they abstain from alchemy, for their motives are objectionable ones, rather practical results of innate ignorance and stupidity than anything else.

The adepts in this art try to keep it concealed, and shrink back from intercourse with those who do not belong to them. Therefore I have not been able to learn from the Hindus which methods they follow in this science, and what element they principally use, whether a mineral or an animal or a vegetable one. I only heard them speaking of the process of *sublimation*, of *calcination*, of *analysis*, and of the *waxing of talc*, which they call in their language *tâlaka*, and so I guess that they incline towards the mineralogical method of alchemy.

The science of Rasâyana.

They have a science similar to alchemy which is quite peculiar to them. They call it *Rasâyana*, a word composed with *rasa*, *i.e.* gold. It means an art which is restricted to certain operations, drugs, and compound medicines, most of which are taken from plants. Its principles restore the health of those who were ill beyond hope, and give back youth to fading old age, so that people become again what they were in the age near puberty; white hair becomes black again, the keenness of the senses is restored as well as the capacity for juvenile agility, and even for cohabitation, and the life of people in this world is even extended to a long period. And why not? Have we not already mentioned on the authority of Patañjali (v. p. 88) that one of the methods leading to liberation is *Rasâyana?* What man would hear this, being inclined to take it for truth, and not dart off into foolish joy and not honour the master of such a wonderful art by popping the choicest bit of his meal into his mouth?

Nâgârjuna, the author of a book on Rasâyana.

A famous representative of this art was Nâgârjuna, a native of the fort Daihak, near Somanâth. He excelled in it, and composed a book which contains the substance of the whole literature on this subject, and is very rare. He lived nearly a hundred years before our time.

Page 93.

The alchemist Vyâḍi in the time of King Vikramâditya.

In the time of the King Vikramâditya, of whose era we shall speak hereafter, there lived in the city of Ûjain a man of the name of Vyâḍi, who had turned his whole attention to this science, and had ruined on account of it both his life and property, but all his zeal did not even avail him so much as to help him to things which, under ordinary circumstances, are easily obtained. Becoming restricted in his means, he conceived a disgust to that which had been the object of all his exertions, and sat down on the bank of a river sighing, sorrowful, and despairing. He held in his hand his *pharmacopœia,* from which he used to take the prescriptions for his medicines, but now he began to throw one leaf of it after the other into the water. A harlot happened to sit on the bank of the same river farther down, who, on seeing the leaves pass by, gathered them, and fished up some relating to *Rasâyana.* Vyâḍi did not notice her till all the leaves of his book had gone. Then the woman came to him, asking why he had done so with his book, whereupon he answered, "Because I have derived no advantage from it. I have not obtained what I ought to have obtained; for *its* sake I have become bankrupt after having had great treasures, and now I am miserable after having so long been in the hope of obtaining happiness." The harlot spoke: "Do not give up a pursuit in which you have spent your life; do not despair of the possibility of a thing which all sages before you have shown to be true. Perhaps the obstacle which prevents you from realising your plans is only of an accidental nature, which may perhaps be removed by an accident. I have much solid cash. It is all yours that you may spend it on the realisation of your plans." Thereupon Vyâḍi resumed his work.

However, books of this kind are written in an enigmatic style. So he happened to misunderstand a word in the prescription of a medicine, which meant *oil* and *human blood*, both being required for it. It was written *raktâmala*, and he thought it meant *red myrobalanon*. When he used the medicine it had no effect whatsoever. Now he began to concoct the various drugs, but the flame touched his head and dried up his brain. Therefore he oiled himself with oil, pouring it in great quantity over his skull. One day he rose to step away from the fireplace for some business or other, but as there happened to be a peg projecting from the roof right above his head, he knocked his head against it, and the blood began to flow. On account of the pain which he felt, he looked downward, and in consequence some drops of blood mixed with oil dropped from the upper part of his skull into the caldron without his noticing it. When, then, the concocting process was finished and he and his wife besmeared themselves with the concoction in order to try it, they both flew up into the air. Vikramâditya on hearing of this affair left his castle, and proceeded to the market-place in order to see them with his own eyes. Then the man shouted to him, "Open thy mouth for my saliva." The king, however, being disgusted, did not do it, and so the saliva fell down near the door, and immediately the threshold was filled with gold.

Vyâḍi and the woman flew to any place they liked. He has composed famous books on this science. People say that both man and wife are still alive.

Story about the piece of silver in the door of the Government-house in Dhâra.

A similar tale is the following:—In the city of Dhâra, the capital of Mâlava, which is in our days ruled by Bhojadeva, there lies in the door of the Government-house an oblong piece of pure silver, in which the outlines of the limbs of a man are visible. Its origin is accounted for by the following story:—Once in olden times a man went to a king of theirs, bringing him a *Rasâyana*, the use of which would make him immortal, victorious, invincible, and capable of doing everything he desired. He asked the king to come alone to the place of their meeting, and the king gave orders to keep in readiness all the man required. Page 94.

The man began to boil the oil for several days, until at last it acquired consistency. Then he spoke to the king: "Spring into it and I shall finish the process." But the king, terrified at what he saw, had not the courage to dive into it. The man, on perceiving his cowardice, spoke to him: "If you have not sufficient courage, and will not do it for yourself, will you allow me myself to do it?" Whereupon the king answered, "Do as you like." Now he produced several packets of drugs, and instructed him that when such and such symptoms should appear, he should throw upon him this or that packet. Then the man stepped forward to the caldron and threw himself into it, and at once he was dissolved and reduced into pulp. Now the king proceeded according to his instruction, but when he had nearly finished the process, and there remained only one packet that was not yet thrown into the mass, he began to be anxious, and to think what might happen to his realm, in case the man should return to life as an *immortal, victorious, invincible* person, as has above been mentioned. And so he thought it preferable not to throw the last packet into the mass. The consequence was that the caldron became cold, and the dissolved man became consolidated in the shape of the said piece of silver.

The Hindus tell a tale about Vallabha, the king of the city of Vallabhî, whose era we have mentioned in the proper chapter.

Story of the fruit-seller Rañka and the king Vallabha.

A man of the rank of a *Siddha* asked a herdsman with reference to a plant called *Thohar*, of the species of the *Lactaria*, from which milk flows when they are torn off, whether he had ever seen *Lactaria* from which blood flows instead of milk. When the herdsman declared he had, he gave him some drink-money that he should show it to him, which he did. When the man now saw the plant, he set fire to it, and threw the dog of the herdsman into the flame. Enraged thereby, the herdsman caught the man, and did with him the same as he had done to his dog. Then he waited till the fire was extinguished, and found both the man and the dog, but turned into gold. He took the dog with him, but left the man on the spot.

Now some peasant happened to find it. He cut off a finger, and went to a fruit-seller who was called *Rañka*, i.e. *the poor*, because he was an utter pauper, and evidently near bankruptcy. After the peasant had bought from him what he wanted, he returned to the golden man, and then he found that in the place where the cut off finger had been, a new finger had grown. He cut it off a second time, and bought again from the same fruit-seller all that he wanted. But when the fruit-seller asked him whence he had the finger, he was stupid enough to tell him. So Rañka went out to the body of the Siddha, and brought it on a carriage to his house. He stayed in his old abode, but managed by degrees to buy the whole town. The king Vallabha desired to own the same town, and asked him to cede it to him for money, but Rañka declined. Being however afraid of the king's resentment, he fled to the lord of Almanṣûra, made him presents of money, and asked him to help him by a naval force. The lord of Almanṣûra complied with his desire, and assisted him. So he made a night-attack upon the king Vallabha, and killed him and his people, and destroyed his town. People say that still in our time there are such traces left in that country as are found in places which were destroyed by an unexpected night-attack.

The greediness of the ignorant Hindu princes for gold-making does not know any limit. If any one of them wanted to carry out a scheme of gold-making, and people advised him to kill a number of fine little children, the monster would not refrain from such a crime; he would throw them into the fire. If this precious science of Rasâyana were banished to the utmost limits of the world, where it is unattainable to anybody, it would be the best.

According to the Eranian tradition, Isfandiyâd is said to have spoken when dying: "Kâûs had been given the power and the miraculous things mentioned in the Book of the Law. Finally he went to the mountain Ḳâf as a decrepit man, bent down by old age, but he returned thence as a lively youth of well-proportioned figure and full of force, having made the clouds his carriage, as God allowed him." An Eranian tradition. Page 95.

As regards charms and incantations, the Hindus have a firm belief in them, and they, as a rule, are much inclined towards them. The book which treats of those things is considered as a work of Garuḍa, a bird on which Nârâyaṇa rode. Some people describe this bird in such a way as to indicate a Ṣifrid-bird and its doings. It is an enemy of fish, catching them. As a rule, animals have by nature an aversion to their opponents, and try to beware of them; here, however, there is an exception to this rule. For when this bird flutters above the water and swims on it, the fish rise from the On the bird Garuḍa.

deep to the surface, and make it easy to him to catch them, as if he had bound them by his spell. Others describe it with such characteristics as might indicate a stork. The *Vâyu Purâṇa* attributes to it a pale colour. On the whole, Garuḍa comes nearer to a stork than to a Ṣifrid, as the stork is by nature, like Garuḍa, a destroyer of snakes.

The effect of charms on the bite of serpents.

Most of their charms are intended for those who have been bitten by serpents. Their excessive confidence in them is shown by this, which I heard a man say, that he had seen a dead man who had died from the bite of a serpent, but after the charm had been applied he had been restored to life, and remained alive, moving about like all others.

Another man I heard as he told the following story: "He had seen a man who had died from the bite of a serpent. A charm was applied, and in consequence he rose, spoke, made his will, showed where he had deposited his treasures, and gave all necessary information about them. But when he inhaled the smell of a dish, he fell down dead, life being completely extinct."

It is a Hindu custom that when a man has been bitten by a venomous serpent, and they have no charmer at hand, they bind the bitten man on a bundle of reeds, and place on him a leaf on which is written a blessing for that person who will accidentally light upon him, and save him by a charm from destruction.

I, for my part, do not know what I am to say about these things, since I do not believe in them. Once a man who had very little belief in reality, and much less in the tricks of jugglers, told me that he had been poisoned, and that people had sent him some Hindus possessing the knowledge of charms. They sang their charms before him, and this had a quieting effect upon him, and soon he felt that he became better and better, whilst they were drawing lines in the air with their hands and with twigs.

I myself have witnessed that in hunting gazelles they caught them with the hand. One Hindu even went so far as to assert that he, without catching the gazelle, would drive it before him and lead it straight into the kitchen. This, however, rests, as I believe I have found out, simply on the device of slowly and constantly accustoming the animals to one and the same melody. Our people, too, practise the same when hunting the ibex, which is more wild even than the gazelle. When they see the animals resting, they begin to walk round them in a circle, singing one and the same melody so long until the animals are accustomed to it. Then they make the circle more and more narrow, till at last they come near enough to shoot at the animals which lie there in perfect rest. Hunting practices.

The shooters of Kaṭâ-birds have a custom of beating copper-vessels during the night with one and the same kind of beat, and they manage to catch them with the hand. If, however, the beat is changed, the birds fly off in all directions.

All these things are peculiar customs which have nothing whatsoever to do with charms. Sometimes the Hindus are considered as sorcerers because of their playing with balls on raised beams or on tight ropes, but tricks of this kind are common to all nations. Page 96.

CHAPTER XVIII.

VARIOUS NOTES ON THEIR COUNTRY, THEIR RIVERS, AND THEIR OCEAN. ITINERARIES OF THE DISTANCES BETWEEN THEIR SEVERAL KINGDOMS, AND BETWEEN THE BOUNDARIES OF THEIR COUNTRY.

The inhabitable world and the ocean.

THE reader is to imagine the inhabitable world, ἡ οἰκουμένη, as lying in the northern half of the earth, and more accurately in one-half of this half—*i.e.* in one of the quarters of the earth. It is surrounded by a sea, which both in west and east is called *the comprehending one;* the Greeks call its western part near their country ὠκεανός. This sea separates the inhabitable world from whatever continents or inhabitable islands there may be beyond it, both towards west and east; for it is not navigable on account of the darkness of the air and the thickness of the water, because there is no more any road to be traced, and because the risk is enormous, whilst the profit is nothing. Therefore people of olden times have fixed marks both on the sea and its shores which are intended to deter from entering it.

The inhabitable world does not reach the north on account of the cold, except in certain places where it penetrates into the north in the shape, as it were, of tongues and bays. In the south it reaches as far as the coast of the ocean, which in west and east is connected with the *comprehending ocean.* This southern ocean is navigable. It does not form the utmost southern limit of the inhabitable world. On the contrary, the latter stretches still more southward in the shape of large and small islands which fill the ocean. In this southern region land and water dispute with each other their position, so that in one place the continent protrudes into the sea, whilst in another the sea penetrates deeply into the continent.

The continent protrudes far into the sea in the western half of the earth, and extends its shores far into the south. On the plains of this continent live the western negroes, whence the slaves are brought; and there are the Mountains of the Moon, and on them are the sources of the Nile. On its coast, and the islands before the coast, live the various tribes of the Zanj. There are several bays or gulfs which penetrate into the continent on this western half of the earth—the bay of Berberâ, that of Klysma (the Red Sea), and that of Persia (the Persian Gulf); and between these gulfs the western continent protrudes more or less into the ocean.

In the eastern half of the earth the sea penetrates as deeply into the northern continent as the continent in the western half protrudes into the southern sea, and in many places it has formed bays and estuaries which run far into the continent—bays being parts of the sea, estuaries being the outlets of rivers towards the sea. This sea is mostly called from some island in it or from the coast which borders it. Here, however, we are concerned only with that part of the sea which is bordered by the continent of India, and therefore is called the *Indian Ocean*.

The orographic system of Asia and Europe.

As to the orographic configuration of the inhabitable world, imagine a range of towering mountains like the vertebræ of a pine stretching through the middle latitude of the earth, and in longitude from east to west, passing through China, Tibet, the country of the Turks, Kâbul, Badhakhshân, Ṭokhâristân, Bâmiyân, Elghôr, Khurâsân, Media, Âdharbaijân, Armenia, the Roman

Empire, the country of the Franks, and of the Jalâlika (Gallicians). Long as this range is, it has also a considerable breadth, and, besides, many windings which enclose inhabited plains watered by streams which descend from the mountains both towards north and south. One of these plains is India, limited in the south by the above-mentioned Indian Ocean, and on

Page 97.

all three other sides by the lofty mountains, the waters of which flow down to it. But if you have seen the

India, a recent alluvial formation.

soil of India with your own eyes and meditate on its nature—if you consider the rounded stones found in the earth however deeply you dig, stones that are huge near the mountains and where the rivers have a violent current; stones that are of smaller size at greater distance from the mountains, and where the streams flow more slowly; stones that appear pulverised in the shape of sand where the streams begin to stagnate near their mouths and near the sea—if you consider all this, you could scarcely help thinking that India has once been a sea which by degrees has been filled up by the alluvium of the streams.

First orientation regarding Madhyadeśa, Kanoj, Mâhûra, and Tânêshar.

The middle of India is the country round Kanoj (Kanauj), which they call *Madhyadeśa, i.e.* the middle of the realms. It is the middle or centre from a geographical point of view, in so far as it lies half way between the sea and the mountains, in the midst between the hot and the cold provinces, and also between the eastern and western frontiers of India. But it is a political centre too, because in former times it was the residence of their most famous heroes and kings.

The country of Sindh lies to the west of Kanoj. In marching from our country to Sindh we start from the country of Nîmrôz, *i.e.* the country of Sijistân, whilst marching to *Hind* or India proper we start from the side of Kâbul. This, however, is not the only possible road. You may march into India from all sides, supposing that you can remove the obstacles in the way.

In the mountains which form the frontier of India towards the west there are tribes of the Hindus, or of people near akin to them—rebellious savage races—which extend as far as the farthermost frontiers of the Hindu race.

Kanoj lies to the west of the Ganges, a very large town, but most of it is now in ruins and desolate since the capital has been transferred thence to the city of Bârî, east of the Ganges. Between the two towns there is a distance of three to four days' marches.

As Kanoj (*Kanyâkubja*) has become famous by the children of Pâṇḍu, the city of Mâhûra (*Mathurâ*) has become famous by Vâsudeva. It lies east of the river Jaun (*Yamunâ*). The distance between Mâhûra and Kanoj is 28 *farsakh*.

Tânêshar (*Sthânêśvara*) lies between the two rivers to the north both of Kanoj and Mâhûra, at a distance of nearly 80 *farsakh* from Kanoj, and nearly 50 *farsakh* from Mâhûra.

The river Ganges rises in the mountains which have already been mentioned. Its source is called *Gaṅgâdvâra*. Most of the other rivers of the country also rise in the same mountains, as we have already mentioned in the proper place.

Hindu method of determining distances.

As for the distances between the various parts of India, those who have not themselves actually seen them must rely upon tradition; but unfortunately it is of such a nature that already Ptolemy incessantly complains of its transmitters and their bias towards story-telling. Fortunately I have found out a certain rule by which to control their lies. The Hindus frequently estimate the burden an ox could bear at 2000 and 3000 *manâ* (which is infinitely more than an ox could carry *at once*). In consequence they are compelled to let the caravan make the same march to and fro during many days—in fact, so long until the ox has carried the whole load assigned to it from one end of the route to the other, and then they reckon as the distance between the two places *a march of such a number of days* as the caravan has altogether spent in marching to and fro. It is only with the greatest exertion and caution that we can to some extent correct the statements of the Hindus. However, we could not make up our mind to suppress that which we know on account of that which we do not know. We ask the reader's pardon where there is anything wrong, and now we continue.

From Kanoj to the Tree of Prayâga (Allahabad) and to the eastern coast. Page 98.

A man marching from Kanoj to the south between the two rivers Jaun and Ganges passes the following well-known places:—*Jajjamau*, 12 *farsakh* from Kanoj, each *farsakh* being equal to four miles or one *kurôh; Abhâpûrî*, 8 *farsakh; Kuraha*, 8 *farsakh; Barhamshil*, 8 *farsakh;* the *Tree of Prayâga*, 12 *farsakh*, the place where the water of the Jaun joins the Ganges, where the Hindus torment themselves with various kinds of tortures, which are described in the books about religious sects. The distance from Prayâga to the place where the Ganges flows into the sea is 12 *farsakh* (*sic*).

Other tracts of country extend from the Tree of Prayâga southward towards the coast. *Arku-tîrtha*, 12 *farsakh* from Prayâga; the realm *Uwaryahâr*, 40 *farsakh; Ûrdabîshau* on the coast, 50 *farsakh*.

Thence along the coast towards the east there are countries which are now under the sway of *Jaur;* first *Daraur*, 40 *farsakh* from *Ûrdabîshau; Kânjî*, 30 *farsakh; Malaya*, 40 *farsakh; Kûnk*, 30 *farsakh*, which is the last of Jaur's possessions in this direction.

From Bârî to the mouth of the Ganges.

Marching from Bârî along the Ganges on its eastern side, you pass the following stations:—*Ajodaha* (Ayodhyâ, Oudh), 25 *farsakh* from Bârî; the famous *Banârasî*, 20 *farsakh*.

Thence changing the direction, and marching eastward instead of southward, you come to *Sharwâr*, 35 *farsakh* from Banârasî; *Pâṭaliputra*, 20 *farsakh; Mungîrî*, 15 *farsakh; Janpa*, 30 *farsakh; Dûgumpûr*,

50 *farsakh*; *Gangâsâyara*, 30 *farsakh*, where the Ganges flows into the sea.

Marching from Kanoj towards the east, you come to *Bârî*, 10 *farsakh*; *Dûgum*, 45 *farsakh*; the empire of *Shilahat*, 10 *farsakh*; the town *Bihat*, 12 *farsakh*. Farther on the country to the right is called *Tilwat*, the inhabitants *Tarû*, people of very black colour and flat-nosed like the Turks. Thence you come to the mountains of Kâmrû, which stretch away as far as the sea. Kanoj through Nepal to Bhôteshar.

Opposite Tilwat the country to the left is the realm of Naipâl. A man who had travelled in those countries gave me the following report:—"When in Tanwat, he left the easterly direction and turned to the left. He marched to Naipâl, a distance of 20 *farsakh*, most of which was ascending country. From Naipâl he came to Bhôteshar in thirty days, a distance of nearly 80 *farsakh*, in which there is more ascending than descending country. And there is a water which is several times crossed on bridges consisting of planks tied with cords to two canes, which stretch from rock to rock, and are fastened to milestones constructed on either side. People carry the burdens on their shoulders over such a bridge, whilst below, at a depth of 100 yards, the water foams as white as snow, threatening to shatter the rocks. On the other side of the bridges, the burdens are transported on the back of goats. My reporter told me that he had there seen gazelles with four eyes; that this was not an accidental misformation of nature, but that the whole species was of this nature.

"Bhôteshar is the first frontier of Tibet. There the language changes as well as the costumes and the anthropological character of the people. Thence the distance to the top of the highest peak is 20 *farsakh*. From the height of this mountain, India appears as a black expanse below the mist, the mountains lying below this peak like small hills, and Tibet and China appear as red. The descent towards Tibet and China is less than one *farsakh.*"

From Kanoj to Banavâs.

Marching from Kanoj towards the south-east, on the western side of the Ganges, you come to the realm of *Jajâhûti*, 30 *farsakh* from Kanoj. The capital of the country is *Kajûrâha.* Between this town and Kanoj there are two of the most famous fortresses of India, Gwâliyar (Gwalior) and Kâlanjar. *Dahâla* [—*farsakh*], a country the capital of which is Tiaurî, and the ruler of which is now Gangeya.

Page 99.

The realm of *Kannakara*, 20 *farsakh*. *Apsûr*, *Banavâs*, on the sea-coast.

From Kanoj to Bazâna.

Marching from Kanoj towards the south-west, you come to *Âsî*, 18 *farsakh* from Kanoj; *Sahanyâ*, 17 *farsakh; Jandrâ*, 18 *farsakh; Râjaurî*, 15 *farsakh; Bazâna*, the capital of Guzarat, 20 *farsakh*. This town is called *Nârâyan* by our people. After it had fallen into decay the inhabitants migrated to another place called Jadûra (?).

From Mâhûra to Dhâr.

The distance between Mâhûra and Kanoj is the same as that between Kanoj and Bazâna, viz. 28 *farsakh*. If a man travels from Mâhûra to Ûjain, he passes through villages which are only five *farsakh* and less distant from each other. At the end of a march of 35 *farsakh*, he comes to a large village called *Dûdahî;* thence to *Bâmahûr*, 17 *farsakh* from Dûdahi; *Bhâilsân*, 5 *farsakh*, a place most famous among the Hindus. The name of the town is identical with that of the idol worshipped there. Thence to *Ardîn*, 9 *farsakh*. The idol worshipped there is called *Mahakâla*. *Dhâr*, 7 *farsakh*.

From Bazâna to Mandagir.

Marching from Bazâna southward, you come to *Maiwâr*, 25 *farsakh* from Bazâna. This is a kingdom the capital of which is *Jattaraur*. From this town to Mâlavâ and its capital, *Dhâr*, the distance is 20 *farsakh*. The city of Ûjain lies 7 *farsakh* to the east of *Dhâr*.

From Ûjain to Bhâilasân, which likewise belongs to Mâlavâ, the distance is 10 *farsakh*.

Marching from Dhâr southward, you come to *Bhûmihara*, 20 *farsakh* from Dhâr; *Kand*, 20 *farsakh; Namâvur*, on the banks of the Narmadâ (Nerbudda), 10 *farsakh; Alîspûr*, 20 *farsakh; Mandagir*, on the banks of the river Gôdâvar, 60 *farsakh*.

From Dhâr to Tâna.

Again marching from Dhâr southward, you come to the valley of *Namiyya*, 7 *farsakh* from Dhâr; *Mahratta-Dêsh*, 18 *farsakh;* the province of *Kunkan*, and its capital, Tâna, on the sea-coast, 25 *farsakh*.

Notes about various animals of India.

People relate that in the plains of Kunkan, called *Dânak*, there lives an animal called *sharava* (Skr. *śarabha*). It has four feet, but also on the back it has something like four feet directed upwards. It has a small proboscis, but two big horns with which it attacks the elephant and cleaves it in two. It has the shape of a buffalo, but is larger than a *gaṇḍa* (rhinoceros). According to popular tales, it sometimes rams some animal with its horns, raises it or part of it towards its back, so that it comes to lie between its upper feet. There it becomes a putrid mass of worms, which work their way into the back of the animal. In consequence it continually rubs itself against the trees, and finally it perishes. Of the same animal people relate that sometimes, when hearing the thunder, it takes it to be the voice of some animal. Immediately it proceeds to attack this imaginary foe; in pursuing him it climbs up to the top of the mountain-peaks, and thence leaps towards him. Of course, it plunges into the depth and is dashed to pieces.

The *gaṇḍa* exists in large numbers in India, more particularly about the Ganges. It is of the build of a buffalo, has a black scaly skin, and dewlaps hanging down under the chin. It has three yellow hoofs on each foot, the biggest one forward, the others on both sides. The tail is not long; the eyes lie low, farther down the cheek than is the case with all other animals. On the top of the nose there is a single horn which is

Page 100. bent upwards. The Brahmins have the privilege of eating the flesh of the *gaṇḍa*. I have myself witnessed how an elephant coming across a young *gaṇḍa* was attacked by it. The *gaṇḍa* wounded with its horn a forefoot of the elephant, and threw it down on its face.

I thought that the *gaṇḍa* was the rhinoceros (or *karkadann*), but a man who had visited Sufâla, in the country of the Negroes, told me that the *kark*, which the Negroes call *impîlâ*, the horn of which furnishes the material for the handles of our knives, comes nearer this description than the rhinoceros. It has various colours. On the skull it has a conical horn, broad at the root, but not very high. The shaft of the horn (lit. its arrow) is black inside, and white everywhere else. On the front it has a second and longer horn of the same description, which becomes erect as soon as the animal wants to ram with it. It sharpens this horn against the rocks, so that it cuts and pierces. It has hoofs, and a hairy tail like the tail of an ass.

There are crocodiles in the rivers of India as in the Nile, a fact which led simple Aljâḥiz, in his ignorance of the courses of the rivers and the configuration of the ocean, to think that the river of Muhrân (the river Sindh) was a branch of the Nile. Besides, there are other marvellous animals in the rivers of India of the crocodile tribe, *makara*, curious kinds of fishes, and an animal like a leather-bag, which appears to the ships and plays in swimming. It is called *burlû* (porpoise ?). I suppose it to be the dolphin or a kind of dolphin. People say that it has a hole on the head for taking breath like the dolphin.

In the rivers of Southern India there is an animal called by various names, *grâha*, *jalatantu*, and *tandua*. It is thin, but very long. People say it spies and lies in wait for those who enter the water and stand in it, whether men or animals, and at once attacks them. First it circles round the prey at some distance, until its length comes to an end. Then it draws itself together, and winds itself like a knot round the feet of the prey, which is thus thrown off its legs and perishes. A man who had seen the animal told me that it has the head of a dog, and a tail to which there are attached many long tentacles, which it winds round the prey, in case the latter is not weary enough. By means of these feelers it drags the prey towards the tail itself, and when once firmly encircled by the tail the animal is lost.

After this digression we return to our subject.

Marching from Bazâna towards the south-west, you come to *Anhilvâra*, 60 *farsakh* from Bazâna; *Somanâth*, on the sea-coast, 50 *farsakh*. From Bazâna to Somanâth.

Marching from Anhilvâra southward, you come to *Lârdêsh*, to the two capitals of the country, *Bihrôj* and *Rihanjûr*, 42 *farsakh* from Anhilvâra. Both are on the sea-coast to the east of Tâna. From Anhilvâra to Loharânî.

Marching from Bazâna towards the west, you come to *Mûltân*, 50 *farsakh* from Bazâna; *Bhâtî*, 15 *farsakh*.

Marching from Bhâtî towards the south-west, you come to *Arôr*, 15 *farsakh* from Bhâtî, a township between two arms of the Sindh River; *Bamhanwâ Almanṣûra*, 20 *farsakh*; *Lôharânî*, at the mouth of the Sindh River, 30 *farsakh*.

Marching from Kanoj towards the north-north-west, you come to *Shirshâraha*, 50 *farsakh* from Kanoj; *Pinjaur*, 18 *farsakh*, situated on the mountains, whilst opposite it in the plain there lies the city of Tânêshar; *Dahmâla*, the capital of Jâlandhar, at the foot of the mountains, 18 *farsakh*; *Ballâwar*, 10 *farsakh*; thence marching westward, you come to *Ladda*, 13 *farsakh*; the fortress *Râjagirî*, 8 *farsakh*; thence marching northward, you come to *Kashmîr*, 25 *farsakh*. From Kanoj to Kashmîr.

Marching from Kanoj towards the west, you come to *Diyâmau*, 10 *farsakh* from Kanoj; *Kutî*, 10 *farsakh*; *Ânâr*, 10 *farsakh*; *Mîrat*, 10 *farsakh*; *Pânipat*, 10 From Kanoj to Ghazna. Page 101.

farsakh. Between the latter two places flows the river *Jaun*; *Kawtal,* 10 *farsakh*; *Sunnâm,* 10 *farsakh.*

Thence marching towards the north-west, you come to *Âdittahaur,* 9 *farsakh*; *Jajjanîr,* 6 *farsakh*; *Mandahûkûr,* the capital of Lauhâwur, east of the river Irâwa, 8 *farsakh*; the river *Candrâha,* 12 *farsakh*; the river *Jailam,* west of the river Biyatta, 8 *farsakh*; *Waihind,* the capital of Kandhâr, west of the river Sindh, 20 *farsakh*; *Purshâwar,* 14 *farsakh*; *Dunpûr,* 15 *farsakh*; *Kâbul,* 12 *farsakh*; *Ghazna,* 17 *farsakh.*

Notes about Kashmîr.

Kashmîr lies on a plateau surrounded by high inaccessible mountains. The south and east of the country belong to the Hindus, the west to various kings, the Bolar-Shâh and the Shugnân-Shâh, and the more remote parts up to the frontiers of Badhakhshân, to the Wakhân-Shâh. The north and part of the east of the country belong to the Turks of Khoten and Tibet. The distance from the peak of Bhôteshar to Kashmîr through Tibet amounts to nearly 300 *farsakh.*

The inhabitants of Kashmîr are pedestrians, they have no riding animals nor elephants. The noble among them ride in palankins called *katt,* carried on the shoulders of men. They are particularly anxious about the natural strength of their country, and therefore take always much care to keep a strong hold upon the entrances and roads leading into it. In consequence it is very difficult to have any commerce with them. In former times they used to allow one or two foreigners to enter their country, particularly Jews, but at present they do not allow any Hindu whom they do not know personally to enter, much less other people.

The best known entrance to Kashmîr is from the town Babrahân, half way between the rivers Sindh and Jailam. Thence to the bridge over the river, where the water of the Kusnârî is joined by that of the Mahwî, both of which come from the mountains of Shamîlân, and fall into the Jailam, the distance is 8 *farsakh.*

Thence you reach in five days the beginning of the ravine whence the river Jailam comes; at the other end of this ravine is the watch-station *Dvâr*, on both sides of the river Jailam. Thence, leaving the ravine, you enter the plain, and reach in two more days Addishtân, the capital of Kashmîr, passing on the road the village Ûshkârâ, which lies on both sides of the valley, in the same manner as Baramûlâ.

The city of Kashmîr covers a space of four *farsakh*, being built along both banks of the river Jailam, which are connected with each other by bridges and ferry-boats. The Jailam rises in the mountains Haramakôt, where also the Ganges rises, cold, impenetrable regions where the snow never melts nor disappears. Behind them there is *Mahâcîn*, *i.e.* Great China. When the Jailam has left the mountains, and has flowed two days' journey, it passes through Addishtân. Four *farsakh* farther on it enters a swamp of one square *farsakh*. The people have their plantations on the borders of this swamp, and on such parts of it as they manage to reclaim. Leaving this swamp, the Jailam passes the town Ûshkârâ, and then enters the above-mentioned ravine.

The upper course of the Sindh river and the north and north-west frontiers of India.

The river Sindh rises in the mountains Unang in the territory of the Turks, which you can reach in the following way:—Leaving the ravine by which you enter Kashmîr and entering the plateau, then you have for a march of two more days on your left the mountains of Bolor and Shamilân, Turkish tribes who are called *Bhattavaryân*. Their king has the title Bhatta-Shâh. Their towns are Gilgit, Aswira, and Shiltâs, and their language is the Turkish. Kashmîr suffers much from their inroads. Marching on the left side of the river, you always pass through cultivated ground and reach the capital; marching on the right side, you pass through villages, one close to the other, south of the capital, and thence you reach the mountain Kulârjak, Page 102.

which is like a cupola, similar to the mountain Dunbâwand. The snow there never melts. It is always visible from the region of Tâkeshar and Lauhâwar (Lahore). The distance between this peak and the plateau of Kashmîr is two *farsakh*. The fortress Râjâgirî lies south of it, and the fortress Lahûr west of it, the two strongest places I have ever seen. The town Râjâwarî is three *farsakh* distant from the peak. This is the farthest place to which our merchants trade, and beyond which they never pass.

This is the frontier of India from the north.

In the western frontier mountains of India there live various tribes of the Afghans, and extend up to the neighbourhood of the Sindh Valley.

The western and southern frontiers of India.

The southern frontier of India is formed by the ocean. The coast of India begins with Tîz, the capital of Makrân, and extends thence in a south-eastern direction towards the region of Al-daibal, over a distance of 40 *farsakh*. Between the two places lies the Gulf of Tûrân. A gulf is like an angle or a winding line of water penetrating from the ocean into the continent, and is dangerous for navigation, specially on account of ebb and flood. An estuary is something similar to a gulf, but is not formed by the ocean's penetrating into the continent. It is formed by an expanse of flowing water, which there is changed into standing water and is connected with the ocean. These estuaries, too, are dangerous for the ships, because the water is sweet and does not bear heavy bodies as well as salt water does.

After the above-mentioned gulf follow the small Munha, the great Munha, then the Bawârij, *i.e.* the pirates of Kacch and Sômanâth. They are thus called because they commit their robberies on sea in ships called *bîra*. The places on the coast are :—*Tawalleshar*, 50 *farsakh* from Daibal; *Lôharânî*, 12 *farsakh*; *Baga*, 12 *farsakh*; *Kacch*, where the *mukl*-tree grows, and *Bâroî*, 6 *farsakh*; *Sômanâth*, 14 *farsakh*; *Kanbâyat*,

30 *farsakh; Asawil*, 2 days; *Bihrôj*, 30 *farsakh* (?); *Sandân*, 50 *farsakh; Súbâra*, 6 *farsakh; Tâna*, 5 *farsakh*.

Thence the coast-line comes to the country *Lârân*, in which lies the city of *Jîmûr*, then to *Vallabha*, *Kânjî*, *Darvad*. Next follows a great bay in which *Singaldîb* lies, *i.e.* the island Sarandîb (Ceylon). Round the bay lies the city of *Panjayâvar* (*sic*). When this city had fallen into ruins, the king, Jaur, built instead of it, on the coast towards the west, a new city which he called *Padnâr*.

The next place on the coast is *Ûmmalnâra*, then *Râmsher* (Râmeshar?) opposite Sarandîb; the distance of the sea between them is 12 *farsakh*. The distance from Panjayâvar to Râmsher is 40 *farsakh*, that between Râmsher and *Setubandha* 2 *farsakh*. Setubandha means *bridge of the ocean*. It is the dike of Râma, the son of Daśaratha, which he built from the continent to the castle Lankâ. At present it consists of isolated mountains between which the ocean flows. Sixteen *farsakh* from Setubandha towards the east is *Kihkind*, the mountains of the monkeys. Every day the king of the monkeys comes out of the thicket together with his hosts, and settles down in particular seats prepared for them. The inhabitants of that region prepare for them cooked rice, and bring it to them on leaves. After having eaten it they return into the thicket, but in case they are neglected, this would be the ruin of the country, as they are not only numerous, but also savage and aggressive. According to the popular belief, they are a race of men changed into monkeys on account of the help which they had afforded to Râma when making war against the demons; he is believed to have bequeathed those villages to them as a legacy. When a man happens to fall in with them, and he recites to them the poetry of Râma and pronounces the incantations of Râma, they will quietly listen to him; they will even

lead on the right path him who has gone astray and give him meat and drink. At all events, thus the matter stands according to popular belief. If there is
Page 103. any truth in this, the effect must be produced by the melody, the like of which we have already mentioned in connection with the hunting of gazelles (v. p. 195).

Islands in the Indian and Chinese Seas.

The eastern islands in this ocean, which are nearer to China than to India, are the islands of the *Zâbaj*, called by the Hindus *Suvarṇa-dvîpa*, *i.e.* the gold islands. The western islands in this ocean are those of the Zanj (Negroes), and those in the middle are the islands *Ramm* and the Dîva islands (Malediva, Laccadiva), to which belong also the Ḳumair islands. It is peculiar to the Dîva islands that they rise slowly; first, there appears a sandy tract above the surface of the ocean; it rises more and more and extends in all directions, till at last it becomes a firm soil, whilst at the same time another island falls into decay and melts away, finally is submerged and disappears in the ocean. As soon as the inhabitants become aware of this process, they search for a new island of increasing fertility, transport there their cocoa-nut palms, date palms, cereals, and household goods, and emigrate to it. These islands are, according to their products, divided into two classes, the *Dîva-kûdha*, *i.e.* the Dîva of the kauri-shells, because there they gather kauri-shells from the branches of the cocoa-nut palms which they plant in the sea, and *Dîva-kanbâr*, *i.e.* the Dîva of the cords twisted from cocoa-nut fibres, and used for fastening together the planks of the ships.

The island of *Alwâḳwâḳ* belongs to the Ḳumair islands. *Ḳumair* is not, as common people believe, the name of a tree which produces screaming human heads instead of fruits, but the name of a people the colour of whom is whitish. They are of short stature and of a build like that of the Turks. They practise the religion of the Hindus, and have the custom of piercing their ears. Some of the inhabitants of the *Wâḳwâḳ* island are of black colour. In our countries there is a great demand for them as slaves. People fetch from thence the black ebony-wood; it is the pith of a tree, the other parts of which are thrown away, whilst the kinds of wood called *mulamma'* and *shauḥaṭ* and the yellow sandal-wood are brought from the country of the Zanj (Negroes).

In former times there were pearl-banks in the bay of Sarandîb (Ceylon), but at present they have been abandoned. Since the Sarandîb pearls have disappeared, other pearls have been found at Sufâla in the country of the Zanj, so that people say the pearls of Sarandîb have migrated to Sufâla.

India has the tropical rains in summer, which is called *varshakâla*, and these rains are the more copious and last the longer the more northward the situation of a province of India is, and the less it is intersected by ranges of mountains. The people of Mûltân used to tell me that they have no *varshakâla*, but the more northern provinces nearer the mountains have the *varshakâla*. In Bhâtal and Indravêdi it begins with the month Âshâḍha, and it rains continually for four months as though water-buckets were poured out. In provinces still farther northward, round the mountains of Kashmîr up to the peak of *Jûdarî* between Dunpûr and Barshâwar, copious rain falls during two and a half months, beginning with the month Śrâvaṇa. However, on the other side of this peak there is no rainfall; for the clouds in the north are very heavy, and do not rise much above the surface. When, then, they reach the mountains, the mountain-sides strike against them, and the clouds are pressed like olives or grapes, in consequence of which the rain pours down, and the clouds never pass beyond the mountains. Therefore Kashmîr has no *varshakâla*, but continual snowfall during two and a half months, beginning with Mâgha, and shortly

On the rainfall in India.

after the middle of Caitra continual rain sets in for a few days, melting the snow and cleansing the earth. This rule seldom has an exception; however, a certain amount of extraordinary meteorological occurrences is peculiar to every province of India.

CHAPTER XIX.

ON THE NAMES OF THE PLANETS, THE SIGNS OF THE ZODIAC, THE LUNAR STATIONS, AND RELATED SUBJECTS.

We have already mentioned, near the beginning of the book, that the language of the Hindus is extremely rich in nouns, both original and derivative, so that in some instances they call *one* thing by a multitude of different names. So I have heard them saying that they have a thousand names all meaning *sun*; and, no doubt, each planet has quite as many, or nearly as many names, since they could not do with less (for the purposes of versification). Page 104.

The names of the days of the week.

The names of the week-days are the best known names of the planets connected with the word *bâra*, which follows after the planet's name, as in Persian the word *shambih* follows after the number of the week-day (*dûshambih*, *sihshambih*, &c.). So they say—

Âditya bâra, *i.e.* Sunday.	*Bṛihaspati bâra*, *i.e.* Thursday.
Soma bâra, *i.e.* Monday.	*Śukra bâra*, *i.e.* Friday.
Maṅgala bâra, *i.e.* Tuesday.	*Śanaiścara bâra*, *i.e.* Saturday.
Budha bâra, *i.e.* Wednesday.	

And thus they go on counting, beginning anew with Sunday, Monday, &c.

On the *Domini dierum*.

Muslim astronomers call the planets the *lords of the days*, and, in counting the *hours* of the day, they begin with the *dominus* of the day, and then count the planets in the order from above to below. For instance, the sun is the *dominus* of the first day, and at the same time the *dominus* of its first hour. The second hour is ruled by the planet of the sphere next under the sphere of the sun, *i.e.* Venus. The third hour is ruled by Mercury, and the fourth by the moon. Therewith the descending from the sun to the *æther*, *i.e.* the atmosphere of the earth, has an end, and in counting they return to Saturn. According to this system, the *dominus* of the twenty-fifth hour is the moon, and this is the first hour of Monday. So the moon is not only the *dominus* of the first hour of Monday, but also the *dominus* of the whole day.

On ὧραι καιρικαί and ὧραι ἰσημεριναί.

In all this there is only one difference between our system and that of the Hindus, viz. that *we* use the ὧραι καιρικαί, so that the thirteenth planet, counted from the *dominus diei*, is the *dominus* of the succeeding night. This is the third planet if you count in an opposite direction, *i.e.* ascending from the lower planet-spheres to the higher. On the contrary, the Hindus make the *dominus diei* the *dominus* of the whole νυχθήμερον, so that day and night follow each other without having each a separate *dominus*. This, at all events, is the practice of the people at large.

Sometimes, however, their chronological methods make me think that the ὧραι καιρικαί were not entirely unknown to them. They call the hour *hora*, and by the same name they call the half of a zodiacal sign in the calculation of the *nímbahra*. The following calculation of the *dominus horæ* is derived from one of their astronomical handbooks:—

"Divide the distance between the sun and the degree of the *ascendens* measured by equal degrees, by 15, and add to the quotient 1, dropping a fraction if there be any. This sum is then counted off from the *dominus diei*, according to the succession of the planets from above to below." (The planet you arrive at in the end is the *dominus* of the hour in question.) This calculation is more of a nature to make us think of ὧραι καιρικαί as having been used, than of ὧραι ἰσημεριναί.

It is a custom of the Hindus to enumerate the planets in the order of the week-days. They will persist in using it in their astronomical handbooks, as well as in other books, and they decline to use any other order, though it be much more correct.

Order of the planets and their notation.

The Greeks mark the planets with figures, to fix thereby their limits on the *astrolabe* in an easily intelligible manner, images which are not letters of the alphabet. The Hindus use a similar system of abridgement; however, *their* figures are not images invented for the purpose, but the initial characters of the names of the planets, *e.g.* *â* = *Âditya*, or the sun; *c* = *Candra*, or the moon; *b* = *Budha*, or Mercury.

The following table exhibits the commonest names of the seven planets :—

Page 105.

The Planets.	Their Names in the Indian Language.
Sun . .	Âditya, sûrya, bhânu, arka, divâkara, ravi, bibatâ (?), heli.
Moon .	Soma, candra, indu, himagu, śîtaraśmi, himaraśmi, śîtâṁśu, śîtadidhiti, himamayûkha.
Mars . .	Maṅgala, bhaumya, kuja, âra, vakra, âvaneya, mâheya, krûrâkshi (?), rakta.
Mercury	Budha, saumya, cândra, jña, bodhana, vitta (?), hemna.
Jupiter .	Vṛihaspati, guru, jîva, devejya, devapurohita, devamantrin, aṅgiras, sûri, devapitâ.
Venus .	Śukra, bhṛigu, sita, bhârgava, âsbati (?), dânavaguru, bhṛiguputra, âsphujit (?).
Saturn .	Śanaiścara, manda, asita, koṇa, âdityaputra, saura, ârki, sûryaputra.

The multiplicity of *names* of the sun as exhibited in the previous table was the cause which led the theologians to assume also a multiplicity of *suns*, so

On the twelve suns.

that according to them there are twelve suns, each of which rises in a particular month. The book *Vishṇu-dharma* says: "Vishṇu, *i.e.* Nârâyaṇa, who is without beginning in time and without end, divided himself for the angels into twelve parts, which became sons to Kaśyapa. These are the suns rising in the single months." Those, however, who do not believe that the multiplicity of names is the source of this theory of twelve suns, point out that the other planets also have many names, but each only one body, and that, besides, the names of the sun are not only twelve, but many more. The names are derived from words with generic meanings, *e.g.* *Âditya, i.e. the beginning,* because the sun is the beginning of the whole. *Savitṛi* means every being which has a progeny, and since all progeny in the world originates with the sun, he is called *Savitṛi*. Further, the sun is called *Ravi*, because he dries wet substances. The juice in the plants is called *rasa*, and he who takes it out of them is called *ravi*.

Names of the moon. Page 106.

The moon too, the companion of the sun, has many names, *e.g.* *Soma*, because she is *lucky*, and everything lucky is called *somagraha*, whilst all that is unlucky is called *pâpagraha*. Further, *Niśeśa*, *i.e.* lord of the night, *Nakshatranâtha*, *i.e.* lord of the lunar stations, *Dvijeśvara*, *i.e.* lord of the Brahmins, *Śîtâṁśu*, *i.e.* having a cold ray, because the moon's globe is *watery*, which is a blessing to the earth. When the solar ray meets the moon, the ray becomes as cool as the moon herself, then, being reflected, it illuminates the darkness, makes the night cool and extinguishes any hurtful kind of combustion wrought by the sun. Similarly the moon is also called *Candra*, which means the *left eye of Nârâyaṇa*, as the sun is his right eye.

The names of the months.

The following table exhibits the names of the months Disturbances and differences in lists of these names proceed from the causes which we shall mention (v. p. 228) when speaking of the enumeration of the different earths.

The Months.	Their Suns according to the *Vishṇu-dharma*.	The Meaning of these Names according to the *Vishṇu-dharma*.	The Suns according to the *Âditya-purana*.	Vernacular Names.
Caitra	Vishṇu	Moving about in heaven, not resting	Aṁśumant	Ravi.
Vaiśâkha	Aryaman	Punishing and beating the rebels. In consequence they do not oppose him, from fear	Savitṛi	Vishṇu.
Jyaishṭha	Vivasvant	He looks at the whole in general, not in detail	Bhânu	Dhâtṛi.
Âshâḍha	Aṁśu	Having rays	Vivasvant	Vidhâtṛi.
Śrâvaṇa	Parjanya	Affording help like the rain	Vishṇu	Aryaman.
Bhâdrapada	Varuṇa	He prepares the whole	Indra	Bhaga.
Âśvayuja	Indra	Companion and lord	Dhâtṛi	Savitṛi.
Kârttika	Dhâtṛi	He gives benefits to men and rules them	Bhaga	Pûshan.
Mârgaśîrsha	Mitra	Beloved by the world	Pûshan	Tvashṭṛi.
Pausha	Pûshan	Nourishment, for he nourishes men	Mitra	Arka.
Mâgha	Bhaga	Lovely, desired by the universe	Varuṇa	Divâkara.
Phâlguna	Tvashṭṛi	He provides the whole with good	Aryaman	Aṁśu.

Page 107.

The names of the months derived from those of the lunar mansions.

People think, with regard to the order of the names of suns as given by the *Vishṇu-dharma*, that it is correct and undisturbed; for Vâsudeva has a separate name in each month, and his worshippers begin the months with Mârgaśîrsha, in which his name is *Keśava*. If you count his names one after the other, you find that one which he has in the month Caitra, Vishṇu, in accordance with the tradition of the *Vishṇu-dharma*.

The names of the months are related to those of the lunar stations. As two or three stations belong to each month, the name of the month is derived from one of them. We have in the following table written these particular stations with red ink (in this translation with an asterisk), in order to point out their relationship with the names of the months.

If Jupiter shines in some lunar station, the month to which this station belongs is considered as *the dominant of the year*, and the whole year is called by the name of this month.

If the names of the month given in the following table differ in some respects from those used heretofore, the reader must know that the names which we have hitherto used are the vernacular or vulgar ones, whilst those given in this table are the classical:—

The Months.		The Lunar Stations.	The Months.		The Lunar Stations.
Kârttika	3	Kṛittikâ.*	Vaiśâkha	16	Viśâkhâ.*
	4	Rohiṇî.		17	Anurâdhâ.
Mârgaśîrsha	5	Mṛigaśîrsha.*	Jyaishṭha	18	Jyeshṭhâ.*
	6	Ârdrâ.		19	Mûla.
Pausha	7	Punarvasu.	Âshâḍha	20	Pûrvâshâḍhâ.*
	8	Pushya.*		21	Uttarâshâḍhâ.
Mâgha	9	Âślêsha.	S'râvaṇa	22	S'ravaṇa.*
	10	Maghâ.*		23	Dhanishta.
Phâlguna	11	Pûrva-phalgunî.*	Bhâdrapadâ	24	S'atabhishaj.
	12	Uttara-phalgunî.		25	Pûrva-bhadrapadâ.*
	13	Hasta.		26	Uttara-bhâdrapadâ.
Caitra	14	Citrâ.*	Âśvayuja	27	Revatî.
	15	Svâtî.		1	Aśvinî.*
				2	Bharaṇî.

The signs of the zodiac have names corresponding to the images which they represent, and which are the same among the Hindus as among all other nations. The third sign is called *Mithuna*, which means a pair consisting of a boy and a girl; in fact, the same as *the Twins*, the well-known image of this sign. On the names of the signs of the Zodiac. Page 108.

Varâhamihira says in the larger book of nativities that the word applies to a man holding a lyre and a club, which makes me think that he identified Mithuna with Orion (*Aljabbâr*). And this is the opinion of common people in general, to such a degree that the station is known as *Aljauzâ* (instead of *the Twins*), though Aljauzâ does not belong to the image of this sign.

The same author explains the image of the sixth sign as *a ship, and in its hand an ear of corn.* I am inclined to think that in our manuscript there is a lacuna in this place, for *a ship* has no *hand.* The Hindus call this sign *Kanyâ*, *i.e.* the virgin girl, and perhaps the passage in question ran originally thus: "*A virgin in a ship holding an ear of corn in her hand.*" This is the lunar station *Alsimâk Al'a'zal* (*Spica*). The word *ship* makes one think that the author meant the lunar station *Al'awwâ* (β, η, γ, δ, ϵ, Virginis), for the stars of Al'awwâ form a line, the end of which is a curve (like the keel of a ship).

The image of the seventh sign he declares to be *fire.* It is called *Tulâ* = balance.

Of the tenth sign Varâhamihira says that it has the face of a goat, whilst the remainder is a *makara* (hippopotamus). However, after having compared the sign with a *makara*, he might have saved himself the trouble of attributing to it the face of a goat. Only the Greeks require the latter description, because they consider the sign as composed of two animals, as a goat in the part above the breast and as a fish in the lower part. But the aquatic animal called *makara*, as people describe it, does not require to be explained as a composition of two animals.

The image of the eleventh sign he calls a bucket, and the name, *Kumbha*, corresponds to this statement. However, if they sometimes enumerate this sign or part of it among *the human figures*, this proves that they, following the example of the Greeks, see in it *Aquarius*.

The image of the twelfth sign he describes as the figure of two fishes, although the name of the sign in all languages signifies only one fish.

Besides the well-known names, Varâhamihira mentions also certain Indian names of the signs which are not generally known. We have united both kinds in the following table :—

The Zodiacal Signs.	Their Common Names.	Names which are not generally known.	The Zodiacal Signs.	Their Common Names.	Names which are not generally known.
0	Mesha.	Kriya.	6	Tulâ.	Jûga.
1	Vṛishan.	Tâmbiru.	7	Vṛiścika.	Kaurba.
2	Mithuna.	Jituma.	8	Dhanu.	Taukshika.
3	Karkaṭa.	Kulîra.	9	Makara.	Agokîru.
4	Siṁha.	Liyaya.	10	Kumbah.	Udruvaga.
5	Kanyâ.	Pârtîna.	11	Mîna.	Anta, *also* Jîtu.

It is the custom of the Hindus in enumerating the zodiacal signs not to begin with 0 for *Aries* and 1 for *Taurus*, but to begin with 1 for *Aries* and 2 for *Taurus*, &c., so that *Pisces* are No. 12.

CHAPTER XX.

ON THE BRAHMÂṆḌA.

The egg of Brahman, its coming forth from the water

Page 109.

BRAHMÂṆḌA means *the egg of Brahman*, and applies in reality to the whole of heaven (αἰθήρ), on account of its being round, and of the particular kind of its motion. It applies even to the whole world, in so far as it is divided into an upper and an under part. When they enumerate the heavens, they call the sum of them Brahmâṇḍa. The Hindus, however, are devoid of training in astronomy, and have no correct astronomical notions. In consequence, they believe that the earth is at rest, more particularly as they, when describing the bliss of paradise as something like worldly happiness, make the earth the dwelling-place of the different classes of gods, angels, &c., to whom they attribute locomotion and the direction from the upper worlds to the lower.

According to the enigmatic expressions of their tradition, the water was before every other thing, and it filled the space of the whole world. This was, as I understand them, at the beginning of the day of the soul (*purushâhorâtra*, p. 332), and the beginning of formation and combination. Further, they say the water was rolling and foaming. Then something white came forth from the water, of which the Creator created the egg of Brahman. Now, according to some, the egg broke; Brahman came forth from it, the one half became the heaven, the other the earth, and the broken bits between the two halves became the rains. If they said *moun-*

tains instead of *rains*, the matter would be somewhat more plausible. According to others, God spoke to Brahman: "I create an egg, which I make for thy dwelling in it." He had created it of the above mentioned foam of the water, but when the water sank and was absorbed, the egg broke into two halves.

Greek parallel: Asclepius.

Similar opinions were held by the ancient Greeks regarding Asclepius, the inventor of the medical art; for, according to Galenus, they represent him as holding an egg in his hand, whereby they mean to indicate that the world is round, the egg an image of the universe, and that the whole world needs the medical art. Asclepius does not hold a lower position in the belief of the Greeks than Brahman in the belief of the Hindus, for they say that he is a divine power, and that his name is derived from his action, *i.e.* protecting against dryness, which means death, because death occurs when dryness and cold are prevalent. As for his natural origin, they call him the son of Apollo, the son of Phlegyas (?), and the son of Kronos, *i.e.* the planet Saturn. By this system of affiliation they mean to attribute to him the force of a threefold god.

Water the first element of creation. The egg of Brahman broken in two halves.

The theory of the Hindus, that the water existed before all creation, rests on this, that it is the cause of the cohesion of the atoms of everything, the cause of the growing of everything, and of the duration of life in every animated being. Thus the water is an instrument in the hand of the Creator when he wants to create something out of matter. A similar idea is propounded by the Koran xi. 9: "And his (God's) *throne was on the water.*" Whether you explain it in an external way as an individual body called by this name, and which God orders us to venerate, or whether you give it the intrinsic meaning of *realm*, *i.e.* God's realm, or the like, in any case the meaning is this, that at that time beside God there was nothing but the water and his throne. If this our book were not restricted to the ideas of one single nation, we should produce from the belief of the nations who lived in ancient times in and round Babel ideas similar to the egg of Brahman, and even more stupid and unmeaning than that.

The theory of the division of the egg into two halves proves that its originator was the contrary of a scientific man, one who did not know that the heaven comprehends the earth, as the shell of the egg of Brahman comprehends its yolk. He imagined the earth to be below and the heaven in only one of the six directions from the earth, *i.e.* above it. If he had known the truth, he might have spared himself the theory of the breaking of the egg. However, he wished by his theory to describe one half of the egg as spread out for the earth, and the other half as placed upon it for a cupola, trying to outvie Ptolemy in the planispheric representation of a globe, but without success. **Page 110.**

Quotation from Plato's *Timæus*.

There have always been similar fancies afloat, which everybody interprets as best suits his religion and philosophy. So Plato says in his *Timæus* something like the Brahmâṇḍa: "The Creator cut a straight thread into halves. With each of them he described a circle, so that the two circles met in two places, and one of them he divided into seven parts." In these words he hints, as is his custom, at the original two motions of the universe (from east to west in the diurnal rotation, and from west to east in the precession of the equinoxes), and at the globes of the planets.

Quotation from Brahmagupta.

Brahmagupta says in the first chapter of the *Brahmasiddhânta*, where he enumerates the heavens, placing the moon in the nearest heaven, the other planets in the following ones, and Saturn in the seventh: "The fixed stars are in the eighth heaven, and this has been created round in order to last for ever, that in it the pious may be rewarded, the wicked be punished, since there is nothing behind it." He indicates in this chapter that the heavens are identical with the spheres, and he gives them in an order which differs from that of the traditional literature of their creed, as we shall show hereafter in the proper place. He indicates, too, that the *round* can only be slowly influenced from without. He evinces his knowledge of the Aristotelic notions regarding the round form and the rotating motion, and that there is no body in existence behind the spheres.

If it is of this description, evidently Brahmâṇḍa is the totality of the spheres, *i.e.* the *αἰθήρ*, in fact, the universe, for retribution in another life takes place, according to the ideas of the Hindus, within it.

Quotation from the *Siddhânta* of Pulisa.

Pulisa says in his *Siddhânta*: "The totality of the world is the sum of earth, water, fire, wind, and heaven. The latter was created behind the darkness. It appears to the eyes as blue, because it is not reached by the rays of the sun and not illuminated by them like the watery non-igneous globes, *i.e.* the bodies of the planet and the moon. When the rays of the sun fall upon these and the shadow of the earth does not reach them, their darkness disappears and their figures become visible in the night. The light-giver is only one, all the others receive the light from him." In this chapter Pulisa speaks of the utmost limit that can be reached, and calls it *heaven*. He places it *in darkness*, since he says that it exists in a place which is not reached by the rays of the sun. The question as to the blue-grey colour of heaven which is perceived by the eye is of too great an extent to be touched upon here.

Quotations from Brahmagupta, Vasishtha, Balabhadra, and Aryabhaṭa.

Brahmagupta says in the above-mentioned chapter: "Multiply the cycles of the moon, *i.e.* 57,753,300,000, by the number of the *yojana* of her sphere, *i.e.* 324,000, and you get as the product 18,712,069,200,000,000, *i.e.* the number of the *yojana* of the sphere of the zodiac." Of the *yojana* as a measure of distance we have already spoken in the chapter on metrology (ch. xv. p. 167). We give the just-mentioned calculation of Brahmagupta, simply reproducing his words without any responsibility of our own, for he has not explained on what reason it rests. Vasishṭha says that the Brahmâṇḍa comprehends the spheres, and the just-mentioned numbers are the measure of the Brahmâṇḍa, since the sphere of the zodiac is connected with it. The commentor Balabhadra says: "We do not consider these numbers as a measure of heaven, for we cannot define its greatness, but we consider them as the utmost limit to which the human power of vision can penetrate. There is no possibility of human perception reaching above it; but the other spheres differ from each other in greatness and smallness, so as to be visible in various degrees." The followers of Âryabhaṭa say: "It is sufficient for us to know the space which is reached by the solar rays. We do not want the space which is not reached by the solar rays, though it be in itself of an enormous extent. That which is not reached by the rays is not reached by the perception of the senses, and that which is not reached by perception is not knowable." Page 111.

Criticisms on the different theories. The question of the ninth sphere.

Let us now examine the bearing of the words of these authors. The words of Vasishṭha prove that the Brahmâṇḍa is a globe comprehending the eighth or so called zodiacal sphere, in which the fixed stars are placed, and that the two spheres touch each other. Now we on our own part were already obliged to assume an eighth sphere, but there is no reason why we should suppose a ninth one.

On this head the opinions of people are divided. Some hold the existence of a ninth sphere to be a necessity on account of the rotation from east to west, in so far as it moves in this direction and compels everything which it comprehends to move in the same direction. Others assume the ninth sphere on account of the same motion, but suppose that it by itself is motionless.

The tendency of the representatives of the former theory is perfectly clear. However, Aristotle has proved that each moving body is brought into motion by something moving which is not within itself. So also this ninth sphere would presuppose a *mover* outside itself. What, however, should prevent this *mover* from putting the eight spheres into motion without the intermediation of a ninth sphere?

Aristotle, Ptolemy, Johannes Grammaticus.

As regards the representatives of the second view, one might almost think that they had a knowledge of the words of Aristotle which we have quoted, and that they knew that the first mover is motionless, for they represent the ninth sphere as motionless and as the source of the east to west rotation. However, Aristotle has also proved that the first mover is not a body, whilst he must be a body, if they describe him as a globe, as a sphere, and as comprehending something else within itself and motionless.

Thus the theory of the ninth sphere is proved to be an impossibility. To the same effect are the words of Ptolemy in the preface of his *Almagest:* "The first cause of the first motion of the universe, if we consider the motion by itself, is according to our opinion an invisible and motionless god, and the study of this subject we call *a divine one.* We perceive his action in the highest heights of the world, but as an altogether different one from the action of those substances which can be perceived by the senses."

These are the words of Ptolemy on the first *mover*, without any indication of the ninth sphere. But the latter is mentioned by Johannes Grammaticus in his refutation of Proclus, where he says: "Plato did not know a ninth, starless sphere." And, according to Johannes, it was this, *i.e.* the negation of the ninth sphere, which Ptolemy meant to say.

Finally, there are other people who maintain that behind the last limit of motion there is an infinite resting body or an infinite *vacuum*, or something which they declare to be neither a *vacuum* nor a *plenum*. These theories, however, have no connection whatsoever with our subject.

Balabhadra gives us the impression of holding the same opinion as those who think that heaven or the heavens are a compact body holding in equilibrium all heavy bodies and carrying them, and that it is above the spheres. To Balabhadra it is just as easy to prefer tradition to eyesight, as it is difficult to us to prefer doubt to a clear proof.

The truth is entirely with the followers of Âryabhaṭa who give us the impression of really being men of great scientific attainments. It is perfectly evident that Brahmâṇḍa means the *αἰθήρ*, together with all products of creation in it.

CHAPTER XXI.

DESCRIPTION OF EARTH AND HEAVEN ACCORDING TO THE RELIGIOUS VIEWS OF THE HINDUS, BASED UPON THEIR TRADITIONAL LITERATURE.

On the seven earths. Page 112.

THE people of whom we have spoken in the preceding chapter think that the earths are seven like seven covers one above the other, and the upper one they divide into seven parts, differing from our astronomers, who divide it into *κλίματα*, and from the Persians, who divide it into *Kishvar*. We shall afterwards give a clear explanation of their theories derived from the first authorities of their religious law, to expose the matter to fair criticism. If something in it appears strange to us, so as to require a commentary, or if we perceive some coincidence with others, even if both parties missed the mark, we shall simply put the case before the reader, not with the intention of attacking or reviling the Hindus, but solely in order to sharpen the minds of those who study these theories.

Differences in the sequence of the earths explained as resulting from the copiousness of the language

They do not differ among themselves as to the number of earths nor as to the number of the parts of the upper earth, but they differ regarding their names and the order of these names. I am inclined to derive this difference from the great verbosity of their language, for they call one and the same thing by a multitude of names. For instance, they call the sun by a thousand different names according to their own statement, just as the Arabs call the lion by nearly as many. Some of these names are original, while others are derived from the changing conditions of his life or his actions and faculties. The Hindus and their like boast of this copiousness, whilst in reality it is one of the greatest faults of the language. For it is the task of language to give a name to everything in creation and to its effects, a name based on general consent, so that everybody, when hearing this name pronounced by another man, understands what he means. If therefore one and the same name or word means a variety of things, it betrays a defect of the language and compels the hearer to ask the speaker what he means by the word. And thus the word in question must be dropped in order to be replaced either by a similar one of a sufficiently clear meaning, or by an epithet describing what is really meant. If one and the same thing is called by many names, and this is not occasioned by the fact that every tribe or class of people uses a separate one of them, and if, in fact, one single name would be sufficient, all the other names save this one are to be classified as mere nonsense, as a means of keeping people in the dark, and throwing an air of mystery about the subject. And in any case this copiousness offers painful difficulties to those who want to learn the whole of the language, for it is entirely useless, and only results in a sheer waste of time.

Frequently it has crossed my mind that the authors of books and the transmitters of tradition have an aversion to mentioning the earths in a definite arrangement, and limit themselves to mentioning their names, or that the copyists of the books have arbitrarily altered the text. For those men who explained and translated the text to me were well versed in the language, and were not known as persons who would commit a wanton fraud.

The earths according to the *Âditya-Purâṇa*.

The following table exhibits the names of the earths, as far as I know them. We rely chiefly on that list, which has been taken from the *Âditya-purâṇa*, because it follows a certain rule, combining every single earth and heaven with a single member of the members of the sun. The heavens are combined with the members from the skull to the womb, the earths with the members from the navel to the foot. This mode of comparison illustrates their sequence and preserves it from confusion :—

Page 113.

The Number of the Earths.	*Âditya-Purâṇa.* What Members of the Sun they Represent.	*Âditya-Purâṇa.* Their Names.	*Vishṇu-Purâṇa.*	*Vâyu-Purâṇa.* Their Names.	*Vâyu-Purâṇa.* Their Epithets.	Vernacular Names.
I.	The navel.	Tâla.	Atala.	Abhâstala.	Kṛishṇa-bhûmi. the dark earth.	Amśu (?)
II.	The thighs.	Sutâla.	Vitala.	Ilâ (?)	S'ukla-bhûmi, the bright earth.	Ambaratâla.
III.	The knees.	Pâtâla.	Nitala.	Nitala.	Rakta-bhûmi, the red earth.	S'arkara (?) (Sakkaru).
IV.	Under the knees.	Âśâla (?)	Gabhastimat.	Gabhastala.	Pîta-bhûmi, the yellow earth.	Gabhastimat.
V.	The calves.	Viśâla (?)	Mahâkhya (?)	Mahâtala.	Pâshâṇa-bhûmi, the earth of marble.	Mahâtala.
VI.	The ankles.	Mṛittâla.	Sutala.	Sutala.	S'ilâtala, the earth of brick.	Sutâla.
VII.	The feet.	Rasâtala.	Jâgara (?)	Pâtâla.	Suvarṇa-varṇa, the gold-coloured earth.	Rasâtala.

THE SPIRITUAL BEINGS LIVING ON THE SEVEN EARTHS ACCORDING TO THE VÂYU-PURÂṆA.

Page 114.

Of the Dânavas—Namuci, Śaṅkukarṇa, Kabandha (?), Nishkukâda (?), Śûladanta, Lohita, Kaliṅga, Śvâpada; and the master of the serpents—Dhanañjaya, Kâliya.

Of the Daityas—Surakshas, Mahâjambha, Hayagrîva, Kṛishṇa, Janarta (?), Śaṅkhâkhsha, Gomukha; and of the Râkshasa—Nîla, Megha, Krathanaka, Mahoshṇîsha, Kambala, Aśvatara, Takshaka.

Of the Dânavas—Rada (?), Anuhlâda, Agnimukha, Târakâksha, Triśira, Śiśumâra; and of the Râkshasa—Cyavana, Nanda, Viśâla. And there are many cities in this world.

Of the Daityas—Kâlanemi, Gajakarṇa, Uñjara (?); and of the Râkshasa—Sumâli, Muñja, Vṛikavaktra, and the large birds called Garuḍa.

Of the Daityas—Virocana, Jayanta (?), Agnijihva, Hiraṇyâksha; and of the Râkshasa—Vidyujjihva, Mahâmegha; the serpent Karmâra, Svastikajaya.

Of the Daityas—Kesari; and of the Râkshasa—Ûrdhvakuja (?), Śataśîrsha, *i.e.* having a hundred heads, a friend of Indra; Vâsuki, a serpent.

The king Bali; and of the Daitya Mucukunda. In this world there are many houses for the Râkshasa, and Vishṇu resides there, and Śesha, the master of the serpents.

On the seven heavens. Quotations from Johannes Grammaticus, Plato, and Aristotle.

After the earths follow the heavens, consisting of seven stories, one above the other. They are called *loka*, which means "*gathering-place.*" In a similar manner also the Greeks considered the heavens as gathering-places. So Johannes Grammaticus says in his refutation of Proclus: "Some philosophers thought that the sphere called γαλαξίας, i.e. *milk*, by which they mean the milky way, is a dwelling-place for rational souls." The poet Homer says: "Thou hast made the pure heaven an eternal dwelling-place for the gods. The winds do not shake it, the rains do not wet it, and the snow does not destroy it. For in it there is resplendent clearness without any covering cloud."

Plato says: "God spoke to the seven planets: You are the gods of the gods, and I am the father of the actions; I am he who made you so that no dissolution

Page 115. is possible; for anything bound, though capable of being loosened, is not exposed to destruction, as long as its order is good."

Aristotle says in his letter to Alexander: "The world is the order of the whole creation. That which is above the world, and surrounds it on the sides, is the dwelling-place of the gods. Heaven is full of the gods to which we give the name of stars." In another place of the same book he says, "The earth is bounded by the water, the water by the air, the air by the fire, the fire by the αἰθήρ. Therefore the highest place is the dwelling-place of the gods, and the lowest, the home of the aquatic animals."

There is a similar passage in the *Vâyu-Purâṇa* to this effect, that the earth is held in its grasp by the water, the water by the pure fire, the fire by the wind, the wind by heaven, and heaven by its lord.

The names of the *lokas* do not differ like those of the earths. There is a difference of opinion only regarding their order. We exhibit the names of the *lokas* in a table similar to the former (p. 230).

The Number of the Heavens.	What members of the Sun they represent according to the *Âditya-Purâṇa*.	Their Names according to the *Âditya*, *Vâyu* and *Vishṇu Purâṇas*.
I.	The stomach.	Bhûrloka.
II.	The breast.	Bhuvarloka.
III.	The mouth.	Svarloka.
IV.	The eyebrow.	Maharloka.
V.	The forehead.	Janaloka.
VI.	Above the forehead.	Tapoloka.
VII.	The skull.	Satyaloka.

Criticisms on the commentator of Patañjali. Page 116. This theory of the earths is the same with all Hindus, except alone the commentator of the book of Patañjali. He had heard that the *Pitaras*, or *fathers*, had their gathering-place in the sphere of the moon, a tradition built on the theories of the astronomers. In consequence he made the lunar sphere the first heaven, whilst he ought to have identified it with *Bhûrloka*. And because by this method he had one heaven too many, he dropped the *Svarloka*, the place of reward.

The same author differs besides in another point. As the seventh heaven, Satyaloka, is in the Purâṇas also called *Brahmaloka*, he placed the Brahmaloka above the Satyaloka, whilst it would have been much more reasonable to think that in this case one and the same thing is called by two different names. He ought to have omitted the Brahmaloka, to have identified Pitṛiloka with Bhûrloka, and not to have left out the Svarloka.

So much about the seven earths and the seven heavens. We shall now speak of the division of the surface of the uppermost earth and of related subjects.

Dîp (*dvîpa*) is the Indian word for *island*. Hence the words *Sangaladîp* (Siṃhaladvîpa), which we call Serendib, and the *Dîbajât* (Maledives, Laccadives). The latter are numerous islands, which become, so to speak, decrepit, are dissolved and flattened, and finally disappear below the water, whilst at the same time other formations of the same kind begin to appear above the water like a streak of sand which continually grows and rises and extends. The inhabitants of the former island leave their homes, settle on the new one and colonise it. The system of Dvîpas and *seas*.

According to the religious traditions of the Hindus, the earth on which we live is round and surrounded by a sea. On the sea lies an earth like a collar, and on this earth lies again a round sea like a collar. The number of dry collars, called *islands*, is seven, and likewise that of the seas. The size of both *dvîpas* and seas rises in such a progression that each *dvîpa* is the double of the preceding *dvîpa*, each sea the double of the preceding sea, *i.e.* in the progression of the powers of two. If the middle earth is reckoned as one, the size of all seven earths represented as collars is 127. If the sea surrounding the middle earth is counted as one, the size of all seven seas represented as collars is 127. The total size of both earths and seas is 254.

The size of the Dvîpas and seas, according to the commentator of Patañjali and the *Vâyu-Purâṇa.*

The commentator of the book of Patañjali has adopted as the size of the middle earth 100,000 *yojana.* Accordingly, the size of all the earths would be 12,700,000 *yojana.* Further he adopts as the size of the sea which surrounds the middle earth 200,000 *yojana.* Accordingly, the size of all the seas would be 25,400,000 *yojana,* and the total size of all the earths and seas 38,100,000 *yojana.* However, the author himself has not made these additions. Therefore we cannot compare his numbers with ours. But the *Vâyu-Purâṇa* says that the diameter of the totality of earths and seas is 37,900,000 *yojana,* a number which does not agree with the above-mentioned sum of 38,100,000 *yojana.* It cannot be accounted for, unless we suppose that the number of earths is only six, and that the progression begins with the number 4 instead of 2. Such a number of seas (*i.e.* 6) may possibly be explained in this way, that the seventh one has been dropped, because the author only wanted to find the size of the continents, which induced him to leave the last surrounding sea out of the calculation. But if he once mentions the continents he must also mention all the seas which surround them. Why he has commenced the progression with 4 instead of 2, I cannot account for by any of the principles of the calculation as they have been laid down.

Each *dvîpa* and sea has a separate name. As far as we know them, we place them before the reader in the following table, and hope that the reader will excuse us for so doing.

The number of the Dvîpas and Seas.	Matsya-Purâṇa.		The Commentator of Patañjali—Vishṇu-Purâṇa.		Vernacular Names.	
	Dvîpas.	Seas.	Dvîpas.	Seas.	Dvîpas.	Seas.
I.	Jambu-dvîpa.	Lavaṇa, *i.e.* salt.	Jambu, the name of a tree.	Kshâra, *i.e.* salt.	Jambu.	Lavaṇa-samudra.
II.	Śâka-dvîpa.	Kshîrodaka, *i.e.* milk.	Plaksha, the name of a tree.	Ikshu, *i.e.* sugar-cane.	Śâka.	Ikshu.
III.	Kuśa-dvîpa.	Ghṛitamaṇḍa, *i.e.* butter.	Śâlmali, the name of a tree.	Surâ, *i.e.* wine.	Kuśa.	Surâ.
IV.	Krauñca-dvîpa	Dadhimaṇḍa, *i.e.* thick milk.	Kuśa, the name of a plant.	Sarpis, *i.e.* butter.	Krauñca.	Sarpis.
V.	Śâlmali-dvîpa.	Surâ, *i.e.* rice-wine.	Krauñca, the hosts.	Dadhi, *i.e.* sour-milk.	Śâlmali.	Dadhisâgara.
VI.	Gomeda-dvîpa	Ikshurasoda, *i.e.* the juice of sugar-cane.	Śâka, the name of a tree.	Kshîra, *i.e.* milk.	Gomeda.	Kshîra.
VII.	Pushkara-dvîpa.	Svâdûdaka, *i.e.* sweet water.	Pushkara, the name of a tree.	Svâdûdaka, *i.e.* sweet water.	Pushkara.	Pânîya.

Page 117.

Page 118. The differences of the traditions as exhibited by this table cannot be accounted for in any rational way. They can hardly have sprung from any other source but from arbitrary, accidental changes of the enumeration. The most appropriate of these traditions is that of the *Matsya-Purâṇa*, because it enumerates the dvîpas and seas one after the other according to a fixed order, a sea surrounding an island, an island surrounding a sea, the enumeration proceeding from the centre to the periphery.

We shall now in this place record some related subjects, though it would perhaps be more correct to treat of them in some other part of the book.

Quotation from the commentator of Patañjali.

The commentator of the book of Patañjali, wishing to determine the dimension of the world, begins from below and says: "The dimension of the *darkness* is one *koṭi* and 85 *laksha* yojana, *i.e.* 18,000,000 *yojana*.

"Then follows *Naraka*, *i.e.* the hells, of the dimension of 13 *koṭi* and 12 *laksha*, *i.e.* 131,200,000 *yojana*.

"Then follows darkness, of one *laksha*, *i.e.* 100,000 *yojana*.

"Above it lies the earth *Vajra*, so called on account of its hardness, because the word means *a diamond*, and *the molten thunder-bolt*, of 34,000 *yojana*.

"Above it lies the middle earth *Garbha*, of 60,000 *yojana*.

"Above it lies *the golden earth*, of 30,000 *yojana*.

"Above this the seven earths, each of 10,000 *yojana*, which makes the sum of 70,000 *yojana*. The upper one of them is that which contains the *dvîpas* and the seas.

"Behind the sweet-water sea lies *Lokâloka*, which means a *not-gathering-place*, *i.e.* a place without civilisation and inhabitants.

"Thereupon follows the gold-earth of one *Koṭi*, *i.e.* 10,000,000 *yojana*; above it the *Pitṛiloka* of 6,134,000 *yojana*.

"The totality of the seven *lokas*, which is called *Brah-*

mâṇḍa, has the dimension of 15 *koṭi, i.e.* 150,000,000 *yojana.* And above this is the darkness *tamas*, similar to the lowest darkness, of 18,500,000 *yojana.*"

We on our part found it already troublesome to enumerate all the seven seas, together with the seven earths, and now this author thinks he can make the subject more easy and pleasant to us by inventing some more earths below those already enumerated by ourselves!

The *Vishṇu-Purâṇa*, when treating of similar subjects, says: "There is a serpent under the seventh lowest earth, which is called *Śeshâkhya*, worshipped among the spiritual beings. It is also called *Ananta.* It has a thousand heads, and bears the earths without being molested by their heavy weight. These earths, one stored above the other, are gifted with good things and happiness, adorned with jewels, illuminated by their own rays, not by those of sun and moon. The latter two luminaries do not rise in them. Therefore their temperature is always equal, they have everlasting fragrant flowers, blossoms of trees and fruits; their inhabitants have no notion of time, since they do not become aware of any motions by counting them. Their dimension is 70,000 *yojana*, the dimensions of each being 10,000. Nârada, the Ṛishi, went down in order to see them, and to acquaint himself with the two kinds of beings which inhabit them, the *Daitya* and *Dânava.* When he then found the bliss of paradise to be rather insignificant in comparison with that of these earths, he returned to the angels, giving his report to them, and rousing their admiration by his description."

Further, the following passage: "Behind the sweet-water sea lies the gold earth, the double of the totality of the *dvîpas* and seas; but not inhabited by men nor by demons. Behind it lies *Lokâloka*, a mountain of the height of 10,000 *yojana*, and of the same breadth. Its Page 119. whole dimension is 50 *koṭi, i.e.* 500,000,000 *yojana.*"

The totality of all this is in the Hindu language

sometimes called *dhâtṛi, i.e. holding all things,* and sometimes *vidhâtṛi, i.e. letting loose all things.* It is also called *the dwelling-place of every living being*, and by various other names, which differ as people differ in their opinions about the *vacuum*. Those who believe in the *vacuum* make it the cause why all bodies are attracted towards it, whilst those who deny the *vacuum* declare that it is not the cause of the attraction.

Then the author of the *Vishṇu-Purâṇa* returns to the *Lokas* and says: "Everything which a foot can tread upon and a ship sail in, is *Bhûrloka.*" This seems to be an indication of the surface of the uppermost earth. The air, which is between the earth and the sun, in which the Siddhas, the Munis, and the Gandharvas, the musicians, wander to and fro, is the *Bhuvarloka.* The whole of these three earths is called *the three pṛithivî.* That which is above them is *Vyâsa-maṇḍala, i.e.* the realm of Vyâsa. The distance between the earth and sun is 100,000 *yojana*, that between the sun and the moon is the same. The distance between the moon and Mercury is two *lakshas, i.e.* 200,000 *yojana*, that between Mercury and Venus is the same. The distances between Venus and Mars, Mars and Jupiter, Jupiter and Saturn, are equal, each being 200,000 *yojana.* The distance between Saturn and the Great Bear is 100,000 *yojana*, and that from the Great Bear to the pole is 1000 *yojana.* Above it is *Maharloka*, at a distance of 20 millions of *yojana*; above it, the *Jinaloka*, at a distance of 80 millions; above it, *Pitṛiloka*, at a distance f 480 millions; above it, *Satyaloka.*"

This sum, however, is more than thrice the sum which we have mentioned on the authority of the commentator of the book of Patañjali, *i.e.* 150,000 *yojana.* But such is the custom of the copyists and scribes in every nation, and I cannot declare the students of the Purâṇas to be free from it, for they are not men of exact learning.

CHAPTER XXII.

TRADITIONS RELATING TO THE POLE.

The origin of the south pole, and the story of Somadatta.

THE pole, in the language of the Hindus, is called *dhruva*, and the axis *śalâka*. The Hindus, with the exception of their astronomers, speak always only of *one* pole, the reason of which is their belief in *the dome of heaven*, as we have heretofore explained. According to *Vâyu-Purâṇa*, heaven revolves round the pole like a potter's wheel, and the pole revolves round itself, without changing its own place. This revolution is finished in 30 *muhûrta*, *i.e.* in one *nychthemeron*.

Regarding the south pole, I have heard from them only one story or tradition, viz. the following. They had once a king called Somadatta, who by his noble deeds had deserved paradise; but he did not like the idea of his body being torn away from his soul when he should depart into the other world. Now he called on the Ṛishi Vasishṭha, and told to him that he loved his body, and did not wish to be separated from it; but the Ṛishi informed him that it was impossible to take along with oneself the material body from this world into paradise. Thereupon he laid his desire before the children of Vasishṭha; however, these spat in his face, scoffed at him, and changed him into a *caṇḍâla* with ear-rings in both ears, and clad in a *kurṭak* (*i.e.* a short shirt worn by the women round the shoulders, reaching down to the middle of the body). When he came in this condition to the Ṛishi, Viśvâmitra, the latter found him to be a disgusting spectacle, and asked him what

was the reason of his appearing so, whereupon Somadatta informed him, and told him the whole story. Now Viśvâmitra became very angry on his account; he
Page 120. ordered the Brahmans into his presence in order to perform a great sacrifice, among those also the children of Vasishṭha, and he spoke to them: "I wish to make a new world, and a new paradise for this pious king, that there he may obtain the fulfilment of his wish." Thereupon he began to make the pole and the Great Bear in the south, but then Indra, the ruler, and the spiritual beings began to fear him. They went to him, humbled themselves before him, and asked him to desist from the work he had commenced on this condition, that they would carry Somadatta *with his body*, just as it was, into paradise. This they did, and in consequence the Ṛishi desisted from making a second world, but that which he had already made up to that moment remained.

It is well known that the north pole with us is called the Great Bear, the south pole Canopus. But some of our people (Muslims) who do not rise above the uneducated mass, maintain that in the south of heaven too there is a Great Bear of the same shape as the northern, which revolves round the southern pole.

Śrîpâla on the star Śûla. Aljaihânî on the fever-star. Brahmagupta on the Śiśumâra.

Such a thing would not be impossible nor even strange, if the report about it came from a trustworthy man, who had made long sea-voyages. Certainly in southern regions stars are seen which we do not know in our latitudes. So Śrîpâla says that the people of Multân see in summer time a red star a little below the meridian of Canopus, which they call *Śûla*, *i.e. the beam of crucifixion*, and that the Hindus consider it as unlucky. Therefore, when the moon stands in the station Pûrvabhadrapada, the Hindus do not travel towards the south, because this star stands in the south.

Aljaihânî relates, in his Book of Routes, that on the

island Langabâlûs there is a large star visible, known as the *fever-star*. It appears in winter about morning dawn in the east as high as a date-palm tree, having an oblong shape, composed of the tail of the Small Bear and his back, and of some small stars situated there; it is called *the axe of the mill*. Brahmagupta mentions it in connection with *the Fish*. The Hindus tell rather ludicrous tales when speaking of the figure in which they represent this group of stars, viz. the figure of a four-footed aquatic animal, which they call *Śakvara* and also *Śiśumâra*. I suppose that the latter animal is the great lizard, for in Persia it is called *Susmâr*, which sounds much like the Indian *Śiśumâra*. Of this kind of animals there is also an aquatic species, similar to the crocodile and the skink. One of those tales is the following.

The story of Dhruva.

When Brahman wanted to create mankind, he divided himself into two halves, of which the right one was called *Virâj*, the left one *Manu*. The latter one is the being from whom the period of time called *Manvantara* has received its name. Manu had two sons, Priyavrata and Uttânapâda, the bow-legged king. The latter had a son called *Dhruva*, who was slighted by one of the wives of his father. On account of this, he was presented with the power to turn round all the stars as he pleased. He appeared in the Manvantara of Svayambhuva, the first of all Manvantaras, and he has for ever remained in his place.

Quotations from *Vâyu-Purâṇa* and *Vishṇu-Dharma*.

The *Vâyu-Purâṇa* says: "The wind drives the stars round the pole, which are bound to it by ties invisible to man. They move round like the beam in the olive-press, for its bottom is, as it were, standing still, whilst its end is moving round.

The *Vishṇu-Dharma* says: "Vajra, one of the children of Balabhadra, the brother of Nârâyaṇa, asked the Ṛishi Mârkaṇḍeya as to the pole, upon which he answered: When God created the world, it was dark and desert. Page 121.

Thereupon he made the globe of the sun shining, and the globes of the stars watery, receiving the light of the sun from that side of his which he turns towards them. Fourteen of these stars he placed round the pole in the shape of a *śiśumâra*, which drive the other stars round the pole. One of them, north of the pole, on the uppermost chin, is Uttânapâda, on the lowest chin Yajna, on the head Dharma, on the breast Nârâyaṇa, on the two hands towards the east the two stars Aśvinî the physicians, on the two feet Varuṇa, and Aryaman towards the west, on the penis Samwatsara, on the back Mitra, on the tail Agni, Mahendra, Marîci, and Kaśyapa."

The pole itself is Vishṇu, the ruler of the inhabitants of paradise; he is, further, the time rising, growing, getting old, and vanishing.

Further, the *Vishṇu-Dharma* says: "If a man reads this and knows it accurately, God pardons to him the sins of that day, and fourteen years will be added to his life, the length of which has been fixed beforehand."

How simple those people are! Among us there are scholars who know between 1020 to 1030 stars. Should those men breathe and receive life from God only on account of their knowledge of stars?

All the stars revolve, whatever may be the position of the pole with regard to them.

If I had found a Hindu able to point out to me with his finger the single stars, I should have been able to identify them with the star-figures known among Greeks and Arabs, or with stars in the neighbourhood in case they did not belong to any of these figures.

CHAPTER XXIII.

ON MOUNT MERU ACCORDING TO THE BELIEF OF THE AUTHORS OF THE PURÂṆAS AND OF OTHERS.

WE begin with the description of this mountain, since it is the centre of the Dvîpas and seas, and, at the same time, the centre of Jambûdvîpa. Brahmagupta says: "Manifold are the opinions of people relating to the description of the earth and to Mount Meru, particularly among those who study the Purâṇas and the religious literature. Some describe this mountain as rising above the surface of the earth to an excessive height. It is situated under the pole, and the stars revolve round its foot, so that rising and setting depends upon Meru. It is called Meru because of its having the faculty of doing this, and because it depends alone upon the influence of its head that sun and moon become visible. The day of the angels who inhabit Meru lasts six months, and their night also six months." Brahmagupta on the earth and Mount Meru.

Brahmagupta quotes the following passage from the book of *Jina*, *i.e.* Buddha: "Mount Meru is quadrangular, not round."

The commentator Balabhadra says: "Some people say that the earth is flat, and that Mount Meru is an illuminating, light-giving body. However, if such were the case, the planets would not revolve round the horizon of the inhabitants of Meru, and if it were shining it would be visible because of its height, as the Balabhadra on the same subject.

pole above it is visible. According to some, Meru consists of gold; according to others it consists of jewels. Âryabhaṭa thinks that it has not absolute height, but only the height of *one yojana*, and that it is round, not quadrangular, the realm of the angels; that it is invisible, although shining, because it is very distant from

Page 122.

the inhabited earth, being situated entirely in the high north, in the cold zone, in the centre of a desert called *Nandana-vana*. However, if it were of a great height, it would not be possible on the 66th degree of latitude for the whole Tropic of Cancer to be visible, and for the sun to revolve on it, being always visible without ever disappearing."

The author criticises Balabhadra.

All that Balabhadra produces is foolish both in words and matter, and I cannot find why he felt himself called upon to write a commentary if he had nothing better to say.

If he tries to refute the theory of the flatness of the earth by the planets revolving round the horizon of Meru, this argument would go nearer proving the theory than refuting it. For if the earth were a flat expanse, and everything high on earth were parallel to the perpendicular height of Meru, there would be no change of horizon, and the same horizon would be the equinox for all places on earth.

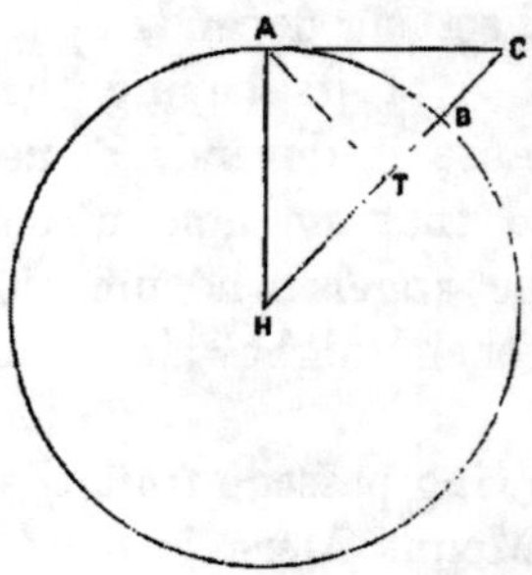

The statements of Âryabhaṭa examined by the author.

On the words of Âryabhaṭa as quoted by Balabhadra we make the following remarks.

Let A B be the globe of the earth round the centre H. Further, A is a place on the earth in the 66th degree of latitude. We cut off from the circle the arc A B, equal to the greatest declination. Then B is the place in the zenith of which the pole stands.

Further, we draw the line A C touching the globe in

the point A. This line lies in the plane of the horizon as far as the human eye reaches round the earth.

We join the points A and H with each other, and draw the line H B C, so that it is met in C by the line A C. Further, we let fall the perpendicular A T on H C. Now, it is evident that—

A T is the sine of the greatest declination ;
T B the versed sine of the greatest declination ;
T H the sine of the complement of the greatest declination.

And as we here occupy ourselves with Âryabhaṭa, we shall, according to his system, change the sines in *kardajât*. Accordingly—

A T = 1397.
T H = 3140.
B T = 298.

Because the angle H A C is a right angle, we have the equation—

H T : T A = T A : T C.

And the square of A T is 1,951,609. If we divide it by T H, we get as quotient 622.

The difference between this number and T B is 324, which is B C. And the relation of B C to B H, the latter being *sinus totus* = 3438, is the same as the relation of the number of *yojanas* of B C to the *yojanas* of B H. The latter number is, according to Âryabhaṭa, 800. If it is multiplied by the just-mentioned difference of 324 we get the sum of 259,200. And if we divide this number by the *sinus totus* we get 75 as quotient, which is the number of *yojanas* of B C, equal to 600 *miles* or 200 *farsakh*.

If the perpendicular of a mountain is 200 *farsakh*, the ascent will be nearly the double. Whether Mount Meru has such a height or not, nothing of it can be visible in the 66th degree of latitude, and it would not cover anything of the Tropic of Cancer at all (so as to intercept from it the light of the sun). And if for those

latitudes (66° and 23°) Meru is under the horizon, it is also under the horizon for all places of less latitude. If you compare Meru with a luminous body like the sun, you know that the sun sets and disappears under the earth. Indeed Meru may be compared with the earth.
Page 123. It is not invisible to us because of its being far away in the cold zone, but because it lies below the horizon, because the earth is a globe, and everything heavy is attracted towards its centre.

Âryabhaṭa further tries to prove that Mount Meru has only a moderate height by the fact that the Tropic of Cancer is visible in places the latitude of which is equal to the complement of the greatest declination. We must remark that this argument is not valid, for we know the conditions of the lines of latitude and other lines in those countries only through ratiocination, not from eyesight nor from tradition, because they are uninhabited and their roads are impassable.

If a man has come from those parts to Âryabhaṭa and told him that the Tropic of Cancer is visible in that latitude, we may meet this by stating that a man has also come to *us* from the same region telling us that one part of it is there invisible. The only thing which covers the Tropic of Cancer is this mountain Meru. If Meru did not exist, the whole tropic would be visible. Who, now, has been able to make out which of the two reports deserves most credit?

In the book of Âryabhaṭa of Kusumapura we read that the mountain Meru is in Himavant, the cold zone, not higher than a *yojana*. In the translation, however, it has been rendered so as to express that it is not higher than Himavant by more than a *yojana*.

This author is not identical with the elder Âryabhaṭa, but he belongs to his followers, for he quotes him and follows his example. I do not know which of these two namesakes is meant by Balabhadra.

In general, what we know of the conditions of the

place of this mountain we know only by ratiocination. About the mountain itself they have many traditions. Some give it the height of one *yojana*, others more; some consider it as quadrangular, others as an octagon. We shall now lay before the reader what the Ṛishis teach regarding this mountain.

The *Matsya-Purâṇa* says: "It is golden and shining like fire which is not dulled by smoke. It has four different colours on its four sides. The colour of the eastern side is white like the colour of the Brahmins, that of the northern is red like that of the Kshatriya, that of the southern is yellow like the colour of the Vaiśya, and that of the western is black like the colour of the Śûdra. It is 86,000 *yojana* high, and 16,000 of these *yojana* lie within the earth. Each of its four sides has 34,000 *yojana*. There are rivers of sweet water running in it, and beautiful golden houses inhabited by the spiritual beings, the Deva, by their singers the Gandharva, and their harlots the Apsaras. Also Asuras, Daityas, and Râkshasas are living in it. Round the mountain lies the pond Mânasa, and around it to all four sides are the *Lokapâla*, *i.e.* the guardians of the world and its inhabitants. Mount Meru has seven *knots*, *i.e.* great mountains, the names of which are Mahendra, Malaya, Sahya, Śuktibâm (?), Ṛikshabâm (?), Vindhya, Pâriyâtra. The small mountains are nearly innumerable; they are those which are inhabited by mankind.

Matsya-Purâṇa on Mount Meru and the mountains of the earth.

"The great mountains round Meru are the following: *Himavant*, always covered with snow, inhabited by the Râkshasa, Piśâca, and Yaksha. *Hemakûṭa*, the golden, inhabited by the Gandharva and Apsaras. *Nishadha*, inhabited by the Nâga or snakes, which have the following seven princes: Ananta, Vâsuki, Takshaka, Karkoṭaka, Mahâpadma, Kambala, Aśvatara. *Nîla*, peacock-like, of many colours, inhabited by the Siddha and Brahmarshi, the anchorites. The mountain

Page 124

Śveta, inhabited by the Daitya and Dânava. The mountain *Śṛiṅgavant*, inhabited by the Pitaras, the fathers and grandfathers of the Deva. Not far to the north of this mountain there are mountain-passes full of jewels and of trees which remain during a whole kalpa. And in the centre of these mountains is Ilâvṛita, the highest of all. The whole is called *Purushaparvata*. The region between the Himavant and the Śṛiṅgavant is called Kailâsa, the play-ground of the Râkshasa and Apsaras."

Quotations from the *Vishṇu*, *Vâyu*, and *Âditya Purâṇas*.

The *Vishṇu-Purâṇa* says: "The great mountains of the middle earth are Śrî-parvata, Malaya-parvata, Mâlyavant, Vindhya, Trikûṭa, Tripurântika, and Kailâsa. Their inhabitants drink the water of the rivers, and live in eternal bliss."

The *Vâyu-Purâṇa* contains similar statements about the four sides and the height of Meru as the hitherto quoted Purâṇas. Besides, it says that on each side of it there is a quadrangular mountain, in the east the Mâlyavant, in the north Ânîla, in the west the Gandhamâdana, and in the south the Nishadha.

The *Âditya-Purâṇa* gives the same statement about the size of each of its four sides which we have quoted from the *Matsya-Purâṇa*, but I have not found in it a statement about the height of Meru. According to this Purâṇa, its east side is of gold, the west of silver, the south of rubies, the north of different jewels.

The commentator of Patañjali on the same subject.

The extravagant notions of the dimensions of Meru would be impossible if they had not the same extravagant notions regarding the earth, and if there is no limit fixed to guesswork, guesswork may without any hindrance develop into lying. For instance, the commentator of the book of Patañjali not only makes Meru quadrangular, but even oblong. The length of one side he fixes at 15 *koṭi*, *i.e.* 150,000,000 *yojana*, whilst he fixes the length of the other three sides only at the third of this, *i.e.* 5 *koṭi*. Regarding the four sides of

Meru, he says that on the east are the mountain Mâlava and the ocean, and between them the kingdoms called Bhadrâśva. On the north are Nîla, Sîta, Śringâdri, and the ocean, and between them the kingdoms Ramyaka, Hiraṇmaya, and Kuru. On the west are the mountain Gandhamâdana and the ocean, and between them the kingdom Ketumâla. On the south are Mrâvarta (?), Nishadha, Hemakûṭa, Himagiri, and the ocean, and between them the kingdoms Bhâratavârsha, Kiṁpurusha, and Harivarsha.

This is all I could find of Hindu traditions regarding Meru; and as I have never found a Buddhistic book, and never knew a Buddhist from whom I might have learned their theories on this subject, all I relate of them I can only relate on the authority of Alêrânshahrî, though, according to my mind, his report has no claim to scientific exactness, nor is it the report of a man who has a scientific knowledge of the subject. According to him, the Buddhists believe that Meru lies between four worlds in the four cardinal directions; that it is square at the bottom and round at the top; that it has the length of 80,000 *yojana*, one half of which rises into heaven, whilst the other half goes down into the earth. That side which is next to our world consists of blue sapphires, which is the reason why heaven appears to us blue; the other sides are of rubies, yellow and white gems. Thus Meru is the centre of the earth.

Buddhistic views.

The mountain *Ḳâf*, as it is called by our common people, is with the Hindus the Lokâloka. They maintain that the sun revolves from Lokâloka towards Meru, and that he illuminates only its inner northern side.

Page 125.

Similar views are held by the Zoroastrians of Sogdiana, viz. that the mountain Ardiyâ surrounds the world; that outside of it is *khôm*, similar to the pupil of the eye, in which there is something of everything, and that behind it there is a *vacuum*. In the centre of the

A tradition of the Zoroastrians of Sogdiana.

world is the mountain *Girnagar*, between our κλίμα and the six other κλίματα, the throne of heaven. Between each two there is burning sand, on which no foot could stand. The spheres revolve in the *climata* like *mills*, but in ours they revolve in an inclined course, because our *clima*, that one inhabited by mankind, is the uppermost.

CHAPTER XXIV.

TRADITIONS OF THE PURÂṆAS REGARDING EACH OF THE SEVEN DVÎPAS.

Description of the Dvîpas according to the *Matsya* and *Vishṇu Purâṇas.*

We must ask the reader not to take any offence if he finds all the words and meanings which occur in the present chapter to be totally different from anything corresponding in Arabic. As for the difference of words, it is easily accounted for by the difference of languages in general; and as regards the difference of the meanings, we mention them only either in order to draw attention to an idea which might seem acceptable even to a Muslim, or to point out the irrational nature of a thing which has no foundation in itself.

1. Jambû-Dvîpa.

We have already spoken of the central Dvîpa when describing the environs of the mountain in its centre. It is called Jambû-Dvîpa, from a tree growing in it, the branches of which extend over a space of 100 *yojana*. In a later chapter, devoted to the description of the inhabitable world and its division, we shall finish the description of Jambû-Dvîpa. Next, however, we shall describe the other Dvîpas which surround it, following, as regards the order of the names, the authority of *Matsya-Purâṇa*, for the above-mentioned reason (v. p. 236). But before entering into this subject we shall here insert a tradition of the *Vâyu-Purâṇa* regarding the central Dvîpa (Jambû-Dvîpa).

The inhabitants of Madhyadeśa, according to *Vâyu-Purâṇa.*

According to this source, "there are two kinds of inhabitants in Madhyadeśa. First the *Kimpurusha*. Their men are known as the gold-coloured ones, their women as *sureṇu*. They live a long life without ever being ill. They never commit a sin, and do not know envy. Their food is a juice which they express from the dates of the palm trees, called *madya* (?). The second kind are the *Haripurusha*, having the colour of silver. They live 11,000 years, are beardless, and their food is sugar-cane." Since they are described as beardless and silver-coloured, one might be inclined to take them for Turks; but the fact of their eating dates and sugar-cane compels us to see in them a more southern nation. But where do we find people of the colour of gold or silver? We know only of the colour of burnt silver, which occurs, *e.g.* among the Zanj, who lead a life without sorrow and envy, as they do not possess anything which gives birth to these passions. They live no doubt longer than we, but only a little longer, and by no means twice as long. The Zanj are so uncivilised that they have no notion of a natural death. If a man dies a natural death, they think he was poisoned. Every death is suspicious with them, if a man has not been killed by a weapon. Likewise it is regarded with suspicion by them, if a man is touched by the breath of a consumptive person.

2. Śâka-Dvîpa.

We shall now describe *Śâka-Dvîpa.* It has, according to the *Matsya-Purâṇa,* seven great rivers, one of which equals the Ganges in purity. In the first ocean there are seven mountains adorned with jewels, some of which are inhabited by Devas, others by demons. One of them is a golden, lofty mountain, whence the clouds rise which bring us the rain. Another contains all the medicines. Indra, the ruler, takes from it the rain. Another one is called Soma. Regarding this mountain they relate the following story:—

Page 126.

The story of Kadrû and Vinatâ. Garuda liberates his mother by means of the Amṛita.

Kaśyapa had two wives, Kadrû, the mother of the snakes, and Vinatâ, the mother of the birds. Both lived in a plain where there was a grey horse. However, the mother of the snakes maintained that the horse was brown. Now they made the covenant that she who was wrong should become the slave of the other, but they postponed the decision till the following day. In the following night the mother of the snakes sent her black children to the horse, to wind themselves round it and to conceal its colour. In consequence the mother of the birds became her slave for a time.

The latter, Vinatâ, had two children, Anûru, the guardian of the tower of the sun, which is drawn by the horses, and Garuḍa. The latter spoke to his mother: "Demand from the children nourished at your breast what may restore you to liberty." This she did. People also spoke to her of the ambrosia (amṛita), which is with the Devas. Thereupon Garuḍa flew to the Devas and demanded it from them, and they fulfilled his wish. For Amṛita is one of those things peculiar to them, and if somebody else gets it, he lives as long as the Devas. He humbled himself before them in order to obtain the Amṛita, for the purpose of freeing therewith his mother, at the same time promising to bring it back afterwards. They had pity upon him, and gave it him. Thereupon Garuḍa went to the mountain Soma, in which the Devas were living. Garuḍa gave the Amṛita to the Devas, and thereby freed his mother. Then he spoke to them: "Do not come near the Amṛita unless you have before bathed in the river Ganges." This they did, and left the Amṛita where it was. Meanwhile Garuḍa brought it back to the Devas, and obtained thereby a high rank in sanctity, so that he became the king of all the birds and the riding-bird of Vishṇu.

The inhabitants of Śâka-Dvîpa are pious, long-lived beings, who can dispense with the rule of kings, since they do not know envy nor ambition. Their lifetime, not capable of any change, is as long as a Tretayuga. The four colours are among them, *i.e.* the different castes, which do not intermarry nor mix with each other.

They live in eternal joy, without ever being sorry. According to *Vishṇu-Purâṇa*, the names of their castes are Âryaka, Kurura, Viviṁśa (Vivaṁśa), and Bhâvin (?), and they worship Vâsudeva.

3. Kuśa-Dvîpa.

The third Dvîpa is Kuśa-Dvîpa. According to the *Matsya-Purâṇa* it has seven mountains containing jewels, fruit, flowers, odoriferous plants, and cereals. One of them, named Droṇa, contains famous medicines or drugs, particularly the *viśalyakaraṇa*, which heals every wound instantaneously, and *mṛitasaṁjîvan*, which restores the dead to life. Another one, called *hari*, is similar to a black cloud. On this mountain there is a fire called *Mahisha*, which has come out of the water, and will remain there till the destruction of the world; it is this very fire which will burn the world. Kuśa-Dvîpa has seven kingdoms and innumerable rivers flowing to the sea, which are then changed by Indra into rain. To the greatest rivers belong *Jaunu* (Yamunâ), which purifies from all sins. About the inhabitants of this Dvîpa, *Matsya-Purâṇa* does not give any information. According to *Vishṇu-Purâṇa* the inhabitants are pious, sinless people, every one of them living 10,000 years. They worship *Janârdana*, and the names of their castes are Damin, Śushmin, Sneha, and Mandeha.

4. Krauñca-Dvîpa.

The fourth, or Krauñca-Dvîpa, has, according to the *Matsya-Purâṇa*, mountains containing jewels, rivers which are branches of the Ganges, and kingdoms the people of which have a white colour and are pious and
Page 127.
pure. According to *Vishṇu-Purâṇa* the people there live in one and the same place without any distinction among members of the community, but afterwards it says that the names of their castes are Pushkara, Pushkala, Dhanya, and Tishya (?). They worship Janârdana.

5. Śâlmala-Dvîpa.

The fifth, or Śâlmala-Dvîpa, has, according to the *Matsya-Purâṇa*, mountains and rivers. Its inhabitants are pure, long-lived, mild, and never angry. They never suffer from drought or dearth, for their food comes to them simply in answer to their wishes, without their sowing or toiling. They come into existence without being born; they are never ill nor sorry. They do not require the rule of kings, since they do not know the desire for property. They live contented and in safety; they always prefer that which is good and love virtue. The climate of this Dvîpa never alters in cold or heat, so they are not bound to protect themselves against either. They have no rain, but the water bubbles up for them out of the earth and drops down from the mountains. This is also the case in the following Dvîpas. The inhabitants are of one kind, without any distinction of caste. Every one lives 3000 years.

According to the *Vishṇu-Purâṇa* they have beautiful faces and worship *Bhagavat*. They bring offerings to the fire, and every one of them lives 10,000 years. The names of their castes are Kapila, Aruṇa, Pîta, and Kṛishṇa.

The sixth, or Gomeda-Dvîpa, has, according to the *Matsya-Purâṇa*, two great mountains, the deep-black *Sumanas*, which encompasses the greatest part of the Dvîpa, and the *Kumuda*, of golden colour and very lofty; the latter one contains all medicines. This Dvîpa has two kingdoms. 6. Gomeda-Dvîpa.

According to *Vishṇu-Purâṇa* the inhabitants are pious and without sin and worship Vishṇu. The names of their castes are Mṛiga, Mâgadha, Mânasa, and Mandaga. The climate of this Dvîpa is so healthy and pleasant that the inhabitants of paradise now and then visit it on account of the fragrancy of its air.

The seventh, or Pushkara-Dvîpa, has, according to the *Matsya-Purâṇa*, in its eastern part the mountain *Citraśâlâ*, *i.e.* having a variegated roof with horns of jewels. Its height is 34,000 *yojana*, and its circum- 7. Pushkara-Dvîpa.

ference 25,000 *yojana*. In the west lies the mountain Mânasa, shining like the full moon; its height is 35,000 *yojana*. This mountain has a son who protects his father against the west. In the east of this Dvîpa are two kingdoms where every inhabitant lives 10,000 years. The water bubbles up for them out of the earth, and drops down from the mountains. They have no rain and no flowing river; they know neither summer nor winter. They are of one kind, without any distinction of caste. They never suffer from dearth, and do not get old. Everything they wish for comes to them, whilst they live quiet and happy without knowing anything else but virtue. It is as if they were in the suburb of paradise. All bliss is given to them; they live long and are without ambition. So there is no service, no rule, no sin, no envy, no opposition, no debating, no toiling in agriculture and diligence in trading.

According to the *Vishṇu-Purâṇa*, Pushkara-Dvîpa is so called from a large tree, which is also called *nyagrodha*. Under this tree is *Brahma-rûpa*, *i.e.* the figure of Brahman, worshipped by the Deva and Dânava. The inhabitants are equal among each other, not claiming any superiority, whether they be human beings or beings associating with the Devas. In this Dvîpa there is only a single mountain, called *Mânasottama*, which rises in a round form on the round Dvîpa. From its top all the other Dvîpas are visible, for its height is 50,000 *yojana*, and the breadth the same.

CHAPTER XXV.

ON THE RIVERS OF INDIA, THEIR SOURCES AND COURSES.

THE *Vâyu-Purâṇa* enumerates the rivers rising in the well-known great mountains which we have mentioned as the knots of Mount Meru (*vide* p. 247). To facilitate the study we exhibit them in the following table:— Page 128. Quotation from *Vâyu-Purâṇa.*

The Great Knots.	Names of the Rivers which rise in them in Nagarasamvṛitta.
Mahendra .	Trisâgâ, Ṛishikulyâ, Ikshulâ, Tripavâ (?), Âyanâ (?), Lâṅgûlinî, Vaṁśavara.
Malaya . .	Kṛitamâlâ, Tâmravarṇâ, Pushpajâti, Utpalavatî (!).
Sahya . .	Godâvarî, Bhîmarathî, Kṛishṇa, Vaiṇyâ, Savañjulâ, Tuṅgabhadrâ, Suprayogâ, Pâjaya (?), Kâverî.
Śukti . .	Ṛishîka, Bâlûka (!), Kumârî, Mandavâhinî, Kirpa (!), Palâśinî.
Ṛiksha . .	Śona, Mahânada, Narmadâ, Surasa, Kirva (?), Mandâkiṇî, Daśârṇâ, Citrakûṭâ, Tamasâ, Pipyala, Sroṇî, Karamoda (?), Piśâbika (?), Çitrapala, Mahâvegâ, Bañjulâ, Bâluvâhiṇî, Śuktimatî, Shakruṇâ (?), Tridivâ.
Vindhya .	Tâpî, Payoshṇî, Nirbindhyâ, Sirvâ (?), Nishadhâ, Vênvâ, Vaitaraṇî, Sini, Hâhu (!) Kumudvatî, Tobâ, Mahâgaurî, Durgâ, Antaśilâ.
Pâriyâtra .	Vedasmṛiti, Vedavatî, Vṛitraghnî (?) Parṇâśâ, Nandanâ, Saddânâ (?), Râmadî (?), Parâ, Carmaṇvatî, Lûpa (?), Vidiśâ.

The rivers of Europe and Asia rising in the Himalaya and its extensions to west and east.

The *Matsya-Purâṇa* and *Vâyu-Purâṇa* mention the rivers flowing in Jambû-Dvîpa, and say that they rise in the mountains of Himavant. In the following table we simply enumerate them, without following any particular principle of arrangement. The reader must imagine that the mountains form the boundaries of India. The northern mountains are the snowy Himavant. In their centre lies Kashmîr, and they are connected with the country of the Turks. This mountain region becomes colder and colder till the end of the inhabitable world and Mount Meru. Because this Page 129. mountain has its chief extension in longitude, the rivers rising on its north side flow through the countries of the Turks, Tibetans, Khazars, and Slavonians, and fall into the Sea of Jurjân (the Caspian Sea), or the sea of Khwârizm (the Aral Sea), or the Sea Pontus (the Black Sea), or the northern Sea of the Slavonians (the Baltic); whilst the rivers rising on the southern slopes flow through India and fall into the great ocean, some reaching it single, others combined.

Rivers of India.

The rivers of India come either from the cold mountains in the north or from the eastern mountains, both of which in reality form one and the same chain, extending towards the east, and then turning towards the south until they reach the great ocean, where parts of it penetrate into the sea at the place called the *Dike of Râma*. Of course, these mountains differ very much in cold and heat.

We exhibit the names of the rivers in the following table:—

Sindh or the river of Vaihand.	Biyatta or Jailam.	Candrabhâgâ or Candrâha.	Biyâha to the west of Lahore.	Irâvati to the east of Lahore.	S'atarudra or Shataldar.
Sarsat, flowing through the country Sarsat.	Jaun.	Gaṅgâ.	Sarayû or Sarwa.	Devikâ.	Kuhû.
Gomati.	Dhutapâpâ.	Viśâlâ.	Bâhudâsa (!).	Kauśiki.	Niścirâ.
Gaṇḍaki.	Lohitâ.	Drishadvati.	Tâmrâ Aruṇâ.	Parnâśâ.	Vedasmṛiti.
Vidâsini.	Candanâ.	Kâwanâ.	Parâ.	Carmaṇvati.	Vidiśâ.
Veṇumati.	S'iprâ, rises in the Pâriyâtrâ and passes Ujain.	Karatoyâ.	Shmâhina.		

In the mountains bordering on the kingdom of Kâyabish, *i.e.* Kâbul, rises a river which is called *Ghorwand*, on account of its many branches. It is joined by several affluents :— Sindh river. Page 130.

1. The river of the pass of Ghûzak.

2. The river of the gorge of Panchîr, below the town of Parwân.

3, 4. The river Sharvat and the river Sâwa, which latter flows through the town of Lanbagâ, *i.e.* Lamghân ; they join the Ghorvand at the fortress of Drûta.

5, 6. The rivers Nûr and Ḳîrâ.

Swelled by these affluents, the Ghorvand is a great river opposite the town of Purshâvar, being there called *the ford*, from a ford near the village of Mahanâra, on the eastern banks of the river, and it falls into the river Sindh near the castle of Bîtûr, below the capital of Alḳandahâr (Gandhâra), *i.e.* Vaihand.

The river Biyatta, known as Jailam, from the city of

Rivers of the Panjâb.

this name on its western banks, and the river Candarâha join each other nearly fifty miles above Jahrâvar, and pass along west of Multân.

The river Biyâh flows east of Multân, and joins afterwards the Biyatta and Candarâha.

The river Irâva is joined by the river Kaj, which rises in Nagarkot in the mountains of Bhâtul. Thereupon follows as the fifth the river Shatladar (Satlej).

After these five rivers have united below Multân at a place called *Pañcanada, i.e.* the meeting-place of the five rivers, they form an enormous watercourse. In flood-times it sometimes swells to such a degree as to cover nearly a space of ten *farsakh,* and to rise above the tree of the plains, so that afterwards the rubbish carried by the floods is found in their highest branches like birds-nests.

The Muslims call the river, after it has passed the Sindhî city Aror, as a united stream, *the river of Mihrân.* Thus it extends, flowing straight on, becoming broader and broader, and gaining in purity of water, enclosing in its course places like islands, until it reaches Almanṣûra, situated between several of its arms, and flows into the ocean at two places, near the city Loharânî, and more eastward in the province of Kacch at a place called *Sindhu-sâgara,* i.e. *the Sindh Sea.*

Eranian tradition.

As the name *union of the five rivers* occurs in this part of the world (in Panjâb), we observe that a similar name is used also to the north of the above-mentioned mountain chains, for the rivers which flow thence towards the north, after having united near Tirmidh and having formed the river of Balkh, are called *the union of the seven rivers.* The Zoroastrians of Sogdiana have confounded these two things; for they say that the whole of the seven rivers is *Sindh,* and its upper course *Barîdîsh.* A man descending on it sees the sinking of the sun on his right side if he turns his face towards the west, as we see it here on our left side (*sic*).

The river Sarsati falls into the sea at the distance of a bowshot east of Somanâth. Various rivers of India.

The river Jaun joins the Ganges below Kanoj, which lies west of it. The united stream falls into the great ocean near Gaṅgâsâgara.

Between the mouths of the rivers Sarsati and Ganges is the mouth of the river Narmadâ, which descends from the eastern mountains, takes its course in a south-western direction, and falls into the sea near the town Bahroj, nearly sixty *yojana* east of Somanâth.

Behind the Ganges flow the rivers Rahab and Kawînî, which join the river Sarwa near the city of Bârî.

The Hindus believe that the Ganges in ancient times flowed in Paradise, and we shall relate at a subsequent opportunity how it happened to come down upon earth.

The *Matsya-Purâṇa* says: "After the Ganges had settled on earth, it divided itself into seven arms, the middle of which is the main stream, known as the Ganges. Three flowed eastward, Nalinî, Hrâdinî, and Pâvanî, and three westward, Sîtâ, Cakshu, and Sindhu. Quotation from *Matsya-Purâṇa*. Page 131.

The river Sîta rises in the Himavant, and flows through these countries: Salila, Karstuba, Cina, Varvara, Yavasa (?), Baha, Pushkara, Kulata, Maṅgala, Kavara, and Saṅgavanta (?); then it falls into the western ocean.

South of Sîta flows the river Cakshuś, which irrigates the countries Cîna, Maru, Kâlika (?), Dhûlika (?), Tukhâra, Barbara, Kâca (?), Palhava, and Bârwancat.

The river Sindh flows through the countries Sindhu, Darada, Zindutunda (?), Gândhâra, Rûrasa (?), Krûra (?), Śivapaura, Indramaru, Sabâtî (?), Saindhava, Kubata, Bahîmarvara, Mara, Mrûna, and Sukûrda.

The river Ganges, which is the middle and main

stream, flows through the Gandharva, the musicians, Kiṁnara, Yakshas, Râkshasa, Vidyâdhara, Uraga, *i.e.* those who creep on their breasts, the serpents, Kalâpagrama, *i.e.* the city of the most virtuous, Kiṁpurusha, Khasa (?), the mountaineers, Kirâta, Pulinda, the hunters in the plains, robbers, Kuru, Bharata, Pañcâla, Kaushaka (?), Mâtsya, Magadha, Brahmottara, and Tâmalipta. These are the good and bad beings through whose territories the Ganges flows. Afterwards it enters into branches of the mountain Vindhya, where the elephants live, and then it falls into the southern ocean.

Of the eastern Ganges arms, the Hrâdinî flows through the countries Nishaba, Ûpakâna, Dhîvara, Prishaka, Nîlamukha, Kîkara, Ushṭrakarṇa, *i.e.* people whose lips are turned like their ears, Kirâta, Kalîdara, Vivarṇa, *i.e.* the colourless people, so called on account of their intense blackness, Kushikâna, and Svargabhûmi, *i.e.* a country like Paradise. Finally it falls into the eastern ocean.

The river Pâvanî gives water to the Kupatha (?), who are far from sin, Indradyumnasaras, *i.e.* the cisterns of the king Indradyumna, Kharapatha, Bîtra, and Saṅkupatha. It flows through the steppe Udyânamarûra, through the country of the Kuśaprâvaraṇa, and Indradvîpa, and afterwards it falls into the salt sea.

The river Nalinî flows through Tâmara, Haṁsamârga, Samûhuka, and Pûrṇa. All these are pious people who abstain from evil. Then it flows through the midst of mountains and passes by the Karṇaprâvaraṇa, *i.e.* people whose ears fall down on their shoulders, Aśvamukha, *i.e.* people with horse-faces, Parvatamaru, mountainous steppes, and Rûmîmaṇḍala. Finally it flows into the ocean.

Vishṇu-Purâṇa.

The *Vishṇu-Purâṇa* mentions that the great rivers of the middle earth which flow into the ocean are Anutapata, Shikhi, Dipâpa, Tridivâ, Karma, Amṛita and Sukṛita.

CHAPTER XXVI.

ON THE SHAPE OF HEAVEN AND EARTH ACCORDING TO THE HINDU ASTRONOMERS.

Page 132.

THIS and similar questions have received at the hands of the Hindus a treatment and solution totally different from that which they have received among us Muslims. The sentences of the Koran on these and other subjects necessary for man to know are not such as to require a strained interpretation in order to become positive certainties in the minds of the hearers, and the same may be said regarding the holy codes revealed before the Koran. The sentences of the Koran on the subjects necessary for man to know are in perfect harmony with the other religious codes, and at the same time they are perfectly clear, without any ambiguity. Besides, the Koran does not contain questions which have for ever been subjects of controversy, nor such questions the solution of which has always been despaired of, *e.g.* questions similar to certain puzzles of chronology.

The Koran, a certain and clear basis of all research.

Islam was already in its earliest times exposed to the machinations of people who were opposed to it in the bottom of their heart, people who preached Islam with sectarian tendencies, and who read to simple-minded audiences out of their Koran-copies passages of which not a single word was ever *created* (*i.e.* revealed) by God. But people believed them and copied these things on their authority, beguiled by their hypocrisy; nay, they disregarded the true form of the book which they had had until then, because the vulgar mind is

Islam falsified: I. By a Judaistic party.

always inclined to any kind of delusion. Thus the pure tradition of Islam has been rendered confused by this Judaistic party.

II. By the dualists.

Islam encountered a second mishap at the hands of the Zindîks, the followers of Mânî, like Ibn Almuḳaffa', 'Abd-alkarîm Ibn 'Abî-al'aujâ', and others, who, being the fathers of criticism, and declaring one thing as *just*, another as *admissible*, &c., raised doubts in weak-minded people as to the One and First, *i.e.* the Unique and Eternal God, and directed their sympathies towards dualism. At the same time they presented the biography of Mânî to the people in such a beautiful garb that they were gained over to his side. Now this man did not confine himself to the trash of his sectarian theology, but also proclaimed his views about the form of the world, as may be seen from his books, which were intended for deliberate deception. His opinions were far-spread. Together with the inventions of the above-mentioned Judaistic party, they formed a religious system which was declared to be *the Islam*, but with which God has nothing whatever to do. Whoso opposes it and firmly adheres to the orthodox faith in conformity with the Koran is stigmatised by them as an infidel and heretic and condemned to death, and they will not allow him to hear the word of the Koran. All these acts of theirs are more impious than even the words of Pharaoh, "I am your highest lord" (Sura, 79, 24), and "I do not know of any god for you save myself" (Sura, 28, 38). If party spirit of this kind will go on and rule for a long time, we may easily decline from the straight path of honour and duty. We, however, take our refuge with God, who renders firm the foot of every one who seeks *Him*, and who seeks the truth about Him.

Veneration of the Hindus for their astronomers.

The religious books of the Hindus and their codes of tradition, the Purâṇas, contain sentences about the shape of the world which stand in direct opposition to scientific truth as known to their astronomers. By these books people are guided in fulfilling the rites of their religion, and by means of them the great mass of the nation have been wheedled into a predilection for astronomical calculation and astrological predictions and warnings. The consequence is, that they show much affection to their astronomers, declaring that they are excellent men, that it is a good omen to meet them, and firmly believing that all of them come into Paradise and none into hell. For this the astronomers requite them by accepting their popular notions as truth, by conforming themselves to them, however far from truth most of them may be, and by presenting them with such spiritual stuff as they stand in need of. This is the reason why the two theories, the vulgar and the scientific, have become intermingled in the course of time, why the doctrines of the astronomers have been disturbed and confused, in particular the doctrines of those authors—and they are the majority—who simply copy their predecessors, who take the bases of their science from tradition and do not make them the objects of independent scientific research.

Astronomers admit popular notions into their doctrines.

General observations on the rotundity of the earth, on Meru and Vadavâmukha.

We shall now explain the views of Hindu astronomers regarding the present subject, viz. the shape of heaven and earth. According to them, heaven as well as the whole world is round, and the earth has a globular shape, the northern half being dry land, the southern half being covered with water. The dimension of the earth is larger according to them than it is according to the Greeks and modern observations, and in their calculations to find this dimension they have entirely given up any mention of the traditional seas and *Dvîpas*, and of the enormous sums of *yojana* attributed to each of them. The astronomers follow the theologians in everything which does not encroach upon their science, *e.g.* they adopt the theory of Mount Meru being under the north pole, and that of the island

Page 133.

Vaḍavâmukha lying under the south pole. Now, it is entirely irrelevant whether Meru is there or not, as it is only required for the explanation of the particular mill-like rotation, which is necessitated by the fact that to each spot on the plane of the earth corresponds a spot in the sky as its zenith. Also the fable of the southern island Vaḍavâmukha does no harm to their science, although it is possible, nay, even likely, that each pair of quarters of the earth forms a coherent, uninterrupted unity, the one as a continent, the other as an ocean (and that in reality there is no such island under the south pole). Such a disposition of the earth is required by the law of gravitation, for according to them the earth is in the centre of the universe, and everything heavy gravitates towards it. Evidently on account of this law of gravitation they consider heaven, too, as having a globular shape.

We shall now exhibit the opinions of the Hindu astronomers on this subject according to our translation of their works. In case, however, one word or other in our translation should be used in a meaning different from that which it generally has in our sciences, we ask the reader to consider only the original meaning of the word (not the technical one), for this only is meant.

Quotation from the *Siddhânta*, of Pulisa.

Pulisa says in his *Siddhânta:* "Paulisa the Greek says somewhere that the earth has *a globular shape*, whilst in another place he says that it has *the shape of a cover* (*i.e.* of a flat plane). And in both sentences he is right; for the plane or surface of the earth is *round*, and its diameter is a straight line. That he, however, only believed in the globular shape of the earth, may be proved by many passages of his work. Besides, all scholars agree on this head, as Varâhamihira, Âryabhaṭa, Deva, Śrîsheṇa, Vishṇucandra, and Brahman. If the earth were not round, it would not be girded with the latitudes of the different places on earth, day and night would not be different in winter and summer, and the conditions of the planets and of their rotations would be quite different from what they are.

"The position of the earth is central. Half of it is clay, half water. Mount Meru is in the dry half, the home of the Deva, the angels, and above it is the pole. In the other half, which is covered by water, lies Vaḍavâmukha, under the south pole, a continent like an island, inhabited by the Daitya and Nâga, relatives of the Deva on Meru. Therefore it is also called Daityântara.

"The line which divides the two earth-halves, the dry and the wet, from each other, is called *Niraksha, i.e. having no latitude,* being identical with our equator. In the four cardinal directions with relation to this line there are four great cities :—

Yamakoṭi, in the east.	Romaka, in the west.
Lankâ, in the south.	Siddhapura, in the north.

"The earth is fastened on the two poles, and held by the axis. When the sun rises over the line which passes both through Meru and Lankâ, that moment is noon to Yamakoṭi, midnight to the Greeks, and evening to Siddhapura."

In the same manner things are represented by Âryabhaṭa.

Brahmagupta, the son of Jishṇu, a native of Bhillamâla, says in his *Brahmasiddhânta:* "Many are the sayings of people about the shape of the earth, specially among those who study the Purâṇas and the religious books. Some say that it is level like a mirror, others say that it is hollow like a bowl. Others maintain that it is level like a mirror, inclosed by a sea, this sea being inclosed by an earth, this earth being inclosed by a sea, &c., all of them being round like collars. Each sea or earth has the double size of that which it incloses. The outside earth is sixty-four times as large as the central earth, and the sea inclosing the outside earth is

Quotation from the *Brahmasiddhânta* of Brahmagupta.

Page 134.

sixty-four times as large as the sea inclosing the central earth. Several circumstances, however, compel us to attribute globular shape both to the earth and heaven, viz. the fact that the stars rise and set in different places at different times, so that, *e.g.* a man in Yamakoṭi observes one identical star rising above the western horizon, whilst a man in Rûm at the same time observes it rising above the eastern horizon. Another argument to the same effect is this, that a man on Meru observes one identical star above the horizon in the zenith of Laṅkâ, the country of the demons, whilst a man in Laṅkâ at the same time observes it above his head. Besides, all astronomical calculations are not correct unless we assume the globular figure of heaven and earth. Therefore we must declare that heaven is a globe, because we observe in it all the characteristics of a globe, and the observation of these characteristics of the world would not be correct unless in reality it were a globe. Now, it is evident that all the other theories about the world are futile."

Quotations from various astronomers.

Âryabhaṭa inquires into the nature of the world, and says that it consists of earth, water, fire, and wind, and that each of these elements is round.

Likewise Vasishṭha and Lâṭa say that the five elements, viz. earth, water, fire, wind, and heaven, are round.

Varâhamihira says that all things which are perceived by the senses, are witnesses in favour of the globular shape of the earth, and refute the possibility of its having another shape.

Âryabhaṭa, Pulisa, Vasishṭha, and Lâṭa agree in this, that when it is noon in Yamakoṭi, it is midnight in Rûm, beginning of the day in Laṅkâ, and beginning of the night in Siddhapura, which is not possible if the world is not round. Likewise the periodicity of the eclipses can only be explained by the world's being round.

Lâṭa says: "On each place of the earth only one-half of the globe of heaven is seen. The more northern our latitude is, the more Meru and the pole rise above the horizon; as they sink down below the horizon, the more southern is our latitude. The equator sinks down from the zenith of places, the greater their latitude is both in north and south. A man who is north of the equator only sees the north pole, whilst the south pole is invisible to him, and *vice versâ.*"

Considerations regarding the rotundity of the earth, the balance of gravity between the northern and southern halves, and the attraction of gravitation.

These are the words of Hindu astronomers regarding the globular shape of heaven and earth, and what is between them, and regarding the fact that the earth, situated in the centre of the globe, is only of a small size in comparison with the visible part of heaven. These thoughts are the elements of astronomy as contained in the first chapter of Ptolemy's *Almagest*, and of similar books, though they are not worked out in that scientific form in which we are accustomed to give them,

(*Lacuna,*)

for the earth is more heavy than the water, and the water is fluid like the air. The globular form must be to the earth a physical necessity, as long as it does not, by the order of God, take another form. Therefore the earth could not move towards the north, nor the water move towards the south, and in consequence one whole half is not *terra firma*, nor the other half water, unless we suppose that the *terra firma* half be hollow. As far as our observation, based on induction, goes, the *terra firma* must be in one of the two northern quarters, and therefore we guess that the same is the case on the adjacent quarter. We admit the possibility of the existence of the island Vaḍavâmukha, but we do not maintain it, since all we know of it and of Meru is exclusively based on tradition. Page 135.

The equatorial line does not, in the quarter of the earth known to us, represent a boundary between *terra firma* and the ocean. For in certain places the continent protrudes far into the ocean, so as to pass beyond the equator, *e.g.* the plains of the negroes in the west, which protrude far towards the south, even beyond the *mountains of the moon* and the sources of the Nile, in fact, into regions which we do not exactly know. For that continent is desert and impassable, and likewise the sea behind Sufâla of the Zanj is unnavigable. No ship which ventured to go there has ever returned to relate what it had witnessed.

Also a great part of India above the province of Sindh deeply protrudes far towards the south, and seems even to pass beyond the equator.

In the midst between both lie Arabia and Yemen, but they do not go so far south as to cross the equator.

Further, as the *terra firma* stretches far out into the ocean, thus the ocean too penetrates into *terra firma*, breaking into it in various places, and forming bays and gulfs. For instance, the sea extends as a tongue along the west side of Arabia as far as the neighbourhood of Central Syria. It is narrowest near Ḳulzum, whence it is also called *the Sea of Ḳulzum.*

Another and still larger arm of the sea exists east of Arabia, the so-called *Persian Sea.* Between India and China, also, the sea forms a great curve towards the north.

Hence it is evident that the coast-line of these countries does not correspond to the equator, nor keep an invariable distance from it,

(*Lacuna,*)

and the explanation relating to the four cities will follow in its proper place.

The difference of the times which has been remarked is one of the results of the rotundity of the earth, and of its occupying the centre of the globe. And if they attribute to the earth, though it be round, inhabitants—for cities cannot be imagined without inhabitants—the existence of men on earth is accounted for by the attraction of everything heavy towards its centre, *i.e.* the middle of the world.

Quotations from the *Vâyu* and *Matsya Purâṇas.*

Much to the same effect are the expressions of *Vâyu-Purâṇa*, viz. that noon in Amarâvatî is sunrise in Vaivasvata, midnight in Sukhâ, and sunset in Vibhâ.

Similar, also, are the expressions of *Matsya-Purâṇa*, for this book explains that east of Meru lies the city Amarâvatîpura, the residence of Indra, the ruler, and his wife; south of Meru, the city Saṁyamanîpura, the residence of Yama, the son of the Sun, where he punishes and requites mankind; west of Meru, the city Sukhâpura, the residence of Varuṇa, *i.e.* the water; and north of Meru, the city Vibhâvarîpura, belonging to the Moon. Sun and planets revolve round Meru. When the sun has his noon position in Amarâvatîpura, it is the beginning of the day in Saṁyamanîpura, midnight in Sukhâ, and the beginning of the night in Vibhâvarîpura. And when the sun has his noon position in Saṁyamanîpura, he rises over Sukhâpura, sets over Amaravatîpura, and has his midnight position with relation to Vibhavarîpura.

Page 136.

A note of the author on the passage from the *Matsya-Purâṇa.*

If the author of the *Matsya-Purâṇa* says that the sun revolves round Meru, he means a mill-like rotation round those who inhabit Meru, who, in consequence of this nature of the rotation, do not know east nor west. The sun does not rise for the inhabitants of Meru in one particular place, but in various places. By the word *east* the author means the zenith of one city, and by *west* the zenith of another. Possibly those four cities of the *Matsya-Purâṇa* are identical with those mentioned by the astronomers. But the author has not mentioned how far they are distant from Meru. What we have besides related as notions of the Hindus is perfectly correct and borne out by scientific methods; however, they are wont never to speak of the pole unless they mention in the same breath also the mountain Meru.

Brahmagupta and Varâhamihira on the law of gravitation.

In the definition of what is *low* the Hindus agree with us, viz. that it is *the centre of the world*, but their expressions on this head are subtle, more particularly as this is one of the great questions which is only handled by the most eminent of their scholars.

So Brahmagupta says: "Scholars have declared that the globe of the earth is in the midst of heaven, and that Mount Meru, the home of the Devas, as well as Vaḍavâmukha below, is the home of their opponents; the Daitya and Dânava belong to it. But this *below* is according to them only a relative one. Disregarding this, we say that the earth on all its sides is the same; all people on earth stand upright, and all heavy things fall down to the earth by a law of nature, for it is the nature of the earth to attract and to keep things, as it is the nature of water to flow, that of fire to burn, and that of the wind to set in motion. If a thing wants to go deeper down than the earth, let it try. The earth is the only *low* thing, and seeds always return to it, in whatever direction you may throw them away, and never rise upwards from the earth."

Varâhamihira says: "Mountains, seas, rivers, trees, cities, men, and angels, all are around the globe of the earth. And if Yamakoṭi and Rûm are opposite to each other, one could not say that the one is *low* in its relation to the other, since the *low* does not exist. How could one say of one place of the earth that it is *low*, as it is in every particular identical with any other place on earth, and one place could as little *fall* as any other. Every one speaks to himself with regard to his own self, '*I* am *above* and the others are *below*,' whilst all of them are around the globe like the blossoms springing on the branches of a Kadamba-tree. They encircle it on all sides, but each individual blossom has the same position as the other, neither the one hanging downward nor the other standing upright. For the earth attracts that which is upon her, for it is the *below* towards all directions, and heaven is the *above* towards all directions."

As the reader will observe, these theories of the

Hindus are based on the correct knowledge of the laws of nature, but, at the same time, they practise a little deceit upon their traditionalists and theologians. So Balabhadra the commentator says: "It is the most correct of the opinions of people, many and different as they are, that the earth and Meru and the zodiacal sphere are round. And the Âpta (?)-purâṇa-kâra, *i.e.* the faithful followers of the Purâṇa, say: 'The earth is like the back of a tortoise; it is not round from below.' They are perfectly right, because the earth is in the midst of the water, and that which appears above the water has the shape of a tortoise-back; and the sea around the earth is not navigable. The fact of the earth being round is proved by eyesight."

Quotations from Balabhadra, and the author's criticisms on them.

Page 137.

Here the reader must notice how Balabhadra declares the theory of the theologians as to the rotundity of the back to be true. He gives himself the air of not knowing that they deny that the womb, *i.e.* the other half of the globe, is round, and he busies himself with a traditional element (as to the earth being like the back of a tortoise), which, in reality, has no connection with the subject.

Further, Balabhadra says: "Human eyesight reaches to a point distant from the earth and its rotundity the 96th part of 5000 *yojana*, *i.e.* 52 *yojana* (exactly $52\frac{1}{12}$). Therefore man does not observe its rotundity, and hence the discrepancy of opinions on the subject."

Those pious men (the Âpta (?)-purâṇa-kâra) do not deny the rotundity of the back of the earth; nay, they maintain it by comparing the earth to the back of a tortoise. Only Balabhadra makes them deny it (by the words, "the earth is not round from below," *supra*), since he understood their words as meaning that the water surrounds the earth. That which rises above the water may either be globular or a plain rising above the water like an inverted drum, *i.e.* like a segment of a round pilaster.

Further, the remark of Balabhadra (v. p. 273), that man, on account of the smallness of his stature, cannot observe the rotundity of the earth, is not true; because even if the human stature were as tall as the plumb-line of the highest mountain, if he were to make his observation only from one single point without going to other places, and without reasoning about the observations made at the different places, even such a height would be of no avail to him, and he would not be able to perceive the rotundity of the earth and its nature.

What, however, is the connection of this remark with the popular theory? If he had concluded from analogy that that side of the earth which is opposed to the *round* one—I mean the lower half—was also round, and if he then had given his theory about the extent of the power of human vision as a result of reflection, not as a result of the perception of the senses, his theory would seem to have a certain foundation.

Calculation on the extent of human vision on the earth.

With regard to Balabhadra's definition of the extent which may be reached by the human eye, we propose the following calculation:—

Let A B round the centre H represent the globe of the earth. B is the standing-point of the observer; his stature is B C. Further, we draw the line C A, so that it touches the earth.

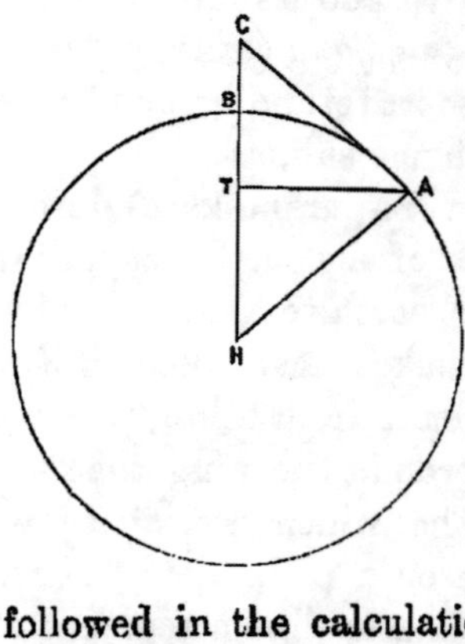

Now it is evident that the field of vision is B A, which we suppose to be equal to $\frac{1}{96}$ of the circle, *i.e.* $3\frac{3}{4}$ degrees, if we divide the circle into 360 degrees.

According to the method followed in the calculation of the mountain Meru (in chap. xxiii.), we divide the square of T A, *i.e.* 50,625, by

H T, *i.e.* 3431′. So we get as quotient T C = 0° 14′ 45″; and B C, the stature of the observer, is 0° 7′ 45″.

Our calculation is based on this, that H B, the *sinus totus*, is 3438′. However, the radius of the earth is, according to the circumference which we have mentioned, 795° 27′ 16″ (*yojana*). If we measure B C by this measure, it is = 1 *yojana*, 6 *krośa*, 1035 yards (= 57,035 yards). If we suppose B C to be equal to four yards, it stands in the same relation to A T, according to the measure of the sine, as 57,035, *i.e.* the yards which we have found as the measure of the stature, to A T according to the measure of the sine, *i.e.* 225. If we now calculate the sine, we find it to be 0° 0′ 1″ 3‴, and its arc has the same measure. However, each degree of the rotundity of the earth represents the measure of 13 *yojana*, 7 *krośa*, and $333\frac{1}{3}$ yards (*sic*). Therefore the field of vision on the earth is $291\frac{2}{3}$ yards (*sic*). Page 138.

(*For an explanation of this calculation see the notes.*)

The source of this calculation of Balabhadra's is the *Pulisa-siddhânta*, which divides the arc of the quarter of a circle into 24 *kardajât*. He says: "If anybody asks for the reason of this, he must know that each of these *kardajât* is $\frac{1}{96}$ of the circle = 225 minutes (= $3\frac{3}{4}$ degrees). And if we reckon its sine, we find it also to be = 225 minutes." This shows us that the sines are equal to their arcs in parts which are smaller than this *kardaja*. And because the *sinus totus*, according to Pulisa and Âryabhaṭa, has the relation of the diameter to the circle of 360 degrees, this arithmetical equality brought Balabhadra to think that the arc was perpendicular; and any expanse in which no convexity protrudes preventing the vision from passing, and which is not too small to be seen, is visible.

This, however, is a gross mistake; for the arc is never perpendicular, and the sine, however small it be, never equals the arc. This is admissible only for such degrees as are supposed for the convenience of calculation, but it is never and nowhere true for the degrees of the earth.

The axis of the earth according to Pulisa.

If Pulisa says (v. p. 267) that the earth is held by an axis, he does not mean thereby that in reality there exists such an axis, and that but for it the earth would fall. How could he say such a thing, since he is of opinion that there are four inhabited cities around the world, which is explained by the fact that everything heavy falls from all sides down towards the earth? However, Pulisa holds this view, that the motion of the peripheric parts is the reason why the central parts are motionless, and that the motion of a globe presupposes two poles, and one line connecting them, which in the idea is the axis. It is as if he meant to say, that the motion of heaven keeps the earth in its place, making it the natural place for the earth, outside of which it could never be. And this place lies on the midst of the axis of motion. For the other diameters of the globe may also be imagined to be axes, since ἐν δυνάμει they are all axes, and if the earth were not in the midst of an axis, there might be axes which did not pass through the earth. Hence one may say metaphorically that the earth is supported by the axes.

Whether the earth moves or is at rest, according to Brahmagupta and the author.

As regards the resting of the earth, one of the elementary problems of astronomy, which offers many and great difficulties, this, too, is a dogma with the Hindu astronomers. Brahmagupta says in the *Brahmasiddhânta:* "Some people maintain that the *first* motion

Page 139.

(from east to west) does not lie in the meridian, but belongs to the earth. But Varâhamihira refutes them by saying: 'If that were the case, a bird would not return to its nest as soon as it had flown away from it towards the west.' And, in fact, it is precisely as Varâhamihira says."

Brahmagupta says in another place of the same book: "The followers of Âryabhaṭa maintain that the earth is moving and heaven resting. People have tried to refute them by saying that, if such were the case, stones and trees would fall from the earth."

But Brahmagupta does not agree with them, and says that that would not necessarily follow from their theory, apparently because he thought that all heavy things are attracted towards the centre of the earth. He says: "On the contrary, if that were the case, *the earth would not vie in keeping an even and uniform pace with the minutes of heaven, the prâṇas of the times.*"

There seems to be some confusion in this chapter, perhaps by the fault of the translator. For the *minutes of heaven* are 21,600, and are called *prâṇa, i.e.* breaths, because according to them each minute of the meridian revolves in *the time of an ordinary human breath.*

Supposing this to be true, and that the earth makes a complete rotation eastward in so many breaths as heaven does according to his (Brahmagupta's) view, we cannot see what should prevent the earth from keeping an even and uniform pace with heaven.

Besides, the rotation of the earth does in no way impair the value of astronomy, as all appearances of an astronomic character can quite as well be explained according to this theory as to the other. There are, however, other reasons which make it impossible. This question is most difficult to solve. The most prominent of both modern and ancient astronomers have deeply studied the question of the moving of the earth, and tried to refute it. We, too, have composed a book on the subject called *Miftâḥ-'ilm-alhai'a* (*Key of Astronomy*), in which we think we have surpassed our predecessors, if not in the words, at all events in the matter.

CHAPTER XXVII.

ON THE FIRST TWO MOTIONS OF THE UNIVERSE (THAT FROM EAST TO WEST ACCORDING TO ANCIENT ASTRONOMERS AND THE PRECESSION OF THE EQUINOXES), BOTH ACCORDING TO HINDU ASTRONOMERS AND THE AUTHORS OF THE PURÂṆAS.

THE astronomers of the Hindus hold on this subject mostly the same views as ourselves. We shall give quotations from them, but shall at once confess that that which we are able to give is very scanty indeed.

Quotation on the subject from Pulisa.

Pulisa says: "The wind makes the sphere of the fixed stars revolve; the two poles keep it in its place, and its motion appears to the inhabitants of Mount Meru as a motion from the left to the right; to the inhabitants of Vaḍavâmukha as one from the right to the left."

In another place he says: "If anybody asks for the direction of the motion of the stars which we see rising in the east and rotating towards the west until they set, let him know that the motion which *we* see as a westward motion appears different according to the places which the spectators occupy. The inhabitants of Mount Meru see it as a motion from the left to the right, whilst the inhabitants of Vaḍavâmukha see it as the opposite, as a motion from the right to the left. The inhabitants of the equator see it exclusively as a westward motion, and the inhabitants of the parts of the earth between the poles and the equator see it more or less depressed, as their places have more or

less northern or southern latitude. The whole of this motion is caused by the wind, which makes the spheres revolve, and compels the planets and the other stars to rise in the east and to set in the west. This, however, is only an *accidens*. As for the *essentia rei*, the motions of the heavenly bodies are directed towards the east, from *Alsharaṭân* towards *Albuṭain*, the latter lying east of the former. But if the inquirer does not know the lunar stations, and is not capable of procuring for him- Page 140.
self by their help an idea of this eastward motion, let him observe the moon herself, how she moves away from the sun once and a second time; how she then comes near him, till she finally joins him. This will give him an idea of the *second* motion."

Quotations from Brahmagupta and Balabhadra.

Brahmagupta says: "The sphere has been created as moving with the greatest rapidity possible about two poles without ever slackening, and the stars have been created where there is no *Baṭn-ḥût* nor *Sharaṭân*, *i.e.* on the frontier between them, which is the vernal equinox."

Balabhadra, the commentator, says: "The whole world hangs on two poles, and moves in a circular motion, which begins with a *kalpa* and ends with a *kalpa*. But people must not therefore say that the world, on account of the continuity of its motion, is without beginning and without end."

Brahmagupta says: "The place without latitude (*Niraksha*), divided into sixty *ghaṭikâ*, is the horizon for the inhabitants of Meru. There east is west; and behind that place (beyond the equator) towards the south is Vaḍavâmukha and the ocean which surrounds it. When the spheres and the stars revolve, the meridian becomes an horizon common to the Devas (in the north) and the Daityas (in the south), which they see together. But the direction of the motion appears to them as different. The motion which the angels see as a motion to the right, the Daityas see as one to the left, and *vice versâ*, just as a man who has a thing on his right side, looking into the water, sees it on his left. The cause of this uniform motion which never increases nor decreases is a wind, but it is not the common wind which we feel and hear; for this is lulled, and roused, and varies, whilst *that* wind never slackens."

In another place Brahmagupta says: "The wind makes all the fixed stars and the planets revolve towards the west in one and the same revolution; but the planets move also in a slow pace towards the east, like a dust-atom moving on a potter's-wheel in a direction opposite to that in which the wheel is revolving. That motion of this atom which is visible is identical with the motion which drives the wheel round, whilst its individual motion is not perceived. In this view Lâṭa, Âryabhaṭa, and Vasishṭha agree, but some people think that the earth moves while the sun is resting. That motion which mankind conceives as a motion from east to west, the angels (Deva) conceive as a motion from left to right, the Daityas as one from right to left."

Criticisms of the author. The wind as the motor of the sphere.

This is all I have read in Indian books on the subject.

Their speaking of the wind as the *motor* (*supra*) has, I think, only the purpose of bringing the subject near to the understanding of people and to facilitate its study; for people see with their own eyes that the wind, when blowing against instruments with wings and toys of this kind, puts them into motion. But as soon as they come to speak of the *first mover* (God), they at once give up any comparison with the natural wind, which in all its phases is determined by certain causes. For though it puts things into motion, the *moving* is not its essence; and besides, it cannot move without being in contact with something, because the wind is a body, and is acted upon by external influences or means, its motion being commensurate with their force.

Their saying that the wind does not rest, simply means that the moving power works perpetually, and does not imply rest and motion such as are proper to bodies. Further, their saying that it does *not slacken* means that it is free from all kinds of accidents; for *slackening* and *weakening* only occur in such bodies or beings which are composed of elements of conflicting qualities. Page 141.

On the two poles *keeping* the sphere.

The expression that the two poles *keep* the sphere of the fixed stars (p. 278) means that they keep or preserve it in its normal state of motion, not that they keep or preserve it from falling down. There is a story of an ancient Greek who thought that once upon a time the Milky Way had been a road of the sun, and that afterwards he had left it. Such a thing would mean that the motions ceased to be normal, and to something like this the expression of *the poles keeping the sphere of the fixed stars* may be referred.

On the relative nature of time.

The phrase of Balabhadra about *the ending of the motion* (that it ends with a *kalpa*, &c., p. 279) means that everything which exists and may be determined arithmetically has no doubt an end, for two reasons: *first*, because it has a beginning, for every number consists of *one* and its reduplications, whilst the *one* itself exists before all of them; and, *secondly*, because part of it exists in the present moment of time, for if days and nights increase in number through the continuation of existence, they must necessarily have a beginning whence they started. If a man maintains that *time* does not exist in the sphere (as one of its immanent qualities), and thinks that day and night have only a *relative* existence, exist only *in relation* to the earth and its inhabitants, that if, *e.g.*, the earth were taken away out of the midst of the world, also night and day would cease to exist as well as the possibility of measuring elements composed of days, he would thereby impose upon Balabhadra the necessity of a digression, and compel him to prove the cause, not of the *first*, but of the *second* motion. The latter cause is the cycles of the planets, which have only a relation to *the sphere*, not to *the earth*. These cycles Balabhadra indicates by the word *kalpa* (v. p. 279), since it comprehends them all, and since all of them begin with its beginning.

The meridian divided into sixty *ghatikâ*.

If Brahmagupta says of the meridian that it is divided into sixty parts (v. p. 279), it is as if any one of us should say, the meridian is divided into twenty-four parts; for the meridian is a medium for measuring and counting time. Its revolution lasts twenty-four hours, or, as the Hindus will have it, sixty *ghaṭikâ* (or *gharî*). This is the reason why they have reckoned the risings of the zodiacal signs in *ghaṭikâ*, not in *times of the meridian* (360 degrees).

On the fixed stars.

If, further, Brahmagupta says that the wind causes the fixed stars and the planets to revolve, if he besides, in particular, attributes a slow eastward motion to the planets (p. 280), he gives the reader to understand that the fixed stars have no such motion, or else he would have said that they, too, have the same slow eastward motion as the planets, not differing from them save in size and in the variation which they exhibit in the retrograde motion. Some people relate that the ancients originally did not understand their (the fixed stars') motions until, in long periods of time, they became aware of them. This opinion is confirmed by the fact that Brahmagupta's book does not, among the various cycles, mention the cycles of the fixed stars, and that he makes their appearing and disappearing depend upon invariable degrees of the sun.

The direction of the heavenly motion, as seen from different points of the earth.

If Brahmagupta maintains (p. 278) that to the inhabitants of the equator the *first motion* is not a motion to the right and left, the reader must bear in mind the following. A man dwelling under either of the two poles, to whatever direction he turns, has always the

moving heavenly bodies *before* himself, and as they move in one direction, they must necessarily first stand opposite one of his hands, and then, moving on, come to stand opposite his other hand. The direction of this motion appears to the inhabitants of the two poles just the very contrary, like the image of a thing in the water or a mirror, where its directions seem to be exchanged. If the image of a man is reflected by the water or a mirror, he appears as a different man standing opposite to the spectator, his right side opposite to Page 142.
the left of the spectator, and his left side opposite to the right of the spectator.

Likewise the inhabitants of places of northern latitude have the revolving heavenly bodies *before* themselves towards the south, and the inhabitants of places of southern latitude have them *before* themselves towards the north. To them the motion appears the same as to the inhabitants of Meru and Vaḍavâmukha. But as regards those living on the equator, the heavenly bodies revolve nearly *above their heads*, so they cannot have them *before* themselves in any direction. In reality, however, they deviate a little from the equator, and in consequence the people there have a uniform motion before themselves on two sides, the motion of the northern heavenly bodies from right to left, and that of the southern bodies from left to right. So they unite in their persons the faculty of the inhabitants of the two poles (viz. of seeing the heavenly bodies moving in different directions), and it depends entirely upon their will, if they want to see the stars move from the right to the left or *vice versâ*.

It is the line passing through the zenith of a man standing on the equator which Brahmagupta means when he says that it is divided into sixty parts (v. p. 279).

The authors of the Purâṇas represent heaven as a

dome or cupola standing on earth and resting, and the stars as beings which wander individually from east to west. How could these men have any idea of the *second* motion? And if they really had such an idea, how could an opponent of the same class of men concede the possibility that one and the same thing individually moves in two different directions?

We shall here communicate what we know of their theories, although we are aware that the reader will not derive any profit from them, since they are simply useless.

Quotation from the *Matsya-Purâna*.

The *Matsya-Purâṇa* says: "The sun and the stars pass along southward as rapidly as an arrow revolving round Meru. The sun revolves round something like a beam, the end of which is burning when its revolution is very rapid. The sun does not really disappear (during the night); he is then invisible only to some people, to some of the inhabitants of the four cities on the four sides of Meru. He revolves round Meru, starting from the north side of Mount Lokâloka; he does not pass beyond Lokâloka, nor illuminate its south side. He is invisible during the night, because he is so far away. Man can see him at a distance of 1000 *yojana*, but when he is so far away, a small object sufficiently near to the eye can render him invisible to the spectator.

"When the sun stands in the zenith of Pushkara-Dvîpa, he moves along the distance of one-thirtieth part of the earth in three-fifths of an hour. In so much time he traverses 21 *laksha* and 50,000 *yojana*, *i.e.* 2,150,000 *yojana*. Then he turns to the north, and the distance he traverses becomes thrice as large. In consequence, the day becomes long. The distance which the sun traverses in a southern day is 9 *koṭi* and 10,045 *yojana*. When he then returns to the north and revolves round *Kshîra*, *i.e.* the Milky Way, his daily march is 1 *koṭi* and 21 *laksha yojana*."

Now we ask the reader to consider how confused these expressions are. If the author of the *Matsya-Purâṇa* says "the stars pass as rapidly as an arrow," &c., we take this for a hyperbole intended for uneducated people; but we must state that the arrow-like motion of the stars is not peculiar to the south to the exclusion of the north. There are limits both in the north and south whence the sun returns, and the time of the sun's passing from the southern limit to the northern is equal to the time of his passing from the northern limit to the southern. Therefore his motion *northward* has the same right of being described as *as rapid as an arrow*. Herein, however, lies a hint of the theological opinion of the author regarding the north pole, for he thinks the north is the *above* and the south the *below*. Hence the stars glide down to the south like children on a see-saw plank.

Criticisms of the author on the theory of the *Matsya-Purâṇa*.

Page 143.

If, however, the author hereby means *the second motion*, whilst in reality it is the *first*, we must state that the stars in the *second motion* do not revolve round Meru, and that the plane of this motion is inclined towards the horizon of Meru by one-twelfth of the circle.

Further, how far-fetched is this simile in which he connects the motion of the sun with a burning beam! If we held the opinion that the sun moves as an uninterrupted round collar, his simile would be useful in so far as it refutes such an opinion. But as we consider the sun as a body, as it were, standing in heaven, his simile is meaningless. And if he simply means to say that the sun describes a round circle, his comparing the sun to a *burning beam* is quite superfluous, because a stone tied to the end of a cord describes a similar circle if it is made to revolve round the head (there being no necessity for describing it as burning).

That the sun rises over some people and sets over others, as he describes it, is true; but here, too, he is not free from his theological opinions. This is shown by his mention of the mountain Lokâloka and his remark that the rays of the sun fall on it, on its *human* or north side, not on its *wild* or south side.

Further, the sun is not hidden during the night on account of his great distance, but because he is covered by something—by the earth according to us, by Mount Meru according to the author of the *Matsya-Purâṇa*. He imagines that the sun marches round Meru, whilst we are on one of its sides. In consequence we are in a varying distance from the sun's path. That this is originally his opinion is confirmed by the later following remarks. That the sun is invisible during the night has nothing whatever to do with his distance from us.

The numbers which the author of the *Matsya-Purâṇa* mentions I hold to be corrupt, as they are not borne out by any calculation. He represents the path of the sun in the north as threefold that in the south, and makes this the cause of the difference of the length of the day. Whilst in reality the sum of day and night is always identical, and day and night in north and south stand in a constant relation to each other, it seems necessary that we should refer his remarks to a latitude where the summer-day is 45 *ghaṭikâ*, the winter-day 15 *ghaṭikâ* long.

Further, his remark that the sun hastens in the north (marches there more rapidly than in the south), requires to be proved. The places of northern latitude have meridians not very distant from each other, because of their being near to the pole, whilst the meridians become more distant from each other the nearer they are to the equator. If, now, the sun hastens in traversing a smaller distance, he wants less time than for traversing the greater distance, more especially if on this greater distance his march is slackening. In reality the opposite is the case.

By his phrase *when the sun revolves above Pushkaradvípa* (p. 284) is meant the line of the winter solstice.

According to him, on this line the day must be longer than in any other place, whether it be the summer solstice or another. All this is unintelligible.

Similar notions are also found in the *Vâyu-Purâṇa*, viz. "that the day in the south is twelve *muhûrta*, in the north eighteen, and that the sun between south and north has a declination of 17,221 *yojana* in 183 days, *i.e.* 94($\frac{19}{183}$) *yojana* for each day." Quotation from the *Vâyu-Purâṇa.*

One *muhûrta* is equal to four-fifths of an hour (=48 minutes). The sentence of the *Vâyu-Purâṇa* applies to a latitude where the longest day is $14\frac{2}{5}$ hours. Page 144.

As regards the numbers of the *yojanas* mentioned by the *Vâyu-Purâṇa*, the author means evidently the *portio* of the double declination of the sphere. According to him, the declination is twenty-four degrees; therefore the *yojanas* of the whole sphere would be $129,157\frac{1}{2}$. And the days in which the sun traverses the double declination are half the solar year, no regard being had to the fractions of days, which are nearly five-eighths of a day.

Further, the *Vâyu-Purâṇa* says "that the sun in the north marches slowly during the day and rapidly during the night, and in the south *vice versâ*. Therefore the day is long in the north, even as much as eighteen *muhûrta*." This is merely the language of a person who has not the slightest knowledge of the eastern motion of the sun, and is not able to measure a day's arc by observation.

The *Vishṇu-Dharma* says: "The orbit of the Great Bear lies under the pole; under it the orbit of Saturn; then that of Jupiter; next Mars, the Sun, Venus, Mercury, and the Moon. They rotate towards the east like a mill, in a uniform kind of motion which is peculiar to each star, some of them moving rapidly, others slowly. Death and life repeat themselves on them from eternity thousands of times." Quotation from the *Vishṇu-Dharma.*

If you examine this statement according to scientific

principles, you will find that it is confused. Conceding that the Great Bear is *under* the pole and that the place of the pole is absolute height, the Great Bear lies *below* the zenith of the inhabitants of Meru. In this statement he is right, but he is mistaken with regard to the planets. For the word *below* is, according to him, to be understood so as to mean a greater or smaller distance from the earth; and thus taken, his statement (regarding the distances of the planets from the earth) is not correct, unless we suppose that Saturn has, of all planets, the greatest declination from the equator, the next greatest Jupiter, then Mars, the Sun, Venus, &c., and that at the same time this amount of their declination is a constant one. This, however, does not correspond to reality.

If we take the sum total of the whole statement of the *Vishṇu-Dharma*, the author is right in so far as the fixed stars are higher than the planets, but he is wrong in so far as the pole is not higher than the fixed stars.

The mill-like rotation of the planets is the *first motion* towards the west, not the *second motion* indicated by the author. According to him, the planets are the spirits of individuals who have gained exaltation by their merits, and who have returned to it after the end of their life in a human shape. According to my opinion, the author uses a number in the words *thousands of times* (p. 287), *either* because he wanted to intimate that their existence is an existence in our meaning of the term, an evolution out of the δύναμις into the πρᾶξις (hence something finite, subject to numeration or determination by measure), or because he meant to indicate that some of those spirits obtain *moksha*, others not. Hence their number is liable to a *more* or *less*, and everything of this description is of a finite nature.

CHAPTER XXVIII.

ON THE DEFINITION OF THE TEN DIRECTIONS.

THE extension of bodies in space is in three directions: *length, breadth*, and *depth* or *height*. The path of any real direction, not an imaginary one, is limited; therefore the lines representing these three paths are limited, and their six end-points or limits are the *directions*. If you imagine an animal in the centre of these lines, *i.e.* where they cut each other, which turns its face towards one of them, the directions with relation to the animal are *before, behind, right, left, above,* and *below*.

If these directions are used in relation to the world, they acquire new names. As the rising and setting of Page 145. the heavenly bodies depend upon the horizon and the *first motion* becomes apparent by the horizon, it is the most convenient to determine the directions by the horizon. The four directions, *east, west, north, south* (corresponding to before, behind, left, and right), are generally known, but the directions which lie between each two of these are less known. These make eight directions, and, together with *above* and *below*, which do not need any further explanation, ten directions.

The Greeks determined the directions by the rising and setting places of the zodiacal signs, brought them into relation to the winds, and so obtained sixteen directions.

Also the Arabs determined the directions by the blowing-points of the winds. Any wind blowing between two cardinal winds they called in general *Nakbâ*. Only in rare cases they are called by special names of their own.

The Hindus, in giving names to the directions, have not taken any notice of the blowing of a wind; they simply call the four cardinal directions, as well as the secondary directions between them, by separate names. So they have eight directions in the horizontal plane, as exhibited by the following diagram:—

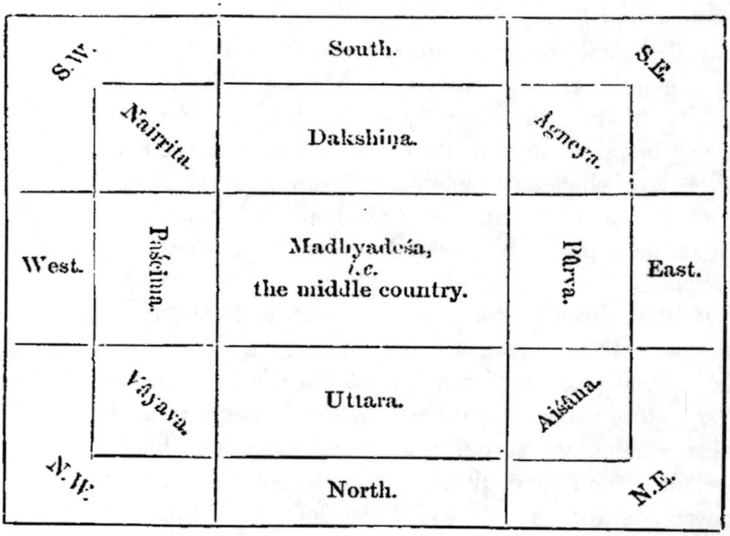

Besides there are two directions more for the two poles of the horizontal plane, the *above* and *below*, the former being called *Upari*, the second *Adhas* and *Tala*.

These directions, and those in use among other nations, are based on general consent. Since the horizon is divided by innumerable circles, the directions also proceeding from its centre are innumerable. The two ends of every possible diameter may be considered as *before* and *behind*, and therefore the two ends of the diameter cutting the former at right angles (and lying in the same plane) are *right* and *left*.

The Hindus can never speak of anything, be it an object of the intellect or of imagination, without representing it as a personification, an individual. They at once marry him, make him celebrate marriage, make his wife become pregnant and give birth to something. So, too, in this case.' The *Vishṇu-Dharma* relates that *Atri*, the star who rules the stars of the Great Bear, married *the directions*, represented as *one* person, though they are eight in number, and that from her the moon was born.

Another author relates: Dakska, *i.e.* Prajâpati, married Dharma, *i.e. the reward*, to ten of his daughters, *i.e.* the ten directions. From one of them he had many children. She was called *Vasu*, and her children the *Vasus*. One of them was the moon.

No doubt our people, the Muslims, will laugh at such a birth of the moon. But I give them still more of this stuff. Thus, *e.g.* they relate: The sun, the son of Kaśyapa and of Âditya, his wife, was born in the sixth Manvantara on the lunar station Viśâkhâ; the moon, the son of Dharma, was born on the station Kṛittikâ; Mars, the son of Prajâpati, on Pûrvâshâḍhâ; Mercury, the son of the moon, on Dhanishṭhâ; Jupiter, the son of Aṅgiras, Page 146.
on Pûrvaphâlgunî; Venus, the daughter of Bhṛigu, on Pushya; Saturn on Revati; the Bearer of the Tail, the son of Yama, the angel of death, on Âślesha, and the Head on Revatî.

According to their custom, the Hindus attribute certain dominants to the eight directions in the horizontal plane, which we exhibit in the following table:—

Their Dominants.	The Directions.	Their Dominants.	The Directions.
Indra . . .	East.	Varuṇa . .	West.
The Fire . .	S.E.	Vâyu . . .	N.W.
Yama . . .	South.	Kuru . . .	North.
Pṛithu . .	S.W.	Mahâdeva .	N.E.

The Hindus construct a figure of these eight directions, called *Râhucakra, i.e.* the figure of the Head, by means of which they try to gain an omen or prophecy for hazard-playing. It is the following diagram :—

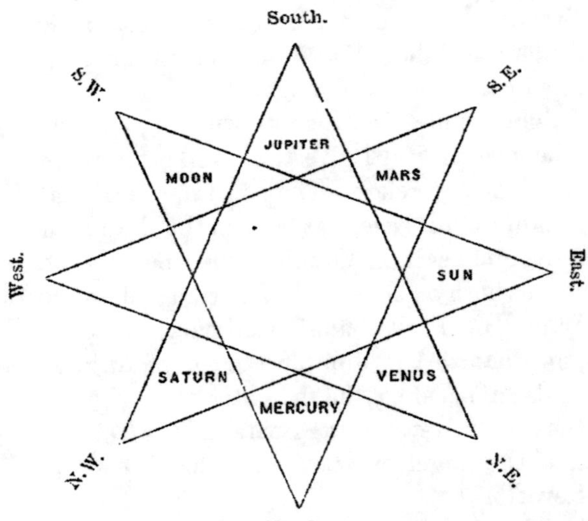

The figure is used in this way : First, you must know the dominant of the day in question, and its place in the present figure. Next you must know that one of the eight parts of the day in which you happen to be. These eighths are counted on the lines, beginning with the dominant of the day, in uninterrupted succession from east to south and west. Thus you find the dominant of the eighth in question. If, *e.g.*, you want to know the fifth eighth of Thursday whilst Jupiter is the *dominus diei* in the south, and the line proceeding from the south terminates in north-west, we find that the dominant of the first eighth is Jupiter, that of the second is Saturn, that of the third the sun, that of the fourth the moon, and that of the fifth Mercury in the north. In this way you go on counting the eighths through the day and the night till the end of the νυχθήμερον. When thus the direction of the eighth of the day in which you are has been found, it is considered by them as Râhu; and when sitting down to play, you must place yourself so that you have this direction at your back. Then you will win, according to their belief. It is no affair of the reader to despise a man who, on account of such an omen, in a variety of games stakes all his chances on one cast of the dice. Suffice it to leave to him the responsibility of his dice-playing.

Page 147.

CHAPTER XXIX.

DEFINITION OF THE INHABITABLE EARTH ACCORDING TO THE HINDUS.

The Ṛishi Bhuvana-kośa on the inhabitable world.

In the book of the Ṛishi Bhuvanakośa we read that the inhabitable world stretches from Himavant towards the south, and is called *Bharata-varsha*, so called from a man, Bharata, who ruled over them and provided for them. The inhabitants of this οἰκουμένη are those to whom alone reward and punishment in another life are destined. It is divided into nine parts, called *Nava-khaṇḍa-prathama*, *i.e.* the primary nine parts. Between each two parts there is a sea, which they traverse from one *khaṇḍa* to the other. The breadth of the inhabitable world from north to south is 1000 *yojana*.

By Himavant the author means the northern mountains, where the world, in consequence of the cold, ceases to be inhabitable. So all civilisation must of necessity be south of these mountains.

His words, that the inhabitants are subject to *reward and punishment*, indicate that there are other people *not* subject to it. These beings he must either raise from the degree of man to that of angels, who, in consequence of the simplicity of the elements they are composed of and of the purity of their nature, never disobey a divine order, being always willing to worship; or he must degrade them to the degree of irrational animals. According to him, therefore, there are no human beings outside the οἰκουμένη (*i.e. Bharata-varsha*).

Bharatavarsha is not India alone, as Hindus think, according to whom *their* country is the world, and their race the only race of mankind: for India is not traversed by an ocean separating one *khaṇḍa* from the other. Further, they do not identify these *khaṇḍa* with the *dvîpas,* for the author says that on those seas people pass from one shore to the other. Further, it follows from his statement that all the inhabitants of the earth and the Hindus are subject to reward and punishment, that they are one great religious community.

The nine parts are called *Prathama, i.e. primary* ones, because they also divide India alone into nine parts. So the division of the οἰκουμένη is a *primary* one, but the division of Bharatavarsha a *secondary* one. Besides, there is still a third division into nine parts, as their astrologers divide each country into nine parts when they try to find the lucky and unlucky places in it.

We find a similar tradition in the *Vâyu-Purâṇa*, viz. that "the centre of Jambu-dvîpa is called Bharatavarsha, which means those *who acquire something and nourish themselves.* With them there are the four *yuga.* They are subject to reward and punishment; and Himavant lies to the north of the country. It is divided into nine parts, and between them there are navigable seas. Its length is 9000 *yojana*, its breadth 1000; and because the country is also called Samnâra (?), each ruler who rules it is called Samnâra (?). The shape of its nine parts is as follows." Quotation from *Vâyu-Purâṇa.*

Then the author begins to describe the mountains in the *khaṇḍa* between the east and north, and the rivers which rise there, but he does not go beyond this description. Thereby he gives us to understand that, according to his opinion, this *khaṇḍa* is the οἰκουμένη. Page 148.
But he contradicts himself in another place, where he

says that Jambu-dvîpa is the centre among the *Nava-khaṇḍa-prathama*, and the others lie towards the eight directions. There are angels on them, men, animals, and plants. By these words he seems to mean the *dvîpas*.

If the breadth of the οἰκουμένη is 1000 *yojana*, its length must be nearly 2800.

Further, the *Vâyu-Purâṇa* mentions the cities and countries which lie in each direction. We shall exhibit them in tables, together with similar information from other sources, for this method renders the study of the subject easier than any other.

Here follows a diagram representing the division of Bharatavarsha into nine parts.

	Nâgadvîpa.	South.	Tâmravarṇa.	
		Gabhastimat.		
West.	Saumya.	Indradvîpa or Madhyadêśa, *i.e.* the middle country.	Kaśerumat.	East.
	Gândharva.		Nagarasaṁvṛitta.	
		North.		

On the figure *Kûrma-cakra.*

We have already heretofore mentioned that that part of the earth in which the οἰκουμένη lies resembles a tortoise, because its borders are round, because it rises above the water and is surrounded by the water, and because it has a globular convexity on its surface. However, there is a possibility that the origin of the name is this, that their astronomers and astrologers divide the directions according to the lunar stations.

Therefore the country, too, is divided according to the lunar stations, and the figure which represents this division is similar to a tortoise. Therefore it is called *Kûrma-cakra*, *i.e.* the tortoise-circle or the tortoise-shape. The following diagram is from the *Samhitâ* of Varâhamihira.

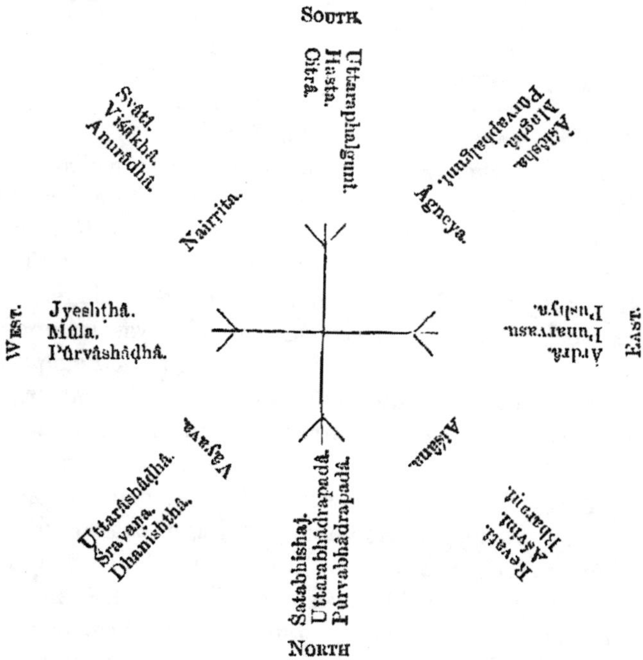

Varâhamihira calls each of the *Nava-khanda* a *varga*. He says: "By them (the *vargas*) Bharatavarsha, *i.e.* half of the world, is divided into nine parts, the central one, the eastern, &c." Then he passes to the south, and thus round the whole horizon. That he understands by Bharatavarsha India alone is indicated by his saying that each *varga* has a region, the king of

Page 149. The division of Bharatavarsha according to Varâhamihira.

which is killed when some mishap befalls it. So belong

To the 1st or central varga,	the region	Pâñcâla.
" 2d varga,	"	Magadha.
" 3d varga,	"	Kaliṅga.
" 4th varga,	"	Avanti, *i.e.* Ujain.
" 5th varga,	"	Ananta.
" 6th varga,	"	Sindhu and Sauvîra.
" 7th varga,	"	Hârahaura.
" 8th varga,	"	Madura.
" 9th varga,	"	Kulinda.

All these countries are parts of India proper.

On the change of geographical names.

Most of the names of countries under which they appear in this context are not those by which they are now generally known. Utpala, a native of Kashmîr, says in his commentary on the book *Saṁhitâ* regarding this subject: "The names of countries change, and particularly in the *yugas*. So Mûltân was originally called Kâśyapapura, then Haṁsapura, then Bagapura, then Sâmbhapura, and then *Mûlasthâna*, i.e. *the original place*, for *mûla* means root, origin, and *tâna* means place."

A *yuga* is a long space of time, but names change rapidly, when, for instance, a foreign nation with a different language occupies a country. Their tongues frequently mangle the words, and thus transfer them into their own language, as is, *e.g.* the custom of the Greeks. Either they keep the original meaning of the names, and try a sort of translation, but then they undergo certain changes. So the city of Shâsh, which has its name from the Turkish language, where it is called Tâsh-kand, *i.e. stone-city*, is called *stone-tower* in the book γεωγραφία. In this way new names spring up as translations of older ones. Or, secondly, the barbarians adopt and keep the local names, but with such sounds and in such forms as are adapted to their tongues, as the Arabs do in Arabising foreign names, which become disfigured in their mouth: *e.g. Bûshang* they call in their books *Fûsanj*, and *Sakilkand* they call in their revenue-books *Fûrfaza* (*sic*). However, what is more curious and strange is this, that sometimes one and the same language changes in the mouth of the same people who speak it, in consequence of which strange and uncouth forms of words spring up, not intelligible save to him who discards every rule of the language. And such changes are brought about in a few years, without there being any stringent cause or necessity for it. Of course, in all of this the Hindus are actuated by the desire to have as many names as possible, and to practise on them the rules and arts of their etymology, and they glory in the enormous copiousness of their language which they obtain by such means.

The following names of countries, which we have taken from the *Vâyu-Purâṇa*, are arranged according to the four directions, whilst the names taken from the *Saṁhitâ* are arranged according to the eight directions. All these names are of that kind which we have here described (*i.e.* they are not the names now in general use). We exhibit them in the following tables:—

The single countries of the middle realm, according to the Vâyu-Purâṇa. Page 150.

Kuru, Pâñcâla, Sâlva, Jaṅgala, Śûrasena, Bhadrakâra (!), Bodha, Patheśvara, Vatsa, Kisadya, Kulya, Kuntala, Kâśi, Kośala, Arthayâshava (?), Puhliṅga (!), Mashaka (!), Vṛika.

The people in the east:—

Andhra, Vâka, Mudrakaraka (?), Prâtragira (?), Vahirgira, Prathaṅga (?), Vaṅgeya, Mâlava (!), Mâlavartika, Prâgjyotisha, Muṇḍa, Âbika (?), Tâmraliptika, Mâla, Magadha, Govinda (Gonanda ?).

The people in the south:—

Pâṇḍya, Kerala, Caulya, Kulya, Setuka, Mûshika, Rumana (?), Vanavâsika, Mahârâshtra, Mâhisha, Ka-

Page 151. liṅga, Abhîra, Îshîka, Âṭavya, Śavara (?), Pulindra, Vindhyamûli, Vaidarbha, Daṇḍaka, Mûlika (!), Asmaka, Naitika (!), Bhogavardhana, Kuntala, Andhra, Udbhira, Nalaka, Alika, Dâkshinâtya, Vaideśa, Sûrpâkâraka, Kolavana, Durga, Tillîta (?), Puleya, Krâla (!), Rûpaka, Tâmasa, Tarûpana (?), Karaskara, Nâsikya, Uttaranarmada, Bhânukacchra (?), Maheya, Sâraswata (?), Kacchîya, Surâshtra, Anartta, Hudvuda (?).

The people in the west :—

Malada (?), Karûsha, Mekala, Utkala, Uttamarṇa, Baśârṇa (?), Bhoja, Kishkinda, Kosala, Traipura, Vaidika, Tharpura (?), Tumbura, Shattumâna (?), Padha, Kar-
Page 152. ṇaprâvaraṇa (!), Hûna, Darva, Hûhaka (!), Trigartta, Mâlava, Kirâta, Tâmara.

The people in the north :—

Vâhlîka (!), Vâḍha, Vâna (?), Âbhîra, Kalatoyaka, Aparânta (?), Pahlava, Carmakhaṇḍika, Gândhâra, Yavana, Sindhu, Sauvîra, *i.e.* Multân and Jahrâwâr, Madhra (?), Śaka, Drihâla (?), Litta (Kulinda), Malla (?), Kodara (?), Âtreya, Bharadva, Jâṅgala, Daseruka (!), Lampâka, Tâlakûna (?), Sûlika, Jâgara.

The names of the countries for the tortoise-figure, as taken from the Saṁhitâ of Varâhamihira.

I. The names of the countries in the centre of the realm :—

Bhadra, Ari, Meda, Mâṇḍavya, Sâlvanî, Pojjihâna, Maru, Vatsa, Ghosha, the valley of the Yamunâ, Sârasvata, Matsya, Mâthura, Kopa, Jyotisha, Dharmâraṇya, Śûrasena, Gauragrîva, Uddehika near Bazâna, Pâṇḍu,
Page 153. Guḍa = Tânêshar, Aśvattha, Pañcâla, Sâketa, Kaṇka, Kuru = Tânêshar, Kâlkoṭi, Kukura, Pariyâtra, Audumbara, Kapishṭhala, Gaja.

II. The names of the countries in the east :—

Añjana, Vṛishabadhvaja, Padma-Tulya (*sic*), Vyâghramukha, *i.e.* people with tiger-faces, Suhma, Karvaṭa, Candrapura, Śûrpakarṇa, *i.e.* people with ears like sieves, Khasha, Magadha, Mount Śibira, Mithilâ, Samataṭa, Oḍra, Aśvavadana, *i.e.* people with horse-faces, Dantura, *i.e.* people with long teeth, Prâgjyotisha, Lohitya, Krîra-samudra (*sic*), *i.e.* the milk-sea, Purushâda, Udayagiri, *i.e.* the mountain of sunrise, Bhadra, Gauraka, Pauṇḍra, Utkala, Kâśi, Mekala, Ambashṭha, Ekapada, *i.e.* the one-footed people, Tâmaliptikâ, Kausalaka, Vardhamâna.

III. The names of the countries of the south-east (*Âgneya*):—

Kosala, Kaliṅga, Vaṅga, Upavaṅga, Jaṭhara, Aṅga, Saulika, Vidarbha, Vatsa, Andhra, Colika (?), Ûrdhvakarṇa, *i.e.* people whose ears are directed upwards, Vṛisha, Nâlikera, Carmadvîpa, the mountain Vindhya, Tripurî, Śmaśrudhara, Hemakûṭya, Vyâlagrîva, *i.e.* Page 154.
people whose bosoms are snakes, Mahâgrîva, *i.e.* people who have wide bosoms, Kishkindha, the country of the monkeys, Kaṇḍakasthala, Nishâda, Râshṭra, Dâśârṇa, Purika, Nagnaparṇa, Śavara.

IV. The names of the countries in the south:—

Laṅkâ, *i.e.* the cupola of the earth, Kâlâjina, Sairîkîrṇa (?), Tâlikaṭa, Girnagara, Malaya, Dardura, Mahendṛa, Mâlindya, Bharukaccha, Kankaṭa, Taṅkaṇa, Vanavâsi on the coast, Śibika, Phaṇikâra, Koṅkana near the sea, Âbhîra, Âkara, Veṇâ a river, Avanti, *i.e.* the city of Ujain, Daśapura, Gonarda, Keralaka, Karṇâṭa, Mahâṭavi, Citrakûṭa, Nâsikya, Kollagiri, Cola, Krauñcadvîpa, Jaṭâdhara, Kauverya, Ṛishyamûka, Vaiḍûrya, Śaṅkha, Mukta, Atri, Vâricara, Jarmapaṭṭana (*sic*), Dvîpa, Gaṇarâjya, Kṛishṇavaiḍûrya, Śibika, Śûryâdri, Kuśumanaga, Tumbavana, Kârmaṇeyaka, Yâmyodadhi, Page 155.
Tâpasâśrama, Ṛishika, Kâñcî, Marucîpaṭṭana, Dîvârśa (!), Siṁhala, Ṛishabha, Baladevapaṭṭana, Daṇḍakâvaṇa, Timingilâśana (?), Bhadra, Kaccha, Kuñjaradarî, Tâmraparṇa.

V. The names of the countries in the south-west (*Nairṛita*):—

Kâmboja, Sindhu, Sauvîra, *i.e.* Multan and Jahrâvâr, Vaḍavâmukha, Âravâmbashṭha, Kapila, Pâraśava, *i.e.* the Persians, Sûdra, Barbara, Kirâta, Khaṇḍa, Kravya, Âbhîra, Cañcûka, Hemagiri, Sindhu, Kâlaka, Raivataka, Surâshṭra, Bâdara, Dramiḍa, Mahârṇava, Nârîmukha, *i.e.* men with women's faces, *i.e.* the Turks, Ânarta, Pheṇagiri, Yavana, *i.e.* the Greeks, Mâraka, Karṇaprâvaraṇa.

VI. The names of the countries in the west:—

Maṇimân, Meghavân, Vanaugha, Astagiri, *i.e.* the country of sunset, Aparântaka, Śântika, Haihaya, Praśastâdri, Vokkâṇa, Pañcanada, *i.e.* the union of the five rivers, Maṭhara, Pârata, Târakruti (?), Jṛinga, Vaiśya, Kanaka, Śaka, Mleccha, *i.e.* the Arabs.

VII. The names of the countries in the north-west (*Vâyava*):—

Page 156. Mâṇḍavya, Tukhâra, Tâlahala, Madra, Aśmaka, Kulûtalahaḍa, Strîrâjya, *i.e.* women amongst whom no man dwells longer than half a year, Nṛisiṁhavana, *i.e.* people with lion-faces, Khastha, *i.e.* people who are born from the trees, hanging on them by the navel-strings, Venumatî (?), *i.e.* Tirmidh, Phalgulu, Guruhâ, Marukucca, Carmaraṅga, *i.e.* people with coloured skins, Ekavilocana, *i.e.* the one-eyed men, Sûlika, Dîrghagrîva, *i.e.* people with long bosoms, which means with long necks, Dîrghamukha, *i.e.* people with long faces, Dîrghakeśa, *i.e.* people with long hair.

VIII. The names of the countries in the north:—

Kailâsa, Himavant, Vasumant, Giri, Dhanushman (!), *i.e.* the people with bows, Krauñca, Meru, Kurava, Uttarakurava, Kshudramîna, Kaikaya, Vasâti, Yâmuna, *i.e.* a kind of Greeks, Bhogaprastha, Ârjunâyana, Agnîtya, Âdarśa, Antardvîpa, Trigarta, Turagânana, *i.e.* people with horse-faces, Śvamukha, *i.e.* people with dog-faces, Keśadhara, Capiṭanâsika, *i.e.* flat-noses, Dâsera, Kavâṭadhâna, Śaradhâna, Takshaśila, *i.e.* Mârîkala, Pushkalâvatî, *i.e.* Pûkala, Kailâvata, Kaṇṭhadhâna,

Ambara, Madraka, Mâlava, Paurava, Kacchâra, Daṇḍa, Piṅgalaka, Mânahala, Hûṇa, Kohala, Śâtaka, Mâṇḍavya, Bhûtapura, Gândhâra, Yaśovati, Hematâla, Râjanya, Khajara, Yaudheya, Dâsameya, Śyâmâka, Kshemadhûrta (?).

IX. The names of the countries in the north-east (*Aiśâna*):—

Meru, Kanashṭharâjya, Paśupâla, Kîra, Kaśmîra, Abhi, Śârada, Taṅgaṇa, Kulûta, Sairindha, Râshṭra, Brahmapura, Dârva, Dâmara, Vanarâjya, Kirâta, Cina, Kauṇinda, Bhalla, Palola, Jaṭâsura, Kunaṭha, Khasha, Ghosha, Kucika, Ekacaraṇa, *i.e.* the one-footed people, Anuviśva, Suvarṇabhûmi, *i.e.* the gold land, Arvasudhana (*sic*), Nandavishṭha, Paurava, Ciranivasana, Trinetra, *i.e.* people with three eyes, Puñjâdri, Gandharva. Page 157.

On Romaka, Yamakoṭi, and Siddhapura.

Hindu astronomers determine the longitude of the inhabitable world by Laṅkâ, which lies in its centre on the equator, whilst Yamakoṭi lies on its east, Romaka on its west, and Siddhapura on that part of the equator which is diametrically opposed to Laṅkâ. Their remarks on the rising and setting of the heavenly bodies show that Yamakoṭi and Rûm are distant from each other by half a circle. It seems that they assign the countries of the West (*i.e.* North Africa) to Rûm or the Roman Empire, because the Rûm or Byzantine Greeks occupy the opposite shores of the same sea (the Mediterranean); for the Roman Empire has much northern latitude and penetrates high into the north. No part of it stretches far southward, and, of course, nowhere does it reach the equator, as the Hindus say with regard to Romaka.

We shall here speak no more of Laṅkâ (as we are going to treat of it in a separate chapter). Yamakoṭi is, according to Ya'ḳûb and Alfazârî, the country where is the city *Târa* within a sea. I have not found the slightest trace of this name in Indian literature. As *koṭi* means *castle* and Yama is the angel of death, the word reminds me of Kangdiz, which, according to the Persians, had been built by Kaikâ'ûs or Jam in the most remote east, behind the sea. Kaikhusrau traversed the sea to Kangdiz when following the traces of Afrâsiâb the Turk, and there he went at the time of his anchorite life and expatriation. For *diz* means in Persian *castle*, as *koṭi* in the Indian language. Abû-Ma'shar of Balkh has based his geographical canon on Kangdiz as the 0° of longitude or first meridian.

How the Hindus came to suppose the existence of Siddhapura I do not know, for they believe, like ourselves, that behind the inhabited half-circle there is nothing but unnavigable seas.

The meridian of Ujain the first meridian.

In what way the Hindus determine the latitude of a place has not come to our knowledge. That the longitude of the inhabitable world is a half-circle is a far-spread theory among their astronomers; they differ (from Western astronomers) only as to the point which is to be its beginning. If we explain the theory of the Hindus as far as we understand it, their beginning of longitude is Ujain, which they consider as the eastern limit of one quarter (of the οἰκουμένη), whilst the limit of the second quarter lies in the west at some distance from the end of civilisation, as we shall hereafter explain in the chapter about the difference of the longitudes of two places.

Page 158.

Other first meridians used by Western astronomers.

The theory of the Western astronomers on this point is a double one. Some adopt as the beginning of longitude the shore of the (Atlantic) ocean, and they extend the first quarter thence as far as the environs of Balkh. Now, according to this theory, things have been united which have no connection with each other. So Shapûrḳân and Ujain are placed on the same meridian. A theory which so little corresponds to reality is quite valueless. Others adopt the *Islands of the Happy Ones* as the beginning of longitude, and the quarter of the οἰκουμένη they extend thence as far as the neighbourhood of Jurjân and Nîshâpûr. Both these theories are totally different from that of the Hindus. This subject, however, shall be more accurately investigated in a subsequent chapter (p. 311).

If I, by the grace of God, shall live long enough, I shall devote a special treatise to the longitude of Nîshâpûr, where this subject shall be thoroughly inquired into.

CHAPTER XXX.

ON LAṄKÂ, OR THE CUPOLA OF THE EARTH.

On the meaning of the term *cupola of the earth.*

THE midst of the inhabitable world, of its longitudinal extension from east to west on the equator, is by the astronomers (of the Muslims) called the *cupola of the earth*, and the *great* circle which passes through the pole and this point of the equator is called the *meridian of the cupola.* We must, however, observe that whatever may be the natural form of the earth, there is no place on it which to the exclusion of others deserves the name of a *cupola;* that this term is only a metaphorical one to denote a point from which the two ends of the inhabitable world in east and west are equidistant, comparable to the top of a cupola or a tent, as all things hanging down from this top (tent-ropes or walls) have the same length, and their lower ends the same distances therefrom. But the Hindus never call this point by a term that in our language must be interpreted by *cupola;* they only say that Laṅkâ is between the two ends of the inhabitable world and without

The story of Râma.

latitude. There Râvaṇa, the demon, fortified himself when he had carried off the wife of Râma, the son of Daśaratha. His labyrinthine fortress is called تنكت درو (?), whilst in our (Muslim) countries it is called *Yâvana-koṭi,* which has frequently been explained as Rome.

The following is the plan of the labyrinthine fortress:—

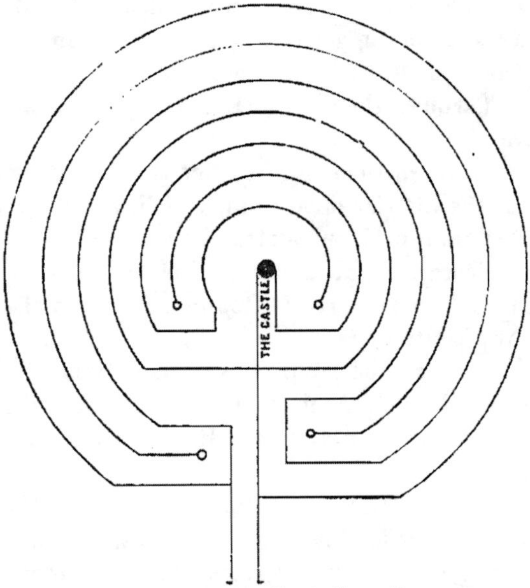

Door of the road leading to the castle.

Page 159.

Râma attacked Râvaṇa after having crossed the ocean on a dyke of the length of 100 *yojana*, which he had constructed from a mountain in a place called *Setubandha*, *i.e.* bridge of the ocean, east of Ceylon. He fought with him and killed him, and Râma's brother killed the brother of Râvaṇa, as is described in the story of Râma and Râmâyana. Thereupon he broke the dyke in ten different places by arrow-shots.

On the island of Laṅkâ.

According to the Hindus, Laṅkâ is the castle of the demons. It is 30 *yojana* above the earth, *i.e.* 80 *farsakh*. Its length from east to west is 100 *yojana*; its breadth from north to south is the same as the height (*i.e.* thirty).

It is on account of Laṅkâ and the island of Vaḍavâmukha that the Hindus consider the south as foreboding evil. In no work of piety do they direct themselves southward or walk southward. The south occurs only in connection with impious actions.

The first meridian.

The line on which the astronomical calculations are based (as 0° of longitude), which passes in a straight line from Laṅkâ to Meru, passes—

(1.) Through the city of Ujain (Ujjayinî) in Mâlava (Mâlvâ).

(2.) Through the neighbourhood of the fortress Rohitaka in the district of Multân, which is now deserted.

(3.) Through Kurukshetra, *i.e.* the plain of Tâneshar (Sthâneśvara), in the centre of their country.

(4.) Through the river Yamunâ, on which the city of Mathurâ is situated.

(5.) Through the mountains of the Himavant, which are covered with everlasting snow, and where the rivers of their country rise. Behind them lies Mount Meru.

The situation of Ujain.

The city of Ujain, which in the tables of the longitudes of places is mentioned as *Uzain*, and as situated on the sea, is in reality 100 *yojana* distant from the sea. Some undiscriminating Muslim astronomer has uttered the opinion that Ujain lies on the meridian of Al-shabûrḳân in Al-jûzajân; but such is not the case, for it lies by many degrees of the equator more to the east than Al-shabûrḳân. There is some confusion about the longitude of Ujain, particularly among such (Muslim) astronomers as mix up with each other the different opinions about the first degree of longitude both in east and west, and are unable to distinguish them properly.

The author's conjecture about Laṅkâ and Langabâlûs.

No sailor who has traversed the ocean round the place which is ascribed to Laṅkâ, and has travelled in that direction, has ever given such an account of it as tallies with the traditions of the Hindus or resembles them. In fact, there is no tradition which makes the thing appear to us more possible (than it is according to the reports of the Hindus). The name Laṅkâ, however, makes me think of something entirely different, viz. that the clove is called *lavang*, because it is imported from a country called *Laṅga*. According to the uniform report of all sailors, the ships which are sent to this country land their cargo in boats, viz. ancient Western *denars* and various kinds of merchandise, striped Indian cloth, salt, and other usual articles of trade. These wares are deposited on the shore on leather sheets, each of which is marked with the name of its owner. Thereupon the merchants retire to their ships. On the following day they find the sheets covered with cloves by way of payment, little or much, as the natives happen to own.

The people with whom this trade is carried on are demons according to some, savage men according to others.

A certain wind as the cause of small-pox.

The Hindus who are the neighbours of those regions (of Laṅkâ) believe that the small-pox is a wind blowing from the island of Laṅkâ towards the continent to carry off souls. According to one report, some men warn people beforehand of the blowing of this wind, and can exactly tell at what times it will reach the different parts of the country. After the small-pox has broken out, they recognise from certain signs whether it is virulent or not. Against the virulent small-pox they use a method of treatment by which they destroy only one single limb of the body, but do not kill. They use as medicine cloves, which they give to the patient to drink, together with gold-dust; and, besides, the males tie the cloves, which are similar to date-kernels, Page 160. to their necks. If these precautions are taken, perhaps nine people out of ten will be proof against this malady.

All this makes me think that the Laṅkâ which the Hindus mention is identical with the clove-country Langa, though their descriptions do not tally. However, there is no communication kept up with the latter, for people say that when perchance a merchant is left behind on this island, there is no more trace found of him. And this my conjecture is strengthened by the fact that, according to the book of Râma and Râmâyana, behind the well-known country of Sindh there are cannibals. And, on the other hand, it is well known among all seamen that cannibalism is the cause of the savagery and bestiality of the inhabitants of the island of Langabâlûs.

CHAPTER XXXI.

ON THAT DIFFERENCE OF VARIOUS PLACES WHICH WE CALL THE DIFFERENCE OF LONGITUDE.

On the Hindu method of determining longitude.

HE who aims at accuracy in this subject must try to determine the distance between the spheres of the meridians of the two places in question. Muslim astronomers reckon by *equatorial times* corresponding to the distance between the two meridians, and begin to count from one (the western one) of the two places. The sum of equatorial minutes which they find is called *the difference between the two longitudes*; for they consider as the *longitude* of each place the distance of its meridian from *the great circle* passing through the pole of the equator, which has been chosen as the limit of the οἰκουμένη, and for this first meridian they have chosen the *western* (not the eastern) limit of the οἰκουμένη. It is all the same whether these *equatorial times*, whatsoever their number for each meridian may be, are reckoned as 360th parts of a circle, or as its 60th parts, so as to correspond to the *day-minutes*, or as *farsakh* or *yojana*.

The Hindus employ in this subject methods which do not rest on the same principle as ours. They are totally different; and howsoever different they are, it is perfectly clear that none of them hits the right mark. As we (Muslims) note for each place its *longitude*, the Hindus note the number of *yojanas* of its distance from the meridian of Ujain. And the more to the west the position of a place is, the greater is the number of *yojanas;* the more to the east it is, the smaller is this number. They call it *deśântara*, i.e. *the difference between the places.* Further, they multiply the *deśântara* by the mean daily motion of *the planet* (the sun), and divide the product by 4800. Then the quotient represents that amount of the motion of the star which corresponds to the number of *yojana* in question, *i.e.* that which must be added to the mean place of the sun, as it has been found for moon or midnight of Ujain, if you want to find the longitude of the place in question.

On the circumference of the earth.

The number which they use as divisor (4800) is the number of the *yojanas* of the circumference of the earth, for the difference between the spheres of the meridians of the two places stands in the same relation to the whole circumference of the earth as the mean motion of the planet (sun) from one place to the other to its whole daily rotation round the earth.

If the circumference of the earth is 4800 *yojanas*, the diameter is nearly 1527; but Pulisa reckons it as 1600, Brahmagupta as 1581 *yojanas*, each of which is equal to eight miles. The same value is given in the astronomical handbook *Al-arkand* as 1050. This number, however, is, according to Ibn Ṭâriḳ, the radius, whilst the diameter is 2100 *yojanas*, each *yojana* being reckoned as equal to four miles, and the circumference is stated as $6596\frac{9}{25}$ *yojanas*.

Page 161.

Quotations from the *Khaṇḍakhâdyaka* and the *Karaṇatilaka*.

Brahmagupta uses 4800 as the number of *yojanas* of the earth's circumference in his canon *Khaṇḍakhâdyaka*, but in the amended edition he uses, instead of this, the *corrected* circumference, agreeing with Pulisa. The correction he propounds is this, that he multiplies the *yojanas* of the earth's circumference by the *sines* of the complement of the latitude of the place, and divides the product by the *sinus totus;* then the quotient is the *corrected* circumference of the earth, or the number of *yojanas* of the parallel circle of the place in question. Sometimes this number is called *the collar of the meri-*

dian. Hereby people are frequently misled to think that the 4800 *yojanas* are the *corrected* circumference for the city of Ujain. If we calculate it (according to Brahmagupta's correction), we find the latitude of Ujain to be 16¼ degrees, whilst in reality it is 24 degrees.

The author of the canon *Karaṇa-tilaka* makes this correction in the following way. He multiplies the diameter of the earth by 12 and divides the product by the equinoctial shadow of the place. The gnomon stands in the same relation to this shadow as the radius of the parallel circle of the place to the sine of the latitude of the place, not to the *sinus totus.* Evidently the author of this method thinks that we have here the same kind of equation as that which the Hindus call *vyastatrairâśika*, i.e. *the places with the retrograde motion.* An example of it is the following. The equation *vyastatrairâśika.*

If the price of a harlot of 15 years be, *e.g.* 10 denars, how much will it be when she is 40 years old?

The method is this, that you multiply the first number by the second ($15 \times 10 = 150$), and divide the product by the third number ($150 : 40 = 3\frac{3}{4}$). Then the quotient or fourth number is her price when she has become old, viz. $3\frac{3}{4}$ denars.

Now the author of the *Karaṇa-tilaka*, after having found that the straight shadow *increases* with the latitude, whilst the diameter of the circle *decreases*, thought, according to the analogy of the just mentioned calculation, that between this increase and decrease there is a certain *ratio.* Therefore he maintains that the diameter of the circle *decreases, i.e.* becomes gradually smaller than the diameter of the earth, at the same rate as the straight shadow *increases.* Thereupon he calculates the corrected circumference from the corrected diameter.

After having thus found the longitudinal difference between two places, he observes a lunar eclipse, and fixes in day-minutes the difference between the time of its appearance in the two places. Pulisa multiplies these day-minutes by the circumference of the earth, and divides the product by 60, viz. the minutes (or 60th parts) of the daily revolution. The quotient, then, is the number of the *yojanas* of the distance between the two places.

This calculation is correct. The result refers to the *great circle* on which Laṅkâ lies.

Brahmagupta calculates in the same manner, save that he multiplies by 4800. The other details have already been mentioned.

Calculation of the *deśântara* according to Alfazârî.

As far as this, one clearly recognises what the Hindu astronomers aim at, be their method correct or faulty. However, we cannot say the same of their calculation of the *deśântara* from the latitudes of two different places, which is reported by Alfazârî in his canon in the following manner:—

"Add together the squares of the sines of the latitudes of the two places, and take the root of the sum. This root is the *portio*.

"Further, square the difference of these two sines and add it to the *portio*. Multiply the sum by 8 and divide the product by 377. The quotient, then, is the distance between the two places, that is to say, according to a rough calculation.

"Further, multiply the difference between the two latitudes by the *yojanas* of the circumference of the earth and divide the product by 360."

Evidently this latter calculation is nothing but the transferring of the difference between the two latitudes from the measure of degrees and minutes to the measure of *yojanas*. Then he proceeds:—

"Now the square of the quotient is subtracted from the square of the roughly calculated *distance*, and of the remainder you take the root, which represents the *straight yojanas*."

Page 162.

Evidently the latter number represents the distance between the spheres of the *meridians* of the two places on the circle of latitude, whilst the *roughly calculated* number is the distance between the two places in longitude.

The author criticises this method.

This method of calculation is found in the astronomical handbooks of the Hindus in conformity with the account of Alfazârî, save in one particular. The here-mentioned *portio* is the *root* of the difference between the squares of the sines of the two latitudes, not *the sum* of the squares of the sines of the two latitudes.

But whatever this method may be, it does not hit the right mark. We have fully explained it in several of our publications specially devoted to this subject, and there we have shown that it is impossible to determine the distance between two places and the difference of longitude between them by means of their latitudes alone, and that only in case one of these two things is known (the distance between two places or the difference between the longitudes of them), by this and by means of the two latitudes, the third value can be found.

Another calculation of the *deśântara*.

Based on the same principle, the following calculation has been found, there being no indication by whom it was invented:—

"Multiply the *yojanas* of the distance between two places by 9, and divide the product by (*lacuna*); the root of the difference between its square and the square of the difference of the two latitudes. Divide this number by 6. Then you get as quotient the number of day-minutes of the difference of the two longitudes."

It is clear that the author of this calculation first takes the distance (between the two places), then he reduces it to the measure of the circumference of the circle. However, if we invert the calculation and reduce the parts (or degrees) of the great circle to *yojanas* according to his method, we get the number 3200, *i.e.* 100 *yojanas* less than we have given on the authority of

Al-arkand (v. p. 312). The double of it, 6400, comes near the number mentioned by Ibn Ṭâriḳ (*i.e.* $6596\frac{9}{25}$, v. p. 312), being only about 200 *yojanas* smaller.

We shall now give the latitudes of some places, as we hold them to be correct.

A criticism of Âryabhaṭa of Kusumapura on the meridian of Ujain.

All canons of the Hindus agree in this that the line connecting Laṅkâ with Meru divides the οἰκουμένη lengthways in two halves, and that it passes through the city of Ujain, the fortress of Rohitaka, the river Yamunâ, the plain of Tâneshar, and the Cold Mountains. The longitudes of the places are measured by their distance from this line. On this head I know of no difference between them except the following passage in the book of Âryabhaṭa of Kusumapura:—

"People say that Kurukshetra, *i.e.* the plain of Tâneshar, lies on the line which connects Laṅkâ with Meru and passes through Ujain. So they report on the authority of Pulisa. But he was much too intelligent not to have known the subject better. The times of the eclipses prove that statement to be erroneous, and Pṛithusvâmin maintains that the difference between the longitudes of Kurukshetra and Ujain is 120 *yojanas.*"

These are the words of Âryabhaṭa.

On the latitude of Ujain.

Ya'ḳûb Ibn Ṭâriḳ says in his book entitled *The Composition of the Spheres*, that the latitude of Ujain is $4\frac{2}{5}$ degrees, but he does not say whether it lies in the north or the south. Besides, he states it, on the authority of the book *Al-Arkand*, to be $4\frac{2}{5}$ degrees. We, however, have found a totally different latitude of Ujain in the same book in a calculation relating to the distance between Ujain and Almanṣûra, which the author calls Brahmaṇavâṭa, *i.e.* Bamhanwâ, viz. latitude of Ujain, 22° 29′; latitude of Almanṣûra, 24° 1′.

According to the same book, the straight shadow in Lohâniyye, *i.e.* Loharânî, is $5\frac{2}{5}$ digits.

On the other hand, however, all the canons of the Hindus agree in this, that the latitude of Ujain is 24 degrees, and that the sun culminates over it at the time of the summer solstice.

Balabhadra, the commentator, gives as the latitude of Kanoj 26° 35′; as that of Tâneshar, 30° 12′. Page 163.

The learned Abû-Aḥmad, the son of Catlaghtagîn, calculated the latitude of the city of Karlî (?), and found it to be 28° 0′, that of Tâneshar 27′, and both places to be distant from each other by three days' marches. What the cause of this difference is I do not know.

According to the book *Karaṇa-sâra*, the latitude of Kashmîr is 34° 9′, and the straight shadow there $8\frac{7}{60}$ digits.

I myself have found the latitude of the fortress Lauhûr to be 34° 10′. The distance from Lauhûr to the capital of Kashmîr is 56 miles, half the way being rugged country, the other half plain. What other latitudes I have been able to observe myself, I shall enumerate in this place:—

Ghazna	33° 35′	Lamghân	34° 43′
Kâbul	33° 47′	Purshâvar	34° 44′
Kandî, the guard-station of the prince	33° 55′	Waihand	34° 30′
Dunpûr	34° 20′	Jailam	33° 20′
		The fortress Nandna	32° 0′

The distance between the latter place and Multân is nearly 200 miles.

Sâlkot	32° 58′
Mandakkakor	31° 50′
Multân	29° 40′

If the latitudes of places are known, and the distances between them have been measured, the difference between their longitudes also may be found according to the methods explained in the books to which we have referred the reader.

We ourselves have (in our travels) in their country not passed beyond the places which we have mentioned, nor have we learned any more longitudes and latitudes (of places in India) from their literature. It is God alone who helps us to reach our objects!

CHAPTER XXXII.

ON THE NOTIONS OF DURATION AND TIME IN GENERAL, AND ON THE CREATION OF THE WORLD AND ITS DESTRUCTION.

On the notion of time according to Alrâzî and other philosophers.

According to the relation of Muḥammad Ibn Zakariyyâ Alrâzî, the most ancient philosophers of the Greeks thought that the following five things existed from all eternity, *the creator, the universal soul, the first* ὕλη, *space in the abstract*, and *time in the abstract*. On these things Alrâzî has founded that theory of his, which is at the bottom of his whole philosophy. Further, he distinguishes between *time* and *duration* in so far as *number* applies to the former, not to the latter; for a thing which can be numbered is finite, whilst duration is infinite. Similarly, philosophers have explained *time* as duration with a beginning and an end, and *eternity* as duration without beginning and end.

According to Alrâzi, those five things are *necessary postulates* of the actually existing world. For that which the senses perceive in it is the ὕλη acquiring shape by means of combination. Besides, the ὕλη occupies some place, and therefore we must admit the existence of *space*. The changes apparent in the world of sense compel us to assume the existence of time, for some of them are earlier, others later, and the *before* and the *afterwards*, the earlier and the later, and the simultaneous can only be perceived by means of the notion of time, which is a necessary postulate of the existing world.

Further, there are *living beings* in the existing world. Therefore we must assume the existence of *the soul.* Among these living beings there are *intelligent* ones, capable of carrying the arts to the highest perfection; and this compels us to assume the existence of a Creator, who is wise and intelligent, who establishes and arranges everything in the best possible manner, and inspires people with the force of intelligence for the purpose of liberation.

On the other hand, some sophists consider eternity and time as one and the same thing, and declare the motion which serves to measure time alone to be finite.

Another one declares eternity to be the circular motion. No doubt this motion is indissolubly connected with that being which *moves* by it, and which is of the most sublime nature, since it lasts for ever. Thereupon he rises in his argumentation from the moving being to its mover, and from the moving mover to the first mover who is motionless.

This kind of research is very subtle and obscure. But for this, the opinions would not differ to such an extent that some people declare that there is no time at all, while others declare that time is an independent substance. According to Alexander of Aphrodisias, Aristotle gives in his book φυσικὴ ἀκρόασις the following argumentation: "Everything moving is moved by a mover;" and Galenus says on the same subject that he could not understand the notion of time, much less prove it.

Page 164.

The notions of Hindu philosophers on time.

The theory of the Hindus on this subject is rather poor in thought and very little developed. Varâhamihira says in the opening of his book *Saṁhitâ*, when speaking of that which existed from all eternity: "It has been said in the ancient books that the first primeval thing was darkness, which is not identical with the black colour, but a kind of non-existence like the state of a sleeping person. Then God created this world for Brahman as a cupola for him. He made it to consist of two parts, a higher and a lower one, and placed the sun and moon in it." Kapila declares: "God has always existed, and with him the world, with all its substances and bodies. He, however, is a cause to the world, and rises by the subtlety of his nature above the gross nature of the world." Kumbhaka says: "The primeval one is *Mahâbhûta*, *i.e.* the compound of the five elements. Some declare that the primeval thing is *time*, others *nature*, and still others maintain that the director is *karman*, *i.e.* action."

In the book *Vishṇu-Dharma*, Vajra speaks to Mârkaṇḍeya: "Explain to me the times;" whereupon the latter answers: "Duration is *âtmapurusha*," *i.e. a breath*, and *purusha*, which means *the lord of the universe*. Thereupon, he commenced explaining to him the divisions of time and their dominants, just as we have propounded these things in detail in the proper chapters (chap. xxxiii. *et seq.*).

The Hindus have divided duration into two periods, a period of *motion*, which has been determined as *time*, and a period of *rest*, which can be determined only in an imaginary way according to the analogy of that which has first been determined, the period of motion. The Hindus hold the eternity of the Creator to be *determinable*, not *measurable*, since it is infinite. We, however, cannot refrain from remarking that it is extremely difficult to imagine a thing which is *determinable* but not *measurable*, and that the whole idea is very far-fetched. We shall here communicate so much as will suffice for the reader of the opinions of the Hindus on this subject, as far as we know them.

The Day of Brahman a period of creation, the Night of

The common notion of the Hindus regarding creation is a popular one, for, as we have already mentioned, they believe matter to be eternal. Therefore, they do

Brahman a period of non-creation.

not, by the word *creation*, understand *a formation of something out of nothing*. They mean by creation only the working with a piece of clay, working out various combinations and figures in it, and making such arrangements with it as will lead to certain ends and aims which are potentially in it. For this reason they attribute the creation to angels and demons, nay, even to human beings, who create either because they carry out some legal obligation which afterwards proves beneficial for the creation, or because they intend to allay their passions after having become envious and ambitious. So, for instance, they relate that Viśvâmitra, the Ṛishi, created the buffaloes for this purpose, that mankind should enjoy all the good and useful things which they afford. All this reminds one of the words of Plato in the book *Timæus:* "The θεοί, *i.e.* the gods, who, according to an order of their father, carried out the creation of man, took an immortal soul and made it the beginning; thereupon they fashioned like a turner a mortal body upon it."

Here in this context we meet with a duration of time which Muslim authors, following the example of the Hindus, call *the years of the world*. People think that at their beginnings and endings creation and destruction take place as kinds of new formations. This, however, is not the belief of the people at large. According to them, this duration is a day of Brahman and a consecutive night of Brahman; for Brahman is intrusted with creating. Further, the coming into existence is a motion in that which grows out of something different from itself, and the most apparent of the causes of this motion are the meteoric motors, *i.e.* the stars. These, however, will never exercise regular influences on the world below them unless they move and change their shapes in every direction (= their *aspects*). Therefore the coming into existence is limited to the *day of Brahman*, because in it only, as the

Hindus believe, the stars are moving and their spheres revolving according to their pre-established order, and in consequence the process of coming into existence is developed on the surface of the earth without any interruption. Page 165.

On the contrary, during *the night of Brahman* the spheres rest from their motions, and all the stars, as well as their apsides and nodes, stand still in one particular place.

In consequence all the affairs of the earth are in one and the same unchanging condition, therefore the coming into existence has ceased, because he who makes things come into existence rests. So both the processes of acting and of being acted upon are suspended; the elements rest from entering into new metamorphoses and combinations, as they rest now in (*lacuna; perhaps:* the night), and they prepare themselves to belong to new beings, which will come into existence on the following day of Brahman.

In this way existence circulates during *the life of Brahman*, a subject which we shall propound in its proper place.

Critical remark of the author.

According to these notions of the Hindus, creation and destruction only refer to the surface of the earth. By such a creation, not one piece of clay comes into existence which did not exist before, and by such a destruction not one piece of clay which exists ceases to exist. It is quite impossible that the Hindus should have the notion of a creation as long as they believe that *matter* existed from all eternity.

Brahman's waking and sleeping.

The Hindus represent to their common people the two *durations* here mentioned, the day of Brahman and the night of Brahman, as his *waking* and *sleeping;* and we do not disapprove of these terms, as they denote something which has a beginning and end. Further, the whole of *the life of Brahman*, consisting of a succession of motion and rest in the world during such a period, is considered as applying only to existence, not to non-existence, since during it the piece of clay exists and, besides, also its shape. The *life of Brahman* is only a *day* for that being who is above him, *i.e.* Purusha (*cf.* chap. xxxv.). When he dies all compounds are dissolved during his *night*, and in consequence of the annihilation of the compounds, that also is suspended which kept him (Brahman) within the laws of nature. This, then, is the rest of Purusha, and of all that is under his control (*lit.* and of his vehicles).

Vulgar and scientific notions on the sleep of Brahman.

When common people describe these things, they make the night of Brahman follow after the night of Purusha; and as Purusha is the name for a man, they attribute to him sleeping and waking. They derive destruction from his snoring, in consequence of which all things that hang together break asunder, and everything standing is drowned in the sweat of his forehead. And more of the like they produce, things which the mind declines to accept and the ear refuses to hear.

Therefore the educated Hindus do not share these opinions (regarding the waking and sleeping of Brahman), for they know the real nature of sleep. They know that the body, a compound of antipathetic *humores*, requires sleep for the purpose of resting, and for this purpose that all which nature requires, after being wasted, should be duly replaced. So, in consequence of the constant dissolution, the body requires food in order to replace that which had been lost by emaciation. Further, it requires cohabitation for the purpose of perpetuating the species by the body, as without cohabitation the species would die out. Besides, the body requires other things, evil ones, but necessary, while simple substances can dispense with them, as also He can who is above them, like to whom there is nothing.

Further, the Hindus maintain that the world will perish in consequence of the conjunction of the twelve suns, which appear one after the other in the different months, ruining the earth by burning and calcining it, and by withering and drying up all moist substances. Further, the world perishes in consequence of the union of the four rains which now come down in the different seasons of the year; that which has been calcined attracts the water and is thereby dissolved. Lastly, the world perishes by the cessation of light and by the prevalence of darkness and non-existence. By all this the world will be dissolved into atoms and be scattered.

Notions regarding the end of the world.

The *Matsya-Purâṇa* says that the fire which burns the world has come out of the water; that until then it dwelt on Mount Mahisha in the Kusha-Dvîpa, and was called by the name of this mountain.

The *Vishṇu-Purâṇa* says that "Maharloka lies above the pole, and that the duration of the stay there is one *kalpa*. When the three worlds burn, the fire and smoke injure the inhabitants, and then they rise and emigrate to Janaloka, the dwelling-place of the sons of Brahman, who preceded creation, viz. Sanaka, Sananda, Sanandanâda (?), Asuras, Kapila, Voḍhu, and Pañća-śikha."

Page 166.

The context of these passages makes it clear that this destruction of the world takes place at the end of a *kalpa*, and hence is derived the theory of Abû-Ma'shar that a deluge takes place at the conjunction of the planets, because, in fact, they stand in conjunction at the end of each *caturyuga* and at the beginning of each *kaliyuga*. If this conjunction is not a complete one, the deluge, too, will evidently not attain the highest degree of its destructive power. The farther we advance in the investigation of these subjects, the more light will be shed on all ideas of this kind, and the better the reader will understand all words and terms occurring in this context.

Abû-Ma'shar uses Indian theories.

Buddhist notions from Alêrânshahrî.

Alêrânshahrî records a tradition, as representing the belief of the Buddhists, which much resembles the silly tales just mentioned. On the sides of Mount Meru there are four worlds, which are alternately civilised or desert. A world becomes desert when it is overpowered by the fire, in consequence of the rising of seven suns, one after the other, over it, when the water of the fountains dries up, and the burning fire becomes so strong as to penetrate into the world. A world becomes civilised when the fire leaves it and migrates to another world; after it has left, a strong wind rises in the world, drives the clouds, and makes them rain, so that the world becomes like an ocean. Out of its foam shells are produced, with which the souls are connected, and out of these human beings originate when the water has sunk into the ground. Some Buddhists think that a man comes by accident from the perishing world to the growing world. Since he feels unhappy on account of his being alone, out of his thought there arises a spouse, and from this couple generation commences.

CHAPTER XXXIII.

ON THE VARIOUS KINDS OF THE DAY OR NYCHTHEMERON, AND ON DAY AND NIGHT IN PARTICULAR.

Definition of day and night.

According to the general usage of Muslims, Hindus, and others, a *day* or nychthemeron means the duration of one revolution of the sun in a rotation of the universe, in which he starts from the one half of a *great circle* and returns to the same. Apparently it is divided into two halves: the *day* (*i.e.* the time of the sun's being visible to the inhabitants of a certain place on earth), and the *night* (*i.e.* the time of his being invisible to them). His being visible and being invisible are relative facts, which differ as the horizons differ. It is well known that the horizon of the equator, which the Hindus call *the country without latitude*, cuts the circles parallel to the meridian in two halves. In consequence, day and night are always equal there. However, the horizons which cut the parallel circles without passing through their pole divide them into two unequal halves, the more so the smaller the parallel circles are. In consequence, there day and night are unequal, except at the times of the two equinoxes, when on the whole earth, except Meru and Vaḍavâmukha, day and night are equal. Then all the places north and south of the line share in this peculiarity of the line, but only at this time, not at any other.

Manushyâhorâtra.

The beginning of the day is the sun's rising above the horizon, the beginning of the night his disappearing below it. The Hindus consider the day as the first, the

Page 167. night as the second, part of the nychthemeron. Therefore they call the former *Sâvana*, *i.e.* a day depending on the rising of the sun. Besides, they call it *Manushyâhorâtra*, *i.e.* a human day, because, in fact, the great mass of their people do not know any other kind of day but this. Now, assuming the *Sâvana* to be known to the reader, we shall in the following use it as a standard and gauge, in order thereby to determine all the other kinds of days.

Day of the fathers.

After *the human day* follows *Pitṛîṇâm ahorâtra*, *i.e.* the nychthemeron of the forefathers, whose spirits, according to the belief of the Hindus, dwell in the sphere of the moon. Its day and night depend upon light and darkness, not upon the rising and setting in relation to a certain horizon. When the moon stands in the highest parts of the sphere with reference to them, this is a day to them; and when it stands in the lowest parts, it is night to them. Evidently their moon is the time of *conjunction* or full moon, and their midnight is *opposition* or new moon. Therefore the nychthemeron of the forefathers is a complete lunar month, the day beginning at the time of half-moon, when the light on the moon's body begins to increase, and the night beginning at the time of half-moon, when her light begins to wane. This follows of necessity from the just-mentioned determination of the noon and midnight of the nychthemeron of the forefathers. Besides, it may be brought near to the reader by a comparison, as the bright half of the light on the moon's body may be compared to the rising of half of the globe of the sun over the horizon, and the other half's setting below the horizon. The day of this nychthemeron extends from the last quarter of a month to the first quarter of the succeeding month; the night from the first to the second quarter of one identical month. The totality of these two halves is the nychthemeron of the forefathers.

Thus the subject is explained by the author of *Vishṇu-Dharma* both at large and in detail, but afterwards he treats it a second time with very little understanding, and identifies *the day of the forefathers* with the *black* half of the month from opposition to conjunction, and their night with its *white* half, whilst the correct statement is that which we have just mentioned. This view is also confirmed by their custom of offering gifts of food to the forefathers on the day of conjunction, for they explain noon to be the time of taking food. For this reason they offer food to the forefathers at the same time when they themselves take it.

Next follows the *Divyâhorâtra, i.e.* the nychthemeron of the angels. It is known that the horizon of the greatest latitude, *i.e.* that of 90 degrees, where the pole stands in the zenith, is the equator, not exactly, but approximately, because it is a little below the visible horizon for that place on earth which is occupied by Mount Meru; for its top and slopes the horizon in question and the equator may be absolutely identical, although the visible horizon lies a little below it (*i.e.* farther south). Further, it is evident that the zodiac is divided into two halves by being intersected by the equator, the one half lying above the equator (*i.e.* north of it), the second half below it. As long as the sun marches in the signs of northern declination it revolves like a mill, since the diurnal arcs which he describes are parallel to the horizon, as in the case of the sun-dials. For those who live under the north pole the sun appears above the horizon, therefore they have day, whilst for those living under the south pole the sun is concealed below the horizon, and therefore they have night. When, then, the sun migrates to the southern signs, he revolves like a mill below the horizon (*i.e.* south of the equator); hence it is night to the people living under the north pole and day to those living under the south pole.

Day of the Devas.

Page 168.

The dwellings of the *Devaka*, *i.e.* the spiritual beings, are under the two poles; therefore this kind of day is called by their name, *i.e.* the nychthemeron *of the Deva.*

Âryabhaṭa of Kusumapura says that the Deva see one half of the solar year, the Dânava the other; that the Pitáras see one half of the lunar month, human beings the other. So one revolution of the sun in the zodiac affords day and night both to the Deva and Dânava, and their totality is a nychthemeron.

In consequence our year is identical with the nychthemeron of the Deva. In it, however, day and night are not equal (as in the nychthemeron of the forefathers), because the sun moves slowly in the half of the northern declination about its apogee, by which the day becomes a little longer. However, this difference is not equal to the difference between the visible horizon and the real one, for this cannot be observed on the globe of the sun. Besides, according to Hindu notions, the inhabitants of those places are raised above the surface of the earth, dwelling on Mount Meru. Whoever holds this view holds regarding the height of Meru the same opinions as those we have described in the proper place (in chap. xxiii.). In consequence of this height of Mount Meru, its horizon must fall a little lower (*i.e.* more southward than the equator), and in consequence the rate of the day's being longer than the night is lessened (as then the sun does not entirely reach his northern apogee, where he makes the longest days). If this were anything else but simply a religious tradition of the Hindus, besides being one regarding which even they do not agree among themselves, we should try to find, by astronomical calculation, the amount of this depression of the horizon of Mount Meru below the equator, but as there is no use in this subject (Mount Meru being simply an invention), we drop it.

Some uneducated Hindu heard people speak of the day of such a nychthemeron in the north, and of its night in the south. In connection with these elements he determined the two parts of the year by the two halves of the zodiac, the one which ascends from the winter solstice, called the northern, and the one which descends from the summer solstice, called the southern. Then he identified the day of this nychthemeron with the ascending half, and its night with the descending half. All of which he has eternised in his books.

Not much better is what the author of the *Vishṇu-Dharma* says:—"The half beginning with Capricornus is the day of the *Asura*, *i.e.* the Dânavas, and their night begins with the sign of Cancer." Previously he had said: "The half beginning with Aries is the day of the Deva." This author acted without any understanding of the subject, for he simply confounds the two poles with each other (for according to this theory the half of the sun's revolution, beginning with Capricornus or the winter solstice, would be the day of the beings under the north pole or the Devas, not that of the beings under the south pole or Asuras, and the revolution of the sun beginning with Cancer or the summer solstice would be the day of the Asuras, not their night). If this author had really understood the sentence, and had known astronomy, he would have come to other conclusions.

Next follows the *Brahmâhorâtra*, *i.e.* the nychthemeron of Brahman. It is not derived from light and darkness (as that of the forefathers), nor from the appearing or disappearing of a heavenly body (like that of the Devas), but from the physical nature of created things, in consequence of which they *move* in the day and *rest* in the night. The length of the nychthemeron of Brahman is 8,640,000,000 of our years. During one half of it, *i.e.* during the day, the æther, with all that is in it, is moving, the earth is producing, and the Day of Brahman.

changes of existence and destruction are constantly going on upon the surface of the earth. During the other half, *i.e.* the night, there occurs the opposite of everything which occurs in the day; the earth is not changing, because those things which produce the changes are resting and all motions are stopped, as nature rests in the night and in the winter, and con-
Page 169. centrates itself, preparing for a new existence in the day and in the summer.

Each day of Brahman is a *kalpa*, as also each night, and a *kalpa* is that space of time which Muslim authors call *the year of the Sindhind*.

Day of Purusha.

Lastly follows the *Purushâhorâtra*, *i.e.* the nychthemeron of the All-soul, which is also called *Mahâkalpa*, *i.e.* the greatest *kalpa*. The Hindus only use it for the purpose of determining duration in general by something like a notion of time, but do not specify it as day and night. I almost feel inclined to think that the day of this nychthemeron means the duration of the soul's being connected with the ὕλη, whilst the night means the duration of their being separated from each other, and of the resting of the souls (from the fatigue of being mixed up with the ὕλη), and that that condition which necessitates the soul's being connected with the ὕλη or its being separated from the ὕλη reaches its periodical end at the end of this nychthemeron. The *Vishṇu-Dharma* says: "The life of Brahman is the day of Purusha, and the night of Purusha has the same length."

The Hindus agree in assigning to the life of Brahman a hundred of *his* years. The number of *our* years which corresponds to *one* of his years betrays itself to be a multiplication of 360 with the number of our years, which correspond to one nychthemeron of his. We have already mentioned (p. 331) the length of the nychthemeron of Brahman. Now the length of *a year of Brahman* is 3,110,400,000,000 of our years (*i.e.*

360 × 8,640,000,000). A hundred years of the same kind, reckoned in *our* years, are represented by the same number increased by two ciphers, so that you get in the whole ten ciphers, viz. 311,040,000,000,000. This space of time is a *day* of Purusha; therefore his nychthemeron is double of it, viz. 622,080,000,000,000 of *our* years.

Parârdha-kalpa.

According to the *Pulisa-Siddhânta*, the life of Brahman is a day of Purusha. However, it has also been mentioned that a day of Purusha is a *parârdhakalpa*. Other Hindus say that *parârdhakalpa* is the *day of kha*, *i.e.* the point, by which they mean the *first cause*, on which all existence depends. The *kalpa* occupies the eighteenth place in the scale of the degrees of the numbers (see p. 175). It is called *parârdha*, which means *the half of heaven*. Now, the double of this would be the *whole* of heaven and the whole nychthemeron. Therefore *kha* is represented by the number 864, followed by twenty-four ciphers, this number representing *our* years (*cf.* p. 331).

These terms must, on the whole, be rather considered as a philosophical means of conveying an abstract notion of time than as mathematical values composed of the various kinds of numbers, for they are derived from the processes of combination and dissolution, of procreation and destruction.

CHAPTER XXXIV.

ON THE DIVISION OF THE NYCHTHEMERON INTO MINOR PARTICLES OF TIME.

Ghaṭî. THE Hindus are foolishly painstaking in inventing the most minute particles of time, but their efforts have not resulted in a universally adopted and uniform system. On the contrary, you hardly ever meet with two books or two men representing the subject identically. In the first instance, the nychthemeron is divided into sixty minutes or *ghaṭî*. We read in the book *Srûdhava* by Utpala the Kashmîrian: "If you bore in a piece of wood a cylindrical hole of twelve fingers' diameter and six fingers' height, it contains three *manâ* water. If you bore in the bottom of this hole another hole as large as six plaited hairs of the hair of a young woman, not of an old one nor of a child, the three *manâ* of water will flow out through this hole in one *ghaṭî*."

Cashaka. Each minute is divided into sixty seconds, called *cashaka* or *cakhaka*, and also *vighaṭikâ*.

Prâṇa. Each second is divided into six parts or *prâṇa*, *i.e.* breath. The above-mentioned book, *Srûdhava*, explains the *prâṇa* in the following manner: "It is the breath of a sleeping person who sleeps a normal sleep, and not like a man who is ill, who suffers from retention of the urine, who is hungry, or has eaten too much, whose mind is occupied with some sorrow or pain; for the breath of a sleeping person varies according to the

Page 170.

conditions of his soul, which originate either from desire or fear, according to the conditions of his body, depending upon the emptiness or fulness of his stomach, and according to various accidents disturbing the kind of *humor* which is considered the most desirable."

It is all the same whether we determine the *prâṇa* according to this rule (one nychthemeron = 21,600 *prâṇa*), or if we divide each *ghaṭî* into 360 parts (60 × 360 = 21,600), or each degree of the sphere into sixty parts (360 × 60 = 21,600).

As far as this all Hindus agree with each other in the matter, though they use different terms. So, for instance, Brahmagupta calls the *cashaka* or seconds *vinâḍî*, likewise Âryabhaṭa of Kusumapura. Besides the latter calls the minutes *nâḍî*. Both, however, did not use particles of time smaller than the *prâṇa*, which correspond to the minutes of the sphere (60 × 360). For Pulisa says: "*The minutes of the sphere*, which are 21,600, resemble the normal breaths of man at the time of the equinoxes, and when man is in perfect health. During one breathing of man the sphere revolves as far as one minute." Vinâḍî.

Other people insert between minute and second a third measure, called *kshaṇa*, which is equal to one-fourth of a minute (or fifteen seconds). Each *kshaṇa* is divided into fifteen *kalâ*, each of which is equal to one-sixtieth of a minute, and this is the *cashaka*, only called by another name. Kshaṇa.

Among the lower orders of these fractions of time there occur three names which are always mentioned in the same sequence. The largest is the *nimesha*, *i.e.* the time during which the eye, in the normal state of things, is open between two consecutive looks. The *lava* is the mean, and the *truṭi* the smallest part of time, the latter word meaning the cracking of the fore-finger against the inside of the thumb, which is with them a gesture expressive of astonishment or admira- Nimesha, lava, truṭi.

tion. The relation between these three measures varies very much. According to many of the Hindus—

2 *truṭi* = 1 *lava*.
2 *lava* = 1 *nimesha*.

Further, they differ as to the relation between the *nimesha* and the next higher order of fractions of time, for according to some the latter (*kâshṭhâ*) contains fifteen, according to others thirty *nimesha*. Others, again, divide each of these three measures into eighths, so that—

8 *truṭi* = 1 *lava*.
8 *lava* = 1 *nimesha*.
8 *nimesha* = 1 *kâshṭhâ* (?).

The latter system is used in the book *Srûdhava*, and has also been adopted by *Ś M Y* (?), one of their learned astronomers. He makes this division still more subtle by adding a further measure, smaller than the *truṭi*, which is called *aṇu*, and eight of which are one *truṭi*.

Kâshṭhâ, kalâ.

The next higher orders, parts of time larger than the *nimesha*, are *kâshṭhâ* and *kalâ*. We have said already (p. 335) that with some Hindus *kalâ* is only another name for *cashaka*, and is considered as equal to thirty *kâshṭhâ*. Further—

1 *kâshṭhâ* = 15 *nimesha*.
1 *nimesha* = 2 *lava*.
1 *lava* = 2 *truṭi*.

Others reckon thus—

1 *kalâ* = $\frac{1}{16}$th minute of the nychthemeron = 30 *kâshṭhâ*.
1 *kâshṭhâ* = 30 *nimesha*.

And the further fractions such as those just mentioned.

Lastly, others reckon thus—

1 *cashaka* = 6 *nimesha*.
1 *nimesha* = 3 *lava*.

Here ends the tradition of Utpala.

According to the *Vâyu-Purâṇa*—

> 1 *muhûrta* = 30 *kalâ*.
> 1 *kalâ* = 30 *kâshṭhâ*.
> 1 *kâshṭhâ* = 15 *nimesha*.

The smaller fractions are disregarded by the *Vâyu Purâṇa*.

We have no means of settling the question as to which of these systems is the most authentic one. Therefore it is the best for us to adhere to the theory of Utpala and *Ś M Y* (?), *i.e.* to divide all measures of time smaller than a *prâṇa* by eight— Page 171

1 *prâṇa* = 8 *nimesha*.	1 *lava* = 8 *truṭi*.
1 *nimesha* = 8 *lava*.	1 *truṭi* = 8 *aṇu*.

The whole system is represented in the following table:—

The names of the measures of time.	How many times the smaller one is contained in the larger one.	How many of it are contained in one day.
Ghaṭî, Nâḍî	60	60
Kshaṇa	4	240
Cashaka, Vináḍî, Kalâ	15	3600
Prâṇa	6	21,600
Nimesha	8	172,800
Lava	8	1,382,400
Truṭi	8	11,059.200
Aṇu	8	88,473,600

The Hindus have also a popular kind of division of the nychthemeron into eight *prahara*, *i.e.* changes of the watch, and in some parts of their country they have clepsydræ regulated according to the *ghaṭî*, by which the times of the eight watches are determined. After a watch which lasts seven and a half *ghaṭî* has elapsed, they beat the drum and blow a winding shell Prahara.

called *śaṅkha*, in Persian *spêd-muhra*. I have seen this in the town of *Purshûr*. Pious people have bequeathed for these clepsydræ, and for their administration, legacies and fixed incomes.

Muhûrta. Further, the day is divided into thirty *muhûrta*, but this division is not free from a certain obscurity; for sometimes you think that the *muhûrtas* have always the same length, since they compare them either with the *ghaṭî*, and say that two *ghaṭî* are one *muhûrta*, or with the *watches*, and say that one *watch* is three and three-quarters *muhûrta*. Here the *muhûrtas* are treated as if they were *horæ æquinoctiales* (*i.e.* so and so many *equal* parts of the nychthemeron). However, the number of such hours of a day or of a night differs on every degree of latitude, and this makes us think that the length of a *muhûrta* during the day is different from its length during the *night* (for if four watches or fifteen *muhûrta* represent a day or a night, the *muhûrtas* cannot be of the same length in the day and in the night, except at the times of the equinoxes).

On the other hand, the way in which the Hindus count the dominants of the *muhûrtas* makes us more inclined to the opposite opinion, that, in fact, the *muhûrtas* are of different length, for in the case of day and night they simply attribute to each of them fifteen dominants. Here the *muhûrtas* are treated like the *horæ obliquæ temporales* (*i.e.* twelve equal parts of the day and twelve equal parts of the night, which differ as day and night differ).

The latter opinion is confirmed by a calculation of the Hindus which enables them to find the number of the *muhûrtas* (which have elapsed of the day) by means of the digits which the shadow of a person at the time measures. From the latter number you subtract the digits of the shadow of the person at noon, and the remaining number you look out in the middle column of the following diagram, which we have taken from some of their metrical compositions. The corresponding field of the upper or lower columns shows the number of *muhûrtas* which you wanted to find.

The *muhûrtas* which have elapsed *before* noon	1	2	3	4	5	6	7	
How many digits the shadow in question is larger than the noon-shadow . . .	96	60	12	6	5	3	2	0
The *muhûrtas* which have elapsed *after* noon . . .	14	13	12	11	10	9	8	

The commentator of the *Siddhânta*, Pulisa, comments on the latter opinion, and blames those who in general declare *one muhûrta* to be equal to *two ghaṭî*, saying that the number of the *ghaṭî* of the nychthemeron varies in the different parts of the year, whilst the number of its *muhûrtas* does not vary. But in another place he contradicts himself, where he reasons about the measure of the *muhûrta*. He fixes one *muhûrta* as equal to 720 *prâṇa* or *breaths*, one breath being composed of two things: the *apâna* or the inhaling, and the *prâṇa* or the exhaling of breath. Two other terms of the same meaning are *niḥśvâsa* and *avaśvâsa*. However, if one thing is mentioned, the other is tacitly included and understood; as, for instance, if you speak of *days*, you include the nights, meaning to express days *and* nights. Accordingly a *muhûrta* is 360 *apâna* and 360 *prâṇa*.

Whether the length of a *muhûrta* is variable or invariable.

Page 172.

In the same manner, when speaking of the measure

of a *ghaṭî*, he only mentions the one species of breath, connoting the other, for he explains it in general as equal to 360 breaths (instead of 180 *apâna* and 180 *prâṇa*).

If now the *muhûrta* is measured by *breaths*, it is dependent upon the *ghaṭî* and the *horæ æquinoctiales* as the gauges of its measure. But this is exactly the contrary of what Pulisa intends, for he argues against his opponents who maintain that a day has fifteen *muhûrtas* only, if he who counts them dwells on the equator or somewhere else, but at the time of the equinoxes. Pulisa observes that the *abhijit* coincides with noon and the beginning of the second half of the day; that, therefore, if the number of the *muhûrtas* of the day varied, the number of the *muhûrta* called *abhijiṭ* and denoting noon would vary too (*i.e.* it would not always be called the eighth *muhûrta* of the day).

Vyâsa says that the birth of Yudhishṭhira took place *in the white half, at noon*, at the eighth *muhûrta*. If an opponent means to infer from this that it was the day of an equinox, we answer by referring him to the statement of Mârkaṇḍeya, viz. that the birth took place at full moon in the month Jyaishṭha, a time of the year which is far distant from an equinox.

Further, Vyâsa says that the birth of Yudhishṭhira took place *at the abhijit, when the youth of the night was gone*, at midnight, *at the eighth* (*muhûrta*) *of the black half*, in the month of Bhâdrapada. This date, too, is far distant from an equinox.

Story of Śiśupâla.

Vasishṭha relates that Vâsudeva killed Śiśupâla, the son of the daughter of Kaṁsa, at the *abhijit*. The Hindus tell the following story of Śiśupâla. He had been born with four hands, and one day his mother heard a voice from above saying, "When that person who will kill him touches him, his two superfluous hands will fall off. Thereupon they put the child to the bosom of each of those who were present, and when it came to be touched by Vâsudeva, the two hands fell off, as had been prophesied. Now the aunt spoke to him, "Assuredly you will one day kill my child;" whereupon Vâsudeva, who was still a child, answered, "I shall not do that except he deserve it for some crime committed intentionally, and I shall not call him to account until his misdeeds exceed *ten*."

Some time afterwards Yudhishṭhira was occupied with preparing a sacrifice to the fire in the presence of the most famous personages. He consulted Vyâsa as to the rank of the guests present and the honours due to the president of such an assembly, consisting in the presentation of water and roses in a cup, and Vyâsa advised him to make Vâsudeva the president. In this assembly also Śiśupâla, his cousin, was present, and now he began to rage, maintaining that he had a better claim to such an honour than Vâsudeva. He boasted much and went even so far as to abuse the parent of Vâsudeva. The latter called the present company to witness as to his bad behaviour, and let him do as he liked. However, when the affair lasted too long, and passed beyond the number of *ten* (*muhûrtas*), Vâsudeva took the cup and threw it at him, as people throw with the *cakra*, and cut off his head. This is the story of Śiśupâla.

He who wants to prove the above-mentioned theory (like Pulisa, viz. that the *muhûrtas* are thirty equal parts of the nychthemeron), will not succeed unless he prove that the *abhijit* falls together with noon and with the middle of the eighth *muhûrta* (so that the day consists of twice seven and a half equal *muhûrtas*, and likewise the night). As long as he does not prove this, the *muhûrtas* differ in length as days and nights, though just in India only very little, and it is possible

Criticisms on Pulisa.

that in times distant from the equinoxes noon falls either at the beginning or at the end of the eighth *muhûrta*, or within it.

How little exact is the learning of the author (Pulisa) who meant to prove this, is evident from the fact that among his arguments he produces a tradition from Garga to this effect, that at the *abhijit* of the equator there is no shadow; for, in the first instance, it is not true save at the two days of the equinoxes; and, secondly, if it were true, it would not have anything to do with the subject he tries to prove (as the question of the different length of day and night and their divisions does not refer to the equator, where day and night always equal each other, but only to southern or northern latitudes of the earth).

Page 173.

Dominants of the *muhûrtas.*

We represent the dominants of the single *muhûrtas* in the following table:—

The number of the Muhûrtas.	The dominants of the Muhûrtas in the day.	The dominants of the Muhûrtas in the night.
1.	Śiva, *i.e.* Mahâdeva.	Rudra, *i.e.* Mahâdeva.
2.	Bhujaga, *i.e.* the snake.	Aja, *i.e.* the lord of all cloven-footed animals.
3.	Mitra.	Ahirbudhnya, the lord of Uttarabhadrapadâ.
4.	Pitṛi.	Pûshan, the lord of Revatî.
5.	Vasu.	Dasra, the lord of Aśvinî.
6.	Âpas, *i.e.* the water.	Antaka, *i.e.* the angel of death.
7.	Viśva.	Agni, *i.e.* the fire.
8.	Viriñçya, *i.e.* Brahman.	Dhâtṛi, *i.e.* Brahma the preserver.
9.	Keśvara (?), *i.e.* Mahâdeva.	Soma, the lord of Mṛigaśîrsha.
10.	Indrâgnî.	Guru, *i.e.* Jupiter.
11.	Indra, the prince.	Hari, *i.e.* Nârâyaṇa.
12.	Niśâkara, *i.e.* the moon.	Ravi, *i.e.* the sun.
13.	Varuṇa, *i.e.* the lord of the clouds.	Yama, the angel of death.
14.	Aryaman.	Tvashṭṛi, the lord of Citrâ.
15.	Bhâgeya (?).	Anila, *i.e.* the wind.

Nobody in India uses *the hours* except the astrologers, for they speak of the *dominants of the hours*, and, in consequence, also of *dominants of the nychthemera*. The dominant of the nychthemeron is at the same time the dominant of the night, for they do not separately establish a dominant for the day, and the night is, in this connection, never mentioned. They arrange the order of the dominants according to the *horæ temporales*.

On the hours in Hindu astrology.

They call the hour *horá*, and this name seems to indicate that in reality they use the *horæ obliquæ temporales;* for the Hindus call the *media signorum* (the centres of the signs of the zodiac) *horá*, which we Muslims call *nímbahr* (cf. chap. lxxx.). The reason is this, that in each day and each night always six signs rise above the horizon. If, therefore, the hour is called by the name of the centre of a sign, each day and each night has twelve hours, and in consequence the hours used in the theory of the dominants of the hours are *horæ obliquæ temporales*, as they are used in our country and are inscribed on the astrolabes on account of these dominants.

Page 174.

This opinion is confirmed by the following sentence of Vijayanandin in the *Karaṇa-tilaka*, i.e. *the first of the canons*. After having explained the rule how to find the dominant of the year and of the month, he says: "To find the *horádhipati*, add the signs which have risen since the morning to the degree of the horoscope, the whole being reckoned in minutes, and divide the sum by 900. The quotient you get count off from the dominant of the nychthemeron, counting the planetary spheres from above to below. The dominant of a day you arrive at, is at the same time the dominant of the hour." He ought to have said, "To the quotient you get add one, and count off the sum from the dominant of the nychthemeron." If he had said, "Reckon the equatorial degrees which have risen," &c., the calculation would have resulted in *horæ æquinoctiales.*

Names of the twenty-four horâs.

The Hindus give certain names to the *horæ obliquæ*, which we have united in the following table. We think they are taken from the book *Śrûdhava.*

The number of the Horâs.	Names of the Horâs in the day.	Whether favourable or unlucky.	Their names in the night.	Whether favourable or unlucky.
1.	Raudra.	Unlucky.	Kâlârâtri.	Unlucky.
2.	Saumya.	Lucky.	Rodhinî.	Lucky.
3.	Karâla.	Unlucky.	Vairahma (?).	Lucky.
4.	Sattra.	Lucky.	Trâsanîya.	Unlucky.
5.	Vega.	Lucky.	Gûhanîya (?).	Lucky.
6.	Viśâla.	Lucky.	Mâyâ.	Unlucky.
7.	Mrityusâra.	Unlucky.	Damarîya (?).	Lucky.
8.	Śubha.	Lucky.	Jîvaharaṇî.	Unlucky.
9.	Kroḍa.	Lucky.	Śoshinî.	Unlucky.
10.	Caṇḍâla.	Lucky.	Vrishṇî.	Lucky.
11.	Krittikâ.	Lucky.	Dâharîya (?).	The most unlucky of all.
12.	Amrita.	Lucky.	Cântima (?).	Lucky.

What time is under the influence of the serpent Kulika.

Page 175.

The book *Vishṇu-Dharma* mentions, among the *nâgas* or serpents, a serpent called *Nâga Kulika.* Certain portions of the hours of the planets stand under its influence. They are unlucky, and everything which is eaten during them hurts and is of no use for anything. Sick people who treat themselves with poisonous medicines do not recover, but die and perish. During these times no incantation is of any avail against the bite of a snake, for the incantation consists in the mention of the Garuḍa, and in those inauspicious times the stork himself cannot help in any way, much less the mention of his name.

These times are represented in the following table

where the planetary hour is reckoned as consisting of 150 parts.

The Dominants of the Hours.	Sun.	Moon.	Mars.	Mercury.	Jupiter.	Venus.	Saturn.
Number of the 150 parts of the hour before the beginning of the time of Kulika . .	67	71	0	0	17	144	86
Number of the parts during which the influence of Kulika lasts.	16	8	37	2	2 1 2	6	64

CHAPTER XXXV.

ON THE DIFFERENT KINDS OF MONTHS AND YEARS.

Definition of the lunar month.

THE *natural* month is the period of the moon's synodical revolution. We call it physical because it develops in the same way as all natural phenomena, rising out of a certain beginning like non-existence, increasing by degrees, and growing, standing still when the climax is attained, then descending, waning away and decreasing, till at last they return to the non-existence whence they came. In the same manner the light develops on the body of the moon, since she appears after the moonless nights as a crescent, then as a young moon (after the third night), and as full moon, and thereafter returns through the same stages to the last night, which is like non-existence, at all events with reference to human senses. It is well known to everybody why the moon continues for some length of time in the moonless nights, but it is not equally known, not even to educated people, why she continues some time as full moon. They must learn how small the body of the moon is in comparison with that of the sun, that in consequence the enlightened portion by far exceeds the dark one, and that this is one of the causes why the moon must necessarily appear as full moon for some length of time.

Effects of moonlight.

That the moon has certain effects on moist substances, that they are apparently subject to her influences, that, for instance, increase and decrease in ebb and flow develop periodically and parallel with the moon's phases, all this is well known to the inhabitants of sea-shores and seafaring people. Likewise physicians are well aware that she affects the *humores* of sick people, and that the fever-days revolve parallel with the moon's course. Physical scholars know that the life of animals and plants depends upon the moon, and experimentalists know that she influences marrow and brain, eggs and the sediments of wine in casks and jugs, that she excites the minds of people who sleep in full moonlight, and that she affects (?) linen clothes which are exposed to it. Peasants know how the moon acts upon fields of cucumbers, melons, cotton, &c., and even make the times for the various kinds of sowing, planting, and grafting, and for the covering of the cattle depend upon the course of the moon. Lastly, astronomers know that Page 176. meteorologic occurrences depend upon the various phases through which the moon passes in her revolutions.

This is the month, and twelve of them are in technical language called *a lunar year*.

Solar month.

The natural year is the period of a revolution of the sun in the ecliptic. We call it the *natural*, because it comprehends all the stages in the process of generation which revolve through the four seasons of the year. In the course of it, the rays of the sun as passing through a window-glass and the shadows of the sun-dials reassume the same size, position, and direction in which, or from which, they commenced. This is the year, and is called *the solar one*, in antithesis to the *lunar* year. As the lunar month is the twelfth part of the lunar year, the twelfth part of the solar year is a solar month in theory, the calculation being based on the mean rotation of the sun. If, however, the calculation is based on his varying rotation, a solar month is the period of his staying in one sign of the zodiac.

These are the well-known two kinds of months and years.

On luni-solar calculation.

The Hindus call the conjunction *amâvâsyâ*, the opposition *pûrṇimâ*, and the two quarters ATVH (?). Some of them use the lunar year with lunar months and days, whilst others use the lunar year but solar months, beginning with 0 degree of each zodiacal sign. The sun's entering a sign is called *saṇkrânti*. This luni-solar calculation is, however, only an approximative one. If they constantly used it, they would soon feel induced to adopt the solar year itself and solar months. In using this mixed system they had only this advantage, that they could dispense with intercalation.

Beginning of the lunar month.

Those who use lunar months begin the month with conjunction or new moon, and this method is *the canonical* one, whilst the others begin it with the opposition or full moon. I have heard people say that Varâhamihira does the latter, but I have not yet been able to ascertain this from his books. The latter method is forbidden. Still it seems as if it were rather old, because the *Veda* says: "Men say the moon has become complete, and by her becoming complete also the month has become complete. Thus they speak because they do not know me nor the interpretation of me, for the Creator of the world commenced creating with the white half, not with the black half." But possibly these words are only a saying of men (not really a sentence taken from the *Veda*).

The month counted as two halves.

The numeration of the days of the month begins with the new moon and the first lunar day is called *BRBA*, and again enumeration begins with full moon (*i.e.* they count twice fifteen days, beginning with new moon and full moon). Each two days which are equidistant from new moon or full moon have the same name (or number). In them, light and darkness on the body of the moon are in corresponding phases of increasing and waning, and the hours of the rising of the moon in one day correspond to the hours of her setting in the other.

For the purpose of finding these times they use the following calculation :—

Multiply the elapsed lunar days of the month, if they are less than 15, or, in case they are more, the difference between them and 15, by the number of the *ghaṭîs* of the night in question. Add 2 to the product, and divide the sum by 15. Then the quotient represents the number of *ghaṭîs* and minor fractions of time between the first night, and *either* the setting of the moon in the night in question, one of the nights of *the white half*, or the rising of the moon in the night in question, one of the nights of *the black half*.

This calculation is based on the fact that the space of time between the first night and the rising or setting of the moon in some following night of the same lunation varies by two minutes (*ghaṭî*), and that the nights vary, lasting either a little longer or a little shorter than thirty minutes. If, therefore, you count thirty minutes for each nychthemeron, and you divide the product by half the number of the minutes, you get two minutes for each nychthemeron. As these two minutes, however, agree with the difference of the nights, they multiplied the number of nychthemera by the measure of the night, *i.e.* the number of its *ghaṭîs* (see above, ll. 6, 7), whilst it would have been more accurate to multiply by the half of the sum of the *ghaṭîs* of the night in question and of the first night of the lunation. It is useless to add the two minutes, Page 177. for they represent the moment when the crescent of the moon first becomes visible, but if this moment were adopted as the beginning of the month, the two minutes would be transferred to the conjunction.

Various kinds of months.

As months are composed of days, there are as many kinds of months as there are kinds of days. Each month has thirty days. We shall here use the *civil* day (*Sâvana*, v. chap. xxxiii.) as a standard.

In agreement with the Hindu calculation of the revolutions of sun and moon in a *kalpa*, *a lunar month* $= 29\frac{189005}{356222}$ nychthemera. You find this number by dividing the sum of the days of the *kalpa* by the number of its lunar months. The number of the lunar months of a *kalpa* represents the difference between the revolutions of sun and moon in it, viz. 53,433,300,000.

A month has 30 lunar days, for this number is canonical, as the number of 360 is canonical for the number of days of a year. The *solar month* has 30 solar days and $30\frac{1,362,987}{3,110,400}$ civil days.

The month of the fathers is equal to 30 of our months, and has $885\frac{163,410}{178,111}$ civil days.

The month of the angels is equal to 30 years, and has $10{,}957\frac{241}{320}$ civil days.

The month of Brahman is equal to 60 *kalpas*, and has 94,674,987,000,000 civil days.

The month of Purusha is equal to 2,160,000 *kalpas*, and has 3,408,299,532,000,000,000 civil days.

The month of Kha has

9,497,498,700,000,000,000,000,000,000,000 civil days.

Various kinds of years.

By multiplying each of these months by twelve, we get the number of days of the corresponding year.

The *lunar* year has $354\frac{65,364}{178,111}$ civil days.

The *solar* year has $365\frac{827}{3200}$ civil days.

The *year of the fathers* has 360 lunar months, or $10{,}631\frac{1899}{178,111}$ civil days.

The *year of the angels* has 360 of our years, or $131{,}493\frac{3}{80}$ civil days.

The *year of Brahman* has 720 *kalpas*, or

1,136,099,844,000,000 civil days.

The *year of Purusha* has 25,920,000 *kalpas*, or

40,899,594,384,000,000,000 civil days.

The *year of Kha* has

113,609,984,400,000,000,000,000,000,000,000 civil days.

The latter number is mentioned by the Hindus, although it is written in their books that there is no

The day of Purusha.

combination of numbers beyond the *day of Purusha*, for

it is the first and the last, and is without a beginning in the past and without an end in the future. The other kinds of days, of which months and years (those of the fathers, the angels, and Brahman) are composed, refer to beings who stand *under* Purusha in the order of beings, and whose duration is defined by certain limits of time. The *day of Purusha* is simply an abstraction of the Hindu mind to denote that which is above the soul (*âtman*), for they make no distinction between *purusha* and *âtman* except in the order or sequence in which they enumerate them. They speak of Purusha in terms resembling those of the Ṣûfîs, viz. the *he* is not the first, and is not something else. It is quite possible Page 178. in imagination to extend the idea of duration from the existing present moment towards both sides, *i.e.* towards the past which no longer exists, and towards the future which possibly will exist, and to measure duration; and if some part of it admits of being determined by days, imagination also admits reduplications of it in the guise of months and years. In all this it is the intention of the Hindus that we should refer the years invented by them to certain periods of life, beginning with the coming into existence, and ending with destruction and death. However, God the Creator is sublime beyond either, and also the simple substances (air, fire, earth, water) do not know coming into existence nor destruction (in periodical returns). Therefore we stop with the day of Purusha, and do not think it necessary to use still larger periods of time.

A tradition relating to the years of the Great Bear and the pole.

Things which do not rest on intrinsic necessity offer a wide field for difference of opinion and arbitrary systematising, so as easily to become the source of numerous theories. Some of them may be developed according to a certain order and rule, whilst others are devoid of such. In the latter class I reckon the following theory, but unfortunately I have forgotten from what source it has come to me: "33,000 human years are one year of the Great Bear; 36,000 human years are one year of Brahman, and 99,000 human years are one year of the pole." However, as regards the year of Brahman, we remember that Vâsudeva speaks to Arjuna on the battlefield between the two ranks: "The day of Brahman is two *kalpas;*" and in the *Brahmasiddhânta* there is a tradition from Vyâsa, the son of Parâśara, and from the book *Smṛiti*, that *kalpa* is a day of Devaka, *i.e.* Brahman, and also a night of his. In consequence the there-mentioned theory is evidently wrong (one year of Brahman being infinitely longer than 36,000 years). Further, 36,000 years are the period of one revolution of the fixed stars in the ecliptic, since they pass one degree in 100 years, and the Great Bear belongs to them. However, in their traditional literature the Hindus separate the Great Bear from the fixed stars, and attribute to it a distance from the earth which differs from the real distance, and therefore they describe it by qualities and conditions which in reality do not belong to it. If the author of that theory meant by the year of the Great Bear one revolution of it, we do not see why it should revolve so much more rapidly than the other fixed stars (for, in that case, the diameter of its course would be much larger than that of the others), nor why it should form an exception to the laws of nature (according to which all fixed stars revolve at the same distance from the earth and in the same time); and the pole has no revolution which might be considered as a year of it. From all this I conclude that the author of the theory was a man entirely devoid of scientific education, and one of the foremost in the series of fools who simply invented those years for the benefit of people who worship the Great Bear and the pole. He had to invent a vast number of years, for the more outrageous it was, the more impression it would make.

CHAPTER XXXVI.

ON THE FOUR MEASURES OF TIME CALLED MÂNA.

Mâna and *pramâna* mean *measure*. The four kinds of measures are mentioned by Ya'ḳûb Ibn Ṭâriḳ in his book *Compositio Sphærarum*, but he did not know them thoroughly, and, besides, the names are misspelled, if this is not the fault of the copyists.

They are—

Saura-mâna, *i.e.* the solar measure.

Sâvana-mâna, *i.e.* the measure depending upon *the rising* (*civil* measure).

Candra-mâna, *i.e.* the lunar measure.

Nakshatra-mâna, *i.e.* the lunar-station measure (*sidereal* measure).

There are days of all four kinds of measure, days of an individual nature, which, when compared with other days, show a certain difference of measure. However, the number 360 is common to all of them (360 days of each class being a year). The civil days are used as a gauge to determine thereby the other days.

As regards the *saura-mâna*, it is known that the solar Measurement of the
year has $365\frac{827}{3200}$ civil days. Dividing this sum by four different kinds of
360, or multiplying it by 10 seconds ($= \frac{1}{360}$ day), you years and
get as the measure of the *solar* day $1\frac{5609}{384,000}$ civil day. days.

According to the *Vishṇu-Dharma*, this is the time of Page 179.
the sun's passing his *bhukti*.

The *civil* day, based on the *sâvana-mâna*, is here used as the unit of a day, for the purpose of measuring thereby the other kinds of days.

The *lunar* day, based on the *candra mâna*, is called *tithi*. Dividing the lunar year by 360 or the lunar month by 30, you get as the measure of the *lunar* day $\frac{5,016,051}{31,558,329}$ civil days (*wrong:* read $\frac{10,519,443}{10,686,860}$ civil day).

According to the *Vishṇu-Dharma*, this is the time during which the moon is visible when she is far distant from the sun.

Nakshatra-mâna is the period of the moon's passing through her twenty-seven stations, viz. $27\frac{11,259}{35,002}$ days. This number is the quotient which you get by dividing the days of a *kalpa* by the number of the revolutions of the moon in a *kalpa*. Dividing it by 27, you get as the time of the moon's passing one station $1\frac{417}{35,002}$ civil days. Multiplying the same number by 12, as we have done with the lunar month, we get $327\frac{15,051}{17,501}$ civil days as the time of the moon's passing twelve times through all her stations. Dividing the first number by 30, we get as the measure of the sidereal day $\frac{318,771}{350,020}$ civil days.

According to the *Vishṇu-Dharma*, the sidereal month has only twenty-seven days, whilst the months of the other measures have thirty days; and if a year is composed of these days, it has $327\frac{15,051}{17,501}$ days (see above). Evidently there is a fault in the text of *Vishṇu-Dharma*, as the month is reckoned too short.

What use is made of the *saura-mâna*, *candra-mâna*, and *sâvana-mâna*.

The *saura-mâna* is used in the computation of the years which compose the *kalpa* and the four *yugas* in the *caturyugas*, of the years of the nativities, of the equinoxes and solstices, of the sixth parts of the year or the seasons, and of the difference between day and night in the nychthemeron. All these things are computed in solar years, months, and days.

The *candra-mâna* is used in the computation of the eleven *karaṇa* (v. chap. lxxviii.), in the determination of the leap month, in the computation of the sum of days of the *ûnarâtra* (v. chap. li.), and of new moon and full moon for lunar and solar eclipses (v. chap. lix.).

In all these things the Hindus use lunar years, months, and days, which are called *tithi.*

The *sâvana-mâna* is used in the calculation of the *vâra, i.e.* the days of the week, of the *ahargaṇa, i.e.* the sum of the days of an era (v. chap. li.); in determining the days of marriage and fasting (v. chap. lxxv.); the *sûtaka, i.e.* the days of childbed (v. chap. lxix.); the days of the uncleanness of the houses and the vessels of the dead (v. chap. lxxii.); the *cikitsâ, i.e.* certain months and years in which Hindu medical science prescribes the taking certain medicines; further in determining the *prâyaścitta, i.e.* the days of the expiations which the Brahmans make obligatory for those who have committed some sin, times during which they are obliged to fast and to besmear themselves with butter and dung (v. chap. lxxi.). All these things are determined according to *sâvana-mâna.*

On the contrary, they do not determine anything by the *nakshatra-mâna,* since it is comprehended in the *candra-mâna.*

Every measure of time which any class of people may choose by general consent to call a day, may be considered as a *mâna.* Some such days have already been mentioned in a preceding chapter (v. chap. xxxiii.). However, the four *mânas par excellence* are those to the explanation of which we have limited the present chapter.

CHAPTER XXXVII.

ON THE PARTS OF THE MONTH AND THE YEAR.

Uttarâyaṇa and dakshinâyana.

As the year is one revolution of the sun in the ecliptic, it is divided in the same way as the ecliptic. The latter is divided into two halves, depending upon the two solstitial points. Correspondingly the year is divided into two halves, each of which is called *ayana*.

Page 180.

When the sun leaves the point of the winter solstice, he begins to move towards the north pole. Therefore this part of the year, which is nearly one half, is referred to the north and called *uttarâyaṇa, i.e.* the period of the sun's marching through six zodiacal signs beginning with *Caper*. In consequence, this half of the ecliptic is called *makarâdi*, i.e. *having Caper as beginning*.

When the sun leaves the point of the summer solstice he begins to move towards the south pole; therefore this second half is referred to the south and called *dakshinâyana, i.e.* the period of the sun's marching through six zodiacal signs beginning with *Cancer*. In consequence, this half of the ecliptic is called *karkâdi*, i.e. *having Cancer as beginning*.

Uneducated people use only these two divisions or year-halves, because the matter of the two solstices is clear to them from the observation of their senses.

Uttarakûla and dakshakûla.

Further, the ecliptic is divided into two halves, according to its declination from the equator, and this division is a more scientific one, less known to the people at large than the former, because it rests on calculation and speculation. Each half is called *kûla*.

That which has northern declination is called *uttarakûla* or *meshâdi*, i.e. *having Aries as beginning;* that which has southern declination is called *dakshakûla* or *tulâdi*, i.e. *having Libra as beginning.*

The seasons.

Further, the ecliptic is by both these divisions divided into four parts, and the periods during which the sun traverses them are called the *seasons of the year*—spring, summer, autumn, and winter. Accordingly, the zodiacal signs are distributed over the seasons. However, the Hindus do not divide the year into four, but into six parts, and call these six parts *ṛitu*. Each *ṛitu* comprehends two solar months, *i.e.* the period of the sun's marching through two consecutive zodiacal signs. Their names and dominants are represented, according to the most widespread theory, in the following diagram.

I have been told that in the region of Somanâth people divide the year into three parts, each consisting of four months, the first being *varshakâla*, beginning with the month Âshâḍha; the second, *śîtakala*, *i.e.* the winter; and the third, *ushnakâla*, *i.e.* the summer.

Uttarâyana, belonging to the Devas or Angels.	The Zodiacal Signs of the Ritu.	Capricornus and Amphora.	Pisces and Aries.	Taurus and Gemini.
	Their name.	S'iśira.	Vasanta or Kusumâkara.	Grishma or Nidâgha.
	Their dominants.	Nârada.	Agni the Fire.	Indra the Ruler.

Scorpio and Sagittarius.	Virgo and Libra.	Cancer and Leo.	The Zodiacal Signs of the Ritu.	Dakshinâyana, belonging to the Pitaras or Fathers.
Hemanta.	S'arad.	Varshakâla.	Their names.	
Vaishṇava.	Prajâpati.	Viśvedevâḥ.	Their dominants.	

Page 181.

I am inclined to think that the Hindus divide the ecliptic by such an opening of the circle which divides the circumference of a circle into six parts, a measure which is equal to the radius, beginning with the two solstitial points, and that therefore they use sixth parts of the ecliptic. If this is really the case, we must not forget that we, too, sometimes divide the ecliptic, beginning with the two solstitial points, at other times beginning with the equinoctial points, and that we use the division of the ecliptic in twelfth parts side by side with that in fourth parts.

The dominants of the single halves of months.

The months are divided into halves from new moon to full moon, and from full moon to new moon. The *Vishṇu-Dharma* mentions the dominants of the halves of the months, as we give them in the following table:—

The Names of the months.	The dominants of the *Bright* half of each month.	The dominants of the *Black* half of each month.
Caitra	Twashṭri	Yâmya.
Vaiśâkha	Indrâgnî	Âgneya.
Jyaishṭha	Śukra	Raudra.
Âshâḍha	Viśvedevâḥ	Sârpa.
Śrâvaṇa	Vishṇu	Pitrya.
Bhâdrapada	Aja	Sânta.
Âśvayuja	Âśana (?)	Maitra.
Kârttika	Agni	Śakra.
Mârgaśîrsha	Saumya	Nirṛiti.
Pausha	Jîva	Vishṇu.
Mâgha	Pitrya	Varuṇa.
Phâlguna	Bhaga	Pûshan.

CHAPTER XXXVIII.

ON THE VARIOUS MEASURES OF TIME COMPOSED OF DAYS, THE LIFE OF BRAHMAN INCLUDED.

Page 182.

Recapitulation of the single measures of time.

THE day is called *dimas* (*dimasu*), in classical language *divasa*, the night *rátrí*, and the nychthemeron *ahorátra*. The month is called *mása* and its half *paksha*. The first or *white* half is called *śuklapaksha*, because the first parts of its nights have moonlight at times when people do not yet sleep, when the light on the moon's body increases and the dark portion decreases. The other or *black* half is called *kṛishṇapaksha*, because the first parts of its nights are moonless, whilst other parts have moonlight, but only then when people sleep. They are the nights when the light on the body of the moon wanes, whilst the dark part increases.

The sum of two months is a *ṛitu*, but this is only an approximative definition, for the month which has two *paksha* is a lunar month, whilst that one the double of which is a *ṛitu* is a solar month.

Six *ṛitu* are a year of mankind, a solar year, which is called *barh* or *barkh* or *barsh*, the three sounds *h*, *kh*, and *sh* being much confounded in the mouth of the Hindus (Skr. *varsha*).

Three hundred and sixty years of mankind are one year of the angels, called *dibba-barh* (*divya-varsha*), and 12,000 years of the angels are unanimously reckoned as one *caturyuga*. There is a difference of opinion only regarding the four parts of the *caturyuga* and regarding the multiplications of it which form a *manvantara* and a *kalpa*. This subject will be fully explained in the proper place (v. chaps. xli. and xliv.).

Two *kalpas* are a day of Brahman. It is the same if we say two *kalpas* or 28 *manvantaras*, for 360 days of Brahman are a year of Brahman, *i.e.* 720 *kalpas* or 10,080 *manvantaras*.

Further, they say that the life of Brahman is 100 of his years, *i.e.* 72,000 *kalpas* or 1,008,000 *manvantaras*.

In the present book we do not go beyond this limit. The book *Vishṇu-Dharma* has a tradition from Mârkaṇḍeya, who answers a question of Vajra in these words: "*Kalpa* is the day of Brahman, and the same is a night of his. Therefore 720 *kalpas* are a year of his, and his life has 100 such years. These 100 years are one day of Purusha, and the same is a night of his. How many Brahmans, however, have already preceded Purusha, none knows but he who can count the sand of the Ganges or the drops of the rain."

CHAPTER XXXIX.

ON MEASURES OF TIME WHICH ARE LARGER THAN THE LIFE OF BRAHMAN.

Want of system regarding the greatest measures of time.

ALL that is devoid of order or contradicts the rules laid down in the preceding parts of this book is repulsive to our nature and disagreeable to our ear. But the Hindus are people who mention a number of names, all—as they maintain—referring to the One, the First, or to some one behind him who is only hinted at. When they come to a chapter like this, they repeat the same names as denoting a multitude of beings, measuring out lives for them and inventing huge numbers, The latter is all they want; they indulge in it most freely, and numbers are patient, standing as you place them. Besides, there is not a single subject on which the Hindus themselves agree among each other, and this prevents us on our part adopting the use of it. On the contrary, they disagree on these imaginary measures of time to the same extent as on the divisions of the day which are less than a *prâṇa* (v. chap. xxxiv.).

Page 183. **The greatest measures of time determined by *kalpas*.**

The book *Srúdhava* by Utpala says that "a *manvantara* is the life of Indra the ruler, and 28 *manvantaras* are one day of Pitâmaha, *i.e.* Brahman. His life is 100 years, or one day of Keśava. The life of the latter is 100 years, or one day of Mahâdeva. The life of the latter is 100 years, or one day of Îśvara, who is near to the Supreme Being. His life is 100 years, or one day of Sadâśiva. The life of the latter is 100 years, or one day of Virañcana, the Eternal, who will last for ever, even when the preceding five beings perish."

We have already mentioned that the life of Brahman is as long as 72,000 *kalpas*. All numbers which we shall here mention are *kalpas*.

If the life of Brahman is a day of Keśava, his year, consisting of three hundred and sixty days, has 25,920,000 *kalpas*, and his life, 2,592,000,000 *kalpas*. The latter is 1 day of Mahâdeva; his life, therefore, 93,312,000,000,000 *kalpas*. The latter is 1 day of Îśvara; therefore his life 3,359,232,000,000,000,000 *kalpas*. The latter is 1 day of Sadâśiva; therefore his life 120,932,352,000,000,000,000,000 *kalpas*. The latter is one day of Virañcana, of which the *parârdhakalpa* is only relatively a very small part (v. p. 175).

The same determined by *truṭis*.

Whatever may be the nature of these calculations, apparently the day and the *centennium* are the elements out of which the whole from beginning to end has been constructed. Others, however, build their system on the small particles of the day which we have previously mentioned (in chap. xxxiv.). In consequence, these people differ among themselves regarding that which they compose, as they differ regarding the particles out of which they compose. We shall here give one system of this kind as invented by those who use the following metrologic system:—

1 *ghaṭî* = 16 *kalâ*.
1 *kalâ* = 30 *kâshṭhâ*.
1 *kâshṭhâ* = 30 *nimesha*.
1 *nimesha* = 2 *lava*.
1 *lava* = 2 *truṭi*.

The reason of this division is, as they maintain, the fact that the day of Śiva is composed out of similar particles; for the life of Brahman is one *ghaṭî* of Hari, *i.e.* Vâsudeva. The life of the latter is 100 years, or one *kalâ* of Rudra, *i.e.* Mahâdeva; the life of the latter is 100 years, or one *kâshṭhâ* of Îśvara; the life of the latter is 100 years, or one *nimesha* of Sadâśiva; the life of the latter is 100 years, or one *lava* of Śakti; the life of the latter is 100 years, or one *truṭi* of Śiva.

If, now, the life of Brahman is
72,000 *kalpas*,
the life of Nârâyaṇa is
155,520,000,000 *kalpas*;
the life of Rudra,
5,374,771,200,000,000,000;
the life of Îśvara,
5,572,562,780,160,000,000,000,000,000;
the life of Sadâśiva,
173,328,992,714,096,640,000,000,000,000,000,000,000;
the life of Śakti,
10,782,449,978,758,523,781,120,000,000,000,000,000,000,000,000,000.
The latter number represents one *truṭi*.

If you compose a day out of it according to the abovementioned system, it has 37,264,147,126,589,458,187, 550,720,000,000,000,000,000,000,000,000,000,000 *kalpas*. The latter number is one day of Śiva, whom they describe as the eternal one, who is exempt from being procreated and from procreating, free from all qualities and attributes which may be applied to created things. The last-mentioned number represents fifty-six orders of number (*i.e.* units, tens, hundreds, thousands, &c. &c.); but if those dreamers had more assiduously studied arithmetic, they would not have invented such outrageous numbers. God takes care that their trees do not grow into heaven.

CHAPTER XL.

ON THE SAṀDHI, THE INTERVAL BETWEEN TWO PERIODS OF TIME, FORMING THE CONNECTING LINK BETWEEN THEM.

Page 184. Explanation of the two *saṁdhis.*

THE original *saṁdhi* is the interval between day and night, *i.e.* morning-dawn, called *saṁdhi udaya, i.e.* the *saṁdhi* of the rising, and evening dawn, called *saṁdhi astamana, i.e.* the *saṁdhi* of the setting. The Hindus require them for a religious reason, for the Brahmans wash themselves during them, and also at noon in the midst between them for dinner, whence an uninitiated person might infer that there is still a third *saṁdhi.* However, none who knows the subject properly will count more than two *saṁdhis.*

The Purâṇas relate the following story of King Hiraṇyakaśipu, of the class of the Daitya :—

Story of King Hiraṇyakaśipu and his son Prahlâda.

By practising devotion for a long period, he had earned the claim that any prayer of his should be granted. He asked for *eternal* life, but only *long* life was granted to him, for eternity is a quality of the Creator alone. Not having obtained the realisation of this wish, he desired that his death should not be effected by the hand of a human being, angel, or demon, and that it should not take place on earth nor in heaven, neither in the night nor in the day. By such clauses he meant to avoid death, which is unavoidable by man. His wish was granted to him.

This wish reminds one of the wish of the devil that he should be allowed to live till the day of resurrection, because on that day all beings would rise from death. However, he did not attain his object, as it was only conceded to him to live till the day of the well-known time, of which it has been said that it is the last of the days of trouble.

The king had a son called Prahlâda, whom he intrusted to a teacher when he grew up. One day the king ordered him into his presence to learn what he was studying. Now the boy recited to him a poem, the meaning of which was that only Vishṇu exists, whilst everything else is illusion. This went much against the opinions of his father, who hated Vishṇu, and therefore he ordered the boy to be intrusted to another master, and that he should learn to distinguish a friend from an enemy. Thereupon he waited a certain time, and then examined him again, when the boy answered, "I have learned what you have ordered, but I do not want it, for I am in friendship alike with everything, not in enmity with anything." Now his father became angry and ordered him to be poisoned. The boy took the poison in the name of God and thought of Vishṇu, and lo! it did not hurt him. His father said, "Do you know witchcraft and incantations?" The boy answered, "No, but the God who has created me and given me to thee watches over me." Now the wrath of the king increased, and he gave orders to throw him into the deep sea. But the sea threw him out again, and he returned to his place. Then he was thrown before the king into a huge blazing fire, but it did not hurt him. Standing in the flame, he began to converse with his father on God and his power. When the boy by chance said that Vishṇu is in every place, his father said, "Is he also in this column of the portico?" The boy said, "Yes." Then his father jumped against the column and beat it, whereupon Narasiṁha came forth from it, a human figure with a lion's head, therefore neither a human being, nor an angel, nor a demon. Now the king and his people began to fight with Narasiṁha, who let them do so, for it was daytime. But when it was towards evening and they were in the *saṁdhi* or twilight, therefore neither in the day nor in the night, then Narasiṁha caught the king, raised him into the air, and killed him there; therefore not on earth nor in heaven. The prince was taken out of the fire and ruled in his place.

Saṁdhi used in astrology. Varâhamihira quoted.

Hindu astrologers require the two *saṁdhi*, because then some of the zodiacal signs exercise the most powerful influence, as we shall explain hereafter in the proper place. They make use of them in a rather superficial way, simply reckoning the time of each *saṁdhi* as one *muhûrta* = two *ghaṭî* = 48 minutes. However, Varâhamihira, excellent astronomer as he is, always only used day and night, and did not allow himself to follow the opinion of the crowd regarding the *saṁdhi*. He explained the *saṁdhi* as that which it really is, viz. as the moment when the centre of the body of the sun stands exactly over the horizontal circle, and this moment he establishes to be the time of the greatest power of certain zodiacal signs.

Page 185.

On the *saṁdhi* of the year-half and its combination with the precession of the equinoxes. Other kinds of *saṁdhi*.

Besides the two *saṁdhi* of the natural day, astronomers and other people assume still other *saṁdhis*, which do not rest on a law of nature nor on observation, but simply on some hypothesis. So they attribute a *saṁdhi* to each *ayana*, *i.e.* to each of the year-halves in which the sun ascends and descends (v. chap. xxxvii.), a *saṁdhi* of seven days before its real beginning. On this subject I have an idea which is certainly possible, and even rather likely, viz. that this theory is of recent origin, not of ancient date, and that it has been brought forward about 1300 of Alexander (= A.D. 989), when the Hindus found out that the real solstice precedes the solstice of their calculation. For Puñjala, the author of the *Small Mânasa*, says that in the year 854 of the Sakakâla the real solstice preceded his calculation by 6° 50′, and that this difference will increase in future by one minute every year.

These are the words of a man who either was himself a most careful practical observer, or who examined the observations of former astronomers which he had at his disposal, and thereby found out the amount of the annual difference. No doubt, also, other people have perceived the same or a similar difference by means of the calculation of the noon-shadows. Therefore (as this observation was already much known) Utpala of Kashmîr has taken this theory from Puñjala.

This conjecture of mine is confirmed by the fact that the Hindus prefix the *saṁdhis* of the solstices to each of the six seasons of the year, in consequence of which they begin already with the twenty-third degree of the next preceding signs.

The Hindus assume a *saṁdhi*, too, between the different *yugas* and between the *manvantaras;* but as the bases of this theory are hypothetical, so everything else derived from them is hypothetical. We shall give a sufficient explanation of these things in the proper place.

CHAPTER XLI.

DEFINITION OF THE TERMS "KALPA" AND "CATURYUGA," AND AN EXPLICATION OF THE ONE BY THE OTHER.

On the measure of a *caturyuga* and a *kalpa*.

TWELVE thousand Divya-years, the length of which has already been explained (v. chap. xxxv.), are one *caturyuga*, and 1000 *caturyugas* are one *kalpa*, a period at the beginning and end of which there is a conjunction of the seven planets and their apsides and nodes in 0° of Aries. The days of the *kalpa* are called the *kalpa-ahargaṇa*, for *âh* means *day*, and *argana* means *the sum*. Since they are *civil days* derived from the *rising* of the sun, they are also called *days of the earth*, for *rising* presupposes an horizon, and an horizon is one of the necessary attributes of the earth.

By the same name, *kalpa-ahargaṇa*, people also call the sum of days of any era up to a certain date.

Our Muslim authors call the days of the kalpa *the days of the Sind-hind* or *the days of the world*, counting them as 1,577,916,450,000 days (*sâvana* or civil days), or 4,320,000,000 solar years, or 4,452,775,000 lunar years. The same sum of days converted into years of 360 civil days is equal to 4,383,101,250 of them, and to 12,000,000 *divya-years*.

The Âditya-Purâṇa says: "*Kalpana* is composed of *kal*, which means the existence of the species in the world, and *pana*, which means their destruction and disappearance. The sum of this existing and perishing is a *kalpa*."

Brahmagupta says: "Since the planets and mankind

in the world came into existence at the beginning of the day of Brahman, and since they both perish at the end of it, we must adopt this day of their existence as a *kalpa*, not another period."

In another place he says: "A thousand *caturyuga* are one day of *Devaka*, *i.e.* Brahman, and a night of his is of the same length. Therefore his day is equal to 2000 *caturyuga*. Page 186.

In the same way Vyâsa the son of Parâśara says: "He who believes that 1000 *caturyugas* are a day and 1000 *caturyugas* a night, knows Brahman."

Relation between *manvantara* and *kalpa*.

Within the space of a *kalpa* 71 *caturyugas* are equal to 1 *manu*, i.e. *manvantara*, or Manu-period, and 14 *manus* are equal to 1 *kalpa*. Multiplying 71 by 14, you get 994 *caturyugas* as the period of 14 *manvantaras*, and a remainder of 6 *caturyugas* till the end of the *kalpa*.

If we, however, divide these 6 *caturyugas* by 15, in order to find the *saṁdhi* both at the beginning and end of each of the 14 *manvantaras*, the number of the *saṁdhis* being by 1 larger than that of the *manvantaras*, the quotient is $\frac{2}{5}$ths. If we now insert $\frac{2}{5}$ *caturyuga* between each two consecutive *manvantaras*, and add the same amount both at the beginning of the first and the end of the last *manvantaras*, the fraction of $\frac{2}{5}$ disappears at the end of 15 *manvantaras* ($\frac{2}{5} \times 15 = 6$). The fractions at the beginning and end of the *kalpa* represent the *saṁdhi*, *i.e.* a common link. A *kalpa*, including its *saṁdhi*, has 1000 *caturyugas*, as we have said in the first part of this chapter.

Conditions of the beginning of a *kalpa*.

The single parts of a *kalpa* stand in a constant relation to each other, one bearing witness regarding the other. For it commences with the vernal equinox, a Sunday, the conjunction of the planets, their apsides and nodes, which takes place there where there is neither Revatî nor Aśvinî, *i.e.* between them, at the beginning of the month Caitra, and in the moment of the sun's rising over Lankâ. When there occurs an irregularity with one of these conditions, all the others become confused and are no longer valid.

We have already mentioned the number of the days and the years of a *kalpa*. Accordingly a *caturyuga*, as $\frac{1}{1000}$th of a *kalpa*, has 1,577,916,450 days and 4,320,000 years. The numbers show the relation between a *kalpa* and a *caturyuga*, and show further how to determine the one by the other.

All we have said in this chapter rests on the theory of Brahmagupta and on the arguments by which he supports it.

Theories of Âryabhaṭa the elder, Pulisa, and Âryabhaṭa the younger.

Âryabhaṭa the elder and Pulisa compose the *manvantara* from 72 *caturyugas*, and the *kalpa* from 14 *manvantaras*, without inserting anywhere a *saṁdhi*. Therefore, according to them, a *kalpa* has 1008 *caturyugas*; further, 12,096,000 *divya years*, or 4,354,560,000 human years.

According to Pulisa, a *caturyuga* has 1,577,917,800 *civil* days. According to him, therefore, the sum of the days of a *kalpa* would be 1,590,541,142,400. These are the numbers which he uses in his book.

I have not been able to find anything of the books of Âryabhaṭa. All I know of him I know through the quotations from him given by Brahmagupta. The latter says in a treatise called *Critical Research on the Basis of the Canons*, that according to Âryabhaṭa the sum of the days of a *caturyuga* is 1,577,917,500, *i.e.* 300 days less than according to Pulisa. Therefore Âryabhaṭa would give to a *kalpa* 1,590,540,840,000 days.

According to Âryabhaṭa and Pulisa, the *kalpa* and *caturyuga* begin with midnight which follows after the day the beginning of which is the beginning of the *kalpa*, according to Brahmagupta.

Âryabhaṭa of Kusumapura, who belongs to the school of the elder Âryabhaṭa, says in a small book of his on

Page 187.

Al-ntf (?), that "1008 *caturyugas* are one day of Brahman. The first half of 504 *caturyugas* is called *utsarpiṇī*, during which the sun is ascending, and the second half is called *avasarpiṇī*, during which the sun is descending. The midst of this period is called *sama*, *i.e.* equality, for it is the midst of the day, and the two ends are called *durtama* (?)."

This is so far correct, as the comparison between day and *kalpa* goes, but the remark about the sun's ascending and descending is not correct. If he meant the sun who makes *our* day, it was his duty to explain of what kind that ascending and descending of the sun is; but if he meant a sun who specially belongs to the day of Brahman, it was his duty to show or to describe him to us. I almost think that the author meant by these two expressions the progressive, increasing development of things during the first half of this period, and the retrograde, decreasing development in the second half.

CHAPTER XLII.

ON THE DIVISION OF THE CATURYUGA INTO YUGAS, AND THE DIFFERENT OPINIONS REGARDING THE LATTER.

The single parts of a *caturyuga* according to *Vishṇu-Dharma* and Brahmagupta.

THE author of the *Vishṇu-Dharma* says: "Twelve hundred *divya years* are one *yuga*, called *tishya*. The double of it is a *dvâpara*, the triple a *tretâ*, the quadruple a *kṛita*, and all four *yugas* together are one *caturyuga*, *i.e.* the four *yugas* or *sums*.

"Seventy-one *caturyugas* are one *manvantara*, and 14 *manvantaras*, together with a *saṁdhi* of the duration of one *kṛitayuga* between each two of them, are one *kalpa*. Two *kalpas* are a nychthemeron of Brahman, and his life is a hundred years, or one day of Purusha, the first man, of whom neither beginning nor end is known."

This is what Varuṇa, the lord of the water, communicated to Râma, the son of Daśaratha, in primeval times, since he knew these things thoroughly. The same information has also been given by Bhârgava, *i.e.* Mârkaṇḍeya, who had such a perfect knowledge of time that he easily mastered every number. He is to the Hindus like the angel of death, who kills them with his seat, being *aprati-dhṛishya* (irresistible).

Brahmagupta says: "The book *Smṛiti* mentions that 4000 *devaka years* are one *kṛitayuga*, but together with a *saṁdhi* of 400 years and a *saṁdhyâṁśa* of 400 years, a *kṛitayuga* has 4800 *devaka years*.

"Three thousand years are one *tretâyuga*, but together

with a *saṁdhi* and a *saṁdhyâṁśa*, each of 300 years, a *tretâyuga* has 3600 years.

"Two thousand years are a *dvâpara*, but together with a *saṁdhi* and a *saṁdhyâṁśa*, each of 200 years, a *dvâpara* has 2400 years.

"A thousand years are one *kali*, but together with a *saṁdhi* and a *saṁdhyâṁśa*, each of 100 years, a *kali-yuga* has 1200 years."

This is what Brahmagupta quotes from the book *Smṛiti*.

"*Divya years* are changed into human years by being multiplied by 360. Accordingly the four *yugas* have the following sums of human years:— **Duration of the single yugas.**

A *kṛitayuga* has	1,440,000 years,	
besides	144,000 ,,	*saṁdhi*,
and	144,000 ,,	*saṁdhyâṁśa*.
Sum total	1,728,000 years = one *kṛitayuga*.	
A *tretâyuga* has	1,080,000 years,	
besides	108,000 ,,	*saṁdhi*,
and	108,000 ,,	*saṁdhyâṁśa*.
Sum total	1,296,000 years = one *tretâyuga*.	
A *dvâpara* has	720,000 years,	
besides	72,000 ,,	*saṁdhi*,
and	72,000 ,,	*saṁdhyâṁśa*.
Sum total	864,000 years = one *dvâpara*.	
A *kali* has	360,000 years,	
besides	36,000 ,,	*saṁdhi*,
and	36,000 ,,	*saṁdhyâṁśa*.
Sum total	432,000 years = one *kaliyuga*.	

Page 188.

"The sum of the *kṛita* and *tretâ* is 3,024,000 years, and the sum of the *kṛita*, *tretâ*, and *dvâpara* is 3,888,000 years."

Further, Brahmagupta says that "Âryabhaṭa considers the four *yugas* as the four equal parts of a *catur-yuga*. Thus he differs from the doctrine of the book *Smṛiti*, just mentioned, and he who differs from us is an **Âryabhaṭa and Paulisa quoted by Brahmagupta.**

opponent." On the other hand, Brahmagupta praises Paulisa for what he does, since he does not differ from the book *Smṛiti*; for he subtracts 1200 from the 4800 years of the *kṛitayuga*, and diminishes the remainder still more and more, so as to get *yugas* which correspond with those of the *Smṛiti*, but *yugas* without *saṁdhi* and *saṁdhyâṁśa*. As regards the Greeks, we may notice that they have nothing like the tradition of the *Smṛiti*, for they do not measure time by *yugas*, *manvantaras*, or *kalpas*.

So far the quotation from Brahmagupta.

As is well known, there is no difference of opinion on the sum of the years of a complete *caturyuga*. Therefore, according to Âryabhaṭa, the *kaliyuga* has 3000 *divya* years or 1,080,000 human years. Each two *yugas* has 6000 *divya* years or 2,160,000 human years. Each three *yugas* has 9000 *divya* years or 3,240,000 human years.

The rule of Paulisa.

There is a tradition that Paulisa in his *Siddhânta* specifies various new rules for the computation of these numbers, some of which may be accepted, whilst others are to be rejected. So in the rule for the computation of the *yugas* he puts 48 as the basis and subtracts one-fourth of it, so as to get 36. Then he again subtracts 12, for this number is his *basis* of subtraction, so as to get 24, and subtracting the same number a third time, he gets 12. These 12 he multiplies by 100, and the product represents the number of *divya* years of the *yugas*.

Criticism thereon.

If he had made the number 60 the basis, for most things may be determined by it, and had made one-fifth of it the basis of subtraction, or if he had subtracted from 60 consecutive fractions of the remaining number, first $\frac{1}{5} = 12$, from the remainder $\frac{1}{4} = 12$, from the remainder $\frac{1}{3} = 12$, and from the remainder $\frac{1}{2} = 12$, he would have obtained the same result which he has found by his method ($60 - \frac{1}{5} = 48, - \frac{1}{4} = 36, - \frac{1}{3} = 24, - \frac{1}{2} = 12$).

It is possible that Paulisa simply mentions this method as one among others, and that it is not that one in particular which he himself adopted. A translation of his whole work into Arabic has not hitherto yet been undertaken, because in his mathematical problems there is an evident religious and theological tendency.

Pulisa calculates how much of the life of Brahman has elapsed before the present *kalpa*.

Pulisa deviates from the rule which he himself gives when he wants to compute how many of our years have elapsed of the life of Brahman before the present *kalpa*. Up to the time of his writing, eight years five months and four days of a new *kalpa* had elapsed. He counts 6068 *kalpas*. As, according to him, a *kalpa* has 1008 *caturyugas*, he multiplies this number by 1008 and gets 6,116,544 *caturyugas*. These he changes into *yugas* by multiplying them by 4, and he gets 24,466,176 *yugas*. As a *yuga*, according to him, has 1,080,000 years, he multiplies the number of *yugas* by 1,080,000, and gets as the product 26,423,470,080,000, *i.e.* the number of years which have elapsed of the life of Brahman before the present *kalpa*. Page 189.

Criticisms on this calculation.

Perhaps it will seem strange to the followers of Brahmagupta that he (Pulisa) has not changed the *caturyugas* into exact *yugas*, but simply changed them into fourth parts (by dividing them by 4), and multiplied these fourth parts by the number of years of a single fourth part.

Now, we do not ask him what is the use of representing the *caturyugas* as fourth parts, inasmuch as they have no fraction which, in this manner, must be reduced to wholes. The multiplication of the whole *caturyugas* by the years of one complete *caturyuga*, *i.e.* 4,320,000, would have been sufficiently lengthy. We, however, say that he would be correct in doing so if he had not been influenced by the wish of bringing the elapsed years of the present *kalpa* into relation with the last-mentioned number, and multiplied the complete elapsed *manvantaras* by 72 in agreement with his theory; further, if he had not multiplied the product by the years of a *caturyuga*, which gives the product of 1,866,240,000 years, and, moreover, had not multiplied the number of the complete *caturyugas* which have elapsed of the current *manvantara* by the years of a single *caturyuga*, which gives the product of 116,640,000 years. Of the current *caturyuga* there have elapsed three *yugas*, *i.e.* according to him, 3,240,000 years. The latter number represents three-fourths of the years of a *caturyuga*. He uses the same number when computing the week-day of a date by means of the number of the days of the here-mentioned number of years. If he believed in the above-mentioned rule, he would use it where it is required, and he would reckon the three *yugas* as nine-tenths of a *caturyuga*.

Brahmagupta's harsh criticisms on Aryabhaṭa.

Now, it is evident that that which Brahmagupta relates on his authority, and with which he himself agrees, is entirely unfounded; but he is blind to this from sheer hatred of Âryabhaṭa, whom he abuses excessively. And in this respect Âryabhaṭa and Pulisa are the same to him. I take for witness the passage of Brahmagupta where he says that Âryabhaṭa has subtracted something from the cycles of the *Caput Draconis* and of the *apsis* of the moon, and thereby rendered confused the computation of the eclipse. He is rude enough to compare Âryabhaṭa to a worm which, eating the wood, by chance describes certain characters in it, without understanding them and without intending to draw them. "He, however, who knows these things thoroughly stands opposite to Âryabhaṭa, Śrîsheṇa, and Vishṇucandra like the lion against gazelles. They are not capable of letting him see their faces." In such offensive terms he attacks Âryabhaṭa and maltreats him.

Different lengths of the solar year.

We have already mentioned (v. chap. xli.) how many civil days (*sâvana*) a *caturyuga* has according to the three scholars. Pulisa gives it 1350 days more than Brahmagupta, but the number of years of a *caturyuga* is the same according to both. Therefore, evidently Pulisa gives the solar year more days than Brahmagupta. To judge from the report of Brahmagupta, Âryabhaṭa gives a *caturyuga* 300 days less than Pulisa, and 1050 more than Brahmagupta. Accordingly, Âryabhaṭa must reckon the solar year longer than Brahmagupta and shorter than Pulisa.

CHAPTER XLIII.

A DESCRIPTION OF THE FOUR YUGAS, AND OF ALL THAT IS EXPECTED TO TAKE PLACE AT THE END OF THE FOURTH YUGA.

THE ancient Greeks held regarding the earth various opinions, of which we shall relate one for the sake of an example.

On natural cataclysms.

Page 190.

The disasters which from time to time befal the earth, both from above and from below, differ in quality and quantity. Frequently it has experienced one so incommensurable in quality or in quantity, or in both together, that there was no remedy against it, and that no flight or caution was of any avail. The catastrophe comes on like a deluge or an earthquake, bringing destruction either by the breaking in of the surface, or by drowning with water which breaks forth, or by burning with hot stones and ashes that are thrown out, by thunderstorms, by landslips, and typhoons; further, by contagious and other diseases, by pestilence, and more of the like. Thereby a large region is stripped of its inhabitants; but when after a while, after the disaster and its consequences have passed away, the country begins to recover and to show new signs of life, then different people flock there together like wild animals, who formerly were dwelling in hiding-holes and on the tops of the mountains. They become civilised by assisting each other against common foes, wild beasts or men, and furthering each other in the hope for a life in safety and joy. Thus they increase to great numbers; but then ambition, circling round them with the wings of wrath and envy, begins to disturb the serene bliss of their life.

Sometimes a nation of such a kind derives its pedigree from a person who first settled in the place or distinguished himself by something or other, so that he alone continues to live in the recollection of the succeeding generations, whilst all others beside him are forgotten. Plato mentions in the *Book of Laws* Zeus, *i.e.* Jupiter, as the forefather of the Greeks, and to Zeus is traced back the pedigree of Hippocrates, which is mentioned in the last chapters added at the end of the book. We must, however, observe that the pedigree contains only very few generations, not more than fourteen. It is the following:—Hippokrates—Gnosidikos—Nebros—Sostratos — Theodoros — Kleomyttades — Krisamis — Dardanas—Sostratos—ابلوسوس (?)—Hippolochos—Podaleirios — Machaon—Asclepios—Apollo—Zeus—Kronos, *i.e.* Saturn.

Pedigree of Hippocrates.

Hindu notions regarding the four ages or *yugas*.

The Hindus have similar traditions regarding the Caturyuga, for according to them, at the beginning of it, *i.e.* at the beginning of Kṛitayuga, there was happiness and safety, fertility and abundance, health and force, ample knowledge and a great number of Brahmans. The good is complete in this age, like four-fourths of a whole, and life lasted 4000 years alike for all beings during this whole space of time.

Thereupon things began to decrease and to be mixed with opposite elements to such a degree, that at the beginning of Tretâyuga the good was thrice as much as the invading bad, and that bliss was three-quarters of the whole. There were a greater number of Kshatriyas than of Brahmans, and life had the same length as in the preceding age. So it is represented by the *Vishṇu-Dharma*, whilst analogy requires that it should be shorter by the same amount than bliss is smaller, *i.e.* by one-fourth. In this age, when offering to the fire, they begin to kill animals and to tear off plants, practices which before were unknown.

Thus the evil increases till, at the beginning of Dvâpara, evil and good exist in equal proportions, and likewise bliss and misfortune. The climates begin to differ, there is much killing going on, and the religions become different. Life becomes shorter, and lasts only 400 years, according to the *Vishṇu-Dharma*. At the beginning of Tishya, *i.e.* Kaliyuga, evil is thrice as much as the remaining good.

The Hindus have several well-known traditions of events which are said to have occurred in the Tretâ and Dvâpara *yugas*, *e.g.* the story of Râma, who killed Ravaṇa; that of Paraśurâma the Brahman, who killed every Kshatriya he laid hold upon, revenging on them the death of his father. They think that he lives in heaven, that he has already twenty-one times appeared on earth, and that he will again appear. Further, the story of the war of the children of Pâṇḍu with those of Kuru.

Page 191.

In the Kaliyuga evil increases, till at last it results in the destruction of all good. At that time the inhabitants of the earth perish, and a new race rises out of those who are scattered through the mountains and hide themselves in caves, uniting for the purpose of worshipping and flying from the horrid, demoniac human race. Therefore this age is called *Kṛitayuga*, which means "Being ready for going away after having finished the work."

Description of the Kaliyuga.

In the story of Śaunaka which Venus received from Brahman, God speaks to him in the following words: "When the Kaliyuga comes, I send Buddhodana, the son of Śuddhodana the pious, to spread the good in the creation. But then the *Muḥammira*, *i.e.* the red-wearing ones, who derive their origin from him, will change everything that he has brought, and the dignity of the Brahmans will be gone to such a degree that a Śûdra, their servant, will be impudent towards them, and that a Śûdra and Caṇḍâla will share with them the presents and offerings. Men will entirely be occupied with gathering wealth by crimes, with hoarding up, not refraining from committing horrid and sinful crimes. All this will result in a rebellion of the small ones against the great ones, of the children against their parents, of the servants against their masters. The castes will be in uproar against each other, the genealogies will become confused, the four castes will be abolished, and there will be many religions and sects. Many books will be composed, and the communities which formerly were united will on account of them be dissolved into single individuals. The temples will be destroyed and the schools will lie waste. Justice will be gone, and the kings will not know anything but oppression and spoliation, robbing and destroying, as if they wanted to devour the people, foolishly indulging in far-reaching hopes, and not considering how short life is in comparison with the sins (for which they have to atone). The more the mind of people is depraved, the more will pestilential diseases be prevalent. Lastly, people maintain that most of the astrological rules obtained in that age are void and false.

Saying of Mânî.

These ideas have been adopted by Mânî, for he says: "Know ye that the affairs of the world have been changed and altered; also priesthood has been changed since the σφαῖραι of heaven, *i.e.* the spheres, have been changed, and the priest can no longer acquire such a knowledge of the stars in the circle of a sphere as their fathers were able to acquire. They lead mankind astray by fraud. What they prophesy may by chance happen, but frequently it does not happen."

Description of the Kṛitayuga according to *Vishṇu-Dharma*.

The description of these things in the *Vishṇu-Dharma* is much more copious than we have given it. People will be ignorant of what is reward and punishment; they will deny that the angels have absolute knowledge. Their lives will be of different length, and none of them will know how long it is. The one will die as an embryo, the other as a baby or child. The pious will be torn away and will not have a long life, but he who does evil and denies religion will live longer. Śûdras will be kings, and will be like rapacious wolves, robbing the others of all that pleases them. The doings of the Brahmans will be of the same kind, but the majority will be Śûdras and brigands. The laws of the Brahmans will be abolished. People will point with their fingers at those who worry themselves with the practice of frugality and poverty as a curiosity, will despise them, and will wonder at a man worshipping Vishṇu; for all of them have become of the same (wicked) character. Therefore any wish will soon be

Page 192.

granted, little merit receive great reward, and honour and dignity be obtained by little worship and service.

But finally, at the end of the *yuga*, when the evil will have reached its highest pitch, there will come forward Garga, the son of J-Ś-V (?) the Brahman, *i.e.* Kali, after whom this *yuga* is called, gifted with an irresistible force, and more skilled in the use of any weapon than any other. Then he draws his sword to make good all that has become bad; he cleans the surface of the earth of the impurity of people and clears the earth of them. He collects the pure and pious ones for the purpose of procreation. Then the Kṛitayuga lies far behind them, and the time and the world return to purity, and to absolute good and to bliss.

This is the nature of the *yugas* as they circle round through the Caturyuga.

The origin of medicine according to the book *Caraka*.

The book *Caraka*, as quoted by 'Alî Ibn Zain of Ṭabaristan, says: "In primeval times the earth was always fertile and healthy, and the elements or *mahabhûta* were equally mixed. Men lived with each other in harmony and love, without any lust and ambition, hatred and envy, without anything that makes soul and body ill. But then came envy, and lust followed.

Driven by lust, they strove to hoard up, which was difficult to some, easy to others. All kinds of thoughts, labours, and cares followed, and resulted in war, deceit, and lying. The hearts of men were hardened, the natures were altered and became exposed to diseases, which seized hold of men and made them neglect the worship of God and the furtherance of science. Ignorance became deeply rooted, and the calamity became great. Then the pious met before their anchorite Kriśa (?) the son of Âtreya, and deliberated; whereupon the sage ascended the mountain and threw himself on the earth. Thereafter God taught him the science of medicine."

All this much resembles the traditions of the Greeks, which we have related (in another place). For Aratus says in his Φαινόμενα, and in his intimations referring to the seventh zodiacal sign: "Look under the feet of the Herdsman, *i.e. Al'awwâ*, among the northern figures, and you see the Virgin coming with a blooming ear of corn in her hand, *i.e. Alsimâk Al'a'zal*. She belongs either to the star-race, which are said to be the forefathers of the ancient stars, or she was procreated by another race which we do not know. People say that in primeval times she lived among mankind, but only among women, not visible to men, being called *Justice*. She used to unite the aged men and those who stood in the market-places and in the streets, and exhorted them with a loud voice to adhere to the truth. She presented mankind with innumerable wealth and bestowed rights upon them. At that time the earth was called *golden*. None of its inhabitants knew pernicious hypocrisy in deed or word, and there was no objectionable schism among them. They lived a quiet life, and did not yet navigate the sea in ships. The cows afforded the necessary sustenance. Quotation from Aratus.

"Afterwards, when the golden race had expired and the silver race come on, Virgo mixed with them, but without being happy, and concealed herself in the mountains, having no longer intercourse with the women as formerly. Then she went to the large towns, warned their inhabitants, scolded them for their evil doings, and blamed them for ruining the race which the *golden fathers* had left behind. She foretold them that there would come a race still worse than they, and that wars, bloodshed, and other great disasters would follow.

Page 193.

"After having finished, she disappeared into the mountains till the silver race expired and a bronze race came up. People invented the sword, the doer of evil; they tasted of the meat of cows, the first who did it. By all this their neighbourhood became odious to Justice, and she flew away to the sphere."

A scholion on Aratus.

The commentator of the book of Aratus says: "This Virgin is the daughter of Zeus. She spoke to the people on the public places and streets, and at that time they were obedient to their rulers, not knowing the bad nor discord. Without any altercation or envy they lived from agriculture, and did not travel on sea for the sake of commerce nor for the lust of plunder. Their nature was as pure as gold.

"But when they gave up these manners and no longer adhered to truth, Justice no longer had intercourse with them, but she observed them, dwelling in the mountains. When, however, she came to their meetings, though unwillingly, she threatened them, for they listened in silence to her words, and therefore she no longer appeared to those who called her, as she had formerly done.

"When, then, after the silver race, the bronze race came up, when wars followed each other and the evil spread in the world, she started off, for she wanted on no account to stay with them, and hated them, and went towards the sphere.

"There are many traditions regarding this Justice,

According to some, she is Demeter, because she has the ear of corn; according to others, she is Τύχη."

This is what Aratus says.

Quotation from the Laws of Plato.

The following occurs in the third book of the Laws of Plato:—

"The Athenian said: 'There have been deluges, diseases, disasters on earth, from which none has been saved but herdsmen and mountaineers, as the remnants of a race not practised in deceit and in the love of power.'

"The Knossian said: 'At the beginning men loved each other sincerely, feeling lonely in the desert of the world, and because the world had sufficient room for all of them, and did not compel them to any exertion. There was no poverty among them, no possession, no contract. There was no greed among them, and neither silver nor gold. There were no rich people among them and no poor. If we found any of their books, they would afford us numerous proofs for all this.'"

CHAPTER XLIV.

ON THE MANVANTARAS.

The single *manvantaras*, their Indras, and the children of Indra.

As 72,000 *kalpas* are reckoned as the life of Brahman, the *manvantara, i.e.* period of Manu, is reckoned as the life of Indra, whose rule ends with the end of the period. His post is occupied by another Indra, who then rules the world in the new *manvantara*. Brahmagupta says: "If a man maintains that there is no *saṁdhi* between two *manvantaras*, and reckons each *manvantara* as 71 *caturyugas*, he will find that the *kalpa* is too short by six *caturyugas*, and the *minus* below 1000 (*i.e.* in 994) is not better than the *plus* above 1000 (*i.e.* in 1008, according to Âryabhaṭa). Both numbers, however, differ from the book *Smṛiti*."

Further he says: "Âryabhaṭa mentions in two books of his, the one of which is called *Daśagîtikâ*, the other *Âryâśtaśata*, that each *manvantara* is equal to 72 *caturyugas*. Accordingly he reckons a *kalpa* at 1008 *caturyugas* (14 × 72)."

In the book *Vishṇu-Dharma* Mârkaṇḍeya gives to Vajra the following answer: "Purusha is the lord of

Page 194.

the universe; the lord of the *kalpa* is Brahman, the lord of the world; but the lord of the *manvantara* is Manu. There are fourteen Manus, from whom the kings of the earth, ruling at the beginning of each *manvantara*, descended."

We have united their names in the following table:—

The Number of the Manvantaras.	The Names of the Manvantaras according to the Vishṇu-Purâṇa.	Their Names according to the Vishṇu-Dharma.	Their Names taken from other Sources.	The Names of Indra according to the Vishṇu-Purâṇa.	The Names of the children of Manu, the kings of the earth who ruled at the beginning of each period, according to the Vishṇu-Purâṇa.
1	Svâyambhuva	Svâyambhuva	Svâyambhuva	Manu, as the ruler of the first manvantara, is Indra, who has nothing in common with any other being.	
2	Svârocisha	Svârociya	Svârocisha	Vipaścit	The first of the children of Manu, Caitraka (?)
3	Auttami	Auttami	Auttami	Suśânti	Sudivya (?)
4	Stâmasa (?)	Stâmasa	Utâmasa (?)	Śikhin	Nara, Khyâti, Śântahaya, Jânujaṅgha.
5	Raivata	Raivata	Raivata	Autata (?)	Balabandhu, Susaṁbhâvya, Satyaka, Sindhu (?), Rebha (?)
6	Câkshusha	Cakshukha	Câkshusha	Manojava	Puru, Muru, Śatadyumna, Pramukha (?)
7	Vaivasvata	Vaivasvata	Vaivasvata	Purandara	Ikshvâku, Nabasa (?), Dhṛishṇa, Śaryâti.
8	Sâvarṇi	Sâvarṇi	These five are called Sâvarṇi: Sâvarṇi	Bali, the imprisoned king	Virajas, Aścârvari, Nirmogha.
9	Daksha	Vishṇu-Dharma	Brahma-putra	Mahâvîrya	Dhṛitaketu, Nirâmaya, Pañcahasta.
10	Brahmasâvarṇi	Dharmaputra	Vishṇu-putra	Śânti	Sukshetra, Uttamaujas, Bhûrisheṇa.
11	Dharmasâvarṇi	Rudraputra	Rudra-putra	Vṛisha	Sarvatraga, Devânîka, Sudharmâtman (?)
12	Rudraputra	Dakshaputra	Daksha-putra	Ṛitadhâman	Devata (?), Vânupadevaś-ca, Deva-śreshṭha.
13	Raucya	Raibhya (?)	Raibhya (?)	Divaspati	Citrasena, Vicitra-âdyâ (!)
14	Bhautya	Bhautya	Bhûmi (?)	Śuci	Urur, Gabhira, Budhnya-âdyâ (!)

Page 195.

The tradition of *Vishnu-Purâṇa* relating to the *manvantaras*.

The difference which the reader perceives in the enumeration of the future *manvantaras* beyond the seventh one, arises, as I think, from the same cause whence the difference in the names of the *Dvîpas* is derived (v. pp. 235, 236), viz. from the fact that the people care more for the *names* than for the *order* in which they are handed down to posterity. We may here rely on the tradition of the *Vishṇu-Purâṇa*, for in this book their number, their names and descriptions, are given in such a way that renders it necessary to us to consider also the *order* in which it gives them as trustworthy. But we have refrained from communicating these things in this place, since they offer only very little use.

The same book relates that King Maitreya, a Kshatriya, asked Parâśara, the father of Vyâsa, about the past and the future *manvantaras*. Thereupon the latter mentions the name by which each Manu is known, the same names which our table exhibits. According to the same book, the children of each Manu will rule the earth, and it mentions the first of them, the names of whom we have given in the table. According to the same source, the Manus of the second, third, fourth, and fifth *manvantaras* will be of the race of *Priyavrata*, an anchorite, who stood in such favour with Vishṇu, that he honoured his children by raising them to this distinction.

CHAPTER XLV.

ON THE CONSTELLATION OF THE GREAT BEAR.

A tradition relating to Arundhati, the wife of Vasishṭha.

THE Great Bear is in the Indian language called *Saptarshayas*, i.e. *the Seven Ṛishis*. They are said to have been anchorites who nourished themselves only with what it is allowable to eat, and with them there was a pious woman, *Al-suhâ* (*Ursa Major*, star 80 by ζ). They plucked off the stalks of the lotus from the ponds to eat of them. Meanwhile came *The Law* (*Dharma ?*) and concealed her from them. Every one of them felt ashamed of the other, and they swore oaths which were approved of by *Dharma*. In order to honour them, *Dharma* raised them to that place where they are now seen (*sic*).

Quotation from Varâhamihira.

We have already mentioned that the books of the Hindus are composed in metres, and therefore the authors indulge in comparisons and *epitheta ornantia*, such as are admired by their countrymen. Of the same kind is a description of the Great Bear in the *Saṁhitâ* of Varâhamihira, where it occurs before the astrological prognostics derived from this constellation. We give the passage according to our translation:[1]—

"The northern region is adorned with these stars, as a beautiful woman is adorned with a collar of pearls strung together, and a necklace of white lotus flowers, a handsomely arranged one. Thus adorned, they are like maidens who dance and revolve round the pole as the pole orders them. And I say, on the authority of

[1] *Saṁhitâ*, chap. xiii. v. 1–6.

Garga, the ancient, the primeval one, that the Great Bear stood in Maghâ, the tenth lunar station, when Yudhishṭhira ruled the earth, and the Śakakâla was 2526 years after this. The Great Bear remains in each lunar station 600 years, and it rises in the north-east. He (of the Seven Ṛishis) who then rules the east is Marîci; west of him is Vasishṭha, then Aṅgiras, Atri, Pulastya, Pulaha, Kratu, and near Vasishṭha there is a chaste woman called Arundhatî."

As these names are sometimes confounded with each other, we shall try to identify them with the corresponding stars in the Great Bear:—

Marîci is the	27th star of this constellation.				
Vasishṭha	,,	26th	,,	,,	,,
Aṅgiras	,,	25th	,,	,,	,,
Atri	,,	18th	,,	,,	,,
Kratu	,,	16th	,,	,,	,,
Pulaha	,,	17th	,,	,,	,,
Pulastya	,,	19th	,,	,,	,,

Criticisms on Garga.

These stars occupy in our time, *i.e.* in the 952nd year of the Śakakâla, the space between $1\frac{1}{3}°$ of Leo and $13\frac{1}{2}°$ of Spica (Virgo). According to the peculiar motion of the fixed stars, as we know it, the same stars occupied at the time of Yudhishṭhira the space between $8\frac{2}{3}°$ Gemini and $20\frac{5}{6}°$ of Cancer.

Page 196.

According to the motion of the fixed stars, as adopted by the ancient astronomers and Ptolemy, these stars occupied at that time the space between $26\frac{1}{2}°$ of Gemini and $8\frac{2}{3}°$ of Leo, and the here-mentioned lunar station (Maghâ) occupied the space between 0–800 minutes in Leo.

Therefore it would be much more suitable *in the present time* to represent the Seven Ṛishis as standing in Maghâ than in the time of Yudhishṭhira. And if the Hindus identify Maghâ with the *Heart of the Lion*, we can only say that this constellation at that time stood in the first degrees of Cancer.

The words of Garga are without any foundation; they only show how little he knew of that which every one must know who wants to fix the places of the stars, either by eyesight or by means of astronomical observation on certain degrees of the signs of the zodiac.

I have read in the almanacs for the year 951 of the Śakakâla which came from Kashmîr the statement that the Seven Ṛishis stand since seventy-seven years in the lunar station Anurâdhâ. This station occupies the space between $3\frac{1}{3}°$ and the end of $16\frac{2}{3}°$ of Scorpio. However, the Seven Ṛishis precede this place by about a whole zodiacal sign and 20 degrees, *i.e.* by $1\frac{2}{3}$ signs (v. p. 390). But what man would be able to learn all the different theories of the Hindus, if he does not dwell among them! Note from a Kashmirian almanac.

Let us now first suppose that Garga is right, that he has not stated the precise place in Maghâ which the Seven Ṛishis occupy, and let us suppose that this place was 0° of Maghâ, which would correspond to 0° of Leo for our time. Further, between the time of Yudhishṭhira and the present year, *i.e.* the year 1340 of Alexander, there is an interval of 3479 years. And lastly, let us suppose that Varâhamihira is right in saying that the Seven Ṛishis dwell 600 years in each lunar station. Accordingly, they ought in the present year to stand in 17° 18′ of Libra, which is identical with 10° 38′ of Svâti. However, if we suppose that they stood in the midst of Maghâ (not in the beginning), they ought at present to stand in 3° 58′ of Viśâkhâ. And if we suppose that they stood *in the end* of Maghâ, they ought at present to stand in 10° 38′ of Viśâkhâ. Examination of the statements regarding the position of the Great Bear.

Hence it is evident that the statement of the Kashmirian calendar does not agree with the statement in the *Saṁhitâ*. Likewise, if we adopt the rule of the said calendar regarding the precession of the equinoxes, and reckon with this measure backward, we do by no means arrive at Maghâ as the lunar station in which the Seven Ṛishis stood in the time of Yudhishṭhira.

Hitherto we used to think that *in our time* the revolution of the fixed stars is more rapid than *in former times*, and we tried to account for this by peculiarities of the shape of the celestial sphere. According to us, they move one degree in 66 solar years. Therefore Varâhamihira highly astonishes us, for, according to him, the rate of this motion would be one degree in forty-five years, *i.e.* much more rapid than at present, whilst *his* time precedes ours only by 525 years.

Rule of the Karaṇasâra to find the position of the Great Bear at any time.

The author of the canon *Karaṇasâra* gives the following rule for the computation of the motion of the Great Bear, and of the place which, at any given time, it occupies:—

"Subtract 821 from the Śakakâla. The remainder is the *basis*, *i.e.* the number of years above 4000 which have elapsed since the beginning of the Kaliyuga.

"Multiply the basis by 47, and add 68,000 to the product. Divide the sum by 10,000. The quotient represents the zodiacal signs and fractions of them, *i.e.* the position of the Great Bear which was sought."

The addition of 68,000, prescribed in this rule, must be the original position of the Great Bear at the beginning of the *basis*, multiplied by 10,000. If we divide 68,000 by 10,000, we get the quotient $6\frac{4}{5}$, *i.e.* six zodiacal signs and twenty-four degrees of a seventh sign.

It is evident that if we divide the 10,000 by 47, the Great Bear has wandered through one zodiacal sign in 212 years, 9 months, and 6 days, according to solar time. Accordingly it wanders through one degree of a sign in 7 years, 1 month, and 3 days, and through one lunar station in 94 years, 6 months, and 20 days.

Now there is a great difference between the values of Varâhamihira and those of Vitteśvara, if there is not a fault in the tradition. If we, by way of an example, make such a computation for the present year (1030 A.D.), we get 9° 17′ in the lunar station Anurâdhâ as the position of the Great Bear.

The people of Kashmîr believed that the Great Bear wanders through a lunar station in 100 years. Therefore the above-mentioned calendar says that of the present *centennium* of the motion of the Great Bear there is still a remainder of twenty-three years.

Theological opinions mixed up with astronomy.

Mistakes and confusion such as we have here laid open arise, in the first place, from the want of the necessary skill in astronomical researches, and secondly, from the way of the Hindus of mixing up scientific questions with religious traditions. For the theologians believe that the Seven Ṛishis stand higher than the fixed stars, and they maintain that in each *manvantara* there will appear a new Manu, whose children will destroy the earth; but the rule will be renewed by Indra, as also the different classes of the angels and the Seven Ṛishis. The angels are necessary, for mankind must offer sacrifices to them and must bring to the fire the shares for them; and the Seven Ṛishis are necessary, because they must renew the Veda, for it perishes at the end of each *manvantara*. Page 197.

The Seven Ṛishis in the different *manvantaras*.

Our information on this subject we take from the *Vishṇu-Purâṇa*. From the same source we have taken the names of the Seven Ṛishis in each *manvantara*, as exhibited by the following table:—

Numbers of the Manvantaras.	The Seven Ṛishis, *i.e.* the Banât-Na'sh, or the Stars of the Great Bear in the Manvantaras.						
	1	2	3	4	5	6	7
1	In this Manvantara there was neither Indra nor the Seven Ṛishis, but only Manu.						
2	Ûrjastambha	Prâṇa	Datta	Niṛishabha	Niśvara	Ṡcorvarî (?)	Vâṁśca (!)
3	The Children of Vasishṭha.						
4	Jyoti	Dhâman	Pṛithu	Kâvya	Caitra and Agni	Varaka	Pîvara
5	Hiraṇyaroman	Vedaśrî	Rûrdhwabâhu (!)	Apara (!)	Vedabâhu	Subâhu	Parjanya
6	Sumedhas	Virajas	Havishmat	Madhu	Atinâman	Sahishṇu	Carshayaḥ (!)
7	Vasishṭha	Kaśyapa	Atri	Jamadagni	Gautama	Viśvâmitra	Bharadvâja
8	Dîptimat	Gâlava	Kṛipa	Aśvatthâman the son of Droṇa	Parâśara	Vyâsa the son of Parâśara	Ṛishyaśriṅga
9	Savana	Dyutimat	Havya	Vasu	Medhâdhṛiti	Jyotishmat	Satya
10	Havishmat	Sukṛiti	Satya	Apâṁmûrti	Nâbhâga	Apratimaujas	Sukshetra
11	Niścara	Agnîdhra	Vapushmat	Vishṇu	Âruṇi	Havishmant	Nagha
12	Tapasvin	Sutaya	Tapomûrti	Taporati	Tapodhṛiti	Dyuti	Iścânyaḥ (!)
13	Nirmoha	Tattvadarśica	Nishprakampa	Nirutsuka	Dhṛitimant	Vyaya	Sutapas
14	Agniba	Śuci	Śukra or Venus	Mâgadha	Agnîdhra	Yuktasta	Jita

CHAPTER XLVI.

ON NÂRÂYAṆA, HIS APPEARANCE AT DIFFERENT TIMES, AND HIS NAMES. Page 198.

On the nature of Nârâyaṇa.

NÂRÂYAṆA is according to the Hindus a supernatural power, which does not on principle try to bring about the good by the good, nor the bad by the bad, but to prevent the evil and destruction by whatever means happen to be available. For this force the good exists prior to the bad, but if the good does not properly develop nor is available, it uses the bad, this being unavoidable. In so doing, it may be compared to a rider who has got into the midst of a cornfield. When he then comes back to his senses, and wants to avoid evil-doing and to get out of the mischief he has committed, he has no other means but that of turning his horse back and riding out on the same road on which he has entered the field, though in going out he will do as much mischief as he has done in entering, and even more. But there is no other possibility of making amends save this.

The Hindus do not distinguish between this force and the *First Cause* of their philosophy. Its dwelling in the world is of such a nature that people compare it to a material existence, an appearance in body and colour, since they cannot conceive any other kind of appearance.

Besides other times, Nârâyaṇa has appeared at the end of the first *manvantara*, to take away the rule of the worlds from Vâlakhilya (?), who had given it the name, and wanted to take it into his own hands. Nârâyaṇa came and handed it over to Śatakratu, the performer of a hundred sacrifices, and made him Indra.

Story of Bali, the son of Virocana.

Another time he appeared at the end of the sixth *manvantara*, when he killed the King Bali, the son of Virocana, who ruled the whole world and had Venus as his vazîr. On having heard from his mother that the time of his father had been much better than *his* time, since it was nearer the *kṛitayuga*, when people enjoyed more profound bliss and did not know any fatigue, he became ambitious and desirous of vying with his father. Therefore he commenced doing works of piety, giving presents, distributing money, and performing sacrifices, which earn the rule of paradise and earth for him who finishes a hundred of them. When he was near this term, or had nearly finished the ninety-ninth sacrifice, the angels began to feel uneasy and to fear for their dignity, knowing that the tribute which men bring them would cease if they stood no longer in need of them. Now they united and went to Nârâyaṇa, asking him to help them. He granted their wish, and descended to the earth in the shape of Vâmana, *i.e.* a man whose hands and feet are too short in comparison with his body, and in consequence his figure is thought to be hideous.

Nârâyaṇa came to the King Bali whilst he was offering, his Brahmans standing round the fires, and Venus, his vazîr, standing before him. The treasure-houses had been opened and the precious stones had been thrown out in heaps, to be given as presents and alms. Now Vâmana commenced to recite the Veda like the Brahmans from that part which is now called *Sâmaveda*, in a melancholy, impressive kind of melody, persuading the king to grant him liberally what he would wish and demand. Upon this Venus spoke stealthily to him: "This is Nârâyaṇa. He has come to rob thee of thy rule." But the king was so excited that he did not mind the words of Venus, and asked Vâmana what was his desire. Thereupon Vâmana said, "As much as four paces of thy realm, that I may live there." The king answered, "Choose what you wish, and how you wish it;" and according to Hindu custom, he ordered water to be brought to pour it over his hands as a sign of the confirmation of the order he had given. Now Venus, because of her love to the king, brought in the jug, but had corked the spout, so that no water should flow out of it, whilst she closed the hole in the cork with the *kuśa* grass of her ring-finger. But Venus had only one eye; she missed the hole, and now the water flowed out. In consequence, Vâmana made a pace towards east, another towards west, and a third towards above as far as Svarloka. As for the fourth pace, there was no more space in the world; he made, by the fourth pace, the king a slave, putting his foot between his shoulders as a sign of making him a slave. He made him sink down into the earth as far as Pâtâla, the lowest of the low. He took the worlds away from him, and handed the rule over to Puraṁdara. Page 199.

The following occurs in the *Vishṇu-Purâṇa*:—

Quotation from *Vishṇu-Purâṇa.*

"The King Maitreya asked Parâśara about the *yugas*. So the latter answered: 'They exist for the purpose that Vishṇu should occupy himself with something in them. In the Kṛitayuga he comes in the shape of Kapila alone, for the purpose of spreading wisdom; in Tretâyuga, in the shape of Râma alone, for the purpose of spreading fortitude, to conquer the bad, and to preserve the three worlds by force and the prevalence of virtuous action; in Dvâpara, in the shape of Vyâsa, to divide the Veda into four parts, and to derive many branches from it. In the end of Dvâpara he appears in the shape of Vâsudeva to destroy the giants; in the Kaliyuga, in the shape of Kali, the son of *J-sh-v* (?) the Brahman, to kill all, and to make the cycle of the *yugas* commence anew. That is his (Vishṇu's) occupation.'"

In another passage of the same book we read: "Vishṇu, *i.e.* another name for Nârâyaṇa, comes at the end of each *dvâpara* to divide the Veda into four parts, because men are feeble and unable to observe the whole of it. In his face he resembles Vyâsa."

Enumeration of the Vyâsas of the seventh *manvantara*.

We exhibit his names in the following table, though they vary in different sources, enumerating the Vyâsas who have appeared in the *caturyugas* of the present or seventh *manvantara* which have elapsed :—

1	Svayaṁbhû	16	Dhanaṁjaya
2	Prajâpati	17	Kṛitaṁjaya
3	Uśanas	18	Riṇajyeshtha (?)
4	Bṛihaspati	19	Bharadvâja
5	Savitṛi	20	Gautama
6	Mṛityu	21	Uttama
7	Indra	22	Haryâtman
8	Vasishṭha	23	Veda-vyâsa
9	Sârasvata	24	Vâjaśravas
10	Tridhâman	25	Somaśushma
11	Trivṛisha	26	Bhârgava
12	Bharadvâja	27	Vâlmîki
13	Antariksha	28	Krishna
14	Vapra (?)	29	Aśvatthâman the son of Droṇa
15	Trayyâruṇa		

Kṛishṇa Dvaipâyana is Vyâsa the son of Parâśara. The twenty-ninth Vyâsa has not yet come, but will appear in future.

Quotation from *Vishṇu-Dharma*.

The book *Vishṇu-Dharma* says: "The names of Hari, *i.e.* Nârâyaṇa, differ in the *yugas*. They are the following: Vâsudeva, Saṁkarshaṇa, Pradyumna, and Aniruddha."

I suppose that the author has not here preserved the proper sequence, for Vâsudeva belongs to the end of the four *yugas*.

The same book says: "Also his colours differ in the *yugas*. In the Kṛitayuga he is white, in the Tretâ-yuga red, in the Dvâpara yellow, the latter is the first phase of his being embodied in human shape, and in the Kaliyuga he is black."

These colours are something like *the three primary forces* of their philosophy, for they maintain that *Satya* is transparent white, *Rajas* red, and *Tamas* black. We shall in a later part of this book give a description of his last appearance in the world. Page 200.

CHAPTER XLVII.

ON VÂSUDEVA AND THE WARS OF THE BHÂRATA.

Analogies of the course of nature to the history of mankind.

THE life of the world depends upon sowing and procreating. Both processes increase in the course of time, and this increase is unlimited, whilst the world is limited.

When a class of plants or animals does not increase any more in its structure, and its peculiar kind is established as *a species* of its own, when each individual of it does not simply come into existence once and perish, but besides procreates a being like itself or several together, and not only once but several times, then this will as a single species of plants or animals occupy the earth and spread itself and its kind over as much territory as it can find.

The agriculturist selects his corn, letting grow as much as he requires, and tearing out the remainder. The forester leaves those branches which he perceives to be excellent, whilst he cuts away all others. The bees kill those of their kind who only eat, but do not work in their beehive.

Nature proceeds in a similar way; however, it does not distinguish, for its action is under all circumstances one and the same. It allows the leaves and fruit of the trees to perish, thus preventing them from realising that result which they are intended to produce in the economy of nature. It removes them so as to make room for others.

If thus the earth is ruined, or is near to be ruined,

by having too many inhabitants, its ruler—for it has a ruler, and his all-embracing care is apparent in every single particle of it—sends it a messenger for the purpose of reducing the too great number and of cutting away all that is evil.

Story of the birth of Vâsudeva.

A messenger of this kind is, according to the belief of the Hindus, Vâsudeva, who was sent the last time in human shape, being called Vâsudeva. It was a time when the giants were numerous on earth and the earth was full of their oppression; it tottered, being hardly able to bear the whole number of them, and it trembled from the vehemence of their treading. Then there was born a child in the city of Mathurâ to Vâsudeva by the sister of Kaṁsa, at that time ruler of the town. They were a Jatt family, cattle-owners, low Śûdra people. Kaṁsa had learned, by a voice which he heard at the wedding of his sister, that he would perish at the hands of her child; therefore he appointed people who were to bring him every child of hers as soon as she gave birth to it, and he killed all her children, both male and female. Finally, she gave birth to Balabhadra, and Yaśodâ, the wife of the herdsman Nanda, took the child to herself, and managed to keep it concealed from the spies of Kaṁsa. Thereupon she became pregnant an eighth time, and gave birth to *Vâsudeva* in a rainy night of the eighth day of the black half of the month Bhâdrapada, whilst the moon was ascending in the station Rohiṇî. As the guards had fallen into deep sleep and neglected the watch, the father stole the child and brought it to *Nandakula*, *i.e.* the stable of the cows of Nanda, the husband of Yaśodâ, near Mathurâ, but separated from this place by the river Yamunâ. Vâsudeva exchanged the child for a daughter of Nanda, which happened to be born at the moment when Vâsudeva arrived with the boy. He brought this female child to the guards instead of his son. Kaṁsa, the ruler, wanted to kill the child, but she flew up into the air and disappeared.

Vâsudeva grew up under the care of his foster-mother Yaśodâ without her knowing that he had been exchanged for her daughter, but Kaṁsa got some inkling of the matter. Now he tried to get the child into his power by cunning plans, but all of them turned out against him. Lastly, Kaṁsa demanded from his parents that they should send him (Vâsudeva) to wrestle in his (Kaṁsa's) presence. Now Vâsudeva began to behave overbearingly towards everybody. On the road he had already roused the wrath of his aunt by hurting a serpent which had been appointed to watch over the lotus flowers of a pond, for he had drawn a cord through its nostrils like a bridle. Further, he had killed his fuller, because the latter had refused to lend him clothes for the wrestling. He had robbed the girl who accom-
Page 201.
panied him of the sandal-wood with which she was ordered to anoint the wrestlers. Lastly, he had killed the rutting elephant which was provided for the purpose of killing him before the door of Kaṁsa. All this heightened the wrath of Kaṁsa to such a degree, that his bile burst, and he died on the spot. Then Vâsudeva, his sister's son, ruled in his stead.

The names of Vâsudeva in the different months.

Vâsudeva has a special name in each month. His followers begin the months with Mârgaśîrsha, and each month they begin with the eleventh day, because on this day Vâsudeva appeared.

The following table contains the names of Vâsudeva in the months :—

The Months.	The Names of Vâsudeva.	The Months.	The Names of Vâsudeva.
Mârgaśîrsha	Keśava	Jyaishṭha	Trivikrama
Pausha	Nârâyaṇa	Âshâḍha	Vâmana
Mâgha	Mâdhava	Śrâvaṇa	Śrîdhara
Phâlguna	Govinda	Bhâdrapada	Hṛishîkeśa
Caitra	Vishṇu	Âśvayuja	Padmanâbhi
Vaiśâkha	Madhusûdana	Kârttika	Dâmodara

Continuation of the story of Vâsudeva.

Now the brother-in-law of the deceased Kaṁsa became angry, went rapidly to Mathurâ, took possession of the realm of Vâsudeva, and banished him to the ocean. Then there appeared near the coast a golden castle called Barodâ, and Vâsudeva made it his residence.

The children of Kaurava (*i.e.* Dhṛitarâshṭra) had the charge of their cousins (the children of Pâṇḍu). Dhṛitarâshṭra received them and played dice with them, the last stake being their whole property. They lost more and more, until he laid upon them the obligation of expatriation for more than ten years, and of concealment in the remotest part of the country, where nobody knew them. If they did not keep this engagement they would be bound to return into banishment for a like number of years. This engagement was carried out, but finally came the time of their coming forward for battle. Now each party began to assemble their whole number and to sue for allies, till at last nearly innumerable hosts had gathered in the plain of Tâneshar. There were eighteen *akshauhiṇî*. Each party tried to gain Vâsudeva as ally, whereupon he offered either himself or his brother Balabhadra together with an army. But the children of Pâṇḍu preferred him. They were five men—Yudhishṭhira, their leader, Arjuna, the bravest of them, Sahadeva, Bhîmasena, and Nakula. They had seven *akshauhiṇî*, whilst their enemies were much stronger. But for the cunning devices of Vâsudeva and his teaching them whereby they might gain victory, they would have been in a less favourable situation than their enemies. But now they conquered; all those hosts were destroyed, and none remained except the five brothers. Thereafter Vâsudeva returned to his residence and died, together with his family, who were called Yâdava. Also the five brothers died before the year had reached its end, at the end of those wars.

End of Vâsudeva and of the five Pându brothers.

Vâsudeva had concerted with Arjuna the arrangement that they would consider the quivering of the left arm or left eye as a mysterious intimation that there was something happening to him. At that time there lived a pious Ṛishi called Durvâsas. Now the brothers and relations of Vâsudeva were a rather malicious, inconsiderate set of people. One of them hid under his coat a new frying-pan, went to the anchorite, and asked him what would be the result of his pregnancy, jeering at the pious man. The latter said, "In thy belly there is something which will be the cause of thy death and that of thy whole clan." When Vâsudeva heard this he became sorry, because he knew that these words would be fulfilled. He gave orders that the pan should be filed away and be thrown into the water. This was done. There was only a small part of it left, which
Page 202.
the artisan who had done the filing considered as insignificant. Therefore he threw it, as it was, into the water. A fish devoured it; the fish was caught, and the fisherman found it in its belly. He thought it would be a good tip for his arrow.

When the predestined time came, Vâsudeva rested on the coast under the shadow of a tree, one of his feet being crossed over the other; the fisherman took him for a gazelle, shot at him, and hit his right foot. This wound became the cause of the death of Vâsudeva. At the same time the left side of Arjuna began to quiver, and then his arm. Now his brother Sahadeva gave orders that he should never any more embrace anybody, that he might not be bereft of his strength (?). Arjuna went to Vâsudeva, but could not embrace him on account of the state in which he was. Vâsudeva ordered his bow to be brought, and handed it over to Arjuna, who tried his strength at it. Vâsudeva ordered him to burn his body and the bodies of his relations when they had died, and to bring away his wives from the castle, and then he died.

Out of the filings or bits of iron which had fallen off when the pan was filed a *bardî* bush had grown. To this there came the Yâdavas, who tied together some bundles of its twigs to sit upon. Whilst they were drinking there arose a quarrel between them; they beat each other with the *bardî* bundles, and killed each other. All this happened near the mouth of the river Sarsatî, where it flows into the sea, near the situation of Somanâth.

Arjuna had done all he had been ordered by Vâsudeva. When he brought away the women, they were suddenly attacked by robbers. When, now, Arjuna was no longer able to bend his bow, he felt that his strength was going. He whirled the bow in a circle above his head, and all who stood under the bow were saved, while the others were seized by the robbers. Now Arjuna and his brothers saw that life was no more of any use to them, therefore they emigrated to the north and entered the mountains, the snow of which never melts. The cold killed them one after the other, till at last only Yudhishṭhira remained. He obtained the distinction of being admitted to paradise, but before that he was to pass through hell in consequence of the sole lie which he had spoken in his life, at the request of his brothers and of Vâsudeva. These were the words which he had spoken within hearing of the Brahman Droṇa: "Aśvatthâman, the elephant, has died." He had made a pause between *Aśvatthâman* and *the elephant*, by which he had led Droṇa to believe that he meant *his son.* Yudhishṭhira spoke to the angels: "If this must be, may my intercession be accepted on behalf of the people in hell; may they be freed from it." After this desire of his had been granted, he went into paradise.

CHAPTER XLVIII.

AN EXPLANATION OF THE MEASURE OF AN AKSHAUHIṆÎ.

Each	*akshauhiṇî*	has	10 *anîkinî*.
,,	*anîkinî*	,,	3 *camû*.
,,	*camû*	,,	3 *pṛitanâ*.
,,	*pṛitanâ*	,,	3 *vâhinî*.
,,	*vâhinî*	,,	3 *gaṇa*.
,,	*gaṇa*	,,	3 *gulma*.
,,	*gulma*	,,	3 *senâmukha*.
,,	*senâmukha*	,,	3 *patti*.
,,	*patti*	,,	1 *ratha*.

IN chess, the latter is called *rukh*, whilst the Greeks call it *chariot of war*. It was invented by *Mankalus* (Myrtilos ?) in Athens, and the Athenians maintain that they were the first who rode on chariots of war. However, before that time they had already been invented by Aphrodisios (*sic*) the Hindu, when he ruled over Egypt, about 900 years after the deluge. They were drawn by two horses.

The following is a tale of the Greeks: Hephæstos loved Athene and desired to possess her, but she refused him, preferring to remain a virgin. Now he concealed himself in the country of Athens, and intended to seize her by force, but she pierced him with a spear and then he let her go. From a drop of his blood, which had dropped to the earth, there grew Erichthonios. He Page 203.
arrived on a chariot like the tower of the sun, the holder of the reins riding together with him. Similar to this are the customs of the hippodrome, as they exist in our time, the running and driving with carriages in the race.

A *ratha* comprehends besides, one elephant, three riders, and five footmen.

All these orders and divisions are necessary for the preparation for battle, for pitching camp and breaking up camp.

An *akshauhiṇî* has 21,870 chariots, 21,870 elephants, 65,610 riders, 109,350 footmen.

To each chariot there belong four horses and their conductor, the master of the chariot, armed with arrows, his two companions armed with spears, a guard who protects the master from behind, and a cartwright.

On each elephant there sits its conductor, and behind him the vice-conductor, a man who has to goad the elephant behind the chair, the master, armed with arrows, in the chair, and together with him his two spear-throwing companions and his jester, *hauhava* (?), who on other occasions runs before him.

Accordingly the number of people who ride on chariots and elephants is 284,323 (*sic*). The number of those who ride on horses is 87,480. The number of elephants in an *akshauhiṇî* is 21,870; the number of chariots, too, is 21,870; the number of horses is 153,090; the number of men, 459,283.

The sum-total of the living beings of one *akshauhiṇî*, elephants, horses, and men, is 634,243; the same number for eighteen *akshauhiṇî* is 11,416,374, viz. 393,660 elephants, 2,755,620 horses, 8,267,094 men.

This is an explanation of the *akshauhiṇî*, and of its single parts.

END OF VOL. I.